# THE POLITICS OF MEXICAN DEVELOPMENT

# THE POLITICS OF
# MEXICAN DEVELOPMENT

*Roger D. Hansen*

*The Johns Hopkins University Press*
*Baltimore and London*

Published for Resources for the Future, Inc.
By The Johns Hopkins University Press
Baltimore and London

The Johns Hopkins University Press, Baltimore, Maryland 21218
The Johns Hopkins Press Ltd., London

Library of Congress Catalog Card Number 77-134300
ISBN 0–8018–1193–7 (clothbound)
ISBN 0–8018–1651–3 (paperbound)

Originally published, 1971
Second printing, 1973
Third printing, 1974

Johns Hopkins Paperbacks edition, 1974
Second printing, 1977
Third printing, 1980
Fourth printing, 1982

*For*
*Mickey*
*and*
*Happy*

# CONTENTS

# TABLES

# PREFACE

Several years ago Wilbert Moore wrote that the problems of economic development "whether theoretical or practical, are mostly 'undisciplined.' Any attempt to deal with them within the strict confines of a single discipline is thus likely to result in sterile formulae and impractical advice."[1] No one interested in the processes of economic development or political "modernization" any longer believes otherwise; yet most studies of economic development in Mexico and elsewhere still confine themselves fairly narrowly to the discipline of economics. This book attempts—for better or worse—to explain the emergence of modern economic growth in Mexico in a much broader context. More than anything else it is an essay on the political, social and cultural parameters of the Mexican development process.

The researching and writing of the study has indebted me to a great many persons. While I should like to acknowledge the contributions which all of them have made, the nature of the book dictates otherwise. The study will inevitably evoke a hostile reaction in certain Mexican circles; therefore, it might well be an unfriendly act for me to thank my Mexican friends here for the most generous assistance they have rendered. Perhaps the best way for me to repay their kindness is to enter a plea that the study be read as an attempt neither to praise nor to blame any individuals or groups involved in the politics of Mexican economic development but rather to *understand* the social, cultural and political ingredients in the Mexican economic "miracle." Wherever the reader feels that a particular passage is value-laden, I would ask him to see if it cannot be more simply interpreted as a piece of social analysis.

To cite but one example, the book notes in some detail the high degree of corruption evidenced in Mexican political life. The theme is em-

[1] Wilbert E. Moore, "Industrialization and Social Change," in Bert F. Hoselitz and Wilbert E. Moore (eds.), *Industrialization and Society* (Paris: UNESCO, Mouton, 1963), p. 364.

phasized not to condemn Mexican political behavior but rather to enable the reader to comprehend a particular socio-economic function which political careers fulfill in Mexican society. Furthermore, I would hope that the general understanding of the relationship of corruption to political life in all nations has reached the degree of sophistication at which discussions of the theme no longer suggest moralizing. Indeed, if corruption is defined as that behavior of public officials which deviates from widely accepted social norms in order to serve private ends, then perhaps the term should not even be used in studying Mexican political life. The use of public position for private gain is so widespread in Mexico—and has been for centuries—that "corruption" may be better understood as a "norm" of political behavior than as a deviation from it.

What *may* distinguish corruption in Mexico (and perhaps in most Hispanic societies) from that in other national settings is its constancy over time. It does not appear to vary a great deal in either scale or incidence with other economic and political variables such as degree of economic development or level of political institutionalization. The study does suggest, however, that political corruption in Mexico developed historically as a response to the lack of opportunities for mobility within the country's economic and social systems. It may well be that the rapid industrialization of the Mexican economy will eventually be reflected in changing norms of political behavior.

I am most grateful to Theodore Geiger and Isaiah Frank, both of whom encouraged me to approach the subject of Mexican economic development from a broad perspective. To three highly respected "Mexicanists" I am indebted for astute and often painstaking comments on a first draft. They are William P. Glade, Stanley R. Ross, and Eric R. Wolf. In addition to their comments, their own published works on Mexico are an indispensable source of intellectual stimulation to all subsequent efforts to interpret Mexican society. My thanks also to James W. Wilkie for having made available to me some revised data on Mexican agrarian reform which appears in the second edition of his *The Mexican Revolution: Federal Expenditure and Social Change Since 1910*. My deepest thanks to Ann L. Hollick, who made substantial and always insightful contributions during all stages of the study's preparation.

A non-Latin Americanist, Barbara M. Bowersox, became one as the book developed. Her talents for organizing an author, his office, his notes, his files, and his manuscript are, to the best of my knowledge, unexcelled.

A final and special word of thanks to Robert W. Tucker, whose interest in this undertaking has been deeply appreciated.

—Washington, D.C.
May, 1970

# INTRODUCTION

*The Politics of Mexican Development* was written during the summer and fall of 1969. In the nearly five years that have elapsed since its completion, the patterns of continuity and change which are Mexico's hallmark have continued to manifest themselves in a legion of ways. Rapid economic growth proceeds, if at a somewhat slower pace, accompanied by an unusual burst of inflation. The regime of the PRI (Partido Revolucionario Institucional) continues to dominate the Mexican political system, though not without signs of some significant stress. The regime's critics express growing doubts about its capacity to survive, while its supporters contend that its incremental approach to the problems of Mexican development—both political and economic—is as sound as ever.

Every student of Mexico will draw a different conclusion from an analysis of the trends and events of the past four years. This, too, is a pattern familiar to Mexico and is a tribute to the mysteries of the Mexican political and socioeconomic systems and their patterns of interaction, which have yet to be understood on anything approaching even an elementary level of comprehensiveness. Therefore, this new introduction will attempt to distinguish between the major events and trends on the one hand and various interpretations of them on the other. A short narrative will precede an effort to view the years since 1969 in an analytical perspective.

With the inauguration of Luis Echeverría as president in December of 1970, Mexico's politics began a "move to the left" in both rhetoric and fact. In the familiar Mexican pattern, a president whose policies had aroused a significant degree of concern and criticism at one end of the political spectrum was succeeded by another who used the change in administration as an opportunity to make a number of alterations in political style and content to defuse dissent. From the first days of Echeverría's tenure he appeared to perceive his role as one of moving the political system back toward the center-left, to try to regain the allegiance of those alienated by the hard-line repressive tactics of the Díaz-Ordaz period.

Echeverría's move to the left has manifested itself in many ways: the rhetorical stress on social and economic justice, including the call for income redistribution in favor of the poor; the release of many political prisoners; Mexico's cordial relations with Chile's Salvador Allende prior to his overthrow and death; and a host of economic policy changes which are presently being implemented. The latter include a relative shift in public sector expenditures toward public housing, regional development projects, and a large rural development program geared to meet the needs of Mexico's small farmers. Similar shifts are developing in the channeling of those credits of the banking system over which the government has control.

Finally, changes in policies affecting public sector revenues, though much more ambiguous, would seem to point in a similar direction. Marginal tax reforms in 1971 and 1972 and major changes of pricing policies of several public sector corporations (notably PEMEX, the state oil monopoly) in 1973 have increased public sector revenues by approximately two percent of gross domestic product, or close to fifteen percent of aggregate public sector revenues. While the initial impact of the price changes may be regressive, the increased revenues will be available, at least indirectly, to finance the slowly growing welfare-oriented programs noted above.

If successfully implemented, all these programs should aid the slow movement toward a more equitable pattern of income distribution and improved standards of living for Mexico's forgotten fifty percent. While interpretations of the data collected during the latter 1960s vary, continued work by Clark Reynolds suggests that there has been some progress made in this direction during the years since 1963—the last year for which figures were available when this study was written.

Significantly, however, major tax reform has not been effected in the first half of the Echeverría administration. As noted in chapter 3 and elsewhere in this study, Mexico has for years had one of Latin America's lowest tax-to-GNP ratios, a ratio significantly below most countries of the world at a similar stage of development. In addition, the tax system contains a vast multitude of omissions and exemptions which favor income from capital over income from labor and contribute to the income distribution problems which President Echeverría apparently set out to relieve during his tenure in office. Yet when presented a major tax reform package by his official financial advisors in December of 1971, Echeverría vetoed the proposal; and as of mid-1974 no serious tax reform measure has been submitted to the Mexican Congress. Although many interpretations exist, no authoritative explanation of the President's refusal to adopt the tax reform proposal so carefully developed within the government has yet been offered.

If the substance of Echeverría's reforms has been rather modest thus far, his rhetoric has been more forceful. The themes of change and "social justice" are constantly sounded, and the business community—both domestic and foreign—is publicly reprimanded for its antisocial behavior. More generally, much of Echeverría's foreign policy—the separation of Mexico's positions from those of the United States on many occasions and in many forums, Mexico's attempts at Third World leadership, and Echeverría's personal role in originating and sponsoring the Charter of Economic Rights and Duties of States before the United Nations—can be interpreted as an integral aspect of the rhetorical "move to the left." The rather unsettling past three years, unsettling at least when measured against recent Mexican standards, would seem to be in large measure attributable to the rhetoric if not the reality of reform.

The most notable stress on the political system occurred in the late spring of 1971. After several months of student unrest and left wing-right wing conflicts triggered by, among other things, the failure of the new administration to release all of the political prisoners jailed following the 1968 student demonstrations, liberal and leftist students from the National University organized a protest march and rally in Mexico City. They planned to demand the release of those prisoners still held by the government, to protest the government's failure to crack down on the well-financed right wing gangs (known as *porras*) that were actively attempting to terminate many forms of liberal student protest movements, and more generally to test the new administration's tolerance of political demonstrations. The march, which took place on Corpus Christi Day (June 10), became the occasion of the bloodiest conflict since the 1968 student demonstrations ended in the Battle of Tlatelolco (see chapter 8). Using automatic weapons, a gang called *Los Halcones* ("the hawks") killed somewhere between ten and twenty marchers while, according to many reports, police at the scene of the violence did nothing to prevent the attack.

One observer of Mexican affairs has presented the following analysis of the event, the political maneuverings involved, and the issues at stake:

> According to unofficial reports [the President] had planned the bold move of meeting with the demonstrators when they arrived at the Zocalo, telling them that he agreed with their views, and asking for their support in the struggle against reactionary elements within the regime. The attack on the marchers, with its indications of official connivance, was clearly designed to force him either to go along with the repression and thus become the prisoner of the irreconcilable elements within the regime, or else to resign, since he was unable to control his own government (indeed, there are indications that orders given by the President at that time were not being carried out).
>
> The situation was saved for Echeverría when he received the unanimous backing of an emergency meeting of senior army commanders. This turned the tide in his favor in the sort of confrontation that had occurred in the 1920's and 1930's, but had not been seen in Mexico in over 30 years. His hand thus strengthened, Echeverría forced the resignation of the Mexico City police chief and of the governor of the

Federal District, Alfonso Martínez Dominguez, a former president of the P.R.I. and a powerful figure thought likely to be a future President.[1]

Another interpretation far less charitable to the new president is given by many Mexican participants in the Corpus Christi affair. They deny that their destination was the Presidential Palace (at the Zocalo); they deny that Echeverría ever intended to meet with them; and they conclude that the president allowed the battle to take place—if he did not conspire in it—in order to rid himself of some holdovers from the Díaz-Ordaz regime.

Since an official investigation revealed very little about either the organization and financing of *Los Halcones* or the degree of responsibility of major political figures for the day's events, many questions concerning this incident (and, much more importantly for our purposes, the evolution of the Mexican political process) remain unanswered. Were the *Halcones* organized and financed entirely within the PRI structure, or were there some elements of direct private sector support for their mobilization? If mobilized entirely within the PRI regime, were all members of its political elite aware of their existence and their "mission," or were these well-kept secrets within some faction or factions of the political elite structure? Was the army aware of their existence, and did it support their organizational and operational efforts in any way? Accurate answers to these questions would tell us much about the present state of the Mexican political system.

In the three years since the event there have been no other such overt challenges to the president's authority from "within" the system. Outside the system both urban and rural guerrilla activities increased during the early 1970s. A pattern of robberies and kidnappings emerged which resembled that in other Latin American countries, in one instance leading to the death of a very prominent member of the Monterrey business community. While the incidence of urban guerrilla activity did not seem to be greater than elsewhere in Latin America it was still novel for Mexico. And while there was little evidence that the political system was in any immediate danger of being eroded through a process of spreading rural unrest, the gradual increase in guerrilla activity in such states as Guerrero was cited by opponents of Echeverría's policies and rhetoric as a reason to return to the hard-line approach of the previous administration.

The performance of the Mexican economy was not unaffected by these political trends. The converse may also be true: major elements in the business community attempted—or at least threatened—to affect the per-formance of the economy in order to influence political trends. With two-thirds of Mexico's annual investment coming from the private sector, and

---

[1] Martin C. Needler, "A Critical Time for Mexico," *Current History* 62 (February 1972): 83.

with wealth and annual income so heavily concentrated in the hands of a small entrepreneurial group, decisions to postpone investment or threats of capital flight continue to represent deeply serious concerns for any Mexican administration. And as the last "leftist" Mexican president, López-Mateos, was forced to come to terms with this economic reality (see chapter 6), so too has President Echeverría been required to recognize the costs involved in pursuing a course of action which might lose all support from the business community, domestic and foreign.

While the Mexican economy has grown at six percent or better per year since 1970, this pace is a bit slower than that of the 1960s. One reason appears to have been a slackening of private investment which has accompanied the verbal duel between the administration and the private sector. Additionally, new Mexican legislation affecting foreign direct investment slowed the pace of foreign capital inflows for at least a year; the longer term effect of this legislation is not at all clear, and may have little or no lasting impact on the magnitude of foreign direct investment flows.

The major new problem for the Mexican economy concerned the rather sudden disappearance of relative price stability in 1973. As noted in chapter 3, the late 1950s and the 1960s were years of remarkable price stabilization for Mexico. But a confluence of circumstances, including the peso devaluations of 1972-73 relative to several major currencies (the peso remained tied to the U.S. dollar), general international price increases, a large increase in governmental deficit spending, and a series of domestic supply bottlenecks produced a twenty-two percent increase in Mexico's official price index for 1973. In September of that year, with talk of a general strike prevalent, the government negotiated a twenty percent wage increase affecting both the public and private sectors.

Among the many challenges for 1974 and beyond will be that of bringing the present inflation under control. Failure to do so will probably do more to inject some militancy into the Mexican labor movement than any event of the past fifteen years, and a militant labor movement would considerably alter the *modus operandi* of the PRI regime, described in chapters 5 and 7. Whether it would eventually impel the system toward the left or the right is highly debatable; that it would force movement in one direction or the other seems indisputable.

In order to bring inflation under control, the administration seems to have decided on an austerity budget for 1974, a return—at least temporarily— to the disciplined approach of the 1960s. It is far too early to hazard a guess at its probability of success or its impact on the moderate impetus toward those economic policy reforms noted above. But it will be interesting to observe whether efforts at reform do survive the present difficult and complex period in Mexican political and economic history, or whether a government-private sector rapprochement will emerge during the final three years of this administration at the expense of the initial targets of Echeverría's attention.

## THE ECHEVERRÍA YEARS: INTERPRETATIONS

It would be difficult to distill much evidence concerning the Mexican development process from the events of the past four years. The time horizon is far too short to separate the cyclical from the secular trends in either the political or economic arenas. However, since the bulk of this book does offer a general interpretation of the Mexican political system, an introductory commentary on certain aspects of the past four years may help to sharpen the focus of its perspective for the reader.

The following chapters suggest that Mexico has evolved a political system with extensive capabilities for meeting the societal demands likely to arise in the process of modern economic growth. In them, I have argued that the country is governed by an authoritarian elite group—the so-called Revolutionary Coalition—and that the "official party," the PRI, is used by that governing elite to legitimize its position of political hegemony, overwhelm any opposition at the polls, co-opt potential opposition leadership, and control the development of demands on the political system in Mexico. I have drawn two general conclusions from this argument. The first is that the leadership of the Revolutionary Coalition, committed to the regime's continued control of Mexican politics, would probably succeed in fostering continued economic growth and the requisite political stability throughout the decade of the 1970s despite the many problems facing a country under-endowed with natural resources and facing an annual population growth rate in excess of 3.5 percent. The second conclusion is that policy changes to manage the problems of political evolution and economic development would be pragmatic and, above all, incremental.

This earlier analysis undoubtedly biases my present interpretation of the events in Mexico since 1969. I find myself developing interpretations to support earlier conclusions and questioning differing versions of others. Having admitted the bias, let me first set forth an interpretation which is fairly compatible with my earlier conclusions, then try to do justice to alternative views.

Liberals in Mexico were deeply disappointed when the Revolutionary Coalition selected Luis Echeverría to succeed Gustavo Díaz-Ordaz as president of Mexico in 1970. As noted in chapter 8, their hopes for reform lay elsewhere, and few observed much in Echeverría's background to suggest anything but "more of the same" with his inauguration. Indeed, as Minister of *Gobernación* during the Díaz-Ordaz administration, Echeverría appeared to have been closely linked to the hard-line policies of his predecessor, including those leading to the Battle of Tlatelolco.

But things turned out quite differently. During the election campaign, views of Echeverría's politics began to shift, and by late 1970, if not earlier, he had become the darling of the liberals, the hope for reform. And, as noted above, Echeverría did embrace change, both rhetorically and programmatically, as he took over the presidency.

What this transition points to is an enduring strength of the PRI regime—the sexennial necessity for the reconsideration of old policies and the consideration of new ones. The evidence available, while fragmented at best, does suggest that Mexico's political leadership makes its choice of a new president—explicitly or implicitly—with an eye to the institutional necessities of the regime for the next six years. And the salient institutional necessity seems to be interpreted as that degree of political stability and quiescence needed for a continuation of the regime's hegemony over the political system.

Many other considerations are undoubtedly in play every six years. The goals, values, and policy preferences of all those consulted in the choosing of a president are bound to cover a broad spectrum. Regime stability is clearly not the sole criterion involved, but the "pendulum pattern" in the Mexican political process apparent since the emergence of the PRI regime strongly suggests the salience of this criterion.

Against this background, one might view the emergence of Echeverría's "liberalism" in the following manner. Toward the end of the 1960s there developed within the coalition a degree of consensus that some changes in direction would have to be made in order to avoid a growing degree of popular discontent with the system. The events of 1968 could have been viewed as portents of the destabilizing things to come if some effort were not made to breathe life back into the symbols of the revolution which had contributed so much to the legitimacy of the PRI regime over the past four decades. If such a consensus did inform the selection process for 1970, then any candidate chosen by the coalition would have been intended to begin some movement back toward the center of the regime's political spectrum.

The change in direction, modest and pragmatic as it might be, would still have been opposed by many within and without the confines of the PRI regime. As noted in chapters 5 and 6, the mutually profitable linkages between the regime and the upper reaches of the Mexican private sector are legion. Any change in governmental direction which might in the slightest way disturb those linkages will always provoke the opposition of many members of the Revolutionary Coalition who identify with orthodox private sector economic policy views and benefit from the symbiotic relationship between government and private sector which has developed in Mexico.

Given these circumstances, Luis Echeverría might well have been viewed as the perfect choice for 1970-76. If there was a fragile consensus within the coalition's leadership that some moves in support of income redistribution, social welfare, and more rapid job creation had to be made, the easiest way to retain that consensus would be to choose a candidate who could be expected to introduce the necessary shifts in policy without excessive enthusiasm. And on the basis of his political track record, Echeverría would have appeared to be just such a man.

Looking at the record of the first three Echeverría years, there are many indications that his intentions have been to keep reforms modest rather than major. Beyond the level of rhetoric, there have been no significant policy changes affecting the vital interests of the Mexican business community. Echeverría's unwillingness to adopt any major tax reforms seems in many ways symbolic of a distinction between marginal and major shifts that has thus far characterized his administration. The tax reforms suggested in late 1971 were not radical; they would simply have rid the present tax laws of some of the anomalies which have long existed to the great benefit of those at the top of the Mexican income scale. And they seemed clearly needed; the government must increase its revenues considerably if it is to be able to finance even those marginal reforms which constitute the central element of Echeverría's policy shifts.

There are at least three plausible explanations for Echeverría's refusal to adopt a serious tax reform package to date. To a degree they are all complementary. The first is that Echeverría may not support major reforms because he is not convinced of their necessity. In the eyes of many, the Mexican "miracle" is not yet dead. Despite some cyclical problems, the economy continues to demonstrate the capacity for healthy growth rates. Those growth rates are presently made possible by the annual investment of about eighteen percent of gross domestic product, over two-thirds of which comes from the private sector, and the equivalent of another two or three percent which comes from abroad. Why should the president risk the loss of private sector confidence, the slowing of investment, or a run on the peso unless he is convinced that Mexico's traditional approach to economic development is clearly unequal to the demands imposed by present patterns of income distribution, unemployment and underemployment, rural poverty and urban discontent, and the probable political consequences of such patterns?

Most of Echeverría's official advisers seem convinced that the old policies will no longer work, to say nothing of their views concerning the issues of equity and justice. But what about the views of his unofficial advisers, many of them linked to the upper reaches of the private sector, and what about his own views? Here one has to be careful not to be misled by the rhetoric of the administration. As this study demonstrates, the gap between government rhetoric and the reality implied by government policies is broader in Mexico than in nearly any other country. The Coalition has for thirty years served up revolutionary rhetoric while it practiced a highly orthodox approach to the problems of economic development. Is there not good reason then to suspect that many of the repeated pronouncements of the present administration were in the standard Mexican tradition, that they were intended to legitimize the continued hegemony of the PRI regime in a period of growing stress on the system, and that they were not a particularly accurate barometer of official intentions? Echeverría's activist and "leftist" foreign policy through 1973 fits well with this interpretation.

A second reason for Echeverría's refusal to adopt major tax reforms may be his concern that unless the action is understood and grudgingly agreed to by the private sector in advance it will seriously undermine Mexican economic growth for some time. There is little question that a complete loss of private sector confidence in the Echeverría administration could have such an effect. Therefore the president may be unwilling to adopt tax or any other economic proposals which could lead to this result until the risks have been considerably narrowed through consultations, explanations, and assurances. Whether, and to what degree such efforts are being made, I do not know.

A third plausible reason for the absence of any major reform thus far concerns the political events of 1971, and goes to the heart of the issue of whether or not the PRI system is nearing a serious regime crisis. Echeverría may have been deeply shaken by the Corpus Christi Day incident and the challenge to the political rules of the game in Mexico which it might have represented. To the degree that Needler's interpretation of the events surrounding the incident is accurate, the president was being fundamentally challenged in a public way from elements *within* the Revolutionary Coalition, probably those most closely allied with the business community; their efforts were apparently directed toward eliminating the administration's potentially reformist tendencies before they were allowed to develop beyond the realm of rhetoric. If this interpretation is correct, and if Echeverría had to appeal to the armed forces to secure his position, then his reasons for approaching any major reform affecting the interests of the business community and the discontented elements of the coalition with extreme caution become obvious. Unless he were prepared for a confrontation which might severely shake the coalition, repoliticize the armed forces in a major way, and have unpredictable results for the political system, he would not undertake any such reforms without building a consensus for them.[2]

---

[2]Even if the "unofficial reports" which Needler cites are inaccurate in suggesting that Echeverría planned to meet with the student demonstrators and seek their support, one need not jump to the conclusion that the president knowingly allowed the confrontation to take place in order to serve his own political purposes. It is doubtful, after all, that any Mexican president would deliberately put himself in the position of having to appeal to the Mexican military in order to control events. The leadership of the Revolutionary Coalition must realize full well that each and every appeal it is forced to make to the military enhances the probability of a major reentry of the military into the Mexican political process.

This probability will be enhanced still further if it becomes necessary to rely increasingly on the army in sporadic campaigns against rural guerrillas. In June of 1974 President Echeverría sent nearly 10,000 troops into the mountains of Guerrero in an attempt

Using the tax reform issue as a proxy for the political intentions of the Echeverría administration in general, it is clear that the first two possible explanations of Echeverría's lack of forcefulness in this field fit far more easily into my general interpretation of Mexican politics than does the third. For the third could signal the potential breakdown of a regime which I suggested in 1969 had a considerable capacity for continued hegemony over Mexican politics. The potential for breakdown merits analysis not only for those interested specifically in Mexican politics but also for those interested more generally in the evolution of authoritarian or patrimonial regimes.

 A political scientist very familiar with the Mexican experience recently suggested that authoritarian regimes are best characterized by (1) limited political pluralism, (2) low subject mobilization of the population, and (3) the predominance of patrimonial rulership on the part of a single leader or a small group.[3] She defines limited political pluralism as a situation in which interest groups are tied to, and highly dependent upon, the regime. Group leaders owe their major allegiance to the regime's elite and depend little upon the support of their followers. Her definition of low subject mobilization includes both the non-participatory attitude developed in the Almond/Verba "subject-participant" dichotomy (see below, chapter 7) and the empty formalism of what participation there is. Citizens are temporarily mobilized to ratify authoritarian elite decisions and to demonstrate support for the regime. Generally, however, such regimes discourage autonomous participation. Finally, patrimonial rulership refers to a style of rulership "in which the ruler grants privileges, goods, or similar 'benefices' to a select portion of the ruled. In return, the individual recipients acknowledge the authority of the ruler and defer to him."[4] Since these characteristics are a close fit with those spelled out at greater length throughout this study, they can be very helpful as a shorthand approach in this new introductory chapter.

What does the Corpus Christi incident highlight about the authoritarian framework in Mexico? First, it adds some further substance to the view that significant elements in Mexico's private sector—in many ways still dependent upon the political regime through the latter's host of controls over the economy—are nevertheless prepared to support challenges to the regime when they perceive major interests to be at stake. In terms of the Purcell model this would imply that the "pluralism" of the business community was less limited

---

to terminate the seven year guerrilla career of Lucio Cabañas and his followers. This largest military campaign in three decades was triggered when Cabañas apparently kidnapped Ruben Figueroa, a millionaire "populist" politician just nominated by the PRI to be the next Governor of Guerrero.

[3] Susan Kaufman Purcell, "Decision Making in an Authoritarian Regime: Theoretical Implications from a Mexican Case Study," *World Politics* 26 (October 1973): 28–54.

[4] *Ibid.*, p. 30.

or "dependent" than required for an authoritarian regime to operate without significant stress upon the system.

Alternatively, one could argue that the financial and organizational support for right-wing paramilitary activity may come strictly from within the confines of the political elite itself, and does not necessarily include the involvement of "outsiders" from the private sector. If this is the case, it suggests that consensus within the Revolutionary Coalition has disintegrated to such an extent that it may no longer be able to provide a relatively stable center of authority. Conflicts within the coalition which go deep enough to produce such clashes risk not only a reentry of the military into Mexican politics but the end to "low subject mobilization" as well.

As David Ronfeldt reminded us recently, the Mexican military never got out of politics altogether.[5] Since 1952 "maintenance of internal order" has been officially posited as the Mexican army's primary mission. Military zone commanders have on many occasions played important roles in state politics, and military officers are often invited to become candidates for office. However, by reentry I am referring to a return to politics brought about by a deterioration of political stability in the process of which clubs once again become trumps and as a result of which the army once again becomes the ultimate arbiter of Mexican politics. The hastiest glance at South America reminds us that the role of the military in politics is intimately related to the problem of regime legitimacy, or consensus on political rules of the game. The institutionalization of political stability in Mexico with the emergence of the PRI regime pushed the army out of an active political role by the early 1940s; the breakup of that stability could, and almost inevitably would, pull the army back in.

This likelihood is increased by the rapid political mobilization which would undoubtedly accompany a breakdown of the present regime. As noted in chapters 6 and 7, the capacity of the PRI regime to smother open political contests and to hide intra-coalition competition from the public has helped to keep the average Mexican citizen politically apathetic. But a return to open bidding for political support, electoral or otherwise, would bring a rather hasty end to the prolonged period of political quiescence. With that change all the old rules of the game would disappear, the bidding for support would polarize Mexican politics, and the military—appealed to from all sides—could hardly avoid being sucked into the vacuum created by the disappearance of a "legitimate" regime.

If conflict within the Revolutionary Coalition—with or without the direct participation of the Mexican private sector—should bring an end to the PRI

---

[5] See David Ronfeldt, "Patterns of Civil-Military Rule," in Luigi R. Einandi, ed., *Latin America in the 1970's.* Rand Corporation, Santa Monica, Calif., December 1972, pp. 74-98.

regime, what would it tell us about the dynamics of authoritarian regimes? Firstly, it would raise an interesting theoretical question about the relationship between an authoritarian government and the private sector of the economy.

Philippe Schmitter has recently speculated about the capacity of authoritarian regimes to endure. He has argued that under present-day circumstances it seems quite plausible to imagine the permanence or persistence of authoritarian rule. Recent developments "in political and material technology have made it vastly easier to establish and implement a consistent set of public policies; to capture evidence of emerging opposition by social indicators and/or survey research and to act preemptively; to regiment political activity into a single official party; to 'corporatize' systems of interest representation; to retain a monopoly over the instruments of organized violence; and to socialize and indoctrinate subjects through media and mass education."[6]

What the Mexican experience might eventually suggest is that if an authoritarian regime does allow the development of a large private sector (in relation to the total size of the economy), that regime may be unable to control it over the long term. Whether because it comes to depend on private sector elites for rapid growth which is a necessary ingredient in its other policies, or because the goals and values of major elements of the ruling regime become closely identified with those of the private sector business groups, it may well prove practically—if not theoretically—impossible for an authoritarian regime to let the private sector genie out of the bottle without losing control of it in the long run.[7] If such an outcome is to be avoided, it would seem necessary for authoritarian regimes to constrain the process by which the private sector's influence on government policies grows faster than that of other "corporate" groups within the societal structure. Whether this can be done remains an interesting question.

Secondly, and closely related, a mortal conflict within the Revolutionary Coalition would raise the issue of the extent to which the military can be "retired" under an authoritarian regime. In Mexico the army has in effect been retired from an active political role for three decades. If the military retains an active role in the governing circles of an authoritarian regime, it may theoretically be able to check the growing influence of business elites in the overall corporate structure. But such a balancing act will then depend upon the military's perceptions of the role of the private sector and its own relationship with it. Is there enough evidence—empirical or theoretical—to

---

[6]Philippe C. Schmitter, "The Portugalization of Brazil," *Authoritarian Brazil: Origins, Policies and Future,* ed. Alfred Stepan (New Haven: Yale University Press, 1973), p. 190.

[7]Of course it must be admitted that the Mexican regime has never approached the problem of retaining control with a dedication to the use of all the available methods noted by Schmitter in the above quotation.

suggest any predictability about that relationship over time in varying socio-economic and cultural contexts? And if the military does retain an active role in the authoritarian structure of government, does this have implications for the "legitimacy" of the regime itself over the long term?

All of this discussion, unrelated as much of it may seem to Mexico of 1974, has been set forth at least in part because many serious students of Mexico are persuaded that this is indeed a time of crisis for Mexico, and that the future for its political system is more in doubt now than it has been at any time since the Revolutionary Coalition stabilized its rule with the aid of the official party in the early 1940s.

The mildest version of this general interpretation is found in Martin Needler's *Politics and Society in Mexico*. Needler suggests that the very success of the PRI regime in fostering economic development has moved the system toward a turning point. Economic development and the resulting change in social structure have undermined the role of the PRI as a party which has guided "the development of a society not yet ready for democracy."[8] Now, in his view, Mexico is prepared for democracy, and the party must choose between resigning its controlled hegemony over Mexican politics and "maintaining the dominant position of the PRI by the use of force. The forces of liberalism that have emerged with the country's development cannot be ignored or cowed like the peasants of the Mexico of yesterday."[9] Needler concludes that by the 1970s Mexico "had arrived at a crossroads," and faced a choice between democracy and dictatorship.[10]

The crisis theme in Needler's work is very softly and cautiously stated. A more pronounced form is sounded in Daniel Cosío Villegas' *El Sistema Político Mexicano*.[11] In this essay the dean of Mexican historians examines many aspects of Mexican political life which disturb him: the absolute power of the Mexican presidency, a "profound dissatisfaction" with the Mexican political system on the part of growing numbers of Mexicans, the antidemocratic bias of Mexico's strongest pressure groups (bankers, industrialists, commercial agriculture, and other business groups), and the difficulties of reforming the PRI from within so that it might forcefully commit itself to "economic development with social justice." But, in his view, the major source of the crisis facing Mexico in the 1970s seems to lie in the radicalizing effects of the confluence of three major trends: (1) a wealthy upper class which is increasingly out of touch with social and economic realities in its own country; (2) a rapidly growing and increasingly important group of

[8]Martin C. Needler, *Politics and Society in Mexico* (Albuquerque: University of New Mexico Press, 1971), p. 35.

[9]*Ibid.*, pp. 35-36.

[10]*Ibid.*, p. 36.

[11]Daniel Cosío Villegas, *El Sistema Político Mexicano* (Mexico: Cuadernos de Juaquin Mortiz, 1972).

*técnicos*, brought more and more into conflict with Mexico's upper class if only because the "torrent" of well-trained graduates exceeds existing opportunities for appropriate employment and socio-economic mobility; and (3), a growing polarization in rural Mexico between those with good land and adequate irrigation on the one hand, and the fast growing number of landless and marginal landholders on the other.

Cosío Villegas argues that such trends will of necessity produce permanent conflict. He stops short of saying that the PRI regime will be unequal to the task of mediating these conflicting interests successfully, but he clearly fears that even success will be costly. For success would be achieved at the price of concentrating even more power in the presidency, and thus moving Mexico further along a course toward an authoritarian or "antidemocratic" regime.[12]

The most unconditional presentation of the Mexico-in-crisis theme is found in Kenneth Johnson's *Mexican Democracy: A Critical View.*[13] There is, says Johnson, "a crisis of legitimacy facing the PRI and it is one to which Alfonso Martínez Dominguez and his successors will be forced to assign a high priority or face certain disaster."[14]

In Johnson's analysis the potential disaster facing the PRI regime is grounded in the following propositions. First, the present governing elite has managed to alienate the "vast masses" of the Mexican population. This lower class alienation stems from the Revolutionary Coalition's political behavior (attempts to co-opt or eradicate leadership of leftist political groups, the handling of the 1968 student demonstrations, etc.) and the "great socio-economic potential for generating expressions of political alienation from the custodians of the state. . . . Political outrage can erupt violently at any time in Mexico and the provocations can vary, but socio-economic wretchedness is in the background of most such expressions."[15]

Johnson's second proposition is that there is a good deal of middle class discontent emerging, and this creates potential leadership for lower class protest movements. He argues that the PRI regime has had "no plan for the burgeoning middle class . . . . that was producing leaders of satellite movements opposed to the PRI."[16]

Johnson's third proposition, a natural consequence of the first two, is that many Mexicans, particularly the young, are transferring loyalties to groups demanding reform of the PRI system. Echoing Cosío Villegas, Johnson warns that the newly educated unemployed (or underemployed) constitute

[12]*Ibid.*, pp. 105–6.

[13]Kenneth F. Johnson, *Mexican Democracy: A Critical View* (Boston: Allyn and Bacon, Inc., 1971).

[14]*Ibid.*, p. 61.

[15]*Ibid.*, p. 171.

[16]*Ibid.*, p. 70.

the regime's most serious challenge. "It has been difficult for a Mexican youth to act the role of a responsible first class citizen when in his eyes the socio-economic-political system is deliberately rigged against him. Awareness of this sparked a mass consciousness among the students, and led to the violence of 1968."[17]

Finally, Johnson argues that the process of urbanization is rapidly increasing the potential for violence inherent in the first three propositions. "The burgeoning of urban areas has made more people acutely aware of their socioeconomic plight, and their proximity to one another has facilitated the articulation and communication of demands for reform that are directed to the political system." The aggregate result is "a new and explosive mood that will prevail throughout the decade of the 1970's. The urban localities and metropolitan areas will be foci of demands for revolutionary change."[18]

There can be little doubt that demands upon the Mexican political system are rising. Such a trend is bound to be positively correlated with other measurable trends in Mexico, e.g., a population growth rate of about 3.7 percent per annum, rising levels of open and disguised unemployment, growing numbers of landless rural laborers, and the appearance of an "educated-underemployed" group in urban Mexico which is now providing leadership for rural as well as urban forms of resistance to the PRI regime. The more important issue is whether or not the capacity of the political system to manage these demands is keeping pace with their growth.

I remain somewhat skeptical of the theory that a crisis stemming from a rapid growth of unfulfilled demands is imminent in Mexico for many reasons, most of which are based upon this study's analysis of the Mexican political system. They include the present state of Mexico's political culture, the expected rate of change in that culture, the continued substantial rate of economic growth in Mexico, and the demonstrated capacity of the PRI system to respond to political demands in an impressive variety of ways.

Additionally, I find it hard to accept the view that the steady increase in the rate of urbanization in Mexico poses a growing threat *per se* to the stability of the present regime. It is an integral element of the Johnson analysis that the process of rapid urbanization is a salient cause of the "crisis" now facing the regime. But he appears to ignore all the contrary evidence regarding the political implications of urbanization in Mexico in particular and Latin America in general. On balance, I still find more convincing the general conclusion that "there is little ground for belief that the swelling urban masses of today's developing nations will prove to be politically radical or violent."[19]

[17]*Ibid.*, p. 163.

[18]*Ibid.*, pp. 172–75.

[19]Joan Robinson, "The Urban Poor: Disruption or Political Integration in Third World Cities?" *World Politics*, 22 (April 1970): 413. Some of the works of Oscar Lewis

For these and other less important reasons I am led to question the degree to which predictions of crisis for Mexico are often at least as much a reflection of normative judgments as they are of empirical analysis. I take issue not with the normative implications but with the analysis. Some of it still seems to suggest that Mexico must choose between two models—democratic or autocratic.[20] A great deal of recent work on Latin America, both theoretical and empirical, suggests otherwise. Whether labeled patrimonial, corporatist, or corporatist-authoritarian, a third modal path of political evolution has characterized the political systems of many Latin American states[21] As Schmitter put the case, Latin American nations "have available a rather rich and wide variety of authoritarian options."[22]

Mexico shares many of the constituent elements of the allegedly determining factors in Latin American authoritarian syndromes—the Ibero-Mediterranean ethos, delayed development, and external dependence. The depth of its "elective affinity" for an enduring authoritarian-corporatist regime is highly uncertain, but must be carefully analyzed if one is to comprehend the range of choices and the relative probabilities at play in the evolution of the Mexican political system.

 Returning for the final time to a theme which has run throughout this introduction, the crucial relationship between the Revolutionary Coalition and Mexico's business elites may well prove the most important variable in the Mexican political equation in the final three Echeverría years and beyond. While most analysts seem to focus on socioeconomic and political demands for change arising from the "masses" and the lower-middle classes in Mexico, I still tend toward the presumption that such demands, whatever their apparent magnitude, will not prove beyond the capacity of the PRI regime to manage successfully *if* the process of incremental reforms to alleviate Mexico's socio-economic problems is allowed to continue. I am more persuaded that the demands from business elites for little or no change, for "more of the same," will prove to be the most difficult demands with which the system is forced to cope.[23] Have those business elites burst the restraints

---

contribute much to an understanding of the conservative aspects of the process of urbanization in Mexico.

[20]The works of Cosío Villegas and Needler are far too sophisticated to fall into this pattern.

[21]Two recent collections of essays present an excellent review of this literature. They are Alfred Stepan, ed., *Authoritarian Brazil: Origins, Policies and Future* (New Haven: Yale University Press, 1973) and *The Review of Politics* 36 (January 1974). See also Riordan Roett, *Brazil: Politics in a Patrimonial Society* (Boston: Allyn and Bacon, 1973) for a persuasive treatment of many of the themes raised throughout this literature.

[22]Philippe C. Schmitter, "Paths to Political Development," in *Changing Latin America: New Interpretations of its Politics and Society*, ed. Douglas A. Chalmers, Proceedings of the Academy of Political Science 30, no. 4, (New York, 1972), p. 93.

[23]Admittedly these demands from the "top" are to a great extent the opposite side of the "demands from the bottom" coin. The distinction is made simply to emphasize

of the corporatist-authoritarian mold in Mexico to be recaptured, if at all, only by a regime change and the chaotic process which would accompany it? One would think that those elites would recognize that the PRI regime's approach to the problems of economic development was about as compatible with their own interests as possible under any stable and legitimate political regime. Nevertheless, it is worth recalling Cosío Villegas' judgment that Mexico's private sector elites are losing touch with the economic and social realities of their own country. If they are, the process can only encourage another Corpus Christi Day affair, more threats of capital flight, and a slowing of domestic investment and economic growth.

Should this scenario eventuate, the Echeverría administration and the Revolutionary Coalition would be faced with two options: either use their full range of policy tools to crack down on those private sector elites in an attempt to "reincorporate" them, or abandon even modest economic and social policy reforms for an interim period. The former option would represent an "all-or-nothing" throw of the dice with incalculable short-term risks for the present regime. The latter option would entail far fewer short-term risks, but might equally threaten the regime in the medium term from the right as well as the left.

Whether, and how close to, this kind of choice the Revolutionary Coalition will come, few people know. And those who do don't talk very much except, presumably, to each other.

—Washington, D.C.
June, 1974

---

the possibility that minimum concessions from the "top" may provide enough policy space for the PRI regime to manage demands from "below" for some time to come.

# THE POLITICS OF MEXICAN DEVELOPMENT

*Chapter 1*

# THE POLITICAL ECONOMY OF
# MEXICAN DEVELOPMENT

Since the mid-1930s the Mexican economy has grown at an annual rate in excess of 6 percent, an accomplishment often referred to as the Mexican "miracle."[1] To maintain this pace for thirty-five years may not be miraculous, but by any standard it is impressive. As table 1-1 demonstrates, the Mexican economic performance over the past several decades has greatly surpassed those of its Latin American neighbors. Moreover, it compares favorably with the growth records of the world's developed economies. This is true even if the growth rates of the latter countries during the decades of their most rapid industrialization are used as the basis for comparison.[2]

Throughout the 1960s, the Mexican economy has continued to exhibit a dynamism which distinguishes it from other large nations in the Latin American setting. As noted in table 1-3, it grew at better than 6.4 percent a year during the first eight years of the decade. Over the same period, the Latin American average was well below 5 percent. In sum, whether measured in aggregate or per capita terms; whether compared with other Latin American countries, or with the developed economies of the world; whether compared over the period since the mid-1930s, or with the decades of rapid industrial growth for each country concerned, Mexican economic growth for the last thirty-five years registers a singular achievement.

This book is a study of that achievement, and is therefore a study of both economic and political development in Mexico. An effort to understand the factors contributing to the Mexican economic miracle inevitably leads to an examination of Mexico's political system, since that is where the seeds of Mexico's economic success have been nurtured. Likewise, major obstacles to

---

[1] Throughout the study aggregate rates of growth for the Mexican economy are given in real terms.

[2] Postwar rates of growth for Japan and some European countries are, of course, an exception.

1

TABLE 1-1. DECADAL RATES OF GROWTH: LATE 1930s TO EARLY 1960s

| Area | Period | Product | Population | Per Capita Product |
|---|---|---|---|---|
| Latin America (total) | 1935-39 to 1954-56 | 55.2 | 24.2 | 25.0 |
| Mexico | 1935-39 to 1960-62 | 79.7 | 31.4 | 36.8 |
| Argentina | 1935-39 to 1960-62 | 27.2 | 20.4 | 6.2 |
| Brazil | 1935-39 to 1959-61 | 59.6 | 30.2 | 22.6 |
| Chile | 1935-39 to 1960-62 | 41.1 | 22.2 | 15.5 |
| Canada | 1939 to 1960-62 | 58.3 | 23.1 | 28.6 |
| U.S.A. | 1939 to 1960-62 | 48.7 | 16.4 | 27.7 |
| U.S.S.R. | 1940 to 1960 | 52.1 | 4.8 | 45.1 |

Source: Simon Kuznets, *Postwar Economic Growth: Four Lectures* (Cambridge: Harvard University Press, Belknap Press, 1964), pp. 129-38.

TABLE 1-2. ECONOMIC GROWTH IN TEN DEVELOPED COUNTRIES

| Country | Initial Period | Terminal Period | Percentage Change per Decade in | | |
|---|---|---|---|---|---|
| | | | Population | Net National Product | NNP per Capita |
| United Kingdom | 1860-1869 | 1949-1953 | 8.0 | 21.5 | 12.5 |
| | 1860-1869 | 1905-1914 | 11.1 | 25.0 | 12.5 |
| France | 1841-1850 | 1949-1953 | 1.3 | 15.3 | 13.8 |
| | 1841-1850 | 1901-1910 | 1.9 | 18.6 | 16.3 |
| Germany | 1860-1869 | 1950-1954 | 10.1 | 27.4 | 15.1 |
| | 1860-1869 | 1905-1914 | 11.5 | 35.6 | 21.6 |
| Denmark | 1870-1878 | 1950-1954 | 11.5 | 30.1 | 16.7 |
| | 1870-1878 | 1904-1913 | 11.3 | 32.7 | 19.3 |
| Sweden | 1861-1868 | 1950-1954 | 6.6 | 36.0 | 27.6 |
| | 1861-1868 | 1904-1913 | 6.8 | 34.8 | 26.2 |
| Italy | 1862-1868 | 1950-1954 | 6.9 | 18.0 | 10.4 |
| | 1862-1868 | 1904-1913 | 7.0 | 15.7 | 8.1 |
| Russia/U.S.S.R. | 1870 | 1954 | 13.4 | 31.0 | 15.4 |
| | 1870 | 1913 | 15.7 | 27.7 | 10.4 |
| U.S.A. | 1869-1878 | 1950-1954 | 17.4 | 41.2 | 20.3 |
| | 1869-1878 | 1904-1913 | 22.3 | 56.0 | 27.5 |
| Canada | 1870-1879 | 1950-1954 | 18.3 | 41.3 | 19.3 |
| | 1870-1879 | 1905-1914 | 17.8 | 47.1 | 24.7 |
| Japan | 1878-1887 | 1950-1954 | 12.7 | 42.3 | 26.3 |
| | 1878-1887 | 1903-1912 | 11.6 | 49.3 | 33.7 |

Source: Simon Kuznets, "Quantitative Aspects of the Economic Growth of Nations. I. Levels and Variability of Growth Rates," *Economic Development and Cultural Change* 5 (October, 1956): 13.

TABLE 1-3.  RECENT LATIN AMERICAN GROWTH RATES

| Area | Gross Domestic Product[a] | | | Per Capita GDP |
| | 1960–66 | 1967 | 1968 | 1960–69 |
|---|---|---|---|---|
| Latin America | 4.6 | 4.5 | 6.1 | 2.2 |
| Mexico | 6.3 | 6.5 | 7.3 | 3.3 |
| Argentina | 2.9 | 1.9 | 4.8 | 1.9 |
| Brazil | 4.1 | 5.0 | 8.3 | 2.6 |
| Chile | 5.4 | 2.0 | 2.7 | 2.0 |
| Venezuela | 5.1 | 6.0 | 5.7 | 1.3 |

Source: Economic Commission for Latin America, "Notas sobre la economía y el desarrollo de América Latina," 16 (April 16, 1969); 42 (May 1, 1970); 44 (May, 1970).
[a]Calculated at factor cost.

sustained economic development in other Latin American countries today may be traced to the structure and operation of their political systems. Politics and economic development are deeply intertwined in these countries because all approaches to economic growth provoke serious political counter-pressures.

Perhaps this point is best understood by characterizing economic systems in two distinct yet inseparable ways: first, as "engines of growth"; second, as "engines of distribution." In order to sustain rapid growth, less developed countries must raise considerably their domestic rates of savings and investment. Mexico, for example, was investing less than 9 percent of its gross domestic product per year as late as 1940; within two decades that figure climbed to 20 percent. It rose in great part as a response to government policies specifically developed to intensify the pace of economic growth.

A second prerequisite for rapid growth, particularly in major Latin American countries, involves the productivity of governmental expenditures. Broadly speaking, the larger the proportion of public sector income which can be channeled into what are often called "bottleneck-breaking" investments, the greater will be the productivity of all capital expenditures, private and public. Investments in industrial and agricultural infrastructure—in power, communication, hydraulic systems—are generally undertaken by governments, not private entrepreneurs. If they are undertaken at the right time and in the right quantities, they can exercise a benign influence both upon aggregate rates of investment and upon the gradual development of a fluid, flexible and competitive economy.

Any country can assemble programs to meet these prerequisites for sustained development. The problem is that policies designed to fuel the savings-investment engine of growth—if they are successful—have a decided impact upon the distribution of welfare within a society. During periods of rapid industrialization the incomes of certain rather small groups tend to rise rapidly, while earnings of the rest, including all those near the bottom of the income scale, increase slowly or not at all or actually decline. Thus the bill for rapid growth is generally paid through forgone consumption on the part of those segments of society who can least afford it.

A natural response of those groups dissatisfied with the welfare distribution during such a period of growth is to demand change through the political system. At this point—with variations depending upon the modus operandi of the political system—governmental tax, expenditure, commercial and wage policies designed to promote growth become the object of bitter political contention. Some governments can contain the pressures for a redistribution of the gains from development without slowing the engine of growth; most cannot. A general Latin American pattern has been one in which the conflicting demands over who is to get what have produced inconsistent and short-lived economic policies detrimental to expanded savings, productive investment and sustained industrialization.

Mexico has been a dramatic exception to this pattern. Its economic policies have fueled the growth process; its political system has successfully absorbed the pressures resulting from the impact of rapid growth on welfare. This is the real Mexican miracle, and the subject of this study. Some have lavishly praised the Mexican government for its contribution to the economic development of Mexico. Many others have condemned it for allowing the benefits of rapid growth to be so inequitably distributed. The purpose of this book is neither to praise nor condemn the miracle, but simply to understand it for what it has been and may yet become.

## THE DEBATE OVER MEXICAN DEVELOPMENT

Any examination of the political roots of the Mexican economic miracle begins on two divergent notes: one of consensus, and another of chaos. The first reflects the general conviction among Mexican scholars that the country's singular economic performance is intimately linked to the political stability which has characterized Mexico since 1930. Nobody who studies the Mexican scene can avoid the intuitive judgment which Dwight Brothers made several years ago: "It seems clear from a comparison with the record of most other Latin American countries that Mexico's remarkable economic progress in the recent past is attributable in no small measure to the political stability that has been achieved."[3] The challenge, of course, is to understand the relationship between Mexico's political stability and its economic develop-

---

[3] Dwight Brothers, review of Raymond Vernon, *The Dilemma of Mexico's Development: The Roles of the Private and Public Sectors,* in *American Economic Review* 54 (March 1964): 157.

ment. At one level the importance of stability for sustained economic growth is self-evident. Since the expansion of both industrial enterprises and physical infrastructure requires large investment well in advance of financial return, reasonable stability in the political system becomes a prerequisite for such innovation. This is especially true if the bulk of new investment is to come from the private sector, as in the case of Mexico: close to 70 percent of Mexican domestic investment since 1940 has been generated by the private sector.

But stable political systems are not always positively correlated with rapid economic growth. Far more common, perhaps, is the pattern set by postwar India, in which—until recently—relative political stability has coincided with low to moderate rates of economic expansion. Furthermore, there is a great deal of evidence to suggest that rapid economic growth itself is a destabilizing force in society. It has been argued that rapid growth leads to political instability in the following ways:

1) it disrupts traditional social structure, increasing the number of individuals who are déclassé, and therefore inclined toward political protest;[4]

2) it expands the number of both gainers and losers, nouveaux riches and nouveaux pauvres. Members of the first group use their growing economic resources in efforts to enhance their social status and increase their political power; those in the second category protest the decline in their economic fortunes through political and other channels;

3) by producing higher incomes and better standards of living it creates rising expectations which outdistance the capacity of the economy to satisfy them;

4) it increases literacy, exposure to mass media, and the capacity for group organization; all these trends produce growing demands on the political system.[5]

The list could be expanded indefinitely, but most students of the development process are convinced that the economic, social and political systems of a single society are interdependent, and that these four major factors describe accurately how rapid changes in one part will produce instability in the others. With these observations in mind, this study will focus on two aspects of Mexican political stability: (1) its relationship to the particularly dynamic economic performance of the past three decades; and (2) its longevity in the face of rapid growth and accompanying social change.

[4] Mancur Olson, Jr., "Rapid Economic Growth as a Destabilizing Force," in *Journal of Economic History* 23 (December 1963): 529–52.

[5] This is only a partial list of the destabilizing aspects of rapid economic growth. See especially Olson, *ibid.*; Lawrence Stone, "Theories of Revolution," *World Politics* 18 (January 1966): 159–76; and Samuel P. Huntington, *Political Order in Changing Societies* (New Haven: Yale University Press, 1968), chap. 1.

The note of chaos which confronts the analyst of Mexico echoes the recent debate over the nature and the modus operandi of the Mexican political system. It is hardly an exaggeration to say that there are as many distinct interpretations of Mexican politics as there are scholars of the subject. One recent analysis of Mexico, for example, concluded that economic development was being jeopardized by a government which lacked the strength to implement policies conducive to continued growth. It pictured the president and his party caught in an impossible effort to meet all political demands, squandering public-sector resources in the process. For each economic ailment vexing Mexico the author proposed a remedy; but he argued that every positive course of action was blocked by political opposition strong enough to immobilize the present political regime. Given the author's picture of the political process, there is little wonder that he was profoundly pessimistic of the chances for continued development.[6]

That interpretation quickly evoked a contrasting one which pictured the Mexican government as formulating and implementing a development strategy from a position of decided strength. It was argued that the present Mexican regime was durable enough to ignore redistribution demands from the political extremes and to concentrate its resources in programs to sustain the growth process.[7] Other views were expressed throughout the 1960s with no sign of an emerging consensus. Economists have varied in their interpretations of Mexico's political economy; political scientists are no closer to agreement when they analyze the Mexican political system. Some see only its weaknesses; others only its strengths. Some portray it as an emerging democratic system; others picture it as rigidly, even harshly, authoritarian. Some attribute to the governing elite the best of liberal intentions; others, the worst of traditional oligarchic behavior. Furthermore, most political interpretations have been produced by foreigners; few qualified Mexicans write about, or even discuss openly, the workings of Mexican politics.

There are obvious difficulties in attempting to analyze the interactions of the political and economic systems in Mexico when there is such fundamental controversy over the nature of the political system itself; yet there may be advantages as well. Given the wide-ranging disagreement with regard to the operation of Mexican politics, an examination of Mexican economic develop-

[6] Raymond Vernon, *The Dilemma of Mexico's Development: The Roles of the Private and Public Sectors* (Cambridge: Harvard University Press, 1963).

[7] William P. Glade, Jr., "The Enigma of Mexico's Dilemma," in *Economic Development and Cultural Change* 13 (April 1965): 366–75. For an excellent exposition of his own views on the process of economic development in Mexico, see Glade, "Revolution and Economic Development," in Charles W. Anderson and William P. Glade, Jr., *The Political Economy of Mexico* (Madison: University of Wisconsin Press, 1963), pp. 3–101.

ment may produce some interesting new evidence against which to measure the conflicting interpretations. An analysis of Mexico's development strategy and its welfare impact reveals a great deal about the manner in which the fruits of thirty years of rapid growth have been distributed, and such knowledge casts considerable light upon the shadow world of Mexican politics. It was, after all, an eminent political scientist who defined politics as who gets what, when and how. Considering the present state of knowledge about the Mexican polity, the approach seems worth attempting.

The first chapters of the book examine the economic and social ingredients of the Mexican miracle. Chapter 2 concentrates on two salient historical contributions to rapid growth: (1) the origins of modern industrial development and indigenous entrepreneurship in the late nineteenth century, and (2) the impact of the Mexican revolution of 1910 upon Mexican social structure and patterns of social and economic mobility.

Chapter 3 analyzes the three decades of rapid economic development in Mexico since 1940. The first half of the chapter examines the role of the public sector and the policies formulated by the government to encourage rapid industrialization; the second half describes the response of the private sector to opportunities for economic growth created by government policy.

Chapter 4 uses data on (1) income distribution, (2) land tenure and agricultural production, and (3) government tax and expenditure policies to examine both the welfare implications of the past three decades of economic development and the role of government policies in distributing the gains from rapid growth.

The following three chapters are devoted to an analysis of the Mexican political system. Chapter 5 examines the leading interpretations of Mexican politics, measures them against the evidence introduced in chapters 4 and 5, and attempts to characterize the regime which has held power since 1929 in light of that evidence. Chapter 6 traces the nineteenth-century origins of the present political system and its governing elite and tries to explain why that elite has followed the development strategy outlined in chapters 3 and 4. In chapter 7 the period since 1930 is studied in some detail to reveal the roots of Mexico's present political stability. This chapter analyzes the major segments of Mexican society in terms of their political orientations and their degrees of political participation. It measures the demands which are made on the Mexican government, the varying degrees of support which Mexican citizens give to the present political regime, and the capacity of that regime to respond to the problems of political stress accompanying rapid economic growth and social change. The relevance of the oft-proclaimed "revolution of rising expectations" and its challenges to political stability are examined in the Mexican setting.

In brief, our examination of Mexico's political economy leads to the following conclusions:

1) Mexico's modern economic growth originated in a flood of foreign investment and the emergence of indigenous entrepreneurship during the years of the Díaz dictatorship. The revolution slowed growth for almost thirty years, but reshaped the Mexican social structure and the opportunities for social mobility in a manner very favorable to the post-1940 economic boom. Finally, a set of government policies highly attractive to the Mexican private sector and conducive to the productivity of investment in general led to more than three decades of growth rates unparalleled in Latin America or elsewhere in the developing world.

2) The concentration of the benefits from rapid growth in the hands of the upper thirty percent of Mexican society in the years between 1940 and the early 1960s left Mexico with an income distribution more inequitable than that prior to 1940, and indeed more inequitable than that of most developing countries in Latin America and elsewhere. While this trend reflects in part the natural economic consequence of the process of industrialization, it also mirrors the impact of a set of government policies which were designed to concentrate rewards at the top of the income scale and do little to ease *directly* the poverty of those at the bottom.

3) The gap between the governing elite's rhetorical dedication to the social goals of the Mexican revolution and the resources it has allocated toward their fulfillment can only be explained by an interpretation of Mexican politics sharply at odds with those which stress governmental commitment to "nation-building," "democratization," and "social justice."

4) The men who rule Mexico today, their goals and values, their political apparatus, and the policies for which they are responsible, are best understood in terms of the nineteenth-century mestizo political heritage. That heritage construed politics as an avenue to socio-economic mobility and personal power. Despite alterations in its outward forms, the substance of twentieth-century mestizo politics reveals little change.

As the last conclusion suggests, much of the political analysis in this study is devoted to an examination of the nineteenth-century origins and development of the mestizo stratum of Mexican society from which today's governing elite group emerged. Since this may seem like an irrelevant exercise in a study devoted to analyzing the success of present-day Mexican economic growth, the rationale of this approach should be stated rather precisely. One major factor arguing in its favor has been summarized by Joseph Spengler in his comments upon the relationship between development and "the content of men's minds." "It is my thesis," he wrote,

> that the state of a people's politico-economic development together with its rate and direction, depends largely upon what is in the minds of its

elites, which reflects in part, as do civilizations, the conceptions men form of the universe .... Accordingly, transformation of an underdeveloped society into a developed one entails transformation of the contents of the minds of the elite who direct and of the men who man such an under-developed society.[8]

One of the most interesting aspects of the Mexican case is that continuity as much as transformation has characterized the outlook of "the elite who direct." This study stresses both the continuity in the value-orientations of the mestizo political elite which emerged toward the end of the nineteenth century, and the manner in which that continuity has contributed to the shaping of the country's strategy of economic development. It points out that the change in values which led to the emergence of Mexico's modern econ-omy is found less in Mexico's political leadership than in its growing in-dustrial-agricultural elites and its broadening middle class. The origins of these two groups lay in the industrial growth of the Díaz period and in the impact of the revolution on Mexico's social structure and elite values.

The second reason for examining the nineteenth-century origins of Mexico's mestizo politicians and their political system is to increase our understanding of the function of politics in Mexican society. Why do individ-uals choose political careers? What do different segments of society expect from their political system? The answers to these questions vary widely from one country to the next, reflecting differing social structures, cultural values, and economic bases. Until these questions are answered in the Mexican case we cannot understand the political stability which has characterized Mexico for the past four decades.

5) A final conclusion, presented in chapter 8, is that the probability for continued rapid growth in Mexico during the 1970s is quite high. This prog-nosis flows directly from the examination of the interaction between today's Mexican economy and its slowly evolving political, social and cultural param-eters. Most important is the complex and crucial relationship between political and economic evolution. To return to the theme which opened this chapter, in all countries this relationship has proved both complicated and paradoxical. The old and naive assumption that the evolution of one rein-forces the other has been challenged by increasing evidence to the contrary. At least during some stages of the modernization process the relationship is one of conflict.

The main contractions may be seen in the fact that growing political modernization [essentially, broadened participation in political life]

---

[8]Joseph J. Spengler, "Theory, Ideology, Non-Economic Values, and Politico-Economic Development," in Ralph Braibanti and Joseph J. Spengler (eds.), *Tradition, Values, and Socio-Economic Development* (Durham, N.C.: Duke University Press, 1961), pp. 4–5.

> *creates demands and pressures for various benefits that may undermine economic development,* while rapid economic development may enhance the power of various traditional and neo-traditional groups who may be opposed to the modern political framework.[9]

This study suggests that a large measure of the success of Mexican economic development is attributable to a political elite which has been at once modernizing and traditional. It has been modernizing in the sense that it has accommodated itself to the social and cultural changes which accompany industrialization. It has attempted neither to freeze the Mexican social structure nor to block access to elite roles. At the same time it has been "traditional" in its own value-orientations and behavioral patterns in the Mexican cultural setting. In retaining these traditional aspects the political elite has contributed directly to the rapid growth process by controlling and containing the "demands and pressures for various benefits" which Eisenstadt noted. Its actions have worked to slow the growth of the Mexican polity, accelerate the growth of the Mexican economy, and stabilize the process of structural change in Mexican society.

---

[9] S. N. Eisenstadt, *Modernization: Protest and Change* (Englewood Cliffs, N.J.: Prentice-Hall, Inc., 1966), pp. 146–47 (emphasis added).

*Chapter 2*

# THE MEXICAN "MIRACLE": ORIGINS

While the phenomenon of Mexico's modern economic growth is relatively recent, its roots are not. Even in a narrow economic sense the origins of twentieth-century Mexican growth are deeply embedded in the later decades of the 1800s. When we examine the social, cultural, and political ingredients of Mexico's recent economic development, it is clearer still that today's headlines are the heritage of yesterday. However, the significance of socio-political contributions to the record of Mexican growth can be better understood after an examination of that record itself.

## *INDEPENDENCE TO 1877*

The period beginning with the Hidalgo revolt against Spanish rule in Mexico (1810) and ending with the assumption of the office of the Mexican presidency by Porfirio Díaz (1876) was one of general economic stagnation. Two factors contributing to economic paralysis stemmed directly from the eleven years of fighting (1810–21) which finally resulted in Mexican independence. The first was the destructiveness of the wars themselves. The armies, guerrillas and bandits loosed by the conflict practically destroyed the mining industry around which much of the colonial economy revolved, devastated agrarian Mexico, and induced capital flight of major proportions. With the liquid wealth went a great majority of the *peninsulares*—those inhabitants of Mexico born in Spain.

The second factor was the prolonged period of political instability which accompanied independence. The Mexican political system both literally and figuratively lost its head, and did not find another for approximately five decades. During its first fifty years of independence Mexico's affairs were directed by more than fifty governments, with some thirty different men serving as president. During one fifteen-year period sixteen men headed twenty-two governments. Often several groups claimed to control the government simultaneously, and such disputes generally resulted in rebellions or coups d'état. In addition to internal struggles, two wars with the French and one with the United States added to the period's chaotic political life. Under these conditions the impact of the political system upon economic growth was inevitably negative. The federal government could provide neither the peace which might have attracted substantial foreign investment nor the internal improvements to stimulate domestic savings and investment.

The internal improvement most sorely needed to develop a domestic market in Mexico was a system of transportation.[1] In 1820 Mexico possessed only three roads which could be called highways, and even they were in a state of decay. The inadequacy of the road system during the period was accurately reflected in prohibitive transport costs. "At a time when cotton sold for 15 cents a pound in U.S. markets, the Veracruz producer spent 13 cents a pound to get his fiber from the field to the buyer."[2] The failure of government to provide an adequate highway network left the country fragmented into thousands of small and isolated communities, each with anywhere from twenty to a thousand inhabitants.

A railway system would have overcome many of these obstacles, but this, too, was lacking. Governments could not afford to finance an undertaking of such scope, and the conditions of political instability cooled the interests of potential foreign investors. In 1837 Mexico's first railway concession—to connect Mexico City with Veracruz—was granted; three years later, when construction had not yet begun, it was rescinded. Other concessions were only slightly more productive, and by 1860, after twenty-three years of effort, Mexico possessed only fifteen miles of serviceable track.

Another impediment to a domestically-oriented pattern of economic growth was reflected in the structure of the Mexican fiscal system. As the conditions existing in the transport sector suggest, budgeting for even the most basic of internal improvements was inadequate. Those scant funds which were directed toward infrastructure expenditures often ended up in the pockets of the government bureaucracy or local *caciques* (bosses). Despite the fact that social overhead and infrastructure expenditures were rarely attempted, the federal government was unable to balance a budget until 1896. As normal revenues failed to match expenditures, reliance both upon loans from abroad and upon special taxes, confiscations, paper money, debasement of currency and forced loans at home increased. By 1867 Mexico's external

---

[1] The following discussion is based upon Daniel Cosío Villegas, ed., *Historia moderna de México, 2, La Rupública restaurada—la vida económica; 7, El Porfiriato—la vida económica,* books 1 and 2 (Mexico: Editorial Hermes, 1965); and Charles C. Cumberland, *Mexico: The Struggle for Modernity* (London: Oxford University Press, 1968).

[2] Cumberland, *Struggle for Modernity,* p. 164.

and internal debt was staggering in terms of the government's capacity to collect revenues. Approximately 95 percent of its customs receipts, themselves constituting over four-fifths of normal government revenues, were hypothecated to debt repayment.

If governmental expenditures were hardly designed to optimize economic growth, the forms in which revenues were raised were positively detrimental. While the federal government relied upon import and export duties for most of its income, the state governments relied heavily upon the *alcabala*, a transactions tax which had originated during colonial times. Together, federal and state transactions taxes and others of a similar nature placed a heavy burden upon internal production for the commercial market, perhaps as high as 20 to 33 percent of the market value of goods sold. This structure of taxation meant that domestic products were often more heavily taxed than their imported competitors, despite the high duties on imported products. Poor transport and internal taxes thus conspired against the domestic producer, and in many cases the total cost of indirect taxation plus transportation was greater for the Mexican entrepreneur than for his European or United States rivals.

These political and economic problems in combination with other less salient factors contributed to the stagnation of the Mexican economy between 1810 and the 1870s. Average annual exports—for the most part silver and gold—fell from 16 million pesos in the 1800–1810 period to 194 thousand in the years between 1861 and 1867; imports dropped from 14 million pesos to 4 million. Not until 1875 were the 1800–1810 averages finally exceeded. The rate of agricultural production expanded no faster than that of population, which increased from about 7 million in 1820 to 9 million by 1867.[3] Only in the manufacturing sector was there any sign of vitality. During these first decades of independence high tariff protection and other forms of federal and state encouragement led Mexican and foreign entrepreneurs to rebuild and expand the textile industry. Statistics on the volume of cotton consumed by these manufacturing firms suggest that textile production in Mexico's most modern industrial sector doubled between 1854 and 1877.

*THE PORFIRIAN PERIOD: 1877–1911*

The final thirty-five years of the 100-year period between the revolt of 1810 and the revolution of 1910 encompassed a period of slow but sustained growth. These years witnessed the spread of commercial agricultural production for both the domestic and the foreign market, the gradual demise of the craftsman in the face of factory competition, growing export diversification, and the importation of producer's goods in ever-increasing proportions. The

[3] Fernando Rosenzweig, "El desarrollo económico de México de 1877 a 1911," *El Trimestre económico* 32 (July–September 1965): 412.

expansion is measurable in both aggregate and per capita terms. While population grew at an annual rate of 1.4 percent over the period, the corresponding rate for gross domestic product was approximately 2.7 percent according to the best available estimate.[4]

Three factors help to explain the transition from stagnation to growth. First, there was the emergence of political stability. Between 1876 and 1911 only two men occupied the presidency: Manuel Gonzáles for one term (1880-84) and Porfirio Díaz for the rest (1876-80; 1884-1911). With stability came pacification, and then a relative peace. The opposition was placated or decapitated, depending upon the circumstances.

Second, the country was inundated with foreign investment which was attracted by Mexico's resources and by the security of the Porfirian peace. In turn that very investment helped to secure the peace. For example, it built the railways which tied the country together, thus enhancing the capacity of federal power centered in Mexico City to penetrate the Mexican periphery to an unprecedented degree. It also filled the government's coffers, enabling Díaz to finance the peace by lining the pockets of power seekers and placemen.[5]

Third, the initial deluge of foreign investment in transport systems integrated the Mexican economy in both an internal and an external sense. While most of the railroads were built by American investors with the express purpose of tying certain sectors of the Mexican economy—especially mining—to the U.S. market, Mexican producers suddenly found themselves in a position to penetrate their own domestic market. In hundreds of cases they did so with alacrity. In addition to improving the efficiency of existing factors of production, the process of internal integration put idle resources to work. In the early Porfirian years, for example, Mexico's system of transport was still so restricted that the country's textile manufacturers located their plants near the east coast and relied heavily on imported cotton for their production; very little was produced locally. But the expansion of the railway system eventually led to an amazing increase in cotton production in Sonora and Nuevo León; by the end of the period Mexico's cotton production had doubled, and self-sufficiency in cotton was virtually achieved.[6]

Foreign investment also integrated the Mexican economy into the world market. The extent of the tie is revealed in both the diversification of Mexican exports and their overall rate of growth. Between 1877 and 1910 the value of Mexican exports rose by more than 600 percent in real terms. As

[4] *Ibid.*, p. 405.

[5] This theme is dealt with in detail in chapter 6.

[6] Raymond Vernon, *The Dilemma of Mexico's Development: The Roles of the Private and Public Sectors* (Cambridge: Harvard University Press, 1963), pp. 41-42; and Cosío Villegas, *El Porfiriato*, book 1, chaps. 1 and 4.

table 2-1 illustrates, the diversification of Mexican exports finally reached the point, in 1904, at which gold and silver accounted for less than 50 percent of export earnings.

TABLE 2-1.  MEXICAN EXPORTS, 1877-1911 (in percent)

| Year | Total | Nondurable Consumer Goods | Durable Consumer Goods | Nondurable Producers Goods[a] | Durable Producers Goods | Precious Metals | Others |
|------|-------|---------------------------|------------------------|-------------------------------|-------------------------|-----------------|--------|
| 1877-78 | 100 | 6.3 | 0.1 | 14.6 | 0.3 | 79.0 | 0.1 |
| 1890-91 | 100 | 12.0 | 0.1 | 24.0 | 0.1 | 63.0 | 0.3 |
| 1900-01 | 100 | 10.5 | 0.1 | 31.0 | 0.4 | 58.0 | 0.5 |
| 1910-11 | 100 | 8.8 | 0.1 | 43.0 | 0.3 | 46.0 | 1.0 |

Source: *Estadísticas económicas del porfiriato, Comercio exterior de México (1877-1911)* (México, D.F.: El Colegio de México, 1960).
[a]Chiefly raw materials.

The key to the economic growth of the period was undoubtedly the Porfirian political system; this can be more logically and comprehensively analyzed when we discuss the Mexican political tradition (chapter 6). For our present purposes, the relevant fact is that civil wars and foreign intervention came to an end, and that an emerging peace gradually provided the requisite conditions for the Porfirian approach to investment and growth. A closer examination of the major factors in that growth reveals a good deal about the mechanics of the Porfirian economy and its legacy for modern-day Mexico.

*Foreign Investment*

Political stability was the essential ingredient in Porfirian growth because of the development strategy adopted by the Díaz government. In essence this strategy was to take all those measures necessary to lure foreign investment into Mexico, "on the theory that the capital, skills, and markets which foreigners had at their command were critical for Mexico's growth."[7] To implement the strategy old restraints on foreign investment were abolished and elaborate sets of incentives were initiated.

In the aggregate, the results were astounding. Although an earlier estimate that U.S. investment alone exceeded 50 percent of Mexico's national wealth seems excessive, there can be no doubt that during the Díaz years foreign capital flowed into the country in quantities proportionately much greater—in relation to national capital and the natural and human resources of Mexico—than the volume of European capital that entered the United States during

[7]Vernon, *Dilemma*, p. 38.

TABLE 2–2. FOREIGN INVESTMENT IN MEXICO, 1911 (in percent by category of investment)

| Category | U.S.A. | Great Britain | France | Germany | Holland | Others | Total | Category as % of Total Investment |
|---|---|---|---|---|---|---|---|---|
| Public Debt | 11.8 | 16.6 | 65.8 | – | 5.2 | – | 100 | 14.6 |
| Banks | 20.4 | 10.8 | 60.2 | 7.2 | 1.7 | – | 100 | 4.8 |
| Railroads | 47.3 | 35.5 | 10.3 | 1.7 | 2.0 | 3.2 | 100 | 33.2 |
| Public Services | 5.5 | 89.1 | 4.2 | – | 1.3 | – | 100 | 6.9 |
| Mining and Metallurgy | 61.1 | 14.3 | 22.0 | – | – | 2.7 | 100 | 24.1 |
| Real Estate | 41.8 | 46.9 | 8.2 | 3.1 | – | – | 100 | 5.7 |
| Industry | 16.0 | 8.4 | 55.0 | 20.6 | – | – | 100 | 3.8 |
| Commerce | 7.4 | – | 65.6 | – | – | 27.0 | 100 | 3.5 |
| Petroleum | 38.5 | 54.8 | 6.7 | – | – | – | 100 | 3.0 |
| Country Total as a Percentage of Total Foreign Investment | 38.0 | 29.1 | 26.7 | 1.9 | 1.6 | 2.7 | 100 | 100 |

Source: Calculated from Daniel Cosío Villegas, ed., *Historia moderna de México, El Porfiriato–la vida económica*, book 2, table 65, p. 1154.

TABLE 2-3. FOREIGN INVESTMENT IN MEXICO, 1911 (in percent by country)

| Category | U.S.A. | Great Britain | France | Germany |
|---|---|---|---|---|
| Public Debt | 4.7 | 8.3 | 36.1 | 3.0 |
| Banks | 2.6 | 1.8 | 11.0 | 18.3 |
| Railroads | 41.3 | 40.6 | 12.8 | 28.4 |
| Public Services | 1.0 | 21.4 | 1.1 | – |
| Mining and Metallurgy | 38.6 | 11.8 | 19.8 | – |
| Real Estate | 6.3 | 9.2 | 1.8 | 9.0 |
| Industry | 1.7 | 1.1 | 7.9 | 41.3 |
| Commerce | 0.7 | – | 8.8 | – |
| Petroleum | 3.1 | 5.8 | 0.7 | – |
| Total | 100 | 100 | 100 | 100 |

Source: Calculated from Cosío Villegas, *El Porfiriato–la vida económica*, book 2, table 66, p. 1155.

its period of most intensive development.[8] Only 100 million pesos as late as 1884, foreign investment rose to 3.4 billion by 1911.[9] Furthermore, it appears that in the 1900–1910 decade foreign investment constituted 66 cents of every dollar invested.[10]

One area of concentration for foreign investment was railway construction. In 1880, Mexico had only 700 miles of track; efforts by both the federal and state governments to promote a railway system had failed. Under Díaz, railway concessions were again opened to foreign investors, and over one-third of all foreign investment during the Díaz period was devoted to railway construction. By 1910, 12,000 miles of track had been built. A second major concentration of foreign investment developed in the extractive industries. Over 24 percent of all foreign funds flowed into mining and metallurgy, and another 3 percent into petroleum production.

United States investments, which by 1911 accounted for 38 percent of all foreign investment, were highly concentrated in railroad construction and the extractive industries. Over 41 percent of American investment was allocated to railway expansion, and over 38 percent to mining and metallurgy. American money accounted for over 47 percent of foreign capital in railway construction and 61 percent in mining. In contrast, British investments included over 21 percent in the public services sector, and another 8 percent in

[8] Ernesto Fernández Hurtado, "Private Enterprise and Government in Mexico," in *Mexico's Recent Economic Growth*, edited by Tom Davis (Austin: University of Texas Press for the Institute of Latin American Studies, 1967), p. 47.

[9] Cosío Villegas, *El Porfiriato*, book 2, p. 1162.

[10] Alfredo Navarrete R., "The Financing of Economic Development," in *Mexico's Recent Economic Growth*, p. 109.

Mexico's public debt. Neither the United States nor Britain allocated as much as 2 percent of their investments to the industrial sector.

It was French capital that flowed into Mexican industrial activities, where it accounted for 55 percent of all foreign investment. A major factor in this pattern of direct investment was a small but energetic and prosperous French "colony," including many families whose roots in Mexico extended back to the early decades of the 1800s. Most of the French worked in commerce and banking, although some were landowners. With the coming of the Porfirian peace and the gradual growth of the domestic market, French merchants began to develop their own sources of supply and gradually moved into various sectors of manufacturing. Some of their investment represented domestic savings; that is, it was earned from their own productive activities in Mexico. But considerable financing came from French banking interests long present in Mexico. Many of the names prominent in Mexican business today can be traced back to this nineteenth-century French-Mexican community which had its origins in early French commercial activity and expanded into the manufacturing field during the Díaz period.

Domestic Mexican investment in the areas of extractive industry, power, transport, and banking was insignificant. Both the size of the investments required in these sectors and the technical aspects represented in their development militated against extensive Mexican participation. In contrast, Mexican investment in the manufacturing sector between 1880 and 1910 was relatively large. This was, in turn, closely related to the growth of domestic and foreign markets.

## Market Growth: Foreign and Domestic

The growth of Mexican exports and the development of a Mexican domestic market were intimately linked. Favorable foreign demand for Mexican foodstuffs and raw materials led to an annual increase in export earnings of 6.1 percent between 1877 and 1911. As exports grew, so too did the demand for production inputs of the export sectors and the purchasing power of those deriving income from those sectors. In both instances the result was to encourage expanded domestic production.

In the mining industry, external demand was the determining factor in growth and modernization during the Porfirian years. In addition to gold and silver, industrial metals began to appear among Mexican exports. Production and export of copper, zinc, graphite, lead and antimony rose rapidly. Foreign demand likewise spurred investment and production in certain agricultural categories. In addition to the export of such traditional items as henequen, wood, wood products, and hides, new export items such as coffee, cattle, cotton, chickpeas, sugar, vanilla and chicle lengthened the list of products earning foreign exchange.

Growing export industries in turn increased the demand for their own production inputs. For example, the demands of the mining industry (and of railway construction) led to the development of Mexico's first iron and steel plant, the Fundidora de Fierro y Acero de Monterrey, which began operation in 1903. It, like many others, was an enterprise undertaken by foreigners resident in Mexico.

In addition to a growing demand linked to the expanding export sectors, improved governmental policies encouraged the development of production for the domestic market. Factors including continued high protective tariffs, a revision of internal taxation, cheaper transport costs, and the falling price of silver help to explain average annual growth rates for the manufacturing sector considerably higher than the aggregate growth rate of 2.7 percent.[11] The high tariff structure inherited from earlier decades was maintained throughout the period; tariffs ranging from 50 to 200 percent of the value of imported products were common. New investment in diverse fields of manufacture was also encouraged by duty-free importation of machinery, raw materials and other processed inputs, tax exemptions, subsidies, and embargoes on the importation of competing products. The various Mexican states, in bidding to attract new investments, added further incentives to those already offered by the federal government.[12]

As external protection continued, internal obstruction diminished. In 1896 the Díaz government attempted—with results far superior to those of earlier governments—to legislate the abolition of the *alcabala*. While the problem represented by an assortment of transactions taxes continued to draw occasional complaints and criticism for several decades, internal free trade was in essence achieved.

Finally, transport costs dropped sharply as the railway system expanded. It cost a textile manufacturer in Mexico City $61 per ton to ship cotton goods to Querétaro in 1877; in 1910 he paid $3 per ton.

Under the combined influence of these market and policy factors, an "industrial sector" emerged in Mexico. The per capita consumption of factory-made cloth grew by 25 percent in a decade; the per capita consumption of refined sugar rose by 50 percent. There was strong growth in the domestic production of such varied items as cement, dynamite, iron and steel products,

[11] Estimates of the annual growth rates for the manufacturing sector during the period range from 12 percent on the high side to 3.6 percent on the low side. Part of the problem, of course, is one of definition. See Cosío Villegas, *El Porfiriato*, book 1, chap. 4; and Leopoldo Solís M., "Hacia un análisis general a largo plazo del desarrollo económico de México," *Demografía y economía* 1 (1967): 43.

[12] See Cosío Villegas, *El Porfiriato*, book 1, chap. 4, "La Industria." Another factor supporting the profitability of domestic production was the falling price of silver on the world market. The Mexican peso was pegged to silver; as the price of silver fell in relation to gold, the price of foreign imports on the Mexican market rose. The process continued until 1905, when Mexico finally adhered to the gold standard.

glass, tobacco products, processed foods and drinks, and many others. Import substitution was perhaps most prominent in the case of cheap cotton products, where the import share of the domestic market dropped from 32 percent in 1889 to 3 percent in 1911.[13]

With low wages and stiff protection came high profits. Comments from foreign embassies as well as Mexican observers place annual profits in Mexican industry in the 10-15 percent range, "never below 10" for the textile industry, according to Peñafiel.[14] It was in this atmosphere that wealthy Mexicans began to be interested in industrial investments. Throughout the early and mid-nineteenth century, French, Spanish, English, German, and U.S. residents in Mexico had contributed in various fields to the development of an entrepreneurial mentality; with the integration of the domestic market consequent to the railroad boom, an increasing proportion of Mexicans joined the capitalist ranks. Sometimes the move was from *hacendado* to industrialist by way of the establishment of a sugar refinery. Sometimes it was from merchant to manufacturer via investment in a small textile factory. Sometimes it was simply by placing capital in a venture initiated by Mexico's European colony of merchant-industrialists, the *criollos nuevos*, "new creoles," as Andrés Molina Enríquez called them.[15]

A study whose estimates are most probably on the low side concludes that Mexican entrepreneurs invested 86 million pesos in the manufacturing sector between 1886 and 1910. This figure includes only initial investments in new companies during these years. A comparison of this figure with the total foreign investment in the manufacturing sector of 131 million pesos by 1911 clearly illustrates the importance of this period for the development of a nucleus of Mexican industrialists. This is all the more true when we observe the blending of Mexican entrepreneurship and capital with that of the *criollos nuevos*, a process which still continues in the modern Mexican setting.

### The Limits of Porfirian Growth

In addition to these achievements, the Díaz regime was able to consolidate its foreign debt and increase governmental revenues to cover both current account outlays and some limited basic infrastructure expenditures. Nevertheless, the bloom deserted the Porfirian rose during the 1900-1910 decade. World demand for Mexican exports—a major factor in the growth rate since the late 1870s—slackened noticeably at the turn of the century. Between

---

[13] See Cumberland, *Struggle for Modernity*, pp. 220-22; Solís, "Hacia un análisis general," pp. 46-49; and Cosío Villegas, *El Porfiriato*, book 1, p. 318.

[14] Cosío Villegas, *El Porfiriato*, book 1, chap. 4.

[15] See Andrés Molina Enríquez, *Los Grandes problemas nacionales* (Mexico: Imprenta de A. Carranza E. Hijos, 1909).

1890 and 1900 export receipts on commercial account had risen by 144 percent; from 1900 through 1910 they rose by less than 75 percent.[16] With the volume of exports growing at a much slower rate, the characteristics of domestic demand assumed a new importance.

Many of the difficulties confronting economic development oriented toward the internal market during the last Porfirian decade are suggested by the evidence presented in table 2-4. First we note that the rate of growth of the total work force slowed perceptibly during the decade. From an annual growth rate of 1.6 percent in the 1895-1900 period, it dropped to 0.9 percent. Since the latter rate was below that of population growth, the labor force as a percentage of total population fell from 35.4 percent in 1900 to 34.8 percent in 1910. These figures suggest that the Porfirian economy was having some difficulty in providing employment opportunities for a slowly growing population.

Further evidence to support this assumption seems to be provided by the sectoral distribution of the labor force.[17] The agricultural sector employed 67 percent of the work force in 1895; in 1900 the corresponding figure was 66 percent. This is a pattern which one would expect to find in an economy in the early stages of industrialization. However, by 1910 the percentage of the labor force in agriculture had risen to 68.1, higher than the figure for 1895, fifteen years before. Employment figures for the industrial sector explain this trend. The percentage of the labor force absorbed by industry rose from 15.6 to 16.6 between 1895 and 1900; by 1910 it had fallen to 15.1. In both the extractive and manufacturing sectors the drop in employment was absolute as well as relative, with the result that the total industrial sector employed 3,000 fewer people in 1910 than it had in 1900. In the textile industry, one of the major sectors of falling employment, factory production was displacing the artisan, and aggregate demand was not increasing fast enough to re-employ those victims of modern production methods. In absolute figures the service sector employed a greater number of workers in 1910 than in 1900, but relatively its absorption of the labor force also registered a slight decline.

Wage increases failed to keep pace with rising prices. Some have suggested that over the 1810-1910 period real wages fell by as much as 75 percent. For the Díaz period the evidence is more solid. Table 2-5 presents a conservative estimate of the decline in real wages during the *Porfiriato*. It indicates that overall real wages fell by approximately one quarter between 1898 and 1911. Only workers in the mining industry seem to have avoided the reduction, which was particularly sharp in agriculture.

[16] Calculated in current prices.

[17] The tentative nature of the statement reflects some hesitation about the reliability of the statistics.

TABLE 2–4. GROWTH OF POPULATION AND WORK FORCE, 1895–1910

| Sector | 1895 | | 1900 | | 1910 | | Annual Growth Rates (%) | | |
|---|---|---|---|---|---|---|---|---|---|
| | Thousands of Persons | % of Work Force | Thousands of Persons | % of Work Force | Thousands of Persons | % of Work Force | 1895–1900 | 1900–1910 | 1895–1910 |
| Total Population | 12,632.4 | – | 13,607.3 | – | 15,160.4 | – | 1.5 | 1.1 | 1.2 |
| Work Force | 4,441.9 | 100.0 | 4,819.2 | 100.0 | 5,272.1 | 100.0 | 1.6 | 0.9 | 1.2 |
| Agricultural Sector | 2,977.8 | 67.0 | 3,182.6 | 66.0 | 3,592.1 | 68.1 | 1.3 | 1.2 | 1.2 |
| Industrial Sector | 691.1 | 15.6 | 798.5 | 16.6 | 795.4 | 15.1 | 2.9 | -0.1 | 0.9 |
| Extractive | 88.5 | 2.0 | 107.3 | 2.2 | 104.1 | 2.0 | 3.9 | -0.6 | 1.1 |
| Manufacturing | 553.0 | 12.4 | 619.3 | 12.9 | 606.0 | 11.5 | 2.3 | -0.2 | 0.6 |
| Construction | 49.6 | 1.2 | 63.0 | 1.3 | 74.7 | 1.4 | 4.9 | 1.7 | 3.0 |
| Other | – | – | 8.9 | 0.2 | 10.6 | 0.2 | – | 1.8 | – |
| Service Sector | 773.0 | 17.4 | 838.1 | 17.4 | 884.6 | 16.8 | 1.6 | 0.5 | 0.9 |
| Commerce | 249.6 | 5.6 | 261.5 | 5.4 | 293.8 | 5.6 | 0.9 | 1.2 | 1.1 |
| Transport | 55.7 | 1.3 | 59.7 | 1.2 | 55.1 | 1.0 | 1.4 | -0.8 | -0.1 |
| Professionals | 112.2 | 2.5 | 137.2 | 2.9 | 146.6 | 2.8 | 4.1 | 0.6 | 2.1 |
| Private Employees | 22.7 | 0.5 | 33.9 | 0.7 | 83.4 | 1.6 | 8.4 | 9.4 | 9.1 |
| Public Employees | 26.3 | 0.6 | 25.2 | 0.5 | 27.7 | 0.5 | -1.0 | 0.9 | 0.3 |
| Armed Forces | 33.2 | 0.7 | 38.6 | 0.8 | 36.7 | 0.7 | 2.2 | -0.5 | 0.7 |
| Servants | 273.3 | 6.2 | 282.0 | 5.9 | 241.3 | 4.6 | 0.6 | -1.5 | -0.8 |

Source: Fernando Rosenzweig, "El Desarrollo económico de México de 1877 a 1911," *El Trimestre económico* 32 (July–September 1965): 438.

TABLE 2-5.  MINIMUM DAILY WAGES, 1877-1911 (in cents, constant 1900 prices)

| Year | Total | Agriculture | Manufacturing | Mining |
|------|-------|-------------|---------------|--------|
| 1877 | 32 | 32 | 32 | 32 |
| 1885 | 29 | 27 | 34 | 31 |
| 1892 | 28 | 26 | 26 | 30 |
| 1898 | 39 | 37 | 50 | 47 |
| 1902 | 33 | 32 | 36 | 43 |
| 1911 | 30 | 27 | 36 | 72 |

Source: Fernando Rosenzweig, "El Desarrollo económico," p. 447.

At certain times in certain countries falling wages foreclose conspicuous consumption; in other instances the pleasures forgone edge closer to life itself. Unfortunately for the vast majority of Mexicans, the latter was the case toward the end of the Díaz period. Later research confirms what was obvious to contemporary observers. Francisco Bulnes warned that the Mexican people were "moving toward death by starvation," and Andrés Molina Enríquez wrote that the growing number of strikes between 1900 and 1909 were "the result of a state of hunger in our lower classes."[18] Between 1895 and 1910 the mortality rate rose from 31 to 33.2 per thousand; infant mortality rose; life expectancy dropped.[19] While growing urbanization without proper health and sanitation facilities provides a partial explanation for these statistics, the fundamental factor is traceable to rural Mexico, to both what *was* happening there, and what *was not*.

*Land Tenure: Changes and Welfare Consequences*

What was happening was an increasing concentration of land ownership. The trend, of course, had begun with the Spanish conquest. What was new and significant was its pace and the resulting consequences for over half of the Mexican population.

By the time that Mexico achieved independence, and indeed long before, rural Mexico was dominated by the hacienda.[20] The characteristic traits of this particular form of landholding included:

1) Large areas under the ownership of a single landlord. Seldom were haciendas less than a thousand hectares in size, and some reached into the hundreds of thousands.

[18] Francisco Bulnes, *El Verdadero Díaz y la revolución* (Mexico: Editora Nacional, 1952), p. 398; and Andrés Molina Enríquez, *Los Grandes problemas*, p. 237.

[19] Rosenzweig, "El Desarrollo económico," p. 439. These statistics reflect the epidemic proportions of some of the diseases that swept urban Mexico during these years.

[20] See Eyler Simpson, *The Ejido: Mexico's Way Out* (Chapel Hill: University of North Carolina Press, 1937), pp. 489-500.

2) Relative self-sufficiency. Crops grown on the hacienda provided for all food needs, and efforts were also made to produce all the tools, building materials and other ingredients of agricultural operations.

3) A permanent resident labor force. The tie between the peon and the hacienda during the course of the nineteenth century increasingly assumed the form of debt bondage. Loans were often advanced by the hacienda store, the *tienda de raya*, with the clear purpose of tying the peasant to the hacienda so that he would be available during the few months when his labor was required. This form of peonage was especially predominant in northern Mexico where the labor supply was scarce, in comparison with the central plateau region in which the Indian population was heavily concentrated. In some regions a sharecropping system developed. In still others, including henequen plantations in Yucatán, tobacco production in the Valle Nacional and coffee plantations in Chiapas, forced labor was employed by the end of the century, consisting predominantly of criminals and conquered Yaqui Indians. Whatever the form, the result was an extremely cheap supply of labor which, given the seasonal nature of the hacienda's labor demands, was severely underemployed.

4) Absentee ownership. The *hacendado* spent little time on his property; for the most part he resided in Mexico City or Europe.

5) Cautious management. "The economic criterion of the *hacendado* in the vast majority of cases is safety first. An assured income, even though it is small and bears little relation to the capital investment represented by the *hacienda*, is prized above any venturing into attempts at increased production and preferred to any trafficking with profits as this term would be understood by a businessman."[21] The nineteenth-century phrase "*hacienda no es negocio*" (a hacienda is not a matter of business) was repeated with approval in elite social circles but with dismay by Mexican economists.[22]

6) Backward production methods. Absentee ownership, exploitation of cheap and underemployed labor, and the precedence of prestige over production dictated continued use of primitive farming methods.

In addition to the hacienda there were two other traditional types of landholding in nineteenth-century Mexico: the *rancho* and the Indian communal village. The average *rancho* was well under a hundred hectares in size, worked by the owner and his family, and perhaps some few sharecroppers or hired laborers. The *rancho* was a post-conquest phenomenon; the landholding village was not. It was, in somewhat different form, the dominant unit in the

---

[21] *Ibid.*, p. 490.

[22] See, for example, Molina Enríquez, *Los Grandes problemas,* part 2, chap. 1. The phrase did not apply to the sugar and henequen plantations of Morelos and other states in southern Mexico. High transport costs and inelastic demand in local markets may have helped to check the emergence of a more entrepreneurial attitude in rural Mexico.

agrarian economy at the time of the Spanish arrival in Mexico.[23] While the original *conquistadores,* their progeny, and later Spanish immigrants soon gained control of most of the productive land in the country, many Indian communities that did not fall under the *encomienda* system managed to keep possession of some land adjacent to their villages. According to Spanish legislation each Indian village was to retain control of lands sufficient for its adequate support. Minimum requirements included a town site and "an *ejido*, varying in size but always encompassing an area of at least one square league. This *ejido* was to include the agricultural land of the village, the woodland, and the pasture land. These lands all were to be inalienable and administered by a town council."[24] While the attempt on the part of the Spanish crown to safeguard the Indian communities was undermined by Spanish settlers, who gained control of Indian lands and reduced the former owners to a condition of virtual serfdom through debt bondage, enough free landholding villages remained in the first half of the nineteenth century to constitute an important aspect of the Mexican agrarian system. These villages were even more self-sufficient than the haciendas, and completed the picture of a rural Mexico isolated from the commercial system of the cities and coastal towns. Only those large plantation units that produced export crops and those haciendas which supplied the agricultural needs of urban areas in their immediate vicinity entered the market economy.

The balance which had developed between hacienda and Indian village was shattered by the Reform Laws of 1855-57 and subsequent Porfirian legislation. The thirty-year struggle between conservative and liberal elements of Mexico's political elite was resolved, as much as any such conflicts ever are, with the defeat of the conservative forces in the Three Years War (1857-60) and the later overthrow of Maximilian's empire by Juárez and his liberal adherents in 1867. The Catholic church, owner of perhaps as much as two-fifths of the nation's wealth and the financial and spiritual mentor of the conservative cause, was divested of its landholdings by the laws of 1857. These properties in turn became the core of the great private haciendas which emerged as a consequence of the confiscations. But added to them were the communal lands of the Indian villages. The famous Lerdo Law of 1856 denied both civil and ecclesiastical corporations the right to hold real estate, and the law was interpreted to mean that all Indian communal property was to be granted in severalty to village members. The Liberals had hoped to create a class of yeoman farmers through the workings of these laws; the result of

---

[23] For a detailed discussion see Simpson, *The Ejido,* pp. 4ff.; and Eric R. Wolf, *Sons of the Shaking Earth* (Chicago: University of Chicago Press, Phoenix Books, 1959), chap. 7.

[24] Nathan L. Whetten, *Rural Mexico* (Chicago: University of Chicago Press, 1948), pp. 80-81.

their efforts was not a rural middle class, but greater concentration at the extremes. When it became clear that *hacendados* were taking advantage of the breakup of village lands to increase their own holdings, the Juárez regime stopped enforcing the law as it applied to the agricultural sections of the *ejidos*. Díaz, however, instructed state governors to prosecute the law to its fullest extent, and the villages were deprived of their last measure of legal protection. It has been estimated that well over two million acres of communal land were allotted in severalty during the Porfirian period, and that literally all of it sooner or later ended up in the hands of land companies or estate owners.[25]

To the growing concentration of former church and communal lands in great estates, a trend he inherited and accelerated, Díaz added in 1883 a new source of polarization: a program for the survey, subdivision and settlement of public lands. Within a decade 20 percent of the entire geographical area of the republic had passed into the hands of land survey companies. Through surveying and the additional purchase of surveyed lands, one individual put together a hacienda of twelve million acres in Baja California and other northern states; another enterprising "surveyor" ended up with over three million acres.

The 1883 law incorporated at least the pretext of surveying for the purpose of colonization, and therefore included some (unenforced) limitations on what lands could be appropriated and how large individual holdings might be; in 1894, new laws dropped all limitations and were openly used by the Díaz regime to reward political favorites and strengthen the hold of the dictator's political machine upon the country.[26] Under the impetus of these new laws *hacendados* renewed their attack on those Indian village lands which had survived the legislation of the Reform period. They also appropriated lands held and worked by private owners who were not members of village communities. Both the land companies and the estate owners could seize all lands which interested them because of the manner in which the new laws operated. The burden of proof concerning ownership lay with the occupant of the land. If the "surveryor" declared a title lacking or invalid, the occupant's only recourse was to take the case to court. But there he had to face court fees as well as a judicial system which never found for the plaintiff. Perhaps nowhere was the inability of occupants to retain lands better illustrated than in the state of Morelos, where the expansion of sugar plantations during the later years of the nineteenth century resulted in the loss of Indian communal lands held for centuries. It was in Morelos that the villagers of

[25] *Ibid.*, p. 86.

[26] Simpson, *The Ejido*, pp. 27ff.; Whetten, *Rural Mexico*, pp. 87ff.; and Moisés González Navarro, *La Confederación nacional campesina* (Mexico: B. Costa-Amic, 1968), pp. 33ff.

Anenecuilco, home of Emiliano Zapata, took their final plea before a judge who fined them for questioning the integrity of the plantation owner who had pushed them off their land. Within a few years the sugar plantations of Morelos and much of the nation's rural economy were laid waste by the revolution which swept Mexico.

The aggregate impact of the Reform Laws and subsequent Díaz legislation upon the structure of land tenure in Mexico was profound. Approximately 27 percent of the total area of the republic was transferred from public to private hands, in return for $12 million. Much of that land was semi-arid and mountainous, but also included were excellent pasture lands, forests, and a considerable amount of good crop land. By 1910, 90 percent of the Indian villages in the central plateau region held no communal lands of any kind. Few *ejidos* were left in Hidalgo, and none were to be found in Tlaxcala or in the Tehuantepec region. The villages of the states of Puebla and México "had not pasturage for a goat." And in Morelos only one village, Tepoztlán, still owned communal lands.[27]

At one extreme, close to 90 percent of Mexico's rural families held no land, and many of them were tied to haciendas through the debt bondage system. Perhaps 15 percent of the communal villages still possessed some land, though in greatly reduced proportions. At no time in history had more Mexicans been landless. In the middle were the *ranchos,* under 50,000 in number, most often described as subsistence-oriented. And at the other extreme were several thousand haciendas, some of them millions of acres in size. About 50 percent of Mexico's rural population lived on these haciendas; together with the land companies, the *hacendados* owned over half of the nation's territory.

What *was* happening in rural Mexico was the ever-increasing concentration of landholding; what *was not* happening was increased per capita production. Between 1877 and 1907 total agricultural output grew by 21.3 percent.[28] This annual average rate of increase of 0.7 percent was scarcely half that of population growth.

The aggregate agricultural production figure is a mix of several different trends. First, the production of raw materials for the domestic market grew at an annual rate of 2.5 percent. Second, production for export increased at 6.5 percent. Finally, production of food and drink for the Mexican market *fell* at an annual rate of 0.5 percent. It was this latter trend which led so many contemporary commentators to warn that the Mexican *campesino* was being pushed toward starvation. Measured on a per capita basis, the decline in corn

[27] Simpson, *The Ejido,* p. 31.

[28] The statistics are taken from Cosío Villegas, *El Porfiriato,* book 1, chap. 1, "La Agricultura."

production between 1877 and 1910 was 50 percent, and corn was the mainstay of the Mexican diet. Bean production, again by a per capita measurement, fell by 75 percent.[29] The Díaz regime resorted to importing large amounts of corn and wheat between 1890 and 1911; nevertheless the great majority of Mexicans ate less toward the end of the Díaz regime than they had at its inception.

Behind these statistics the following picture of rural Mexico emerges. A limited number of large landowners responded to the opportunities for commercial production created during the Porfirian peace. Their estates produced for export and for internal industrial needs. In Morelos and other states, sugar cane plantations grew and profits were reinvested in increased acreage and cane processing plants. In Yucatán henequen growers wrested lands from former occupants—mostly Mayan Indians—and increased production in response to growing world demand. In the Bajío region cotton production rose at astounding rates. And further to the north—where *hacendados* sent their sons to Europe and the United States for their education, and some, like Francisco Madero, took graduate courses in agricultural economics at the University of California—commercial agriculture responded to growing market opportunities. But for the great majority of landowners prestige continued to prevail over production. Even those who availed themselves of the new transport systems to produce some export crops still held large sections of their arable lands fallow, often refusing to rent them to idle and hungry *campesinos*. At the same time, they chained those peasants to the hacienda so that they could be seasonally employed.

It is an interesting question whether, over time, the Porfirian pattern of economic development could have overcome the debilitating effects of a generally stagnant rural economy. Table 2–6 reflects the obstacles to continued economic growth which the hacienda system presented. Mexico in 1910 was still 80 percent rural, and close to one half of the total population was bound directly to the great estates. Those so situated seldom entered the market economy. Even those not directly tied to the hacienda, the small farmers (*pequeños agricultores*), had little or no purchasing power.

At the other extreme the *hacendados* directed their purchasing power toward luxury imports and European vacations. The result was to narrow the effective domestic market to the three million of Mexico's fifteen million inhabitants who lived in towns and cities. And even there the prevailing wage and price trends, as we have noted, were contracting the size of the population which could purchase anything beyond the barest necessities. Only continued export demand and foreign investment could have sustained the Díaz system of growth over the short and medium term.

---

[29] Cumberland, *Struggle for Modernity*, p. 204.

TABLE 2-6. POPULATION, 1895-1910

| Division of Population | Thousands of inhabitants | | % of Total | | Annual Growth Rates (%) |
|---|---|---|---|---|---|
| | 1895 | 1910 | 1895 | 1910 | 1895-1910 |
| Total Population | 12,637 | 15,160 | 100.0 | 100.0 | 1.2 |
| Rural | | | | | |
| Less than 5,000 | 10,085 | 12,216 | 79.8 | 80.0 | 1.2 |
| Urban | 2,552 | 3,034 | 20.2 | 20.0 | 1.2 |
| 5,000-20,000 | 1,392 | 1,366 | 11.0 | 9.0 | -0.1 |
| More than 20,000 | 1,160 | 1,668 | 9.2 | 11.0 | 2.5 |

Source: Fernando Rosenzweig, "El desarrollo económico," p. 418.

But the question is entirely academic. The strains on the Mexican social system, induced in great part by the developments in rural Mexico discussed above, combined with an emerging challenge to the Díaz political system to precipitate a revolution which bled Mexico for fourteen years. Among the casualties of the revolution was the Porfirian pattern of economic development.

## REVOLUTION AND REFORM: 1911-1940

With the overthrow of Porfirio Díaz, Mexico again lost its head. But history was not to repeat itself; within fifteen years, rather than fifty, the foundations of a political system capable of integrating mosaic Mexico were laid. During those years, however, the country endured untold destruction. Indicative of the level of violence is the fact that between 1910 and 1921 the population of Mexico actually fell from 15.2 million to about 14.5 million.[30] Deaths caused by the revolution probably ran well over one million, close to one out of every fifteen persons in the country. The failure of the de la Huerta revolt in 1924 brought the worst violence to an end. Although there were further insurrections during the following fourteen years, almost always linked to the problem of presidential succession, a slowly emerging political stability limited their impact and gradually drained them of their raison d'être—a high probability of success.

The long years of upheaval seriously disrupted the Mexican economy. Destruction of the railways, for instance, was particularly severe, since at any given moment the losers in a struggle attempted to slow the movement of victorious armies. The social upheaval and political change which characterized the period combined with the impact of the depression to slow

[30] The census estimate for 1921 was 14.3 million, but various scholars have suggested that the true figure was somewhat higher.

perceptibly—in some years to halt or reverse—the growth process in Mexico. Even those changes within the economy which were to promote rapid development in later decades, such as land reform, tended to slow the pace of growth in the short run.

During the first decade of the revolution the Mexican economy suffered from sharp production declines in mining and manufacturing, the former falling during the period by 40 percent and the latter by 9 percent. Agricultural production fell as well.[31] By the mid-1920s, the volume of Mexican production was only slightly above that of the last years of Díaz.

The period from the mid-1920s to 1940 was characterized by a low aggregate real growth rate, 1.6 percent (-0.2 percent per capita), according to the most recent and comprehensive study.[32] The only sector which exhibited any strength was manufacturing. Production of traditional manufactures grew rapidly, and so did the output of iron, steel and cement. The other sectors of the Mexican economy remained generally stagnant until the late 1930s.

Several factors serve to explain this sluggish performance. The first was the impact of the Depression on the Mexican economy. By 1932 Mexico's real gross national product had fallen below that of 1910. Again the mining industry, which accounted for 10 percent of total output in 1929, was particularly hard-hit; over the next five years production fell by 32 percent.[33]

A second factor involved the increasing tension between the Mexican government and foreign investors during the 1930s. Throughout the years of the Cárdenas presidency (1934-40) the government actively supported the organization of labor and generally sided with Mexican workers in their disputes with foreign ownership and management. The wave of strikes which inundated Mexico during the mid-1930s became a major concern of the foreign business community. Government support for organized labor, policies of nationalization and threats of expropriation led many foreign investors to withdraw profits from Mexico rapidly and to slow the replacement rate of plants and equipment.

When Cárdenas expropriated the foreign-owned oil industry in 1938, capital flight increased rapidly. From a high point of 3.5 billion pesos in 1926, direct foreign investment fell to 2.6 billion by 1939. The drop was influenced not only by Mexican labor policies and the oil expropriation, but also by the crash of 1929 in the United States and the international oil

---

[31] Enrique Pérez López, "The National Product of Mexico: 1895 to 1964," in *Mexico's Recent Economic Growth*, edited by Tom Davis (Austin: University of Texas Press, for the Institute of Latin American Studies, 1967), pp. 27-28.

[32] Clark Reynolds, *The Mexican Economy: Twentieth Century Structure and Growth* (New Haven: Yale University Press, forthcoming).

[33] Pérez López, "The National Product of Mexico," pp. 29-31.

companies' search for cheaper oil fields in Venezuela prior to the troubles of 1937-38.

Capital flight merely compounded the foreign exchange crisis which Mexico faced throughout the 1930s. Between 1929 and 1940 the market for Mexico's traditional exports was severely depressed, and export earnings dropped considerably during those years in which U.S. economic activity was stagnant. Adding to the problem was the fact that the attacks on foreign ownership in Mexico—particularly in mining—were depressing output in some of Mexico's major export sectors. Between 1925 and 1940 receipts on merchandise exports actually declined on an average of 1.4 percent per year. By the latter date, and despite two significant devaluations, Mexico's international reserves had dropped to $20 million.

A final factor tending to depress the rate of economic growth during these years was the environment within which agrarian reform took place. As the half-century from 1860 to 1910 was characterized by concentration in ownership of land, so the fifty-year period between 1920 and 1970 has witnessed a reversal of that process. While there was a good deal of disagreement within the revolutionary elite over the issue of land redistribution, the tide of events determined that a reform program would be adopted in one form or another. Peasants formed the bulwark of the revolutionary armies, while most *hacendados* fought for the old order. With peasants armed and conservative forces in retreat, de facto forms of redistribution flourished from the earliest days of the revolution. At one extreme Indian villages reclaimed ancient communal lands; at the other victorious revolutionary generals confiscated great landed estates. De jure forms of redistribution were also instituted shortly after the revolution began. The famous decree of 1915, issued by Venustiano Carranza in an effort to strengthen his position vis-à-vis the Emiliano Zapata-Francisco Villa alliance, declared that all communal lands alienated since 1856 should be returned to their former owners and that villages without former titles, but in need of lands, should also receive them. Such lands were to be expropriated from private owners. The constitution of 1917 incorporated and expanded upon the 1915 decree, and additional provisions were added to the agrarian code first established in the 1930s.

Most of the land distributed under the decree of 1915, article 27 of the constitution, and subsequent legislation has taken the *ejido* form. Both the name and the substance of this mode of redistribution clearly identify it with the pre-conquest and colonial forms of land tenure which had been destroyed during the Díaz period. Under the *ejido* form of tenure land is granted to a village rather than to individuals. While the pastures and woodlands are generally held in common, cropland is in most cases worked individually. According to the 1960 census, for example, only 3 percent of all *ejidal* croplands are organized collectively, and only 2 percent of the 1.6 million *ejidatarios* (*ejido* members) are members of crop-growing cooperatives. Where croplands are cultivated individually, each *ejidatario* is assigned a parcel of land to work, and he may pass it on to one of his dependents. According to law his parcel cannot be taken from him unless he fails to work it for two successive years.

It was not until the 1930s that the land reform program had a significant impact upon the structure of Mexican land tenure. Tables 2-7 and 2-8 present an aggregate measure of the redistributive process; they can be misleading, however, since much of the land which has been granted to the Mexican peasant is not arable. Table 2-9 measures the reform program in terms of the distribution of arable land and acreage actually cultivated.

All three tables testify to the tremendous change which took place in rural Mexico during the decade of the 1930s. As late as 1930 the *ejidos* held only 13 percent of aggregate Mexican cropland; by 1940 they composed 47 percent of the total. Measured in terms of hectares actually cultivated, the *ejidal* proportion rose from 15 percent to 49 percent. Furthermore, table 2-9 reveals that these changes entailed transfer of lands already in use, since the totals for cropland and land under cultivation rose very little during the 1930-40 decade. Finally, by 1940 virtually one-half of Mexico's rural population lived on *ejidos,* while the population living on haciendas had shrunk to less than one million.

Anarchic conditions prevailed in much of rural Mexico during years between 1925 and 1940. Throughout the country peasants attempted to stake claim to nearby private holdings; in response most *hacendados* employed private armies to keep the *campesinos* off their properties. Villages fought not only with the landowners, but often with other villages laying claim to the same lands. The rural conflict was reflected in revolutionary elite circles, where one wing (the *veteranos*) was inclined to terminate the *ejido* program while the other (the *agraristas*) sought to make the *ejido* the central—indeed the sole—mode of land reform. The inevitable result of this conflict and the uncertainty which it engendered was a low rate of growth in agricultural production. The best available estimate suggests a growth rate in agriculture (including forestry, fishing and animal husbandry) of 1.9 percent between 1925 and 1940, just enough to keep pace with population growth (1.8 percent). In a period characterized by insecurity of land tenure and consequent low levels of investment and land use, it is surprising that the agricultural sector performed as well as it did.

However accurate they may be, sectoral and aggregate growth rates between 1925 and 1940 cannot and do not reflect the true contribution of that period to the Mexican economic record since 1940. That contribution is to be found in several crucial institutional developments, some political, others economic, and still others social-psychological in nature.

TABLE 2-7. LAND DISTRIBUTION SINCE CARRANZA DECREE OF 1915

| President | End of Term | Approximate Number of Months | Total Hectares Distributed | Average per Month | Total as a Percentage of Mexico's Surface | Cumulative Total | Percent of Mexico's Surface |
|---|---|---|---|---|---|---|---|
| Carranza | May 21, 1920 | 66.5 | 167,936 | 2,525 | 0.1 | 167,936 | 0.1 |
| De la Huerta | November 30, 1920 | 6.0 | 33,696 | 5,616 | – | 201,632 | 0.1 |
| Obregón | November 30, 1924 | 48.0 | 1,100,117 | 22,919 | 0.6 | 1,301,749 | 0.7 |
| Calles | November 30, 1928 | 48.0 | 2,972,876 | 61,935 | 1.5 | 4,274,625 | 2.2 |
| Portes Gil | February 4, 1930 | 14.1 | 1,707,750 | 121,117 | 0.9 | 5,982,375 | 3.0 |
| Ortiz Rubio | September 3, 1932 | 30.8 | 944,538 | 30,667 | 0.5 | 6,926,913 | 3.5 |
| Rodríguez | November 29, 1934 | 27.0 | 790,694 | 29,285 | 0.4 | 7,717,607 | 3.9 |
| Cárdenas | November 29, 1940 | 72.0 | 17,906,429 | 248,700 | 9.1 | 25,624,036 | 13.0 |
| Avila Camacho | November 30, 1946 | 72.0 | 5,944,449 | 82,562 | 3.0 | 31,568,485 | 16.1 |
| Alemán | November 30, 1952 | 72.0 | 4,844,123 | 67,279 | 2.5 | 36,412,608 | 18.5 |
| Ruiz Cortines | November 30, 1958 | 72.0 | 4,936,668 | 68,565 | 2.5 | 41,349,276 | 21.0 |
| López Mateos | November 30, 1964 | 72.0 | 11,361,370 | 157,797 | 5.8 | 52,710,646 | 26.8 |

Source: James W. Wilkie, *The Mexican Revolution: Federal Expenditure and Social Change Since 1910* (Berkeley and Los Angeles: University of California Press, 1967), p. 188, as revised for second edition.

TABLE 2-8.  RECIPIENTS OF LAND BY PRESIDENTIAL TERM SINCE 1915

| End of Term (Year) | President | Recipients Number | Recipients Average Hectares | Cumulative Number of Recipients |
|---|---|---|---|---|
| 1920 | Carranza | 46,398 | 3.6 | 46,398 |
| 1920 | De la Huerta | 6,330 | 5.3 | 52,728 |
| 1924 | Obregón | 128,468 | 8.6 | 181,196 |
| 1928 | Calles | 297,428 | 10.6 | 478,624 |
| 1930 | Portes Gil | 171,577 | 10.0 | 650,201 |
| 1932 | Ortiz Rubio | 64,573 | 14.6 | 714,774 |
| 1934 | Rodríguez | 68,556 | 11.5 | 783,330 |
| 1940 | Cárdenas | 811,157 | 22.1 | 1,594,487 |
| 1946 | Avila Camacho | 157,536 | 37.7 | 1,752,023 |
| 1952 | Alemán | 97,391 | 49.7 | 1,849,414 |
| 1958 | Ruiz Cortines | 231,888 | 21.1 | 2,081,302 |
| 1964 | López Mateos | 304,498 | 37.3 | 2,385,800 |

Source: Wilkie, *The Mexican Revolution*, p. 194, as revised for second edition.

TABLE 2-9.  DISTRIBUTION OF CROPLAND AND CULTIVATED LAND

| Land Category | 1930 | 1940 | 1950 | 1960 |
|---|---|---|---|---|
| Total Cropland (in millions of hectares) | 14.6 | 14.9 | 19.9 | 23.8 |
| *Ejido* Cropland (% of total) | 13 | 47 | 44 | 43 |
| Total Land Cultivated (in millions of hectares) | 7.3 | 7.9 | 10.9 | 13.8 |
| *Ejido* Land Cultivated (% of total) | 15 | 49 | 49 | 47 |

Source: Calculated from decennial agricultural censuses.

Within the political sphere it is hardly an overstatement to say that political stability itself was institutionalized. The mechanism of stability assumed the form of a political party now called the Party of Revolutionary Institutions, or PRI. From the date of its inception in 1929 it has been utilized to control the political evolution of Mexican society in a manner so conducive to the Mexican pattern of economic development that for the past thirty years no major pressures or crises of a socio-political nature have emerged to obstruct the course of economic growth. This virtuoso performance would engender admiration—though not necessarily approbation—in any socio-cultural setting; in the Latin American context it is particularly impressive.[34]

[34] The workings of the present political system as well as the manner in which it developed are examined in chapters 5-7.

In the economic sphere certain institutions emerged which were also to play prominent roles in the post-1940 phase of economic development. Among them were the Bank of Mexico, the Nacional Financiera, and several lesser financial organizations. In 1925 the Banco de México was organized as the country's central bank. Before its establishment some thirty commercial banks had been granted the right to issue bank notes; since that time that right has been limited to the central bank. During the first years of existence the bank established itself as the major institution of the Mexican financial superstructure and developed a variety of financial controls which were used after 1940 to influence economic growth. A system of graduated and flexible reserve requirements was increasingly relied upon to influence both the aggregate money supply and the allocation of bank credit. In 1941 the bank received greater authority to vary reserve requirements, alter discount rates, and buy and sell public and private securities.

A second major institutional innovation in the financial field was the organization of the Nacional Financiera in 1934. It has been characterized by one scholar specializing in the area of finance as "the most important original contribution made by Mexico to the types of financial institutions participating in financing economic development and promoting economic growth."[35] Since its inception, Nacional Financiera has concentrated its investment activities in long-term debt financing of basic sectors of the economy. It has been said of the organization that between 1934 and 1940 it "tried out in incipient form every role it was later to play and one or two which it was to discard."[36] During that period it became the most important operator in the Mexican securities market, particularly in support of federal government obligations. It also made industrial loans, underwrote bond issues, channeled funds to some public welfare projects, performed the first of its many entrepreneurial roles by organizing a bank, and issued its own securities. Between 1940 and 1950 Nacional Financiera concentrated its resources in a number of basic industries, extending long-term credits or acquiring equity securities. The funds for this large-scale investment banking role were supplied by the federal government, domestic investors in Nacional Financiera's securities, and U.S. governmental institutions such as the Export-Import Bank. After 1950 an increasing proportion of its resources was directed toward the financing of infrastructure investment, particularly electric power and railroads.

[35] Raymond W. Goldsmith, *The Financial Development of Mexico* (Paris: Development Centre of the Organization for Economic Co-operation and Development, 1966), p. 21.

[36] Calvin P. Blair, "Nacional Financiera: Entrepreneurship in a Mixed Economy," in *Public Policy and Private Enterprise in Mexico*, edited by Raymond Vernon (Cambridge: Harvard University Press, 1964), p. 205.

Beginning in the late 1920s, several other financial institutions were organized which were to promote various aspects of economic development in the following years. Prominent among them were the Agricultural Credit Bank and the Ejidal Credit Bank organized to support agricultural production, and the Foreign Trade Bank to facilitate the growth of Mexican exports.

Another fundamental institutional change in the economic sphere during this period was the growth of a free labor market. In many regions of Mexico the power of the Mexican *hacendados* did not collapse with the revolution; it was only with the coming of the Cárdenas agrarian reform program in the 1930s that their domination of significant portions of rural Mexico was finally broken. By 1940 fewer than a million peasants still lived on haciendas. No longer tied by debt to an estate on which he was generally underemployed, the rural Mexican who received land was free to work it to his own best advantage. Those for whom there was no land at least gained mobility; some remained on the land as agricultural laborers, while others drifted toward the cities where they were gradually integrated into the urban labor force. In either case, post-1940 growth rates were to benefit. Those Mexicans who received even the smallest plots of land worked longer and harder than they had before the land reform program, with the result that their agricultural output increased even without other production inputs, which most of the *ejidatarios* could not afford. The migration to the cities expanded the urban labor supply, keeping wages low and profits high and encouraging the reinvestment of earnings throughout the 1940s and 1950s.

Perhaps the least measurable of those developments which were to have a major influence on the post-1940 growth performance was what might be called the institutionalization of new avenues and incentives for economic and social advancement. This characterization is in some ways both inadequate and inaccurate, for it is meant to cover a wide range of changes, both social and psychological. Furthermore, the evidence with regard to those changes is fragmentary at best. Nevertheless, enough individual features of the phenomenon are evident to attempt a portrait of the whole.

Rapid economic growth in nontotalitarian countries can only occur if their social systems reward those who work, save, invest, and innovate. And since the rewards of any social system in large part reflect the goals and values of its elite groups, elite value-orientations significantly affect the course and pace of economic development. Throughout Latin America during the nineteenth century the landed aristocracy formed the apex of the social structure. We have already noted the *rentier* mentality and patterns of luxury consumption of this class in Mexico, which were so bitterly criticized by contemporary observers. The Catholic church, with an appetite for land and conspicuous consumption voracious enough to rival any *hacendado,* reinforced a social structure and value-orientations that were clearly incompatible with rapid economic development.

The victory of Juárez and the Liberal party during the Reform period broke the landed creole control over Mexican politics, and Díaz in particular drew upon mestizos in forming his political and military machine. But it was not until the revolution and the ensuing programs of land reform that the economic power of the *hacendados* was broken. Since the revolution considerably weakened the influence of the church as well, Mexico was presented with an opportunity for change in social structure and elite values unparalleled in the rest of Latin America.

Those who bid for the vacated room at the top of the socio-economic scale came from three distinct groups. First, there was the indigenous commercial-industrialist group whose origins we have traced to the Díaz period. Members of that group already possessed capital, initiative and experience; what they needed was political stability and proper assurances that there was a place for a profit-oriented private sector in the new postrevolutionary Mexico. Second, there were the sons of the self-exiled aristocracy. Some of them retained ownership of relatively small portions of former haciendas; others were left in control of commercial holdings. Both these farm and nonfarm enterprises often blossomed into profitable and expanding businesses, utilizing modern methods of production. The third group was more closely linked than the first two with the emerging Mexican political elite. It comprised friends and relatives of the successful revolutionary politicians and generals, and its early sources of wealth were highly profitable government contracts. As one Mexican scholar has noted, "its members were buccaneering, risk-taking entrepreneurs par excellence. The rough, crude middle-class backgrounds of the friends of the new political leaders not only added to their avarice, but also stimulated them to risky efforts. They did not have high status positions to maintain and, if they were to rise to positions of prestige, they had to strike boldly."[37] And for those who struck it rich, the temptation to assimilate the values of the traditional aristocracy by investing in rural real estate was removed as a result of the land reform program.

These changes in structure and values at the apex of the Mexican social system found their counterparts in the lower levels as well; perhaps the evidence is most striking in rural Mexico. Many sociologists and anthropologists studying Mexican and Central American Indian communities have commented upon the—at least latent—acquisitive nature of these various subcultures. Yet they have also noted the relative absence of any achievement motivation. Some experts have argued that the apparent lack of a will to achieve and accumulate is an inherent cultural trait. Others have noted that where real economic opportunity has presented itself, such communities

[37] James G. Maddox, "Economic Growth and Revolution in Mexico," *Land Economics* 36 (August 1960). See also Sanford A. Mosk, *Industrial Revolution in Mexico* (Berkeley and Los Angeles: University of California Press, 1954), on origins of this "new group."

reveal a pronounced pecuniary orientation.[38] This has led them to argue that peasant "indifference" has been to a considerable extent a rational response to a social and economic system which restricted the range of economic opportunities available to them and quickly deprived them of any surpluses which they managed to accumulate. Thus "a paralysis of productive motivation and a weak interest in exertion would derive from simple ignorance of available opportunities, malnutrition, limited economic capabilities, and the lack of any clear-cut correspondence between expended effort and accruing results . . . as well as from such factors as habit, tradition, and 'prerational' or 'precommercial' values."[39]

The response of those Mexican villagers who gained lands through the reform program clearly supports the contention of those who have argued the latter case. As Oscar Lewis points out in his study of the Indian village of Tepoztlán, the world view of the Tepoztecan reflects a knowledge of and an adaptation to the constraints imposed by his environment. When economic and political liberties increase, as they did following the revolution, the villagers respond to the new opportunities. The breakup of the hacienda system and the creation of *ejidos* removed many obstacles to social mobility, encouraged industrious activity on the part of the Indian peasant, and resulted in a significant increase in the size of the middle and upper income group in Tepoztlán.[40] As the following chapter will demonstrate, by any of several diverse measurements the *ejidal* sector of Mexican agriculture has been as productive as that under private ownership.

For the vast majority of the Mexican population—the mestizo element which found its place above the Indian and below the creole in the Mexican social structure—evidence has always indicated a drive for mobility and socio-economic advancement. In fact, this trait seems to be shared by the mestizo (or Ladino) segments of all Latin American societies.[41] The problem with regard to the mestizo in Mexico has never been one of motivation, but rather one of opportunity. Throughout the nineteenth century wealth in Mexico was concentrated in very few hands: those of the creoles, the church and foreigners. This initial situation was further exacerbated by the Porfirian

---

[38] See Sol Tax, *Penny Capitalism: A Guatemalan Indian Economy* (Chicago: University of Chicago Press, 1953); and Robert Redfield, *A Village that Chose Progress* (Chicago: University of Chicago Press, 1950).

[39] William P. Glade, Jr., "Revolution and Economic Development," in Charles W. Anderson and William P. Glade, Jr., *The Political Economy of Mexico* (Madison: University of Wisconsin Press, 1963), pp. 38-39.

[40] Oscar Lewis, *Life in a Mexican Village: Tepoztlán Restudied* (Urbana: University of Illinois Press, 1963), pp. 116, 177, 477 and *passim*.

[41] John Gillin, "Ethos Components in Modern Latin American Culture," in *Contemporary Cultures and Societies of Latin America*, edited by Richard N. Adams and Dwight B. Heath (New York: Random House, 1965), pp. 503-17.

pattern of growth which concentrated wealth to a still greater degree. Both social structure and economic system conspired against mestizo advancement. As later chapters will suggest, about the only avenue of socio-economic mobility remaining to the mestizo was politics, including positions in the army and the government bureaucracy.

With the revolution the situation began to change. The old elites were displaced, and their wealth was in part redistributed through land reform, confiscation of church properties, and nationalization of some foreign concessions. Furthermore, as indicated above, the beneficiaries of the upheaval could not invest their gains in the old nonproductive ways. Once wealth began to be channeled in increasing proportions into productive investments in industry, commerce and commercial agriculture, opportunities for socio-economic mobility multiplied at a rate hitherto unknown in Mexico. Table 2-10 measures the structural change in Mexican society between 1895 and 1940. During those years we note that middle class Mexico grew proportionally in excess of 100 percent, while both the upper and lower class proportions decreased. The drop in the size of the rural upper class gives us some measure of the effect of the revolution and agrarian reform on Mexico's landed elite. The growing urban orientation of Mexico's upper class is also revealed when we compare the two years. What the table fails to reveal is the rapid growth of the middle class between 1925 and 1940. Since much of the pre-revolution middle class was undoubtedly ruined between 1910 and the early 1920s, the greater part of the growth of that segment of the social structure took place after 1925.

TABLE 2-10. CHANGES IN CLASS STRUCTURE, 1895-1940

| Social Class | 1895 | | 1940 | | Proportional Change |
|---|---|---|---|---|---|
| | Number | Percent | Number | Percent | |
| Total Population | 12,698,330 | 100.00 | 19,653,552 | 100.00 | |
| Upper | 183,006 | 1.44 | 205,572 | 1.05 | -27.1 |
| Urban | 49,542 | 0.39 | 110,868 | 0.57 | +46.2 |
| Rural | 133,464 | 1.05 | 94,704 | 0.48 | -54.3 |
| Middle | 989,783 | 7.78 | 3,118,958 | 15.87 | +104.0 |
| Urban | 776,439 | 6.12 | 2,382,464 | 12.12 | +98.0 |
| Rural | 213,344 | 1.66 | 736,494 | 3.75 | +125.9 |
| Lower | 11,525,541 | 90.78 | 16,329,022 | 83.08 | -8.5 |
| Urban | 1,799,898 | 14.17 | 4,403,337 | 22.40 | +58.1 |
| Rural | 9,725,643 | 76.61 | 11,925,685 | 60.68 | -20.8 |

Source: José E. Iturriaga, *La Estructura social y cultural de México* (Mexico: Fondo de Cultura Económica, 1951), pp. 28-30.

New opportunities evoked new responses, and in both urban and rural Mexico increased social and economic mobility resulted. The case studies of Oscar Lewis provide many individual examples, including one of a millionaire industrialist emerging from a childhood of urban slum poverty.[42] At a more generalized level his investigation of the village of Tepoztlán portrays the gradual blurring of sharp economic and social class lines and an acceleration in the process of socio-economic mobility.[43]

The literature on economic development is studded with references to the "vicious circle" of poverty that obstructs growth: low income → low savings → low investment → low productivity → low income. Yet at differing times, under differing circumstances, in differing places, growth occurs. In the Mexican case, the years between 1910 and 1940 reveal the gradual emergence of a "virtuous circle" which suggests that development as well as stagnation can feed upon itself. The revolution removed an economically nonproductive elite, foreclosed old patterns of nonproductive investment, and redistributed some wealth. After 1940 the new elites, literally forced into new investment patterns, coincidentally opened a broad variety of new channels of socio-economic mobility for lower class and middle class Mexico. Enhanced mobility prospects within the Mexican economy lessened the traditional demands on the Mexican political system to provide advancement for the society's middle segments. The lowering of these demands increased political stability, which in turn encouraged accelerated rates of savings and investment. And so the pace of economic growth after 1940 quickened, as did the capacity to satisfy the mobility desires of the Mexican people.

It has been argued that "if we have to look for one factor which would explain more than any other the economic retardation of all of Latin America, we are more likely to find it in Latin American social structure and the values deriving from it."[44] The greater the accuracy of this assertion—and nothing in the Mexican case controverts it—the more crucial becomes the change in structure and values of Mexican society during the years preceding 1940 as a factor contributing to the pace of economic development since that date.

---

[42] Oscar Lewis, *Five Families: Mexican Case Studies in the Culture of Poverty* (New York: Science Edition, 1962).

[43] Lewis, *Life in a Mexican Village.*

[44] Bert F. Hoselitz, "Economic Growth in Latin America," *First International Conference of Economic History* (The Hague: Mouton & Co., 1960), p. 88.

*Chapter 3*

# THE MEXICAN "MIRACLE": FRUITION

In the three decades since 1940 the Mexican economy has grown at an annual rate of more than 6 percent. On a per capita basis, the rate has exceeded 3 percent. Throughout the period manufacturing production has risen approximately 8 percent a year. Agricultural output grew at an even faster rate over the first decade of the period, then dropped to an annual rate of increase of 4.3 percent during the following decade. Between 1940 and 1962 the average product per person employed in the agricultural sector rose by 68 percent, or 2.4 percent a year.[1]

Sectoral shifts in both output and employment over the past thirty years illustrate the fundamental nature of the changes which the Mexican economy has experienced. The agricultural sector employed 65 percent of Mexico's work force and constituted over 23 percent of gross domestic product in 1940; three decades later it employs less than half the work force and accounts for 16 percent of aggregate domestic product. In contrast manufacturing activity has raised its share of the total domestic product from 17.8 percent to 26 percent and now employs more than 16 percent of the labor force.[2] Except for mining, the industrial sectors annually register the highest rates of growth. From 1965 through 1968, for example, the manufacturing, construction and electrical energy sectors all grew at average annual rates of 9 percent or better. By 1970 Mexico was largely self-sufficient in the production of foodstuffs, basic petroleum products, steel, and most consumer goods.

Indicative of the extent of Mexican industrialization is the fact that the most rapid growth is now being experienced in the producers' goods fields.

[1] See Leopoldo Solís M., "Hacia un análisis general a largo plazo del desarrollo económico de México," *Demografía y economía* 1 (1967): 74.

[2] Alfredo Navarrete R., "Mexico's Balance of Payments and External Financing," *Weltwirtschaftliches Archiv* 101 (1968): 74.

TABLE 3-1. MEXICAN GROWTH, 1940-1968 (average annual growth rates)

| Item | 1940-50 (1) | 1950-60 (2) | 1960-68 (3) |
|---|---|---|---|
| Gross Domestic Product | 6.7 | 5.8 | 6.4 |
| Population | 2.8 | 3.1 | 3.3 |
| Per Capita Product | 3.9 | 2.7 | 3.1 |
| Agricultural Production | 8.2 | 4.3 | 4.0 |
| Manufacturing Production | 8.1 | 7.3 | 8.2 |

Sources: Columns 1 and 2 from Clark Reynolds, *The Mexican Economy: Twentieth Century Structure and Growth* (New Haven: Yale University Press, forthcoming). Column 3 derived from statistics of the Economic Commission for Latin America and recent issues of the Banco de México's *Informe anual.*

Between 1950 and 1966 production of steel and other metal products grew at an annual rate of 11.5 percent, machinery production by 10 percent, vehicles and transport equipment output by 10.7 percent, and chemicals production by 12.5 percent.[3] The manufacturing sector now produces such items as automobile motors, rear axles, hydraulic brakes, tractors, industrial motors, mechanical shovels, color television, electrical transformers, air conditioning units and electrical office equipment.

Both the rapid growth rate and the structural transformation of the Mexican economy since 1940 are in great part a consequence of trends in Mexican savings and investment. The combined investment efforts of Mexico's public and private sectors have financed a technological revolution in both agriculture and industry. In sharp contrast with the Porfirian years, the savings which Mexicans have invested have been their own. During the 1900-1910 period possibly as much as two-thirds of all investment was foreign in origin; since 1940 close to 90 percent of all gross fixed investment has been financed from domestic savings. The marginal rate of internal saving has been high enough to raise the ratio of domestic savings to gross domestic product from 8 percent in 1940 to 17 percent in 1967.[4]

The figures on savings and investment reflect more clearly than any others the extent to which the Mexican economy has been developing since 1940. Growth rates measure changes in total output, and are often cited in misleading ways. They are a composite of cyclical and secular trends in supply and demand, of ephemeral as well as fundamental forces affecting the productive capacity of economic systems. Four or five good crop years can produce high growth rates in developing economies which are still essentially agricultural; a few years of bad weather will result in apparent stagnation.

[3] *Ibid.*, p. 75.
[4] Estimates of Nacional Financiera. See *ibid.*, p. 76.

TABLE 3-2. OCCUPATIONAL STRUCTURE (percent of total employment)

| Year | Agriculture | Industry | Services |
|------|-------------|----------|----------|
| 1940 | 65.4 | 12.7 | 21.9 |
| 1950 | 58.3 | 15.9 | 25.7 |
| 1960 | 54.1 | 19.0 | 26.9 |
| 1964 | 52.3 | 20.1 | 27.6 |

Source: Various issues of Nacional Financiera, *La Economía mexicana en cifras.*

TABLE 3-3. STRUCTURE OF PRODUCTION
(percent of gross domestic product, 1960 prices)

| | Year | | | | | |
|---|---|---|---|---|---|---|
| Category | 1940 | 1945 | 1950 | 1955 | 1962 | 1967 |
| Agricultural Production | 23.2 | 18.6 | 20.8 | 20.3 | 17.2 | 15.8 |
| Industrial Production | 31.0 | 34.0 | 31.0 | 31.3 | 33.9 | 36.7 |
| Manufacturing | 17.8 | 20.8 | 20.7 | 21.1 | 23.3 | 26.5 |
| Mining | 4.6 | 3.5 | 2.4 | 2.2 | 1.6 | 1.5 |
| Electricity | 0.9 | 0.8 | 0.9 | 1.0 | 1.3 | 1.5 |
| Petroleum | 2.8 | 2.4 | 2.7 | 2.7 | 3.2 | 3.2 |
| Construction | 4.9 | 6.5 | 4.3 | 4.3 | 4.5 | 3.9 |
| Services | 45.8 | 47.4 | 48.2 | 48.4 | 48.9 | 47.5 |
| Total | 100.0 | 100.0 | 100.0 | 100.0 | 100.0 | 100.0 |

Sources: Leopoldo Solís M., "Hacia un análisis general a largo plazo del desarrollo económico de México," *Demografía y economía* 1 (1967): 73; and Banco de México, *Informe anual*, 1968.

Growth rates measure changes in physical output; economic development measures the institutionalization of the growth process itself. Development entails the better use of natural and human resources, changes in the structure of an economy, and the enhanced capacity to increase production through the savings-investment process. Investment may take many forms: fixed capital formation (including expenditure on infrastructure), programs of research and technology, broadened systems of education, and so forth. All increase a society's productive base. All have expanded in Mexico since 1940, and help to distinguish this period from earlier phases of Mexican history that were characterized by some economic *growth* but little economic *development.*

## ECONOMIC DEVELOPMENT: PUBLIC-SECTOR INITIATIVES

Since 1940 the Mexican public sector has accounted for 30 percent of all gross fixed capital formation (table 3-4). During the early years public investment exceeded 50 percent of the total. The quantity of this investment alone had a direct catalytic effect in Mexico's recent growth. But the government

TABLE 3-4.  GROSS FIXED CAPITAL FORMATION, 1940-1967 (in current prices)

| | Percent of Gross Domestic Product | | | Percent Distribution | |
| Period | Total | Public | Private | Public | Private |
|---|---|---|---|---|---|
| (1) 1940-46 | 8.6 | 4.4 | 4.2 | 52 | 48 |
| (2) 1947-53 | 16.2 | 5.9 | 10.3 | 36 | 64 |
| (3) 1954-60 | 20.5 | 5.3 | 15.2 | 26 | 74 |
| (4) 1961-62 | 19.1 | 6.5 | 12.6 | 34 | 66 |
| (5) 1940-62 | 18.6 | 5.6 | 13.0 | 30 | 70 |
| (6) 1963-67 | 20.7 | 6.2 | 14.5 | 30 | 70 |

Sources: Rows 1-5, Grupo Secretaría de Hacienda, Banco de México, Estudios sobre Proyecciones, *Manuel de estadísticas básicas para el análisis del desarrollo económico de México,* as presented in Raymond Goldsmith, *The Financial Development of Mexico* (Paris: Development Centre of the Organisation for Economic Cooperation and Development, 1966), p. 74. Row 6, from data published by the Mexican Ministry of Finance and Public Credit, the Banco de México, and the Agency for International Development.

has also developed institutions and implemented policies that have indirectly encouraged and sustained a dynamic Mexican private sector.

*Direct Impact*

Shifts in the pattern of direct government investment in the economy since 1930 reflect the changes in priorities that resulted from economic growth during that period. Before 1930, state ownership and control predominated in the railway and banking sectors. During the Cárdenas presidency (1934-40) state entrepreneurship spread to rural industry, petroleum and electric power. Since 1940 this trend has continued to the point where some four hundred operations are public or mixed public-private sector enterprises. The government owns the petroleum and electric power industries and the railways, major steel and fertilizer plants, railway equipment factories, and a number of banks. Its proportion of ownership is also significant in petrochemicals, aviation, motion pictures, newsprint, and mineral exploitation.

Between 1935 and 1960 over half of the public sector's investment was channeled into crucial infrastructure expenditures in agriculture, transport, and communications. Most of the money invested in the agricultural sector was spent on the construction of vast irrigation networks. As a result the acreage irrigated under publicly financed hydraulic systems has risen at a rate of 4.9 percent a year since 1950. It now includes over 60 percent of all irrigated land in Mexico, in comparison with 13 percent in 1940.[5] One of the largest of its kind in the world, the Mexican program has reclaimed and

[5]*Ibid.,* p. 79; Frank Brandenburg, *The Making of Modern Mexico* (Englewood Cliffs, N.J.: Prentice-Hall, 1964), p. 259.

TABLE 3-5. DISTRIBUTION OF GROSS PUBLIC CAPITAL FORMATION,
1935-1960 (in percent)

| Years | Total | Agri-culture | Industry | Transport and Com-munication | Social Welfare | Admin-istration and Defense | Unspecified |
|-------|-------|--------------|----------|------------------------------|----------------|----------------------------|-------------|
| | (1) | (2) | (3) | (4) | (5) | (6) | (7) |
| 1935-39 | 100 | 19.7 | 4.9 | 55.7 | 8.2 | 0.0 | 13.1 |
| 1940-46 | 100 | 15.5 | 10.8 | 51.1 | 12.7 | 1.7 | 8.2 |
| 1947-53 | 100 | 21.2 | 19.8 | 40.7 | 12.3 | 1.1 | 4.9 |
| 1954-60 | 100 | 11.0 | 31.4 | 36.0 | 15.9 | 2.7 | 2.9 |
| 1935-60 | 100 | 14.1 | 26.7 | 38.5 | 14.6 | 2.2 | 3.9 |

Source: Nacional Financiera, *50 Años de revolución mexicana en cifras* (Mexico, 1963), p. 133.

irrigated more land than any other Latin American country. Between 1940 and 1946 alone, croplands covered by government-financed irrigation tripled in size. Together with government investments in road systems in rural Mexico, this public investment in irrigation and land reclamation has revolutionized Mexican agricultural production and greatly accelerated agricultural output.

Close to 30 percent of all public investment since 1940 has occurred in the industrial sector. During the 1940s and early 1950s, Nacional Financiera directed most of its long-term financing to basic import-substitution industries, including iron, steel, and oil. Often these investments were made to alleviate critical supply shortages created by wartime conditions.

Since 1940, large portions of the public investment have been channeled into the electrical power and petroleum fields, with resulting annual growth rates of 10 percent for installed electrical power capacity and 6.6 percent for gas and oil production.[6] Particularly during the Ruiz Cortines administration (1952-58), public-sector investment continued to exhibit the "bottleneck-breaking" quality which has characterized it throughout the post-1940 period. Public investment priorities turned from the newly flourishing agricultural sector to transport and industry. Large capital investments in the railway system resolved a critical problem in internal transport which had arisen with the country's economic boom. Public investment also increased installed electrical capacity by 80 percent and oil refining capacity by 50 percent over the six-year period.[7]

[6] Navarrete R., "Mexico's Balance of Payments," p. 79.

[7] Raymond Vernon, *The Dilemma of Mexico's Development: The Roles of the Private and Public Sectors* (Cambridge: Harvard University Press, 1963), p. 111.

During the years between 1939 and 1960, the public sector financed over three-quarters of its investment programs from its own savings, that is, government revenues net of current account expenditures and the surpluses of the decentralized state enterprises and agencies. Initially, domestic borrowing covered much of the deficit, but during the 1950s the Mexican government increasingly relied upon foreign borrowing (table 3-6). During the 1960s the capacity of the public sector to finance investment programs with its own savings fell to about 68 percent. One reason was that the size of those investments rose slightly as a proportion of the gross national product while public-sector saving, similarly measured, fell from 4.4 percent in 1961 to 3.5 percent in 1966 and 1967; it rose again in 1968 (tables 3-4 and 3-7). The

TABLE 3-6. FINANCING OF PUBLIC-SECTOR INVESTMENT, 1939-1959
(percent of total investment)

| Period | Total | Public Sector Savings | Domestic Borrowing | Foreign Borrowing |
|---|---|---|---|---|
| 1939-50 | 100 | 77 | 14 | 9 |
| 1950-59 | 100 | 76 | 10 | 14 |

Source: Derived from Alfredo Navarrete R., "The Financing of Economic Development" in *Mexico's Recent Economic Growth,* edited by Tom Davis (Austin: University of Texas Press for the Institute of Latin American Studies, 1967), pp. 105-30.

TABLE 3-7. FINANCING OF PUBLIC-SECTOR INVESTMENT, 1961-1968

| Means of Financing | Year | | | | | | | |
|---|---|---|---|---|---|---|---|---|
| | 1961 | 1962 | 1963 | 1964 | 1965 | 1966 | 1967 | 1968[a] |
| Public-sector investment (% of GNP) | 5.4 | 5.9 | 6.5 | 7.5 | 5.8 | 5.3 | 6.3 | 6.4 |
| Public-sector net savings (% of GNP) | 4.4 | 4.6 | 4.5 | 4.4 | 4.3 | 3.5 | 3.5 | 4.2 |
| Net savings (% of investment) | 81.2 | 77.1 | 68.8 | 59.0 | 73.9 | 67.2 | 56.0 | 63.1 |
| Financing of deficit (% of investment) | | | | | | | | |
| Domestic | 16.6 | 29.7 | 26.1 | 28.7 | 33.1 | 40.5 | 29.2 | 28.7 |
| Foreign | 22.5 | 15.9 | 18.9 | 26.7 | – | 7.8 | 18.5 | 15.4 |
| Less "financial investment"[b] | 20.4 | 22.7 | 13.9 | 14.4 | 7.0 | 8.0 | 17.9 | 7.2 |

Sources: Derived from data published by the Ministry of Finance and Public Credit, and the Banco de México.
[a]Preliminary estimates.
[b]A residual item including changes in inventory and working capital, and financial investments.

public sector's capacity to finance a major share of its investments with its own savings has held government debt in Mexico to very moderate levels. Measured against total GNP and aggregate national wealth, the debt is below corresponding ratios for the United States. The rise in the public debt since World War II represents approximately 10 percent of Mexican net savings during the period. Since about half of that increase has been covered by foreign saving, the proportion of Mexico's aggregate private-sector savings absorbed by the government has remained well under 10 percent.[8]

One of the striking features of the Mexican public-sector performance in recent decades is how much it has done with how little. While data on total public-sector income are fragmentary at best, the figures presented in table 3-8 are in close agreement with most published estimates. At no time between 1940 and 1960 did the public sector absorb more than 13 percent of total gross domestic product. During most of the period the figure was less than 11 percent. Yet the government managed to save approximately 40 percent of that income for public investment. Most other Latin American governments have taxed substantially more, yet invested less over the same three decades.[9]

[8]Raymond W. Goldsmith, *The Financial Development of Mexico* (Paris: Development Centre of the Organisation for Economic Co-operation and Development, 1966), pp. 37ff.

[9]One notable reason has been the low level of expenditures for defense in Mexico. Defense expenditures since 1950 have remained well below 10 percent of aggregate federal government outlays. See James W. Wilkie, *The Mexican Revolution: Federal Expenditure and Social Change since 1910* (Berkeley and Los Angeles: University of California Press, 1968), pp. 102-3.

TABLE 3-8.  PUBLIC-SECTOR INCOME

| Public-Sector Category | 1940 % | 1940 % of GDP | 1950 % | 1950 % of GDP | 1960 % | 1960 % of GDP | 1964 % | 1964 % of GDP |
|---|---|---|---|---|---|---|---|---|
| I. Total | 100.0 | 10.0 | 100.0 | 10.94 | 100.0 | 12.43 | 100.0 | 14.80 |
| II. Government sector—total | | | | | 77.0 | 9.57 | 69.6 | 10.31 |
| a. Federal government | | | | | 57.3 | 7.12 | 52.0 | 7.70 |
| b. Federal district | | | | | 7.0 | 0.87 | 6.3 | 0.94 |
| c. States & territories | | | | | 9.7 | 1.20 | 8.6 | 1.27 |
| d. Municipalities | | | | | 3.0 | 0.38 | 2.7 | 0.40 |
| III. Rest of public sector—total | | | | | 23.0 | 2.86 | 30.4 | 4.49 |
| a. Surplus of public enterprises | | | | | 13.6 | 1.69 | 18.6 | 2.75 |
| b. Net income of other state agencies | | | | | 9.4 | 1.17 | 11.8 | 1.74 |

Sources: For 1940 and 1950, Combined Mexican Working Party, *The Economic Development of Mexico* (Baltimore: Johns Hopkins Press, for the International Bank for Reconstruction and Development, 1953), p. 363, table 121. For 1960 and 1964, Roberto Anguiano Equihua, *Las Finanzas del sector Público en México* (Mexico: Universidad Nacional Autónoma de México Ciudad Universitaria, 1968), pp. 104-5.

*Indirect Impact*

Beyond the direct impact of its own expenditure on economic development, the Mexican government designed a series of policies to encourage private-sector initiative. Some of those policies reflected a standard Latin American response to the possibilities for industrialization resulting from the depression and further trade dislocations during World War II. Others have been quite unique.

Mexico most closely resembles her southern neighbors in the area of commercial policy. Her domestic market is highly protected, reflecting the commitment of the Mexican government to industrialization since the Cárdenas years (1934-40)—and particularly during the presidencies of Manuel Avila Camacho (1940-46), Miguel Alemán (1946-52) and Adolfo Ruiz Cortines (1952-58). Two major policies have been used to insulate the domestic producer from foreign competition. In the earlier years tariff protection was relied upon to a considerable extent to entice domestic investors into import-substitution enterprises. During the 1940s rising tariff protection was viewed as the logical corollary to the widely stated goal of industrialization. The policy of the Avila Camacho administration was to offer protection for practically every new industry that appeared in Mexico during the war years. Miguel Alemán, even more committed to Mexican industrialization than his predecessor, continued to rely heavily upon expanded tariff protection to encourage private sector investment.[10] Since the 1940s, nominal import duties on raw materials have been kept low while rates for finished manufactures have often exceeded 100 percent. When calculated to measure effective tariff protection, that is, the protection granted to the value-added process in Mexico, the rates on finished products are even higher.

By the late 1950s an elaborate system of import licensing had been developed, and this direct control over imports now constitutes the major mode of Mexican protection. The program began in the 1940s with the double objective of increasing the pace of industrialization and conserving scarce foreign exchange for the importation of nonluxury items. Approximately 80 percent of Mexican imports are now subject to licensing requirements. Under the licensing system the mere capacity to produce domestically has generally been deemed sufficient reason to suspend the importation of competing products.[11] During the past half decade the Ministry of Industry

---

[10] Sanford A. Mosk, *Industrial Revolution in Mexico* (Berkeley and Los Angeles: University of California Press, 1954), pp. 67–83.

[11] See Ariel Buira, "Development and Price Stability in Mexico," *Weltwirtschaftliches Archiv* 101 (1968): 67; Rafael Izquierdo, "Protectionism in Mexico," in *Public Policy and Private Enterprise in Mexico,* edited by Raymond Vernon (Cambridge: Harvard University Press, 1964), pp. 243–89.

and Commerce, which administers the import licensing program, has insisted publicly that domestic producers will be exposed to import competition if they cannot manage to market their products at a "reasonable" price within a "reasonable" period of time. As yet, however, there is little evidence that the ministry has moved much beyond the "pronouncement" stage in its attempt to revive the concept of efficient production in many areas of the Mexican manufacturing sector.[12]

A final form of protection was provided by the exchange devaluations of 1949 and 1954, which lowered the value of the Mexican peso from 4.85 per U.S. dollar to the present rate of 12.5. Most studies suggest that the second devaluation considerably undervalued the peso.

Commercial policies assuring the Mexican entrepreneur a protected domestic market have been complemented by other incentives to private investment. From the earliest years of the period, industrialists have been given significant tax concessions. Beginning in 1941, exemptions from the payment of all major forms of taxation for periods varying from five to ten years were granted to new enterprises and to others deemed necessary for the development of manufacturing in Mexico. Duties on imported raw materials and machinery for manufacturing firms have also been rebated. Investment subsidies and a ceiling on nominal rates of interest have further encouraged Mexican entrepreneurs. As a result of the latter policy, the cost of borrowing may even have reached negative levels during the inflationary years of the late 1940s and early 1950s.

One final and highly significant element in the program to stimulate industrialization was the impact of fiscal policy on the distribution of national income. Throughout the late 1930s and 1940s the Mexican government relied on inflationary financing of public sector expenditures. Revenues remained low, investment programs grew in size, and central bank lending covered a major portion of the growing deficits. While there is a good deal of debate with regard to the wisdom of the particular fiscal policy mix that contributed substantially to annual price increases of between 6 and 22 percent during the period, there is agreement that government officials made a quite conscious choice to finance public sector programs through inflation rather than direct taxation. At least one major study of the period has argued that Mexico could have achieved even higher rates of growth during the period if taxes had matched expenditures and prices had been held stable.[13] Those responsible for government policy, however, apparently felt that

[12] In the past reasonable prices have been interpreted to mean no more than 100 percent above international market price.

[13] Barry N. Siegel, *Inflación y desarrollo: las experiencias de México* (Mexico, D.F.: Centro de Estudios Monetarios Latinoamericanos, 1960), pp. 179–87.

growth with price stability was impossible at that time; they feared that increases in taxation would simply undermine all the other investment incentives. So taxes were not raised and price increases continued to average 10 percent a year through 1955. The best statistical evidence available suggests that during the 1940–1950 period real wages fell in both agricultural and nonagricultural activities while the real incomes of entrepreneurs rose rapidly.[14]

Wage increases lagged well behind price increases for two reasons. First, migration from rural to urban areas presented the industrial and service sectors with an almost infinitely elastic labor supply. Second, by the mid-1940s the Mexican labor movement was firmly controlled by the ruling *Partido Revolucionario Institucional* and the governing elite that dominated it.[15] Union leaders who objected too openly to the falling trend in real wages were often replaced by others more amenable to the dictates of the new political elite. By then committed to a program of rapid industrialization, that elite was in a position to assure increased capital formation through the mechanism of inflation.[16]

The Mexican government's contribution to economic development has diverged most significantly from the Latin American pattern (typified by Argentina, Brazil and Chile) in financial policy. Of the four, Mexico is the only country to move from an extended period of inflation to one of relative price stability. Since 1955 Mexican prices have risen at less than 3 percent a year, a record of stability which compares favorably with price trends in most developed economies over the same period. Furthermore, the pace of growth has not noticeably slackened as a result of this transition.

The goals of Mexican monetary and financial policy throughout the period since 1940 have included both internal and external price stability, but before 1955 this *desideratum* was sacrificed to that of expanding Mexico's productive capacity as rapidly as possible. The decision to grant a higher priority to price stability resulted in great part from the economic and political effects of the 1954 devaluation. Prices rose by 30 percent in the twenty-month period following the devaluation; protests among middle and lower

---

[14] See Ifigenia M. de Navarrete, *La distribución del ingreso y el desarrollo económico de México* (Mexico, D.F.: Instituto de Investigaciones Económicas, Escuela Nacional de Economía, 1960), chaps. 2 and 3; and Adolf Sturmthal, "Economic Development, Income Distribution, and Capital Formation in Mexico," *Journal of Political Economy* 63 (June 1955). As both authors indicate, the decade was also one of rising per capita income in the form of wages and salaries. The apparent contradiction in trends is explained by shifts in the structure of employment from agriculture to industry, and from lower- to higher-skilled jobs.

[15] See below, chaps. 5, 6, and 7.

[16] This is not to argue that the process necessarily operated by design but more simply that it did operate and that the workings of PRI politics assured its success.

income groups occurred throughout the country, and private sector confidence in the government's development policies seemed broken. Perhaps in no other period since the PRI assumed command of the Mexican presidency and politics had criticism of the present system of government been so harsh and outspoken.

The response of the political elite to the 1954–55 *crise de confiance* is revealed in the record of price stability since that time. Stability has been achieved essentially through (1) a more vigorous application of monetary and financial tools developed during the 1940s, and (2) an increasing dependence upon external financing of the public sector deficit. The major instrument of monetary policy in Mexico has been the Banco de México's control over legal reserve requirements of the private banking system. At times reserve requirements on additional deposits have reached 100 percent. Using this instrument, the bank has been able to control effectively the aggregate levels of money supply and credit. In addition there has developed in Mexico a very intricate system of selective credit controls designed specifically to minimize the inflationary effects of public-sector deficit financing and to encourage growth in key areas of the economy. Through regulations on reserve requirements and portfolio distributions the private banking system was forced to acquire increasingly larger shares of outstanding government and other public securities.[17]

Some trends during the 1950s will illustrate the effect of these selective controls. Between 1950 and 1955, over 33 percent of the increase in total banking system claims on the government sector was acquired by the central bank. Between 1956 and 1961, the holdings of the central bank fell—not only relatively, but absolutely—from 2.1 billion pesos to 1.3 billion. Over the latter period private financial institutions increased their share of the banking system's claims on government from 23 percent to 63 percent of the total.[18] As the burden of financing public-sector deficits shifted from the central bank to private financial institutions, the degree of direct monetization of the deficits was significantly lowered.

In addition to minimizing the inflationary effects of deficit financing, the selective credit controls have regulated portfolio composition of private financial institutions in favor of investments in agriculture and industry. As a result those sectors have obtained access to credit in greater amounts and at lower

---

[17] See Dwight S. Brothers and Leopoldo Solís M., "Recent Financial Experience in Mexico," *Economía latinoamericana* 2 (July 1965): 77–98; and Leopoldo Solís M., "The Financial System in the Economic Development of Mexico," *Weltwirtschaftliches Archiv* 101 (1968): 36–47.

[18] Brothers and Solís M., "Recent Financial Experience," pp. 84–86; and Dwight S. Brothers and Leopoldo Solís M., *Mexican Financial Development* (Austin: University of Texas Press, 1966), chap. 4.

rates of interest than would have prevailed in the absence of such controls.[19] The Mexican stabilization program has also included an increased reliance on foreign borrowing to cover public sector deficits, as reflected in tables 3-6 and 3-7.

The relationship between Mexico's recent economic development and the financial policies just described is literally impossible to measure. The difficulty is not one of data, but of the present state of economic knowledge. As Raymond Goldsmith has put it, the relation between financial and economic development in the process of economic growth has been severely neglected in both theoretical and empirical analysis. Economic theory has been increasingly conducted in "real" terms, for example, national product in physical units; production functions; input-output coefficients; and capital-output ratios. Empirical research has moved in the same direction. As a consequence "we are not even certain that financial structure and development do exert a significant influence on economic growth. Still less are we in a position to say how, when and why the financial superstructure and the real infrastructure interact, or to make confident statements about the effects such interactions have on economic growth."[20]

On the particular question of the relationship between inflation and economic growth there is no general agreement despite two decades of academic discussion, most of it focusing on recent Latin American experience.[21] All that can be said with certainty is that among those Latin American countries with high rates of inflation some have grown rapidly while others have not. Brazil and Mexico did experience annual price increases of 10 to 20 percent with growth rates in excess of 6 percent during the 1940s and 1950s. Argentina, on the other hand, combined annual price increases of 25 percent with a growth rate of less than 2 percent during the 1950s. During the same period the comparable figures for Chile were 38 percent and 3 percent, respectively.

Despite the indeterminate nature of such evidence, there are several reasons for believing that a country like Mexico, which has managed to combine price stability with rapid growth, is in the best possible position to sustain the development process over an extended period of time. Inflation seems generally compatible with rapid growth only if prices increase faster than wages and salaries. So long as they do, and so long as other market conditions buoy profit expectations, inflation may indeed encourage rapid capital formation. However, a growing sophistication on the part of the labor force will often narrow the lag between price and wage increases to the point

---

[19] Solís M., "The Financial System," p. 46.

[20] Goldsmith, *The Financial Development of Mexico*, p. 53.

[21] The literature is voluminous. Perhaps the best introduction is still provided by Werner Baer and Isaac Kerstenetzky (eds.), *Inflation and Growth in Latin America* (Homewood, Ill.: Richard D. Irwin, 1954).

where the redistributive effect of inflation—away from consumption and toward investment—is nullified.[22]

When this point is reached the compatibility between inflation and growth tends to disintegrate, and the potentially distortive effects of inflation are likely to develop. Savings will be channeled into unproductive investments like real estate, luxury housing, and inventory accumulation unless specific government policies are developed to prevent such patterns of resource allocation.[23] Rising costs of domestic production will also increase import demand while discouraging exports. A worsening balance of payments position may lead to currency speculation, adding to the pressures for devaluation. Even when devaluations are undertaken, they are often accompanied by exchange (or import) controls which introduce distortions into the price mechanism and discourage foreign investment.

Another significant source of price distortion appears in Latin American countries endeavoring to limit the effects of rapid inflation. In Argentina, Brazil and Chile, for example, governments control the rates charged by public utilities and set prices on basic foodstuffs. Since these governments are exposed to severe criticism when any of these controlled prices are raised, they tend to lag far behind the general price increases. There are two results, both detrimental to growth: first, increasing public-sector deficits directly attributable to the pricing of the services involved; and second, growing bottlenecks in the utilities fields where pricing policies discourage further investment. All these problems have attended inflation in various Latin American countries, and have led their governments to attempt stabilization programs. What makes the Mexican case so interesting is that only Mexico has managed to move from a period of inflation to one of stability, and without paying a heavy price in terms of forgone capital formation and growth. In Argentina, Brazil, and Chile government policies have yet to produce either stabilization or growth rates comparable to those of Mexico.

One reason that Mexico accomplished the transition without sacrificing growth to stability was that public-sector infrastructure investments were not curtailed. Deficits were simply financed in a far less inflationary manner. Thus Mexico developed an approach to the financing of economic development which reflected the wisdom of both the "monetarist" and "structuralist" schools of thought on inflation in Latin America.[24] It heeded both

[22] See Werner Baer, *Industrialization and Economic Development in Brazil* (Homewood, Ill.: Richard D. Irwin, 1965), for an analysis of the Brazilian experience revealing this pattern.

[23] See *ibid.*

[24] See essays by David Felix and Joseph Grunwald in *Latin American Issues: Essays and Comments,* edited by Albert O. Hirschman (New York: Twentieth Century Fund, 1961); and Baer and Kerstenetzky, *Inflation and Growth,* for a discussion of the major schools of thought on inflation in Latin America.

the monetarist warning that government deficits are the principal cause of inflation in Latin America and the structuralist admonition that a slowdown in infrastructure expenditure may create bottlenecks which will slow the general growth rate.

Another reason for the successful transition was that stabilization itself gradually increased the resources available for the financing of Mexican development. External financing is now available to Mexico as to few other less-developed countries of the world. Since 1963 Mexico has placed more than twelve bond issues in the U.S. and European capital markets, and direct foreign investment has eagerly entered the country on terms established by the Mexican government.

Internal resources have also responded to the stability of the peso. Since 1962 the liabilities of the Mexican banking system (private domestic savings and inflows of funds from nonresidents) have increased at better than 18 percent per year. As table 3-9 demonstrates, since 1958 liabilities have been

TABLE 3-9.  STRUCTURE OF THE LIABILITIES OF THE BANKING SYSTEM, 1950-1965[a] (percent of national income at current prices)

| Year | Monetary liabilities | Savings deposits and other demand deposits | Bonds and lien obligations | Long-term | In Foreign Currency | Columns 1-4 |
|------|------|------|------|------|------|------|
|      | In Domestic Currency | | | | | |
|      | (1) | (2) | (3) | (4) | (5) | (6) |
| 1950 | 16.6 | 2.3 | 1.2 | 2.4 | 3.3 | 22.5 |
| 1955 | 13.7 | 2.2 | 1.2 | 3.6 | 4.8 | 20.7 |
| 1958 | 11.7 | 2.0 | 1.0 | 3.0 | 6.5 | 17.7 |
| 1960 | 12.3 | 2.0 | 1.4 | 5.1 | 7.4 | 20.8 |
| 1964 | 13.6 | 2.6 | 4.6 | 8.4 | 7.6 | 29.2 |
| 1965 | 13.4 | 2.8 | 6.4 | 9.2 | 7.0 | 31.8 |

Source: Leopoldo Solís M., "The Financial System in the Economic Development of Mexico," in *Weltwirtschaftliches Archiv* 101 (1968): 43.
[a]Excluding interbank operations.

growing far more rapidly than the gross national product. Furthermore, the changing structure of the banking system's liabilities demonstrates a steadily expanding capacity to provide long-term financing (table 3-10). Price and exchange stability and high interest rates have combined to encourage the investment of savings in liabilities issued in Mexican currency. With these growing savings the Mexican banking system has increased its capacity to finance both public- and private-sector development progress.

TABLE 3-10. STRUCTURE OF THE LIABILITIES OF THE BANKING SYSTEM, 1950-1965[a] (percent of the total liabilities of the banking system)

| Year | In Domestic Currency | | | | In Foreign Currency | Columns 1-4 |
| | Monetary liabilities | Savings deposits and other demand deposits | Bonds and lien obliga-tions | Long-term | | |
| | (1) | (2) | (3) | (4) | (5) | (6) |
|---|---|---|---|---|---|---|
| 1950 | 64.2 | 8.9 | 4.8 | 9.4 | 12.7 | 87.3 |
| 1955 | 53.7 | 8.5 | 4.8 | 14.4 | 18.6 | 81.4 |
| 1958 | 48.4 | 8.2 | 3.9 | 12.5 | 27.0 | 73.0 |
| 1960 | 43.7 | 7.0 | 5.1 | 18.1 | 26.1 | 73.9 |
| 1964 | 37.1 | 6.9 | 12.5 | 22.8 | 20.7 | 79.3 |
| 1965 | 34.6 | 7.1 | 16.6 | 23.7 | 18.0 | 82.0 |

Source: Leopoldo Solís M., "The Financial System in the Economic Development of Mexico," p. 43.
[a]Excluding interbank operations.

The very success of Mexican monetary and financial policy in supporting public investment while stabilizing prices has led critics to emphasize that this policy is a substitute for what is really needed, that is, tax reform to increase government revenues.[25] Their argument assumes that tax rates in Mexico can now be raised significantly without lowering domestic rates of savings and investment. The assumption has not yet been tested, since no major tax reform has been undertaken. If the critics are correct, then developments in Mexican monetary and financial policy represent a second-best solution to the problem posed by public sector deficit financing of infrastructure investment. But what is second best in a strictly economic sense may well be optimal in a broader socio-political framework. The fact is that Mexican financial innovations have for over twelve years minimized the misallocations and bottlenecks which would undoubtedly have arisen either from continued rapid inflation or from lowered public sector investment. The capacity for constructive adaptation to political constraints thus demonstrated by Mexican policy-makers is surely not the least of the public sector's contributions to economic development since 1940.

## ECONOMIC DEVELOPMENT: PRIVATE-SECTOR RESPONSE

The programs and policies of the Mexican government since 1940 have been designed to stimulate private-sector efforts in the development process.

[25] See, for example, Brothers and Solís M., "Recent Financial Experience."

The positive response to those policies is perhaps best illustrated by the growing participation of private-sector investment in total Mexican capital formation. Between 1940 and 1946 gross fixed capital formation amounted to 8.6 percent of gross domestic product. Private investment contributed less than half of that investment, or 4.2 percent of gross domestic product. Fourteen years later, and over a comparable time period (1954-60), average annual rates of capital formation had risen to 20.5 percent of GDP, and three-quarters of it, or 15.2 percent of GDP, was private investment. Since 1963 the comparable figures have been 20.7 percent and 14.5 percent (table 3-4).

## The Industrial Sector

Private response to government incentives has resulted in a substantial growth in Mexican industry. Industrial production now represents approximately 37 percent of aggregate domestic product. The industrial sector presently employs over one-fifth of the labor force, a 58 percent increase over the corresponding 1940 figure (table 3-2). Manufacturing output alone now represents more than 26 percent of total national product, employs more than 16 percent of the labor force, and is the fastest growing sector of the Mexican economy. The growth of the industrial sector is reflected in the changing structure of Mexican imports. In 1940 consumer goods accounted for 23 percent of total merchandise imports. During the later 1960s that proportion had fallen to 15 percent, while capital goods imports had risen from 35 percent to 46 percent of the total.

Mexican exports are also beginning to reflect the diversification of the Mexican economy. Manufactured products now earn over 25 percent of Mexico's total merchandise export receipts. While food processing industries account for almost half of that total, the rest comprises such manufactured items as textiles, chemical and rubber products, copper and steel tubing, wood and metal furniture, automobile parts, typewriters, and electrical equipment. More important than the present percentage of manufactured exports is their upward trend in aggregate export sales. They have risen from 3 percent of that total in 1940 to approximately 14 percent by 1969 (exclusive of

TABLE 3-11. MERCHANDISE IMPORTS (percent of total)

| Type of Merchandise | 1940 | 1967 |
|---------------------|------|------|
| Consumer Goods      | 23   | 15   |
| Producers Goods     | 77   | 85   |
| Capital Goods       | 35   | 46   |
| Primary Materials   | 42   | 39   |

Source: Banco de México, *Informe anual,* various issues.

processed food products). The capacity to export industrial products is the final test of protective policies which encourage import substitution. The continuing diversification of Mexican manufactured exports clearly indicates that for a marginal but growing number of industrial products the Mexican economy is becoming competitive in foreign markets.

Mexican industrial development policies and the growing size of the Mexican consumer market have attracted United States as well as Mexican investors. Over two-thirds of all U.S. direct investment in Mexico between 1950 and 1959 flowed into manufacturing activity.[26] In 1950 less than one-third of U.S. direct investment in Mexico was in the manufacturing sector; by 1959 the proportion had reached 47 percent. For all of Latin America, the corresponding figure was 17 percent. During those years U.S. direct investment in manufacturing rose from $133 to $355 million, double the rate at which it increased in Latin America as a whole.

These trends in U.S. direct private investment in Mexico have continued throughout the 1960s. By 1967 U.S. private investment in the Mexican manufacturing sector had reached $890 million, more than twice as much as in 1959. And by 1967 two-thirds of all U.S. direct investment in Mexico was in the manufacturing sector. It has been estimated that during the early 1960s U.S.-controlled enterprises accounted for approximately one-sixth of Mexican manufacturing output.[27]

A further measurement of private-sector response to public-sector incentives in industry has recently been provided by Clark Reynolds. He compared Mexican levels of output for fifteen manufacturing industries in 1950 and 1960 with output levels of Hollis Chenery's "hypothetical economy." Chenery's model, based on data from thirty-eight countries, assumes that the pattern of industrial production in a country can be explained by the size of the population and its per capita income.[28] Using the coefficients of the Chenery model, Reynolds found that in both 1950 and 1960 actual Mexican industrial output exceeded predicted levels for an "average" country with the same population and income level in at least twelve of the fifteen industries. In 1950 Mexican production in printing and transportation equipment was below expected levels; in 1960 the printing, wood products and textiles sectors registered outputs less than predicted by Chenery's coefficients. Reynolds' study further showed that between 1950 and 1960 nine of the

[26] United States, Department of Commerce, *U.S. Business Investment in Foreign Countries* (Washington, D.C.: Government Printing Office, 1960), pp. 89–92. The figures for the 1960s come from U.S. Department of Commerce, *Survey of Current Business* (October 1968), p. 24.

[27] Vernon, *Dilemma*, p. 22.

[28] Hollis Chenery, "Patterns of Industrial Growth," *American Economic Review* 50 (September 1960): 625–54.

fifteen industries measured grew at rates in excess of those suggested by the Chenery model.[29] These comparative statistics on industrial growth, unlike those on exports, tell us nothing about the efficiency of new resource allocation. But they do provide some measurement of the aggressive response of Mexico's new entrepreneurial elite to the government's development policies since 1940.

## The Agricultural Sector

The crucial role played by the agricultural sector in the course of industrialization has been stressed ever since the study of economic development became fashionable two decades ago. It has been pointed out repeatedly that the agricultural sector must provide (1) increased food production for a rapidly expanding urban population, (2) increased production of raw materials and/or (3) export production to finance imported industrial inputs, (4) a growing labor supply to meet the demands of the urban industrial and service sectors, (5) savings to be used in infrastructure and industrial investment, and (6) a market for industrial sector outputs. The failure of agriculture to fulfill these various requirements has been cited just as often to explain many of the difficulties encountered by industrializing countries in Latin America, Asia, and Africa.

The "miracle" of modern Mexican economic growth, to the extent that there is one, is to be found in the performance of Mexican agriculture. Since 1935 agricultural production has risen at an annual real rate of 4.4 percent.[30] In the process the agricultural sector has made the following contributions to Mexico's economic development:

1) It has lifted Mexico to virtual self-sufficiency in food production and in doing so has supplied a fast-growing population with higher levels of food consumption and better diets.

2) Its production of several manufacturing sector inputs has grown rapidly (cotton at 8.7 percent a year, sugar cane at 6.3 percent, and coffee at 4.3 percent).

3) Agricultural exports have risen at better than 6 percent a year in real terms since 1940, and have grown from 25 percent to 50 percent of total merchandise export receipts. Cotton, coffee, vegetables, fruits and livestock are among Mexico's leading exports; cotton alone accounts for 18 percent of commodity earnings abroad. The rapidly expanding foreign exchange earnings

[29] Clark Reynolds, *The Mexican Economy: Twentieth Century Structure and Growth* (New Haven: Yale University Press, forthcoming).

[30] Salomon Eckstein, *El Marco macroeconómico del problema agrario mexicano* (Mexico: Centro de Investigaciones Agrarias, 1968), as cited in Sergio Reyes Osorio, "El Desarrollo polarizado de la agricultura mexicana," *Comercio exterior* 19 (March 1969): 236.

of the agricultural sector have been used to finance the import requirements for Mexican industrialization, and are in great part responsible for the absence of a foreign exchange bottleneck in Mexican development efforts to date.

4) A rapidly growing proportion of Mexico's rural population has become available for urban employment. Over the past three decades the labor force in the industrial and service sectors has grown at twice the rate of that employed in agriculture. This internal migration has kept wages low, sustained high profits, and encouraged further investment.[31]

5) The agricultural sector has transferred savings to the rest of the Mexican economy. Between 1942 and 1961 public expenditure on rural development was greater than tax revenues taken from rural Mexico, resulting in a net flow of resources to the agricultural sector.[32] But this flow was far less than the net transfer of savings from agriculture to industry and services effected by the banking system and the changing terms of trade between agriculture and industry. A recent attempt to render a combined accounting of the fiscal system, banking system and internal terms-of-trade over the twenty-year period indicates a net transfer from agriculture to the rest of the economy of approximately $250 million (1960 prices).[33] This figure represents 2–3 percent of total fixed domestic investment over the period, and a substantially higher proportion of private investment in the industrial and service sectors alone. It thus seems fair to say that the savings of the agricultural sector not only financed its own growth, but also provided a significant source of investible funds for the rest of the economy.[34]

6) Finally, the increasing purchasing power of rural Mexico provided a growing market for the products of Mexican industry. A proportionally small but growing rural middle class can afford to purchase most products of Mexican industry, including consumer durables. *Ejidatarios* in some regions of Mexico are able to afford many of the nondurable products.[35] And some manufactured products—shoes, basic agricultural implements and processed foodstuffs, for example—are purchased even by the poorer segments of rural Mexican society.[36]

[31] Information on profit levels is very scarce, and often contradictory. The best evidence that they were high is the rapid rise in private sector investment since 1940.

[32] Solís M., "Hacia un análisis general," p. 63.

[33] Eckstein, *Marco macroeconómico.*

[34] The data upon which these estimates are made are admittedly incomplete, especially that on the transfers effected by changes in the rural-urban terms of trade. See discussion in *ibid.*

[35] See Clarence Senior, *Land Reform and Democracy* (Gainesville: University of Florida Press, 1958), for a discussion of change in buying habits of the *ejidatarios* of the Bajío as early as 1940.

[36] Census material since 1940 reveals these trends. See discussion in Wilkie, *The Mexican Revolution*, chap. 9; and Pablo Gonzáles Casanova, *La Democracia en México* (Mexico: Ediciones ERA, 1965), chap. 5.

Census data on rural Mexico are collected in such a manner that analysis of economic trends in agriculture focuses upon three types of landholdings: private holdings over five hectares (12.5 acres) in size; private holdings of less than five hectares; and *ejidos*. Each has contributed significantly to post-1940 economic development.

The incentives which led to the appearance of large commercial farming were developed during the 1935–1950 period. Massive irrigation projects were begun, and rural road networks were expanded at a rapid pace. In addition, land tenure laws were changed to accommodate private commercial producers. Certificates of "inaffectibility" were granted which exempted landowners from further expropriation for holdings up to 100 hectares of irrigated land or 200 hectares of seasonal land. For the production of certain specified crops the size of "inaffectible" holdings was made even larger: 150 hectares for cotton, and up to 300 hectares for bananas, grapes, coffee, sugarcane, henequen, and others.

TABLE 3-12. PERCENTAGE OF TOTAL FEDERAL INVESTMENT IN
IRRIGATION AND ROADS, 1930-1963

| Period | Investment in Irrigation | Investment in Roads | Roads and Irrigation as % of Total Federal Investment |
|---|---|---|---|
| 1930–34 | 11.3 | 16.2 | 27.5 |
| 1935–39 | 18.6 | 26.6 | 45.2 |
| 1940–44 | 15.1 | 27.3 | 42.4 |
| 1945–49 | 16.5 | 19.9 | 36.4 |
| 1950–54 | 15.9 | 16.7 | 32.6 |
| 1955–59 | 11.9 | 13.9 | 25.8 |
| 1960–63 | 8.2 | 10.7 | 18.9 |

Source: Derived from data supplied by the Dirección de Inversiones Públicas, Secretaría de la Presidencia.

Approximately three-quarters of the newly irrigated land was located in northern and northwestern Mexico. Over 50 percent of it is held by private owners, and this new cropland has become the center of Mexican commercial agriculture. Yields on irrigated lands are generally three to four times greater than those on unirrigated land, and each irrigation project has been associated with the production of at least one major export crop. Much of this newly irrigated land is now farmed in a partially or totally mechanized manner. Aggregate output of those farms exceeding five hectares in size has grown by 364 percent in a twenty-year period (table 3-13), and much of that growth is a reflection of production increases on private commercial farms developed after 1940.

TABLE 3-13.    GROSS OUTPUT INDICES OF CROPS AND ANIMAL PRODUCTS,
1940-1960

| Category of Farms | Crop Production | Animal Products | Total of 1 and 2 |
|---|---|---|---|
| | (1) | (2) | (3) |
| | 1960 over 1940 | | |
| Over 5 hectares | 323 | 531 | 364 |
| 5 hectares and under | 168 | 135 | 142 |
| Ejidos | 223 | 176 | 210 |
| Total | 262 | 237 | 256 |
| | 1960 over 1950 | | |
| Over 5 hectares | 166 | 253 | 184 |
| 5 hectares and under | 112 | 87 | 93 |
| Ejidos | 170 | 105 | 154 |
| Total | 163 | 137 | 155 |
| | 1950 over 1940 | | |
| Over 5 hectares | 195 | 210 | 198 |
| 5 hectares and under | 150 | 155 | 152 |
| Ejidos | 131 | 168 | 136 |
| Total | 161 | 173 | 165 |

Source: Folke Dovring, "Land Reform and Productivity: The Mexican Case, Analysis of Census Data," (Madison: University of Wisconsin, Land Tenure Center) 63 (January 1969).

The *ejido* sector has matched the pace set by the private commercial sector. This is true despite the contrary inference that might be drawn from table 3-13. *Ejidal* production grew by 210 percent over the same 1940-60 period, but it lacked many of the inputs which swelled the private production figure. Table 3-14 demonstrates the disparity in some of the major inputs during the years in question. Quite clearly the moderately larger increases in output on private holdings over five hectares were accompanied by significantly larger production inputs.

According to the 1960 census, *ejidatarios* held 43 percent of all cropland and 40 percent of all irrigated land; their crop production totaled 43 percent of Mexican aggregate production for that year.[37] They produced 36 percent of total agricultural output, and supplied 34 percent of all farm products marketed.[38] Finally, over 25 percent of total *ejidal* crop production was exported. These figures reveal that *ejidal* agriculture in the aggregate is as

[37] *IV Censo agrícola ganadero y ejidal. 1960 resumen general* (Mexico, D.F.: Departamento General de Estadísticas, 1965).

[38] D. E. Horton, "Land Reform and Economic Development in Latin America, the Mexican Case," *Illinois Agricultural Economics* 8 (January 1968): 20.

TABLE 3-14.  CHANGES IN MAJOR INPUTS AND PRODUCTION BETWEEN 1940
AND 1960 ON *EJIDOS* AND PRIVATE FARMS OF MORE THAN 5
HECTARES[a]

| Item | Value in 1940 | Value in 1960 | Percentage Increase | Increase on Private Farms as % of Increase on *Ejidos*[b] |
|---|---|---|---|---|
| Cropland area (million hectares) | | | | |
| *Ejidos* | 7.0 | 10.3 | 47 | |
| Private farms[b] | 6.8 | 12.2 | 79 | 168 |
| Labor force (millions) | | | | |
| *Ejidos* | _[c] | 3.5 | _[c] | _[c] |
| Private farms[b] | 1.1 | 2.2 | 100 | 100-200[d] |
| Value of machinery, implements, and vehicles (billion pesos)[e] | | | | |
| *Ejidos* | 51 | 1,331 | 2,510 | |
| Private farms[b] | 50 | 2,893 | 5,686 | 227 |
| Gross value of total crop output (billion pesos)[f] | | | | |
| *Ejidos* | 2.6 | 5.8 | 123 | |
| Private farms[b] | 2.3 | 7.4 | 222 | 180 |

Source: D. E. Horton, "Land Reform and Economic Development in Latin America,
the Mexican Case," *Illinois Agricultural Economics* 8 (January 1968): 19.

[a]Mexican Census of Agriculture, 1940 and 1960.
[b]Private farms of more than 5 hectares.
[c]Data not available.
[d]Estimated.
[e]Prices in 1940 and 1960.
[f]Prices in 1960.

commercially oriented as private agriculture. Approximately 85 percent of all
*ejido* plots are subsistence-oriented, but so too are close to 100 percent of
those private farms under five hectares, and 50 percent of the larger private
units. Since the 1930s it has generally been the quality of the land rather than
the form of ownership which has demarcated subsistence and commercial
agriculture in Mexico.

The third type of holding for which aggregate data are available is the
private plot under five hectares in size. While production on these *minifundia*
increased far less than on the other two types of holdings—142 percent over
the two decades—they were almost always farmed without irrigation, credit,
farm machinery, or any other of the inputs available to some *ejidatorios* and
most large commercial farmers. Despite these disadvantages the 1960 census
figures reveal that the holdings under five hectares produced higher yields per

hectare in several crops, including corn, cotton and beans, than either the *ejidos* or the large commercial farms. A study by Salomon Eckstein demonstrates that in terms of output per unit of all inputs save the owner's labor, the *minifundista* is the most efficient of all Mexican agricultural producers, followed by *ejidatarios* and the owners of the large private farms in that order.[39] His study lends support to the findings of other economists that, while absolute productivity increases have been greatest in the newly opened and irrigated northern and northwestern regions of Mexico, productivity residuals—that is, those increases in production unexplained by increases in land, capital and measureable labor inputs—have been highest in the overpopulated agricultural regions of central Mexico.

Each of the three types of Mexican landholders has contributed in a substantial way to the country's record of rapid agricultural growth. The large commercial farmers and those *ejidatarios* possessing good cropland supplied both Mexico's domestic needs and a growing foreign market. The *minifundistas,* applying in greater quantities the one input at their disposal—their own labor—also increased yields on their marginal plots of land. As table 3-15

TABLE 3-15. CROP PRODUCTION, 1940-1967 (average annual rates of growth)

| | Period | | | | |
|---|---|---|---|---|---|
| Item | 1940–45 | 1945–52 | 1952–56 | 1956–61 | 1961-67[a] |
| Production (quantum index) | 3.5 | 6.5 | 6.5 | 3.6 | 4.0 |
| Acreage harvested | 0.6 | 4.3 | 2.9 | 1.5 | 1.6 |
| Yields | 2.8 | 2.0 | 3.8 | 2.2 | 2.4 |

Source: Salomon Eckstein, *El Marco macroeconómico del problema agrario mexicano* (Mexico: Centro de Investigaciones Agrarias, 1968), as cited in Sergio Reyes Osorio, "El Desarrollo polarizado de la agricultura mexicana," *Comercio exterior* 19 (March 1969): 233.
[a]Preliminary.

reveals, increased acreage accounts for far less than half of the increased production in Mexican agriculture since 1940. The rest is attributable to increased yields, and reflects the impact on Mexican agriculture of invest-

---

[39] Eckstein's rationale for deleting an imputed input for owner's labor in his calculations of productivity is that such labor in Mexican agriculture does not represent a scarce resource, and his study and others on the growing rate of underemployment in rural Mexico support that rationale. Eckstein calculates that the average holding of less than five hectares can occupy only some 10 percent of the yearly man-hours represented by the owner and his family.

ments in irrigation and roads, the use of new seeds, fertilizers, and pesticides, improved production techniques, and greater labor inputs. The aggregate result of social and economic change in rural Mexico has been a record of agricultural growth far surpassing the rest of Latin America and most other countries in the world since 1940. Whatever the transitional costs of agrarian reform in terms of lost production during the 1920s and 1930s, the economic returns on that reform over the last three decades have been exceptional.[40]

In a broader socio-political context the contribution of rural Mexico to the course of economic development goes far beyond the benefits deriving from production increases. Mexico's development strategy, whether by design or default, has programmed a major role for the Mexican private sector. The public sector is omnipresent, whether directly through ownership and invest-- ment, or indirectly through the maze of government policies ranging from commercial import licenses to banking portfolio requirements. As presently constituted, however, the success of the Mexican strategy depends ultimately upon the response of the private sector, upon private saving and induced private investment. From this dependence certain consequences follow, the most important being the necessity of political stability. In a less-developed country, especially one with no restrictions on capital outflows, only the continuously demonstrated capacity of the political system to ensure stability and profitable economic opportunity can induce growing rates of private domestic investment.

Mexico has enjoyed the political stability without which the present development strategy would have failed, and rural Mexico has created the conditions fundamental to that stability. The haciendas have disappeared from the heavily populated central plateau regions, thus removing the major source of social and economic friction which had plagued Mexico since the conquest. The agrarian reform program has directly benefited over two and a half million peasant families, who now possess their own land. Many of those yet to receive acreage still live in hope, and hope has proved to be as conservative a force as ownership itself.[41] *Ejidatarios* and other *minifundistas* who possess land are concerned only with conserving their sparse holdings. "The peasants are still as poor as ever but they remain attached to the revolution which gave them what they desired most: a patch of ground. . . . They re-

---

[40] Recent evidence suggests that production losses during the 1930s have been grossly exaggerated. Eckstein's study, for example, reveals an annual growth rate in agricultural production of 5.2 percent between 1935 and 1942. Eckstein, *Marco macroeconómico.*

[41] See the comments of Moisés T. de la Peña, *El Pueblo y su tierra: mito y realidad de la reforma agraria en México* (Mexico, D.F.: Cuadernos Americanos, 1964), p. 330; and François Chevalier, "The Ejido and Political Stability in Mexico," in *The Politics of Conformity*, edited by Claudio Veliz (London: Oxford University Press, 1967), especially pp. 186–87 on the conservative effects of Mexican land reform.

member Cárdenas and they wait patiently for better days."[42] Their patience is a crucial ingredient in a development strategy which has concentrated resources and rewards in industrial activity and large commercial farming, with little thought to needs of the *campesino*. Without it, the strategy could not have succeeded.[43]

## MEXICAN DEVELOPMENT IN THE
## LATIN AMERICAN PERSPECTIVE

Mexican economic development over the past three decades has clearly outstripped that of the other large, industrializing Latin American countries. A number of factors have contributed to this more rapid pace of development. Perhaps the most important are Mexico's geographical location, the nature and extent of government expenditure in Mexico, the government's monetary and financial policy, and the performance of the agricultural sector.

Mexico's proximity to the United States has had a number of effects on the Mexican economy. First, a common border with the world's largest single market has undoubtedly encouraged Mexican interest and investment in export opportunities. Since 1940 the United States' share of Mexican commodity exports has averaged more than 75 percent. Second, that same proximity has facilitated the flow of technology. The U.S. investor, the Mexican graduate student at Harvard, Yale or California, and the *bracero* all serve as conduits in the transfer of technology. Third, U.S. tourist expenditures have helped the Mexican balance of payments. By 1968 Mexico was earning as much foreign exchange through tourism and border transactions as it was on its merchandise account. Finally, and much more generally, it has been suggested that the presence of a great power on its borders may have stimulated a dynamic response in Mexico similar to that of Japan when confronted by the West after 1856.

It is impossible to measure the impact of the U.S. "presence" on Mexican development in a comprehensive and quantitative fashion, but two of the issues raised deserve a word of comment. First, Mexican earnings on tourism are often presented in a misleading way. Since the proximity of the United States to Mexico encourages Mexicans to travel in the United States, balance of payments disadvantages as well as gains are involved in the border relation-

---

[42] Chevalier, "The Ejido and Political Stability," pp. 186-87.

[43] Mexican agrarian reform has also served indirectly to minimize the growth of one urban problem which often accompanies industrialization and hinders economic development: the rapid increase in social overhead expenditures. The redistribution of land ownership and the accompanying increases in agricultural production slowed the pace of rural-urban migration in Mexico after 1940, and in doing so contributed to the public sector's capacity to concentrate its resources in vital infrastructure investments and to postpone expenditures on housing, social security and other welfare programs.

ship. The important figure is that of net Mexican earnings on tourism, and it is significantly smaller than that for gross receipts. Nonetheless, the capacity to augment foreign exchange earnings revealed in the net balance on tourism and export receipts from border trade has in large part accounted for the absence of a serious foreign exchange bottleneck to Mexican development over the past three decades. (See appendix, tables 2 and 4.)

Second, the influence of history's great powers on physically less powerful countries has more often proved debilitating than invigorating. Some societies have disintegrated under the impact; others have experienced reactive forms of nationalism which have proved detrimental to the process of economic growth. Japan and Mexico may indeed have benefited in some economic sense from these confrontations of disparity; if so they are in the creative minority.

TABLE 3-16. AVERAGE PERCENTAGE OF FEDERAL BUDGETARY EXPENDI-
TURE BY FUNCTIONAL CATEGORY (actual expenditures)

| Period | President | Total | Economic | Social | Administration |
|---|---|---|---|---|---|
| 1900-1911 | Díaz[a] | 100.0 | 16.0 | 6.6 | 77.4 |
| 1911-1912 | Madero | 100.0 | 17.6 | 9.9 | 72.5 |
| 1912-1913 | De la Huerta | 100.0 | 15.2 | 8.9 | 75.9 |
| 1917-1919 | Carranza | 100.0 | 16.3 | 2.0 | 81.7 |
| 1920 | De la Huerta | 100.0 | 17.2 | 2.3 | 80.5 |
| 1921-1924 | Obregón | 100.0 | 17.9 | 9.7 | 72.4 |
| 1925-1928 | Calles | 100.0 | 24.8 | 10.1 | 65.1 |
| 1929 | Portes Gil | 100.0 | 23.2 | 12.9 | 63.9 |
| 1930-1932 | Ortiz Rubio | 100.0 | 28.1 | 15.8 | 56.1 |
| 1933-1934 | Rodríguez | 100.0 | 21.7 | 15.4 | 62.9 |
| 1935-1940 | Cárdenas | 100.0 | 37.6 | 18.3 | 44.1 |
| 1941-1946 | Avila Camacho | 100.0 | 39.2 | 16.5 | 44.3 |
| 1947-1952 | Alemán | 100.0 | 51.9 | 13.3 | 34.8 |
| 1953-1958 | Ruiz Cortines | 100.0 | 52.7 | 14.4 | 32.9 |
| 1959-1963 | López Mateos | 100.0 | 39.0 | 19.2 | 41.8 |

Source: James W. Wilkie, *The Mexican Revolution: Federal Expenditure and Social Change Since 1910* (Berkeley and Los Angeles: University of California Press, 1967), p. 32.
[a]1900-1901 and 1910-11.

Mexico has differed markedly from other Latin American nations in the nature and extent of governmental expenditure. Between 1940 and 1960 the ratio of taxes to GNP was lower in Mexico than in any other country in Latin America, with the possible exceptions of Guatemala and Honduras.[44] At the

[44] For a recent ranking of less-developed countries see Jorgen R. Lotz, and Elliott R. Morss, "Measuring 'Tax Effort' in Developing Countries," reprinted from International Monetary Fund, *Staff Papers* (November 1967).

same time, the Mexican public sector was accounting for between 30 and 55 percent of gross fixed domestic investment. As noted earlier, much of the investment developed vital infrastructures for Mexican agricultural and industrial expansion. This capacity to concentrate the minimal resources at its command on expenditures for economic growth is reflected in the federal government's budgetary expenditures since the Cárdenas period. Federal expenditures on economic development as a proportion of the total budget rose from 22 percent in 1933-34 to an average of 52 percent for the twelve-year period from 1947 through 1958.[45]

During these same years a far different trend in governmental budgets was being experienced in other Latin American countries. As Tom Davis has noted, public expenditures in Chile and Argentina were being devoted to the expansion of government bureaucracies, "to defraying costs of a comprehensive social security system (complete with full pension benefits for white collar employees after thirty to thirty-five years of service), and to constructing middle income housing, primarily for public employees."[46] A detailed examination of the Argentine economy between 1945 and 1955 reveals that 69 percent of all capital formation—public and private—was channeled into housing, government services and other services. Over the same period the agricultural sector was allocated only 2.7 percent of aggregate investment (in Mexico public investment alone in agriculture was close to 10 percent of aggregate Mexican investment); electricity and communications received only 2.3 percent, and there was a net disinvestment of 2.7 percent in the Argentine railways.[47] Furthermore, Argentine industrialization policies favored the light consumer goods industries which should have been nearing maturity. "If the public sector had been in earnest about a policy of industrialization and growth, it would have devoted more of its attention to those industries which were just struggling to start in Argentina (steel, capital goods, petro-chemicals, etc.) and to the social overhead capital required by such industries."[48] The Mexican government was in earnest, and its attention and resources were devoted to precisely those new industrial activities.

The same study makes several interesting observations about Argentine development policies which serve to highlight the contrasts between Argen-

[45] For a complete breakdown of these economic activities see Wilkie, *The Mexican Revolution*, p. 13, and chap. 6.

[46] Tom Davis, introduction to *Mexico's Recent Economic Growth*, edited by Tom Davis (Austin: University of Texas Press for the Institute of Latin American Studies, 1967), pp. 8-9. For an analysis of Chilean social expenditures see the same author's "Dualism, Stagnation and Inequality: The Impact of Pension Legislation in the Chilean Labor Market," *Industrial and Labor Relations Review* 17 (April 1964): 380-98.

[47] Carlos F. Díaz-Alejandro, "An Interpretation of Argentine Economic Growth Since 1930," part 1, *Journal of Development Studies* 3 (October 1966): 162.

[48] *Ibid.*, p. 164.

tina and Mexico during the 1940s and 1950s. Argentine investment was channeled primarily into industries producing "wage commodities" and activities which Díaz-Alejandro has called "wage services" (such as low cost housing, health, and education). Policies affecting the rural sector were shaped to ensure cheap foodstuffs for urban workers, generally at the expense of agricultural exports and the foreign exchange proceeds which were vital for the importation of machinery and equipment. Finally, wage policies led to a rise in the wage share of national income far beyond that which might have been expected by the growth of the manufacturing sector. "These policies taken together present a picture of a government not so much interested in industrialization as in a nationalistic and 'populist' policy of increasing the real consumption and employment and economic security of the masses and of the (kept) entrepreneurs even at the expense of capital formation and the capacity to transform the economy."[49]

These policies, together with others which overvalued Argentina's currency and thus discouraged exports, created a series of bottlenecks from which Argentina has not yet recovered. The Argentine growth rate has averaged less than 3 percent a year since 1940, despite gross savings ratios of 20 percent over much of the period.[50] We have seen that Mexican industrialization policies have differed sharply from their Argentine counterparts in almost every detail. These differences undoubtedly account in large part for the greater productivity of Mexican investment over the past three decades.

The contrast between Mexico and other major Latin American nations in the field of financial policy is equally vivid. In Argentina, Brazil and Chile central-bank financing of persistent public-sector deficits has been the major cause of price increases well in excess of 20 percent a year since the 1940s.[51] In each country rates of inflation have accelerated to the point where "stop and go" policies to brake price increases have induced long periods of stagnation while failing to achieve price stability. Since currency devaluations have not kept pace with internal price increases, exports have been discouraged and foreign exchange bottlenecks have been magnified. In Mexico the trends have been significantly different. First, monetary and financial policies have reduced the role of the central bank in financing the public sector's deficit, thus minimizing the inflationary impact of government borrowing. Second,

[49] *Ibid.*, pp. 166–67.

[50] *Ibid.*, p. 174.

[51] On the role of government deficits in inflation see *ibid.*; Tom Davis, "Eight Decades of Inflation in Chile, 1879–1959: A Political Interpretation," *Journal of Political Economy* 71 (August 1963): 389–97; and Mario Henrique Simonsen, "Brazilian Inflation: Postwar Experience and Outcome of the 1964 Reforms," in *Economic Development Issues: Latin America* (New York: Committee for Economic Development, 1967).

two swift and sizable devaluations of the Mexican peso prevented the over-valuation of Mexican currency on the world market and encouraged the continued production of exportable commodities. The growth and diversification of Mexican merchandise exports since 1940 is at least in part a reflection of the success of these financial policies. Commodity exports have risen throughout the period at an average annual rate of more than 4 percent in real terms. In this context it is interesting to note that between 1930–39 and 1957–61 the quantum index of Argentine exports actually *fell* from 94 to 74 (1925–29 = 100).[52]

Mexico has also had far greater success than other large Latin American countries in expanding agricultural output. Mexican agricultural production has grown at twice the rate of that in Argentina and Chile, and considerably faster than that of all other Latin American nations save Costa Rica.[53] As we have seen, this rapid and sustained increase in production has enabled the Mexican agricultural sector to contribute to aggregate economic development in diverse ways, and particularly in the capacity to earn foreign exchange.

A final interesting contrast lies in the realm of defense expenditures. Of all the Latin American nations only Costa Rica and Panama spend less (as a ratio of total government expenditure) than Mexico. During the 1960s, for example, the average Latin American country spent slightly more than 12 percent of total central government expenditure on defense; the average for Mexico was less than 9 percent.[54]

These contrasts between Mexico and other major Latin American countries in the process of industrialization can do no more than suggest needed research on the causes of the disparities in rates of economic development in Latin America. But such research cannot be profitably undertaken until the social and political parameters of the development process in the Latin American context are better understood. Mexican development strategy has thus far succeeded because the country's sociopolitical evolution has supported rather than negated public policies and private responses designed to accelerate growth. At various times other Latin American nations have adopted similar policies; generally, however, these policies have fallen victim to political and social pressures which have been better contained in Mexico. Why has Mexico succeeded where others have failed?

[52] Díaz-Alejandro, "An Interpretation of Argentine Economic Growth," p. 20.

[53] See United States, Department of Agriculture, *Changes in Agriculture in 26 Developing Nations: 1948 to 1963* (Washington, D. C.: Department of Agriculture, Economic Research Service, November 1965), p. 6.

[54] United States, Agency for International Development, *A Review of Alliance for Progress Goals* (Washington, D. C.: Government Printing Office, 1969), p. 66.

*Chapter 4*

# FRUITION: FOR WHOM?

Thus far we have examined only one facet of the Mexican economic "miracle." The analysis in chapter 3 sought to characterize the "engine of growth" aspects of the Mexican economy. If economic growth depended solely upon the development of policies to fuel the savings-investment process there would be few "underdeveloped" countries in Latin America today. All could follow the Mexican example, and gross national product throughout the region would be doubling every fifteen years.

But the Mexican economy, like all basically free-enterprise economic systems, is at the same time an "engine of distribution." And perhaps the most fundamental obstructions to the development process arise in Latin America because policies designed to nurture engines of growth also influence the distribution of welfare within a society. Monetary, fiscal, commercial and labor policies in Mexico have generally been designed to entice the business community to save and invest increasing proportions of its expanding profits in the domestic market. But these same policies, effectively implemented to accelerate growth, have tended to produce—or at least, to reinforce—a highly inequitable pattern of income distribution. In other words, a large part of the bill for the past thirty years of rapid industrialization has been paid in terms of forgone increases in consumption by the large majority of Mexican society located toward the bottom of the income scale. Between 1940 and the early 1960s the rich in Mexico became richer and the poor poorer, some in a relative sense and some absolutely. Measurements of income distribution in recent decades indicate that at least as late as 1963 Mexico continued to lead almost all other Latin American countries in terms of income inequality. Even in the realm of government services that improve lower-class standards of living, Mexico has lagged well behind other major Latin American countries in providing for the well-being of the poorer half of its society.

Because every development strategy has its attendant pattern of welfare distribution, growth policies inevitably become the matrix of political contention. Politics is, after all, a matter of "who gets what, when and how," and every strategy of economic development affects the whats, whens, and hows. More importantly, it divides the "whos" into the "haves" and the "have nots," the temporary gainers and losers in the development process. To distinguish the gainers from the losers is to begin to understand the reality of Mexican politics. As we complete our discussion of Mexican economic development, therefore, we will inevitably raise some fundamental questions about the Mexican political system which will concern us throughout the remaining chapters.

## TRENDS IN MEXICAN INCOME DISTRIBUTION

During the 1940s income distribution in Mexico was characterized by (1) rapidly rising entrepreneurial incomes, (2) slowly rising *per capita* wage and salary earnings, and (3) a fall in real wage rates.[1] The result was an increasingly unequal distribution of income accompanied by a slow rise in the general standard of living. The redistribution of income in favor of profits resulted from both the achievement of full employment of capital resources and the process of inflation.[2] Prior to World War II many Mexican industrial concerns were operating at well below capacity. But the difficulty in obtaining imports plus the export demand for certain products which accompanied the war soon yielded large increases in production without proportionate investment growth. This phenomenon was particularly marked in the steel, textile and cement industries. In aggregate terms industrial production rose by 46 percent between 1939 and 1943. Industrial output for the domestic market rose by 36 percent and for foreign markets by 600 percent.[3]

Rapid price increases throughout the 1940s also influenced the redistribution of income in favor of Mexican entrepreneurs. The cost of living index for working-class families in Mexico City rose from 21.3 in 1940 to 75.3 in 1950 (1954=100).[4] Increases in money wages did not keep pace with price rises,

[1] For studies of these trends during the 1940s, see Adolf Sturmthal, "Economic Development, Income Distribution, and Capital Formation in Mexico," *Journal of Political Economy* 63 (June 1955): 183–201; Diego López Rosado, and Juan F. Noyola Vázquez, "Los Salarios reales en México, 1939–1950," *El Trimestre económico* 18 (April–June 1951): 201–209; and Ifigenia M. de Navarrete, *La Distribución del ingreso y el desarrollo económico de México* (Mexico, D.F.: Instituto de Investigaciones Económicas, Escuela Nacional de Economía, 1960).

[2] Sturmthal, "Economic Development, Income Distribution, and Capital Formation," p. 190.

[3] Combined Mexican Working Party, *The Economic Development of Mexico* (Baltimore: Johns Hopkins Press, for the International Bank for Reconstruction and Development, 1953), p. 276.

[4] Ariel Buira, "Development and Price Stability in Mexico," *Weltwirtschaftliches Archiv* 101 (1968): 59. Like any such index, this one is subject to considerable qualifica-

and real wages fell by perhaps as much as one-third between 1940 and 1950.[5] The lag in wage increases reflected both the elastic supply of labor and the captive nature of Mexican labor unions during the period. Real wage rates in urban Mexico remained well above those in the rural sector; as a result the urban labor supply continued to exceed the demand for it in the industrial sector. Migrants from rural Mexico drifted into the urban service sector, and from there were slowly absorbed into industrial occupations as the process of economic development created new jobs in industry. Between 1940 and 1950 employment in the industrial sector calculated as a percentage of the total labor force rose from 13 to 16 percent, while employment in the service sector rose from 22 to 26 percent (table 3-2). During the period in question collective wage agreements were negotiated every other year, and minimum wage rates were set by the government at the same intervals. Even if full adjustments for price rises were made in wage rates every two years, the reduction in real wages consequent to the rapid inflation would have been significant.[6] Thus there is little reason to question the finding that real wages in agriculture and industry dropped considerably during the decade.[7]

At the same time the average real earnings of Mexican wage and salaried labor rose slightly. This increase in real income per worker at a time when real wage rates were falling reflected the shifting occupational structure in Mexico. Employment in the low-wage agricultural sector fell, relative to the growing industrial and service sectors. Over 65 percent of the labor force was employed in agriculture in 1940; by 1950 the proportion had fallen to 58 percent. A second type of shift was occurring within the industrial sector, from lower- to higher-productivity occupations. A further factor which may have improved the standard of living of some of the Mexican labor force while not influencing wages was a rise in the level of public services. Between 1939 and 1950 the per capita volume of educational services rose by 58 percent, and that of public health and welfare services by 134 percent.[8] The 1940s thus witnessed both a slow rise in the overall standard of living and an increasingly unequal distribution of personal income.[9]

---

tion. The figures cited should therefore be taken to indicate a general order of magnitude.

[5] *Ibid.*

[6] As Sturmthal points out, if we assume that the price level rose at a steady rate over the two-year period and that a full adjustment was made at the end of that time, real wages would have been reduced throughout the period by one-half the price rise. Sturmthal, "Economic Development, Income Distribution, and Capital Formation," p. 195.

[7] López Rosado and Noyola Vázquez, "Los Salarios reales," p. 206.

[8] Combined Mexican Working Party, *Economic Development of Mexico*, p. 326.

[9] Two wage earning groups that did not participate in the rising standard of living were agricultural wage earners and those workers in the industrial and service sectors

A continuation of the latter trend well into the 1950s is suggested by the evidence presented in table 4-1. Between 1950 and 1957 there was a significant drop in the proportion of aggregate personal income received by the poorer 50 percent of Mexican families. Their share dropped from 19.1 percent of the total in 1950 to 15.6 percent in 1957, and remained practically unchanged in 1963. By this same measure the degree of income inequality in Mexico as late as the early 1960s was greater than in most other Latin American countries. The 50 percent of the population in the lower income brackets in Argentina (1961) and Brazil (1960) received 20 percent of total income, while in Chile the figure approximated that of Mexico.[10] If we consider the income shares of the lower six deciles, which were 24.6 percent, 21.2 percent, and 21.5 percent in Mexico during the three years for which data are available, the relatively high degree of inequality in Mexico is again apparent. Similar postwar shares (1948-1950) calculated for India, Ceylon and Puerto Rico were 28 percent, 30 percent, and 24 percent respectively.[11] Figures for industrialized countries, of course, reveal far less income inequality. In recent years the proportion of income going to the lower 50 percent of the population in the United States has been over 23 percent and in the United Kingdom about 25 percent.

Table 4-1 indicates that the relative share of total income going to the lower income families has declined substantially since 1950.[12] It is less clear that *real incomes* of the poorest families have also dropped. Both the Navarrete study and Bank of Mexico's investigation indicate a decline in real in-

---

who did not advance in terms of occupational categories. See de Navarrete, *La Distribución del ingreso,* chap. 3.

[10] United Nations, Economic Commission for Latin America, "Income Distribution in Latin America," *Economic Bulletin for Latin America* 12 (October 1967): 41.

[11] Simon Kuznets, "Economic Growth and Income Inequality," *American Economic Review* 45 (March 1955): 1-27.

[12] It is again best to treat the statistics in table 4-1 as suggesting orders of magnitude. The 1950 figures were estimated on the basis of information on income in the 1950 census and calculations of personal income made in connection with an input-output study of the Mexican economy. The 1957 calculations were based upon a sampling survey using 5,000 questionnaires on income and expenditures. Señora de Navarrete has said that "even though the survey was less comprehensive than studies of this type should be, it was decided to make use of it because it constituted the first source of overall information about a problem crucial to the country's economy and politics." [Ifigenia M. de Navarrete, "Income Distribution in Mexico," in *Mexico's Recent Economic Growth,* edited by Tom Davis (Austin: University of Texas Press for the Institute of Latin American Studies, 1967), p. 144.] The budget study upon which the 1963 estimates are based involved a somewhat broader sampling and is apparently more reliable than that of 1956. All three estimates had to deal with the problem of discrepancies between reported personal incomes in the samplings and the estimate of personal income made by the Bank of Mexico. One highlight of the table is that the 1963 calculations, based upon a budget study unconnected with the 1956 investigation, lend support to some of the trends suggested in Señora Navarrete's earlier work.

TABLE 4-1. PERSONAL INCOME DISTRIBUTION, 1950, 1957, 1963 (in percent by deciles of families)

| Deciles | Percent of Families[a] | | | 1950 | | 1957 | | 1963 | |
|---|---|---|---|---|---|---|---|---|---|
| | 1950 | 1957 | 1963 | % of Total Income | Cumulative Income | % of Total Income | Cumulative Income | % of Total Income | Cumulative Income |
| I | 10.0 | 10.0 | 10.0 | 2.7 | 2.7 | 1.7 | 1.7 | 2.0 | 2.0 |
| II | 10.0 | 10.0 | 10.0 | 3.4 | 6.1 | 2.7 | 4.4 | 2.0 | 4.0 |
| III | 10.0 | 10.0 | 10.0 | 3.8 | 9.9 | 3.1 | 7.5 | 2.5 | 6.5 |
| IV | 10.0 | 10.0 | 10.0 | 4.4 | 14.3 | 3.8 | 11.3 | 4.5 | 11.0 |
| V | 10.0 | 10.0 | 10.0 | 4.8 | 19.1 | 4.3 | 15.6 | 4.5 | 15.5 |
| VI | 10.0 | 10.0 | 10.0 | 5.5 | 24.6 | 5.6 | 21.2 | 6.0 | 21.5 |
| VII | 10.0 | 10.0 | 10.0 | 7.0 | 31.6 | 7.4 | 28.6 | 8.0 | 29.5 |
| VIII | 10.0 | 10.0 | 10.0 | 8.6 | 40.2 | 10.0 | 38.6 | 11.5 | 41.0 |
| IX | 10.0 | 10.0 | 10.0 | 10.8 | 51.0 | 14.7 | 53.3 | 17.5 | 58.5 |
| X | 5.2 | 5.1 | 5.0 | 9.2 | 60.2 | 10.1 | 63.4 | 14.5 | 73.0 |
| | 2.4 | 2.6 | 2.5 | 7.5 | 67.7 | 12.6 | 76.0 | 11.0 | 84.0 |
| | 2.4 | 2.3 | 2.5 | 32.3 | 100.0 | 24.0 | 100.0 | 16.0 | 100.0 |
| Totals | 100.0 | 100.0 | 100.0 | 100.0 | | 100.0 | | 100.0 | |

Sources: For 1950 and 1957, Ifigenia M. de Navarrete, *La Distribución del ingreso y el desarrollo económico de México* (Mexico, D.F.: Instituto de Investigaciones Económicas, Escuela Nacional de Economía, 1960), table 12. For 1963, Banco de México, *Encuesta sobre ingresos y gastos familiares en México—1963* (Mexico, Banco de México, 1967), table 1.

[a] Decile I contains the lowest income families; decile X those with the highest income.

comes for the bottom 20 percent of Mexican families (table 4-2). As Raymond Vernon has argued, however, two statistical problems involved in these calculations may be responsible for the apparent decline.[13] First, the consumption patterns of low-income groups are so dissimilar to those at the opposite end of the income scale that it may be misleading to apply the same price deflator to the income of both groups. Yet this procedure has been followed with regard to the calculations in table 4-2, since more sophisticated data are lacking. Second, no comprehensive attempt has been made to measure and include imputed income, a procedure which would undoubtedly raise the income of those on the bottom of the income scale relative to the rest. It is also probable that the slow growth of government services has somewhat improved the standard of living of Mexicans at the lower end of the income ladder. Only in smaller rural communities are most of these services still totally lacking.

TABLE 4-2. DISTRIBUTION OF PERSONAL INCOME BY DECILES OF FAMILIES 1950, 1957, and 1963

| Deciles | Percent of Families | Average Monthly Income (1957 pesos) | | |
|---|---|---|---|---|
| | | 1950 | 1957 | 1963 |
| I | 10.0 | 247 | 192 | 223 |
| II | 10.0 | 311 | 304 | 223 |
| III | 10.0 | 348 | 350 | 279 |
| IV | 10.0 | 403 | 429 | 502 |
| V | 10.0 | 440 | 485 | 502 |
| VI | 10.0 | 504 | 632 | 669 |
| VII | 10.0 | 641 | 835 | 892 |
| VIII | 10.0 | 788 | 1,128 | 1,282 |
| IX | 10.0 | 989 | 1,658 | 1,952 |
| X | 5.2 | 1,621 | 2,233 | 3,234 |
| | 2.4 | 2,858 | 5,460 | 4,907 |
| | 2.4 | 12,329 | 11,765 | 7,137 |

Sources: For 1950 and 1957, Ifigenia M. de Navarrete, *La Distribución del ingreso*, table 9. For 1963, Banco de México, *Encuesta sobre ingresos.*

X

While those on the lower half of the Mexican income scale have clearly lost ground in a relative sense, and possibly in absolute terms for the lowest 20-30 percent, shifts in the upper income brackets have benefited the emerging Mexican middle and upper-middle class. As table 4-1 indicates, the share of total personal income going to the top decile of Mexican families has

[13] Raymond Vernon, *The Dilemma of Mexico's Development: The Roles of the Private and Public Sectors* (Cambridge: Harvard University Press, 1963), p. 208, n. 10.

fallen from 49 percent in 1950 to 41.5 percent in 1963. The share of the top 2.4 percent has dropped by over half, from 32.3 percent of total income in 1950 to less than 16 percent in 1963. Gainers in the redistribution of relative shares appear in the seventh, eighth and ninth deciles. These groups increased their share of total income from 26.4 percent in 1950 to 37 percent in 1963. One result of these changes is that income in Mexico is now less concentrated within the top 5 percent of the population than it is in Argentina or Brazil, although it still surpasses many other Latin American countries.[14] More important in terms of Mexican economic development is the emergence of an income group which provides an effective market for Mexican domestic manufactures. The familes within the upper-middle deciles which have gained from recent trends in income distribution are increasingly able to purchase those durable consumer goods now being manufactured in Mexico. Many of these products cannot yet meet international competitive standards, and must be sold in Mexico. By providing a growing domestic market for them, the redistribution of income away from both the top and the bottom of the Mexican income scale toward the upper-middle sectors has undoubtedly supported the process of Mexican industrialization as it has developed since 1940.[15]

## RURAL MEXICO: THE FRUITS OF REFORM

The gross inequality in income distribution in Mexico is above all a reflection of the new dualism in the Mexican agricultural sector. While a small segment of Mexican agriculture is modernized, perhaps as many as 85 percent of the aggregate private and *ejidal* holdings are still farmed primitively. As a result, product per worker in the agricultural sector is only one-sixth that for the rest of the economy.[16] Average monthly per capita income in agriculture is $11; in the industrial, commercial and service sectors it is $22, $26 and $25 respectively. In 1963, 43 percent of Mexico's families had a monthly income

[14] Economic Commission for Latin America, "Income Distribution in Latin America," p. 41.

[15] Raymond Vernon and others who have argued that the lack of purchasing power in the hands of the lower 50 percent of Mexico's population represents a major bottleneck—in a market sense—to growth in Mexico seem premature in their judgments. Income concentration in the upper 50 percent may better support the Mexican industrialization strategy *if* the distribution within the upper brackets provides a sufficient market for the products of protected industries. In any case it is not argued here that Mexican income distribution has in any sense been optimal for continued growth, but merely that trends in distribution within the upper brackets have thus far been sufficient to sustain that growth.

[16] This and the following measurements are derived from the Banco de México, *Encuesta sobre ingresos y gastos familiares en México, 1963* (Mexico: Banco de México, 1967).

of $48 or less; two-thirds of those families derived their income from the agricultural sector.

Within agriculture income is less equitably distributed than in any of the other sectors.[17] This fact may seem surprising in view of the extensive nature of the Mexican land reform program, but the present structure of land tenure and other factors affecting rural incomes since 1940 explain the increasing polarization.

Table 4-3 reveals the extent to which private cropland in Mexico is still concentrated in a few holdings. Slightly over 1 percent of the farm units occupy more than 50 percent of the total. In some states—Quintana Roo,

TABLE 4-3. DISTRIBUTION OF PRIVATE CROPLAND, 1960

| Size of Holdings (in hectares) | Number of Holdings | | Total Area | |
|---|---|---|---|---|
| | Thousands | % | Thousands | % |
| Up to 5 | 929 | 77.2 | 1,461 | 10.8 |
| 5.1-10 | 95 | 8.0 | 665 | 4.9 |
| 10.1-25 | 103 | 8.6 | 1,581 | 11.7 |
| 25.1-50 | 37 | 3.1 | 1,280 | 9.5 |
| 50.1-100 | 22 | 1.8 | 1,499 | 11.1 |
| 100.1-200 | 10 | 0.8 | 1,329 | 9.9 |
| 200.1-400 | 3 | 0.3 | 888 | 6.6 |
| 400.1 and over | 2 | 0.2 | 4,787 | 35.5 |
| Total | 1,201 | 100.0 | 13,490 | 100.0 |

Source: *IV censo agrícola ganadero y ejidal. 1960 resumen general* (Mexico, D.F.: Departamento General de Estadísticas, 1965), pp. 25ff.

Guerrero and Oaxaca, for instance—between 75 and 94 percent of private croplands are held by less than 1.5 percent of the private landowners.[18] And despite the fact that the agrarian statutes have set maximum size limits on private holdings at 300 hectares, the 1960 census registered 2,053 units with an average of 2,331 hectares of cropland.[19] At the other extreme, 77 percent of all private landowners control only 11 percent of private croplands. The average size of such holdings is 1.6 hectares, or 4 acres of land. These one million farmers constitute the core of the *minifundia* problem in Mexico today. Close to a million *ejidatarios* also farm plots incapable of sustaining a single family.

[17] *Commercio exterior* (September 1967), p. 724.

[18] Carlos Tello, "Agricultural Development and Land Tenure in Mexico," *Weltwirtschaftliches Archiv* 101 (1968): 24.

[19] *Ibid.*

TABLE 4-4. DISTRIBUTION OF *EJIDAL* CROPLAND, 1960

| Cropland per *Ejidatario* (in hectares) | *Ejidos* | | *Ejidatarios* | |
|---|---|---|---|---|
| | Number | % | Number | % |
| Up to 1 | 1,124 | 6.2 | 147,118 | 9.7 |
| 1.1–4 | 5,681 | 31.0 | 521,044 | 34.5 |
| 4.1–10 | 7,878 | 43.0 | 612,984 | 40.5 |
| Over 10.1 | 3,618 | 19.8 | 230,979 | 15.3 |
| Total | 18,301 | 100.0 | 1,512,125 | 100.0 |

Source: *IV censo agrícola.*

Table 4–5 combines the figures for *ejidal* and private holdings. In 1960, 1.4 percent of all holdings contained over 36 percent of Mexico's croplands, while half of the landholders worked less than 12 percent. Over 90 percent of all holdings up to 10 hectares can be classed as *minifundia.* Only a very small proportion of them receive an adequate supply of water, whether from rain or irrigation, to produce enough food for minimum family needs.

TABLE 4-5. DISTRIBUTION OF TOTAL CROPLAND, 1960

| Size of Holdings (hectares) | Number of Holdings (thousands) | Total Area (thousand hectares) | Number of Holdings (percent) | Area (percent) |
|---|---|---|---|---|
| Up to 5 | 1,332.2 | 2,759.5 | 49.45 | 11.75 |
| 5.1–10 | 1,079.9 | 7,991.5 | 40.09 | 34.04 |
| 10.1–25 | 201.1 | 2,803.5 | 7.47 | 11.94 |
| 25.1–50 | 42.5 | 1,422.7 | 1.58 | 6.06 |
| 50.1–100 | 22.0 | 1,498.6 | 0.82 | 6.38 |
| 100.1–200 | 10.4 | 1,328.5 | 0.39 | 5.66 |
| 200.1–400 | 3.3 | 888.1 | 0.12 | 3.78 |
| Over 400 | 2.1 | 4,785.9 | 0.08 | 20.39 |
| Total | 2,693.5 | 23,478.3 | 100.0 | 100.0 |

Source: *IV censo agrícola.*

The concentration of income suggested by the pattern of land tenure is confirmed by statistics on the distribution of other agricultural inputs and production itself. Table 4–6 reveals that in 1960, 54.3 percent of total agricultural output was attributable to 3.3 percent of Mexican farm units. More important in terms of the trend toward an increasing dualism in the agricultural sector is the fact that this same 3.3 percent accounted for 80 percent of the increase in production between 1950 and 1960. Over the same decade the first group represented in table 4–6 suffered an absolute loss in production

TABLE 4-6. LAND TENURE AS MEASURED BY AGRICULTURAL PRODUCTION, 1960 (in percent)

| Type of Holding (by value of 1960 production) | Number of Holdings | Arable Land | Irrigated Land | Value of Machinery | Value of Holdings | Value of Production | Change in Value of Production, 1950–1960 |
|---|---|---|---|---|---|---|---|
| 1) Below subsistence, $0–80 | 50.3 | 13.6 | – | 1.3 | 6.7 | 4.2 | -1.0 |
| 2) Subsistence, $80–400 | 33.8 | 24.5 | 3.9 | 6.5 | 13.8 | 17.1 | +10.0 |
| 3) Family, $400–2,000 | 12.6 | 19.2 | 27.0 | 17.0 | 22.6 | 24.4 | +11.0 |
| 4) Multi-family, $2,000–8,000 | 2.8 | 14.4 | 31.5 | 31.5 | 19.3 | 22.0 | +35.0 |
| 5) Large multi-family, above $8,000 | 0.5 | 28.3 | 37.6 | 43.7 | 37.6 | 32.3 | +45.0 |
| Total | 100.0 | 100.0 | 100.0 | 100.0 | 100.0 | 100.0 | 100.0 |

Source: Derived from Salomon Eckstein, *El Marco macroeconómico del problema agrario mexicano*, (Mexico: Centro de Investigaciones Agrarias, 1968), as cited in Sergio Reyes Osorio, "El Desarrollo polarizado de la agricultura mexicana," *Comercio exterior* 19 (March 1969): 234–35.

and the following two groups lost ground relative to Mexico's large commercial farmers.

The growing number of landless agricultural workers in Mexico constitutes a final contributing factor to the highly skewed distribution of income in Mexico in general and in the agricultural sector in particular. In 1950 there were approximately 2.3 million laborers in rural Mexico who did not possess lands; by 1960 their numbers exceeded 3.3 million. Employment opportunities in the industrial and service sectors have been growing too slowly to absorb them, as has the continuing program of land redistribution. While the number of landless workers is increasing, the opportunity of employing them all in agriculture is decreasing. It has recently been estimated that their per capita rate of employment has fallen from 194 days per year in 1950 to 100 days in 1960, and that the annual real income per worker from such employment fell from $68 to $56.[20] Without permanent jobs, these rural laborers obtain work wherever they can and whenever they can, following seasonal agricultural employment opportunities. Some find openings as unskilled workers in cities, but never enough of them to stem the steady growth of this poorest segment of the Mexican labor force. Present projections suggest that another fifteen years will pass before the trend can be reversed, by which time the landless agricultural work force will have been swelled by an additional two million persons.[21]

Just as the Mexican government's inflationary financing of public-sector investment tended to increase inequality in Mexico's income distribution, so too did several other policies whose impact was more directly felt in the agricultural sector. One such policy involved the location of Mexico's major irrigation projects. Most of them have been developed in the rather sparsely populated north and northwest, where large private holdings predominated over *ejidal* lands. In fact much of the land directly benefited by the new hydraulic systems is owned, directly or indirectly, by prominent Mexican politicians and their friends and relatives.[22] This pattern was particularly evident during the presidency of Miguel Alemán, when investment in irrigation absorbed 17 percent of total federal investment. In contrast, little has been done to bring water to the heavily populated central mesa region where most of the land is held by *ejidatarios* and the owners of small private plots.

[20] Salomon Eckstein, *El Marco macroeconómico del problema agrario Mexicano* (Mexico: Centro de Investigaciones Agrarias, 1968), p. 222.

[21] Sergio Reyes Osorio, "Estructura agraria, demografía y desarrollo económico," *Planificación* 1 (January 1968).

[22] For confirmation of this point see Robert E. Scott, *Mexican Government in Transition*, rev. ed. (Urbana: University of Illinois Press, 1964), p. 252, and chap. 5 below. It is also true, however, that the decision to carry out large irrigation projects in the northwest was very sensible from a technical point of view.

A second policy which favored the more advantaged was that of rural credit. Since *ejidatarios* do not actually own their land (it is deeded to the village), they have not been able to use it as collateral with which to raise crop loans. Therefore, the only credit available to them at normal interest rates has come from various government agencies, most notably the Ejidal Credit Bank. Statistics on government credit to the *ejidal* sector reveal just how limited the government commitment to *ejido* agriculture has been. Aggregate government credit to agriculture fell from about 4 percent of the federal budget during the Cárdenas years to less than 1 percent in the 1950s. And during the same period the percentage of the total funds which was allocated to the Ejidal Credit Bank also fell from over 90 percent to about 63 percent. Only after 1960 were these downward trends reversed. Furthermore, even those funds available to ejidal agriculture have been channeled to the few highly productive, commercially oriented *ejidos*. The proportion of *ejidatarios* actually receiving credit from the government fell from 30 percent in 1936 to 14 percent by 1960.[23]

[23] Rodolfo Stavenhagen, "Social Aspects of Agrarian Structure in Mexico," *Social Research* 33 (Autumn 1966): 471. It is also worth noting that until very recently almost all the Ejidal Bank's loans have been crop loans. As a result there has been literally no long-term credit available to *ejidatarios* with which they could make permanent improvements or purchase equipment.

TABLE 4-7. GOVERNMENT AGRICULTURAL CREDIT (in percent)

| Year | % of Federal Budget | Ejidal Bank Share as % of Total Government Credit | Year | % of Federal Budget | Ejidal Bank Share as % of Total Government Credit |
|------|------|------|------|------|------|
| 1935 | 7.2 | – | 1950 | 0.8 | 69.1 |
| 1936 | 9.5 | – | 1951 | 0.6 | 66.7 |
| 1937 | 3.3 | – | 1952 | 0.5 | 66.9 |
| 1938 | 3.6 | – | 1953 | 1.3 | 29.8 |
| 1939 | 3.8 | 90.9 | 1954 | 0.4 | 66.1 |
| 1940 | 3.4 | 97.1 | 1955 | 0.9 | 62.5 |
| 1941 | 4.3 | 84.9 | 1956 | 0.8 | 62.5 |
| 1942 | 2.9 | 82.5 | 1957 | 0.7 | 62.5 |
| 1943 | 2.3 | 80.2 | 1958 | 0.6 | 62.5 |
| 1944 | 1.6 | 83.5 | 1959 | 0.6 | 62.5 |
| 1945 | 1.5 | 83.5 | 1960 | 0.4 | 62.5 |
| 1946 | 1.4 | 80.0 | 1961 | 0.7 | 77.8 |
| 1947 | 1.4 | 66.7 | 1962 | 2.1 | 93.1 |
| 1948 | 0.2 | 66.4 | 1963 | 2.2 | 93.2 |
| 1949 | 0.9 | 72.7 | | | |

Source: James W. Wilkie, *The Mexican Revolution: Federal Expenditure and Social Change Since 1910* (Berkeley and Los Angeles: University of California Press, 1968), pp. 139-41.

Finally, as the statistics on land tenure above illustrate, since the Cárdenas years the government has moved slowly to implement the land reform program. While the pace of redistribution has increased since 1958, there are still millions of hectares of cropland in Mexico which would be subject to expropriation if the laws were strictly enforced. Countless forms of evasion have been allowed to develop, and only occasionally do public scandals over the size of some holdings or the means by which they have been obtained lead to the enforcement of agrarian statutes.[24]

Since 1940 the Mexican government has subordinated agrarian reform to agricultural production even though it is not clear that reform and increased productivity are incompatible in the Mexican case. Two general guidelines have been developed to implement this agricultural strategy. The first includes a continued public commitment to agrarian reform. As mentioned above, the pace of redistribution has actually accelerated during the 1960s, although an increasing amount of the land so affected is very marginal cropland or is not cropland at all. The second policy has been to encourage the emergence of large private commercial farms through public financing of irrigation projects, raising maximum legal limits on the size of private farms, and overlooking gross violations of these limits when the violators possess the proper political connections. The first policy has proved the opiate of the Mexican *campesino*, whether he be a present or prospective beneficiary of agrarian reform; the second has proved a stimulant to Mexico's booming commercial agriculture.

## THE PARADOX OF MEXICAN DEVELOPMENT

The degree of inequality in the distribution of Mexican income, no matter how it is measured, exceeds that of most of the world's developing countries. Only within the top 5 percent of Mexico's income brackets is a trend toward a more equal distribution noticeable. Those families in the bottom two or three deciles have clearly lost ground relatively, and perhaps absolutely, since the beginning of the Mexican "miracle."

In many developing countries the severe and often growing inequalities in income distribution that can accompany the early stages of industrialization are somewhat mitigated by the impact of government tax and expenditure policies.[25] In Mexico, however, neither has been geared to redistribute the

---

[24] For a discussion of several such incidents in recent years see Moisés González Navarro, *La Confederación nacional campesina* (Mexico: B. Costa-Amic, 1968) chaps. 10–12. The newspaper *El Día* carries weekly accounts of the conflict between landowners and the landless over the implementation of agrarian reform.

[25] For theoretical reasons, increasing inequality in income distribution might be expected during the early years of rapid industrialization. At the same time government

gains from rapid growth. In the first place, taxation in Mexico is so light that there is sorely little to redistribute. Over the past thirty years the tax burden in Mexico has generally been lower than in any other country of Latin America save Guatemala, Paraguay and possibly Colombia. Table 4-8 actually places Mexico last, but it reflects certain accounting techniques that somewhat understate total Mexican revenues. During the mid-1960s the correct proportion for Mexico would be about 14 percent of the gross national product.

TABLE 4-8.  REVENUES OF ALL LEVELS OF GOVERNMENT IN LATIN AMERICA, 1965[a] (% of gross national product)

| Country | Percent | Country | Percent |
|---------|---------|---------|---------|
| Brazil | 30.4 | Bolivia | 14.7 |
| Chile | 25.8 | Nicaragua | |
| Venezuela | 23.0 | El Salvador | |
| Ecuador | 22.9 | Dominican Republic | 14.3 |
| Uruguay | 22.5 | Honduras | |
| Peru | 19.9 | Colombia | 13.4 |
| Argentina | 18.9 | Paraguay | 13.0 |
| Panama | 18.6 | Guatemala | 10.7 |
| Costa Rica | 16.9 | Mexico | 10.4 |

Source: United States, Agency for International Development, *A Review of Alliance for Progress Goals* (Washington, D.C.: Government Printing Office, 1969), p. 62.
[a]Including social insurance.

A recent attempt to measure the "tax effort" among the world's developing countries points up the lightness of the Mexican tax burden. Three different measurements were made of taxation in seventy-two countries. The first was a simple revenue-to-GNP ratio; the other two introduced refinements with regard to level of economic development and size of the foreign trade sector. The countries were then ranked in descending order, the first country collecting the highest relative proportion of taxes, the seventy-second, the lowest. On these three measurements Mexico ranked 66th, 70th and 67th, respectively. Brazil's ranking scores were 21, 4 and 1; Argentina's were 27, 31 and 17; while Chile ranked 23, 23 and 14.[26]

---

policies in many countries have tended to forestall trends toward a growing inequality. See Kuznets, "Economic Growth and Income Inequality." The paradox that such trends did develop in Mexico and that little was done to halt them is discussed below.

[26] Jorgen R. Lotz and Elliott R. Morss, "Measuring 'Tax Effort' in Developing Countries," reprinted from International Monetary Fund, *Staff Papers* (November 1967).

In addition to the low level of the tax burden, the structure of the Mexican tax system may still be somewhat regressive. Until the very recent past Mexico has relied rather heavily on indirect taxes, and the operation of its income-tax schedules is at present very favorable to persons with high non-wage incomes.[27] However, toward the end of the 1960s income taxes (personal and corporate) were contributing close to 50 percent of Mexico's tax revenues (exclusive of public-enterprise savings).[28] With the ratio of taxes to GNP slowly rising, and direct taxation growing as a proportion of total revenues, it is probable that during the next decade the Mexican tax system will gradually introduce a degree of redistribution in favor of Mexico's lower-income groups. This change will come more than fifty years after the "victory" of Mexico's social revolution.

On the expenditure side of the equation, we have already noted that the concentration of public sector funds in infrastructure investments left little for those "social" expenditures which might have directly raised lower-class standards of living. Public-sector investment in all the social welfare fields as a percentage of total public investment averaged less than 15 percent a year during the period from 1935 to 1960; only in the late 1950s did the figure rise above 13 percent (table 3-5). Since 1960 just over 20 percent of aggregate investment has been allocated to the welfare field. The Mexican government did gradually extend the coverage of such public services as free education, social security, health and welfare services, and housing, food and transportation subsidies. But what most foreign commentators who praise such achievements have failed to note is the extremely limited nature of these efforts when measured against total public-sector expenditures, GNP, or against similar efforts in other Latin American countries.[29] The arresting contrast between Mexico and Argentina in the realm of governmental allocation of funds has already been examined in chapter 3.

Additional evidence on this point can be found wherever one looks among various budgetary indicators. For example, total expenditure on education in Mexico as late as the end of the 1950s was averaging only 1.4 percent of Mexico's gross national product. Corresponding figures for other

[27] See Victor L. Urquidi, "An Overview of Mexican Economic Development," *Weltwirtschaftliches Archiv* 101 (1968): 5; and Roberto Anguiano Equihua, *Las Finanzas del sector público en México* (Mexico: Universidad Nacional Autónoma de México Ciudad Universitaria, 1968), chaps. 10–13.

[28] Anguiano Equihua, *Las Finanzas*, p. 145; and annual reports of the Social Progress Trust Fund, Washington, D.C.

[29] Howard Cline and Robert Scott extol the virtues of Mexican social expenditures in Howard F. Cline, *Mexico: Revolution to Evolution, 1940–1960* (London: Oxford University Press, 1962); and Robert E. Scott, *Mexican Government in Transition*, rev. ed. (Urbana: University of Illinois Press, 1964).

Latin American countries in these same years were as follows: Argentina, 2.5 percent; Brazil, 2.6 percent; Chile, 2.4 percent; Peru, 2.9 percent; and Venezuela, 4.1 percent. In the Soviet Union, "revolutionary" leaders were directing 7.1 percent of the GNP toward education.[30]

In a related field, it is indicative of how little Mexico has done directly for those in the lowest income sectors that the proportion of agricultural extension agents to Mexico's farm families is approximately 1 to 10,000. Even in the republics of Central America where—with the exception of Costa Rica—almost nothing has been done for the *campesino*, corresponding ratios are generally much more favorable. The ratios of agents to farm families in Central America as of the 1950s and early 1960s were as follows: 1:1,600 in Costa Rica; 1:1,900 in Nicaragua; 1:3,200 in El Salvador; 1:5,000 in Honduras and 1:11,000 in Guatemala.[31] Almost no effort has been made over the past four decades in Mexico to train an adequate number of extension agents or to pay those with the proper education high enough salaries to keep them in the extension service.[32]

A third example is provided by comparing figures on the number of persons covered by social security systems in various Latin American countries. Mexico was Latin America's pioneer in the field of legislation protecting workers and enhancing their bargaining powers vis-à-vis management. Yet, as of 1967, only 6.1 percent of the total Mexican population, or 18.9 percent of the Mexican work force, was covered by social security benefits. For other Latin American countries in the same year the corresponding figures were as follows: Argentina, 24.9 percent and 66.3 percent; Brazil, 6.6 percent and 20.4 percent; Chile, 21.8 percent and 67.4 percent; Peru, 8.4 percent and 26.5 percent; and Venezuela, 6.9 percent and 21.9 percent. By either measurement—as a proportion of total population or of those economically active—the Mexican efforts to extend social security coverage have fallen behind those of all her major Latin American neighbors whether relatively rich (Argentina) or poor (Brazil or Peru), relatively industrialized or agrarian.[33] In the light of such comparisons it is not an exaggeration to say

[30] Frederick Harbison and Charles N. Myers, *Education, Manpower and Economic Growth* (New York: McGraw-Hill Book Co., 1964), pp. 46–47. The figures include both public and private expenditures on education.

[31] Eduardo L. Venezian and William K. Gamble, *The Agricultural Development of Mexico: Its Structure and Growth Since 1950* (New York: Frederick A. Praeger, 1969), p. 165; Roger D. Hansen, *Central America: Regional Integration and Economic Development* (Washington, D.C.: National Planning Association, 1967), p. 73.

[32] See discussions of this point in Charles N. Myers, *Education and National Development in Mexico* (Princeton, N. J.: Princeton University, Industrial Relations Section, 1965), pp. 61ff.; Venezian and Gamble, *Agricultural Development of Mexico,* pp. 137ff., 165ff., 186ff.

[33] Inter-American Institute of Statistics, *Boletín Estadístico* 47 (May 1969): 1. Those organized workers in Mexico who do benefit from social security and from the coverage

that in terms of using tax and expenditure policies to arrive at a more equal distribution of income, over the past several decades Mexico has *done* less *with* less than have all the other major Latin American nations. Two generalizations with regard to the course of economic development in Mexico seem valid. The first is that no other Latin American political system has provided more rewards for its new industrial and commercial agricultural elites. Their taxes and their wage costs have been low, their profits have been high, and the expanding public infrastructure which supports their productive endeavors has kept pace with their needs. Regardless of the friction which may have existed between the public and private sectors thirty years ago, it is hard to imagine a set of policies designed to reward private entrepreneurial activity more than those of the Mexican government since 1940. In this sense, and despite the continued prominence of public-sector activity, the Mexican government is as much a "businessman's government" as any in the United States during the decades of the Republican ascendancy (1860–1932).

The second generalization is that, excepting the impact of land redistribution, in no other major Latin American country has less been done directly by the government for the bottom quarter of society. Trends in prices, wages and occupational opportunities in Mexico have probably left most of the families within this stratum with a standard of living at or below that which they enjoyed in 1940. Even for those families within the next quarter of the population, real wage rates remained below 1940 levels until the early 1960s.[34] While certain labor unions favored by the government were granted periodic pay increases to keep abreast of rising prices, most wage earners suffered a decline in their earnings relative to other segments of the population as a result of the income redistribution which accompanied inflationary growth between 1940 and 1955. Finally, social service expenditures in Mexico measured as a percentage of GNP have lagged well behind those in other industrializing nations of the region.[35]

---

of other labor law legislation are compensated under these programs as well as most other Latin American workers, and better than some. See Carlos M. Terry and John M. Vivian, "Remuneration and Motivation in Latin America," *Columbia Journal of World Business* 4 (January–February 1969): 41–53.

[34] Mike Everett has found that real wage levels for 33 industries in six major industrial cities remained below their 1939–40 level until 1963. See Mike Everett, *The Evolution of the Mexican Wage Structure, 1939-63*, manuscript, revised version (Mexico, D.F.: El Colegio de Mexico, February 1968).

[35] No attempt is being made here to argue that an increased allocation of government resources to the social welfare fields through higher taxation or a reallocation of available public sector funds would necessarily have benefited *absolute* standards of living of Mexico's lower income groups over any extended time period. When policies consciously aimed at redistributing wealth lead to stagnant growth rates, less-developed countries may succeed only in equalizing levels of poverty. Furthermore, as James W. Wilkie has

It is the paradox of modern Mexico that such a development strategy has been devised and implemented in the only major Latin American nation to undergo a profound and bloody social revolution. In some other country the hard-nosed and unsentimental Mexican model of development might seem natural; in Mexico itself it appears incongruous. The constitution under which Mexico is ruled today reveals the depth of the revolutionary commitment to a better life for the Mexican *campesino* and laborer, as did many Mexican governmental policies during the presidential term of Lázaro Cárdenas (1934-40). How can we reconcile that commitment with the distribution of the gains from Mexico's economic development since 1940?

It has recently been suggested that the constitution of 1917 "is a most unremarkable document. It provides Mexico with a quite conventional system of liberal democracy along federal lines. This is not surprising, for those who drafted the document were in large measure urbane men of law and letters rather than the immediate leaders of an agrarian revolt."[36] This characterization is distorted on two counts. First, the Mexican constitution may not seem a radical document by today's standards, but it was in 1917. Second, the "urbane men of law and letters" were consistently outvoted at the constitutional convention of Querétaro, and the fact that they were in the minority accounts for the radical nature of the fundamental law which the convention produced.[37]

It is true that the great majority of the victorious revolutionaries who attended the Querétaro convention were middle-class in origin, but a fundamental division in outlook soon divided them into two opposing groups. The

demonstrated recently, the percentage of aggregate Mexican families living below a hypothesized "poverty level" has diminished more rapidly since 1940 than prior to that date. This correlation between rapid economic growth and diminishing aggregate levels of poverty will not be viewed with surprise by any Anglo-Saxon economist, and emphasizes that there is more to the "trickle-down" theory of economic development than often meets the leftist eye in Mexico and elsewhere. To the extent that governmental policies of incentives and rewards "at the top" created the conditions requisite for Mexico's rapid growth, they have served to raise the living standards of many groups not directly aided by tax and expenditure policies.

The "performance gap" being noted above lies not between Mexican development strategy and some optimum growth *vs.* welfare tradeoff—which may or may not have existed—but rather, as the remainder of the chapter suggests, between the chosen Mexican approach and the revolutionary rhetoric of the country's political leadership.

[36] Charles W. Anderson, "Bankers as Revolutionaries: Politics and Development Banking in Mexico," in Charles W. Anderson and William P. Glade, Jr., *The Political Economy of Mexico: Two Studies* (Madison: University of Wisconsin Press, 1963), p. 113.

[37] For an analysis of the convention and the constitution, consult the following works: H. N. Branch, *The Mexican Constitution of 1917 Compared with the Constitution of 1857* (Philadelphia: American Academy of Political and Social Science, 1917); *Diario de los debates del congreso constituyente, 1916-1917* (Mexico, D. F.: Talleres Gráficos de la Nación, 1960); and Charles C. Cumberland, *Mexico: The Struggle for Modernity* (London: Oxford University Press, 1968), pp. 261-272.

moderates supported the general features of the draft constitution submitted to the convention by Venustiano Carranza, the leader of the victorious faction in the revolutionary struggle. Their perception of the state was Gladstonian in nature: they envisioned a neutral government that would play no positive role in the development of society. Surprisingly, they found themselves outnumbered by the more radical group, referred to as the Jacobins, which looked to Alvaro Obregón for leadership and completely rewrote the draft constitution. On many major issues they outvoted the moderates by a four-to-one margin. The Jacobins viewed the government as "an active force—perhaps *the* active force—in instituting the social and economic changes which all members of the assembly accepted as necessary for the eventual good of the nation."[38] As it finally emerged, the constitution of 1917 defined democracy as "not only a judicial structure and a political regime, but a way of life founded in the steady economic, social, and cultural improvement of the people,"[39] and included many articles designed specifically to promote the social and economic betterment of the less advantaged segments of Mexican society. Particularly relevant for the purpose of understanding the paradox involved in Mexican development strategy since 1940 are those articles dealing with land reform and the rights of labor.

Article 27 of the constitution asserted state ownership of all lands and waters in Mexico. The state claimed both the right to transmit land titles to private persons and the right to expropriate property for redistribution. Also vested with the nation was the ownership of all minerals and other subsoil wealth. The article specifically stated that:

> The Nation shall have at all times the right to impose on private property such limitations as the public interest may demand as well as the right to regulate all natural resources, which are susceptible to appropriation, in order to conserve them and equitably to distribute the public wealth. For this purpose necessary measures shall be taken to divide larger landed estates; to develop small landed holdings; to establish new centers of rural population with such lands and waters as may be indispensable to them.... Settlements, hamlets situated on private property and communes which lack lands or water or do not possess them in sufficient quantities for their needs shall have the right to be provided with them from adjoining properties, always having due regard for small landed holdings.[40]

Article 27 charged the states with the responsibility for setting a maximum limit to the size of private landholdings. Expropriated lands were to be paid for through the issue of 20-year agrarian bonds with a maximum

---

[38] Cumberland, *Struggle for Modernity*, p. 261.

[39] Quoted in Alfredo Navarrete R., "The Financing of Economic Development," in Davis (ed.), *Mexico's Recent Economic Growth*, p. 105.

[40] Branch, *Mexican Constitution of 1917*, p. 16.

interest rate of 5 percent, and land prices were set at declared tax values plus 10 percent. This constitutional commitment to agrarian reform was broadened in later years to benefit not only existing villages but also peasants living on haciendas. Article 27 and the later legislative enactments on the subject of land reform set the stage for the revolutionary change in the structure of land tenure which took place during the 1930s.

Article 123, a hybrid of Mexican radicalism and contemporary European ideas on labor legislation, constituted the most advanced labor code in the world at its time. It not only allowed labor to organize, but prescribed in detail the eight-hour day, the protection of women and children in the labor force, and the most modern ideas on the safeguarding of labor rights.[41] The article stated that the minimum wage should be "that considered sufficient, according to the conditions in each region, to satisfy normal necessities of life of the worker."[42] It established the principle of equal pay for equal work regardless of sex or nationality, and called for double pay for any work over the eight-hour day. Employers were obliged to furnish housing for their employees at a rent which could not exceed 0.5 percent a month of the taxable value of the property. Employers were also made responsible for all industrial accidents.

Article 123 and others in the constitution also clarified labor's right to strike. Strikes were recognized as legal when their purpose was to establish "equilibrium between the diverse factors of production, harmonizing the rights of labor with those of capital."[43] Arbitration and conciliation procedures were introduced. A board consisting of equal numbers of management and labor representatives and one government representative was established to hear and determine all cases brought to it by mutual consent of the adversaries. If management refused to negotiate by means of arbitration or to accept the award of the board, however, it was obliged to pay all workers involved in a dispute the equivalent of three months' salary.[44] The effect of these provisions was to advance the legal rights of the Mexican laborer beyond those in any other country at the time; his constitutional rights were still issues for negotiation in the United States, Europe, and elsewhere.

All the principles contained in Article 123 and others dealing with the rights of labor were incorporated in the Federal Labor Law of 1931. This statute legalized collective bargaining and the closed shop, prohibited lockouts, restricted management's rights to discharge workers, guaranteed ample dismissal wages for any employee fired without just cause, and provided for

[41] See ibid., pp. 94–103; and Joe C. Ashby, Organized Labor and the Mexican Revolution under Lazaro Cárdenas (Chapel Hill: University of North Carolina Press, 1963), pp. 58–64.

[42] Quoted in Ashby, Organized Labor and the Mexican Revolution, p. 58.

[43] Ibid., p. 59.

[44] Ibid.

the establishment of government boards of conciliation and arbitration. Under the 1931 legislation employers had to enter into collective contracts when requested to do so, and once a strike had been declared legal by the labor board, management was forced to pay workers' wages for the duration of the work stoppage.[45]

Since Latin American constitutions are classically honored only in the breach, why emphasize the social goals expressed in the Mexican document? Because, as is most often the case, the Mexican experience is *sui generis*. In the first place, the Mexican commitment to improved standards of living and life chances for the peasant and the laborer was made in a country in which the social, economic and political dominance of the "oligarchs" had been, or was soon to be, broken. Therefore the air of unreality which has surrounded so many other Latin American constitutional conventions and charters was far less noticeable at Querétaro in 1917. While the self-designated constitutional chief, Venustiano Carranza, disapproved of the radical changes made in his proposed constitution, the fact that the second most powerful figure in Mexico at that time—Alvaro Obregón—supported the revisions which were demanded by large majorities suggested that the provisions of the new constitution might be enforced. In the second place, the time eventually came when they were indeed implemented. Between 1934 and 1940 the social content of the revolution as expressed in Articles 27 and 123 of the Querétaro document was revived with such force and vigor that the course of Mexican development after 1940 seems all the more incongruous because of that brief renaissance.

During his six-year term as president, Cárdenas crushed the power of the remaining Mexican *hacendados*. He redistributed more than 10 percent of Mexico's entire territory, three times as much as had been touched by agrarian reform between 1915 and 1934. By the end of his term the *ejido* proportion of total Mexican cropland had risen from 13 percent to 47 percent, and it included some of the finest agricultural land in Mexico. In the rich Bajío region huge commercial farms were expropriated and turned into communally organized and operated *ejidos*.[46] By 1940 the newer *ejidos* were producing significant proportions of such commercial crops as cotton, henequen, wheat and coffee. As a result of the changes in land tenure, the number of recipients of land—over 800,000 families in six years—rose from 21 percent to 42 percent of the population employed in agriculture.[47]

[45] *Ibid.*, p. 61.

[46] See Clarence Senior, *Land Reform and Democracy* (Gainesville: University of Florida Press, 1958) for the story of the expropriations and their results.

[47] James W. Wilkie, *The Mexican Revolution: Federal Expenditure and Social Change Since 1910* (Berkeley and Los Angeles: University of California Press, 1968), p. 194.

During those same years government expenditures on social programs rose from an average of 10 percent of the federal budget in the 1920s to 18 percent. Over 12 percent of total budget expenditures was allocated to public education, a proportion not reached again until the presidency of Adolfo López Mateos almost twenty years later.[48]

Social and economic gains on the part of the *campesino* were matched by those of organized labor. Several aspects of President Cárdenas' policies with regard to labor and labor-management problems contributed to the improvement of the Mexican worker's social and economic opportunities.[49] First, the government encouraged and sponsored the unification of all industrial workers into a central labor confederation, the Confederación de Trabajadores Mexicanos (CTM). Given such encouragement the CTM, under the vigorous leadership of leftist Vicente Lombardo Toledano, became the dominant force in Mexican organized labor. Second, the government promoted the ideas that every worker in the country should be a member of a trade union, and that all should be covered by collective contracts. In the process of organizing labor, more strikes were experienced in the Cárdenas years than at any other point in Mexican history. Most of them were declared legal by the boards of arbitration and conciliation on which the government had the deciding vote, and employers most often accepted the arbitration process as the only practicable way out of the labor-management controversies. "Hence, by far the majority of significant disputes between labor and management over terms of collective contracts were settled by arbitrary awards handed down by officials of the Labor Department or even by the chief executive himself."[50]

A third aspect of the Cárdenas policies which produced workers' gains was his insistence that wages should be based upon "the ability of the companies to pay."[51] During the later years of the Cárdenas presidency it became an established practice in labor-management conflicts to appoint a commission of experts to investigate the financial capacity of the industry involved. The report of the commission was subsequently used to determine the award made by the board of arbitration. Appeals from such awards could be taken to the Supreme Court, but the judges were all Cárdenas appointees and their rulings were generally favorable to labor.

Finally, Cárdenas, in a famous speech in Monterrey, told those employers whom he classified as "tired of the social struggle" to turn their properties over to workers or to the government to run for the benefit of the workers.

[48] *Ibid.*, pp. 158–161.
[49] See Ashby, *Organized Labor and the Mexican Revolution*, pp. 284–90.
[50] *Ibid.*, p. 286.
[51] Quoted in *ibid.*

In several major instances the Expropriation Law of 1936 was used to those ends. Sugar and lumber mills were expropriated, as were the cotton lands of the Laguna district. The government also turned the management of the National Railways Company over to the Railroad Workers Union and granted the Oil Workers Union minority representation on the directive board of the nationalized oil industry.

Under government sponsorship, labor found itself playing an economic and political role never before achieved in Mexican history. Its material benefits grew, but even more importantly for the long run it appeared that its socio-political position was rapidly improving. As one historian of the period noted, "the primary achievement of Cárdenas and organized labor lay . . . in the field of obtaining for the workers of Mexico a position of dignity in the national life and in making the organized labor movement an important influence over national economic policy."[52] Little wonder that Jesús Silva Herzog should have labeled the Cárdenas government "the culminating moment of the Mexican revolution. Never before had land been distributed at such a rapid rate; never before had the labor movement been so encouraged from above."[53] And more importantly, never before had Mexican *campesinos* and workers been incorporated to such a degree into Mexican political life.

Between 1934 and 1940 some seemingly revolutionary changes took place within both the "official party" of Mexico and the system of Mexican politics.[54] The National Revolutionary Party (later to be called the Partido Revolucionario Institucional) was formed in 1929 during a crisis situation. Mexico's leading caudillo and president-elect, Alvaro Obregón, was assassinated in July 1928. The outgoing president, Plutarco Elías Calles, used the opportunity presented by the crisis to unite the regional strongmen of the revolutionary coalition into a national political party. Initially the party was primarily a coalition of regional military chiefs and their various state organizations, and labor and peasant associations were subordinate to them. Each leader controlled politics in his own region, supported always by his troops, and in many cases by small peasant and labor groups. The party provided an institution within which the clashing interests represented by these regional *caciques* could be reconciled without resort to civil war.[55] With the passage of

[52] *Ibid.*, p. 289.

[53] Jesús Silva Herzog, "La Revolución mexicana en crisis," reprinted from *Cuadernos americanos* (1944): 18.

[54] The PRI is often called the "official" party because it always wins elections and therefore is always the governing party.

[55] For a discussion of the origins of the PRI, see Cline, *Revolution to Evolution,* pp. 149ff.; Vicente Fuentes Díaz, *Los Partidos políticos en México*, book 2 (Mexico: Edición del Autor, 1956), pp. 65ff.; and Patricia McIntire Richmond, *Mexico: A Case Study of One-Party Politics*, Ph.D. dissertation, University of California, 1965, pp. 250ff.

a few years the institution became much more than an instrument of conciliation. Calles, operating through the party organization, was able to undermine
much of the strength of the agrarian and labor organizations affiliated with
the party through the membership of their leaders; he also weakened the
independence of the military *caciques* who had operated with great
autonomy in the 1920s. By 1934 Calles was using the party to manipulate
Mexican politics and control the Mexican government. The degree of centralization of political power was greater than at any time since the fall of
Porfirio Díaz.

Between 1934 and 1940, an intense struggle for political control
developed between Calles and the new president, Lazaro Cárdenas. At the
time Calles represented the conservative elements of the Revolutionary Coalition while Cárdenas drew his support from the more radical and often the
younger elements active in Mexican politics. To strengthen his hand against
Calles and those elements of the military forces loyal to the former president,
Cárdenas began to reunite and strengthen those same labor and agrarian mass
organizations which Calles had fragmented earlier.[56] He encouraged the
formation of militant labor and peasant unions, and the grouping of each into
national organizations. The local *ejido* organizations became members of state
peasant leagues, and the leagues themselves were united by 1938 into the
National Campesino Confederation (CNC). Most of the reformist and radical
labor unions were organized and centralized in the Workers Confederation of
Mexico (CTM).

Having developed these bases of support, Cárdenas proceeded to reconstruct the official party. In 1938 the old National Revolutionary Party, based
on a geographical and individual membership structure, was replaced by the
Party of the Mexican Revolution (PRM). The new party was organized into
four sectors: labor, agrarian, military and popular. The CTM, the largest of
Mexico's labor confederations, represented the bulk of the labor movement
within the party, and the National Campesino Confederation became the core
of the agrarian sector. The popular sector of the party consisted primarily of
government employees who had organized their own labor confederation, the
FSTSE.

The newly formed party claimed over four million members at its inception: 1,250,000 from the labor sector, 2,500,000 from the agrarian sector,
55,000 from the military, and 500,000 from the popular sector. Government
workers and the military had always had articulate voices in Mexican politics;
the participation of organized labor and peasant leagues in political activity at
the national level was a novelty. They supported Cárdenas' reforms, he sup-

---

[56] See Fuentes Díaz, *Los Partidos políticos*, Vol. 2, 54ff.; and Frank Brandenburg,
*The Making of Modern Mexico* (Englewood Cliffs, N.J.: Prentice-Hall, 1964), pp. 64ff.

ported their organizations, and the Mexican political scene was permanently altered. Indeed, the apparent emergence of two new strata of Mexican society as effective political forces in the struggle over who gets what, when and how led one prominent scholar of Mexican politics to state quite recently that "Cárdenas accomplished the feat of bringing off a class war, while at the same time subordinating it to the overriding theme of Mexican nationalism."[57]

Thus the paradox of Mexican development emerges. By 1940 the social goals of the revolution were finally being implemented, and at a dramatic pace. Organized labor and the rural masses were directly represented in the official party, and were numerically the most important of that party's four sectors. The vast majority of the Mexican population was at long last beginning to share in the distribution of Mexican wealth. After 1940 the trends reversed. A development strategy emerged which tightly controlled labor union activity, slowed the pace of agrarian reform, and reduced the relative share of total income of the bottom 60 percent of the Mexican population. How is it that the only Latin American country to have experienced a profound revolution before the 1950s chose to follow an approach to economic development which combined sustained sacrifices at the bottom of the socioeconomic scale with growing rewards at the top?

[57] L. Vincent Padgett, *The Mexican Political System* (Boston: Houghton Mifflin Co., 1966), p. 39.

*Chapter 5*

# THE PRI AND MEXICAN POLITICS: LA COSA NUESTRA

Many Mexican scholars see no paradox in Mexico's approach to the problems of economic development. They view the upheaval of 1910-20 as a "bourgeois revolution" and argue that it put a new Mexican upper-middle class in power. From their point of view, the course of economic development since 1920 flows quite naturally from this interpretation of the revolution and its impact upon the Mexican social structure.[1] Their analysis, like much Latin American social science, assumes that politics is a rather uncomplicated reflection of class structure and conflict. They see post-1940 Mexican social structure as characterized by a very wealthy elite at the top of the socioeconomic scale, a vast majority of the population at the poverty level, and a small but growing middle class.[2] This structure quite naturally suggests to Marxist-oriented scholars that Mexico's economic elite controls Mexican politics, and therefore dictates the policies shaping the course of Mexican economic development.

The basic trouble with the analysis is that it doesn't fit all of the facts. At no time since the revolution has the Mexican political system passively reflected the interests of an emerging industrial elite, and in the Mexican cultural setting there is little reason why it should have done so. Political power remained the special preserve of the revolutionary coalition which eventually consolidated its power in the official party in 1929. Both the personal and

[1] For the most sophisticated presentation of this view, see Moisés González Navarro, "La Ideología de la revolución mexicana," *Historia mexicana* 10 (April-June 1961): 628-36; "Social Aspects of the Mexican Revolution," *Cahiers d'histoire mondiale* 8 (1964): 281-89; and "Le Developpement economique et social du Mexique," *Annales economies sociétés civilisations* 21 (July-August 1966): 842-58.

[2] Estimates for the Mexican "middle class" vary from 16.9 percent (a Mexican government estimate) to 33.5 percent (estimate by Cline). See Howard F. Cline, *Mexico: Revolution to Evolution, 1940-1960* (London: Oxford University Press, 1962), chap. 11.

institutionalized interests of this coalition predate the emergence of Mexico's new industrial-agricultural elite groups. As late as 1930 most of today's new wealthy and influential businessmen "were barely scratching out an existence."[3] Furthermore, the revolutionary coalition did not need the political support of the new economic group, since it already had the backing of the organized labor and peasant sectors of the Partido Revolucionario Institucional (PRI).

A leading American scholar of political development has recently expounded an interpretation of the Mexican political process which sharply contradicts the Mexican leftist analysis.[4] The views of Samuel Huntington are worth considering in some detail both because they offer an excellent general framework from which to examine the process of politics in Mexico and because they focus our attention upon a revealing discrepancy between Huntington's theory and Mexican reality.

## MEXICAN "MODERNIZATION"

Urbanization, industrialization, secularization, education and exposure to the mass media together constitute what is generally referred to as the process of modernization in society. Perhaps most important in terms of politics is that process which Karl Deutsch has labeled "social mobilization," in which "major clusters of old social, economic and psychological commitments are eroded or broken and people become available for new patterns of socialization and behavior."[5] The erosion of traditional values and norms which accompanies social mobilization and modern economic growth tends to create increasing social conflict and political instability. As societies become larger in membership and more complex in structure and activity, new industrial elite groups rise to challenge traditional aristocracies; at the same time political demands are articulated by those at the bottom of the social scale whose community life patterns are also subjected to change. Huntington's basic thesis is that during this process of modernization "the maintenance of a high level of community becomes increasingly dependent upon political institutions."[6] Where those institutions do not develop, he argues, the result is most often a form of "praetorian society," one in which all kinds of social forces and groups (ethnic, religious, territorial, economic, or status) become directly engaged in national politics.

[3]Frank Brandenburg, *The Making of Modern Mexico* (Englewood Cliffs, N.J.: Prentice-Hall, 1964), p. 135.

[4]Samuel P. Huntington, *Political Order in Changing Societies* (New Haven: Yale University Press, 1968); see especially chap. 5, "Revolution and Political Order."

[5]Karl W. Deutsch, "Social Mobilization and Political Development," *American Political Science Review* 55 (September 1961): 494.

[6]Huntington, *Political Order*, p. 10.

Specialized social groups engage in the political process in all societies. What makes them seem more "politicized" in a praetorian society, Huntington believes, is the absence of political institutions capable of moderating and mediating group political action. Without such institutions social forces confront each other nakedly, and no agreement exists among the competing groups with regard to legitimate and authoritative methods for resolving conflicts. Therefore each group employs its own peculiar capabilities to achieve its goals in the socio-political arena. "The wealthy bribe; students riot; workers strike; mobs demonstrate; and the military coup. . . . The techniques of military intervention are simply more dramatic and effective than the others because, as Hobbes put it, 'When nothing else is turned up, clubs are trumps.' "[7]

The praetorian pattern of politics characterized much of nineteenth-century Latin American history. The heritage of Spanish and Portuguese rule left Latin America with no indigenous political institutions of any strength, and the attempts to build French and U.S. political systems upon alien social and cultural foundations failed. The result for Mexico as well as for most other Latin American states was the dominance of entrenched social forces and the absence of political institutions capable of balancing the demands of newly emerging social groups with the vested interests of the old elites.

Set against this historical background, the Mexican revolution's great achievement, in Huntington's view, was to prepare the way for *political development* and *political modernization* in Mexico. He defines political development as the creation of complex, autonomous, coherent, and adaptable political organizations and procedures; political modernization he defines as the centralization of power necessary for social reform and the expansion of power necessary for group assimilation.[8] "In the three decades after 1910 . . . the weak, personal, uninstitutionalized system of rule which had prevailed before the revolution in which personal interests and social forces dominated was replaced by a highly complex, autonomous, coherent, and flexible political system, with an existence of its own clearly apart from social forces and with a demonstrated capacity to combine the reasonably high centralization of power with the expansion of power and the broadened participation of social groups in the political system."[9]

The major institutional innovation was the official party. As the revolution served to demote the interests of the church, the landed elite, and eventually the army, it also promoted the interests of newer social and economic groups in business, labor, agriculture and the professions. The political problem for Mexico was "to subordinate autonomous social forces to an

[7]*Ibid.*, p. 196.
[8]*Ibid.*, p. 324.
[9]*Ibid.*, pp. 316–17.

effective political institution. This was accomplished in the 1930s by the incorporation of these organized social forces into the revolutionary party and by the organization of the party into four sectors: agrarian, labor, popular, and military."[10] Through the PRI the Mexican political system established its autonomy from and authority over the diverse social groupings in Mexico. Conflicts between various segments of Mexican society "now had to be resolved within the framework of the party and under the leadership of the president and the central leadership of the party."[11] Each segment was allotted a specified number of offices in local, state and national politics, and each supported the chosen candidates of the party as a whole. A system of institutional bargaining and compromise replaced the praetorian politics of open conflict, and the interests of the various sectors "were subordinated to and aggregated into the interests of the party."[12] Particularly noteworthy was the gradual decline in the role and power of the military, which was dropped as a sector of the party in the reforms of 1940.

The Cárdenas years were a particularly important period for Mexico's political modernization, that is, for the centralization of power for reform, and the expansion of power through the incorporation of new groups into the political system. In his struggle with Calles, the conservative "*jefe máximo,*" Cárdenas reorganized both the party and the army leadership to strengthen the powers of the president. At the same time he led the mobilization and organization of urban labor and the *campesinos.* Often he did this personally; it was Cárdenas who inaugurated the practice of traveling extensively through Mexico while campaigning for the presidency. Subsequently much of his time as president was spent touring rural Mexico and impressing upon peasants throughout the country that the Mexican government was their own.

Huntington is on firm ground in suggesting that the capacity of Mexico's major political institution—the PRI—to assimilate new groups into the political system has been a contributing factor in the process of Mexico's recent economic development. It has blessed Mexico with a political stability unmatched throughout the rest of Latin America. To use Argentina again as a contrast, the absence there of a similar institution has exacerbated the social conflict arising from the emergence of new social groups in the process of industrialization and has contributed to the adoption of economic policies which could only result in the creation of bottlenecks to economic development.[13]

[10] *Ibid.*, p. 318.

[11] *Ibid.*

[12] *Ibid.*, p. 319.

[13] See Gino Germani, *Política y sociedad en una época de transición: de la sociedad tradicional a la sociedad de masas* (Buenos Aires: Editorial Paidos, 1962); and Kalman H. Silvert, "The Costs of Anti-Nationalism: Argentina," in *Expectant Peoples,* edited by Kalman H. Silvert (New York: Random House, Vintage Books, 1967), pp. 347–72.

There is one aspect of Huntington's analysis, however, which raises a serious problem with regard to his interpretation of Mexican political development. If, as he claims, the development of the official party effectively broadened the participation of new social groups in the political system and introduced the practice of "institutionalized bargaining and compromise" between the four politically prominent sectors, how can the fruits of Mexican development have been distributed so unequally? Mexico's *ejidatarios* comprise the largest sector of the official party. What has the system of institutionalized bargaining produced for them? We know that in the early 1960s 86 percent of them received not a single peso from the government in the form of agricultural credit. We know that 85 percent of them live at the subsistence level, and that many of the government's agricultural policies have contributed to this result. What has the party's bargaining process allocated to organized labor, the second largest sector of the PRI? Some favored unions have done well, but the membership of most suffered relative income declines along with the rest of Mexican wage earners during twenty years of inflation. And what group has reaped most of the harvest? The country's new industrial and agricultural entrepreneurs, who are not even members of the official party.

What appears to have happened in Mexico since 1940 is that one particular social group, a new industrial-agricultural elite, has been consistently favored by government policy. It is for this reason that so many Mexican analysts argue that the "new bourgeoisie" controls the political system. But Huntington's general theory specifically precludes this outcome. Mexico is one of his prime examples of an institutionalized political system, and he argues that

> in institutionalized systems, politicians expand their loyalties from social group to political institution and political community as they mount the ladder of authority. In the praetorian society the successful politician simply transfers his identity and loyalty from one social group to another. In the most extreme form, a popular demagogue may emerge, develop a widespread but poorly organized following, threaten the established interests of the rich and aristocrats, be voted into political office, and then be bought off by the very interests which he has attacked. In less extreme forms, the individuals who mount the ladder to wealth and power simply transfer their allegiance from the masses to the oligarchy. They are absorbed or captured by a social force with narrower interests than that to which they previously owed allegiance. The rise to the top in an institutionalized civic polity broadens a man's horizons; in a praetorian system it narrows them.[14]

Mexico's pattern of economic development and its impact on Mexican society suggest that Huntington's analysis of Mexican politics as well as his

[14] Huntington, *Political Order*, p. 197. Emphasis added.

general theory concerning political behavior within institutionalized systems is at best a partial reflection of the social reality which he is trying to comprehend. He offers Mexico as the very model of an "institutionalized civic polity"; yet the behavior of successful Mexican politicians as measured by the governmental policies for which they are responsible clearly exhibits some rather pronounced "praetorian" tendencies. Leftist critics of the Mexican government are in fact arguing precisely that the leaders of the Revolutionary Coalition have been "absorbed or captured by a social force with narrower interests than that to which they previously owed allegiance." Only a much closer examination of the structure and functioning of the PRI and its leadership can reveal which point of view is closer to the reality of Mexican politics.

## THE PARTIDO REVOLUCIONARIO INSTITUCIONAL

The Partido Revolucionario Institucional, Mexico's "official" party, was founded in 1929. Since that date the PRI has held the Mexican presidency, all state governorships, and all federal senatorial seats without interruption. The PRI candidate for the presidency normally polls close to 90 percent of the total vote; only in 1946 and 1952 did the party's proportion of the votes cast fall below 80 percent. In the two most recent presidential elections, 1958 and 1964, the PRI candidates, Adolfo López Mateos and Gustavo Díaz Ordaz, polled 90 percent and 89 percent respectively.[15]

For many years the PRI also held all but five or six of the 162 seats in the federal Chamber of Deputies, but a recent change in the electoral law has enlarged the representation of the opposition parties in the chamber. In addition to winning seats by direct popular election in single member districts, a party which gains 2.5 percent of the total vote for the chamber throughout the country receives five seats. And for each additional 0.5 percent a party receives another seat, up to a maximum of twenty. Thus a party might win no places in the chamber by direct election, but obtain as many as twenty seats on the basis of its proportional vote throughout the country. Table 5-1 illustrates the effect of the new provision. In 1958, prior to the electoral reform, opposition parties won only nine of 162 seats; in 1964 they were able to gain thirty-five places. But the PRI majority continues to be overwhelming. In the most recent election, 1967, it won 176 seats out of a total of 211.

The official party's hold over state and local government is equally impressive. It controls all the governorships and all the state legislatures, and has done so since the 1930s. Of the more than 2,300 mayoralties in Mexico, only 17 are now held by members of other parties.[16] And of the 700 major

[15] These are the "official" results. Few observers in Mexico believe they are accurate, although most concede that the PRI does receive a majority of those votes cast.

[16] *Visión*, March 14, 1969, p. 24.

TABLE 5-1. SEATS IN THE CHAMBER OF DEPUTIES

| Party | 1958 Seats | 1964 Seats |
|-------|------------|------------|
| PRI | 153 | 175 |
| PAN | 6 | 20 |
| PPS | 1 | 10 |
| Others | 2 | 5 |
| Total | 162 | 210 |

Mexican municipal councils the rightist Party of National Action (PAN) holds majorities in 18, the leftist Popular Socialist Party (PPS) controls 5, and the PRI runs the rest.[17]

The forty-year supremacy of the PRI in Mexican politics is a matter of public record. Some analysts explain it by denying the possibility of a fair vote count; others charge that even the existing opposition parties are financed and manipulated by the PRI leadership to provide the appearance of a contest when in reality there is none.[18] While these charges are widely made, they remain generally unsubstantiated.

The makeup of Mexico's ruling party has changed little since the four-sector system was introduced by President Cárdenas in 1937. One sector, the military, has been dropped, and the three other sectors, agrarian, labor and "popular," remain. The agrarian sector claims a membership of about three million, and is the largest of the three. All *ejidatarios* are counted as members of the party, and constitute the overwhelming majority of the agrarian sector membership. Most of them are incorporated in the National Campesino Confederation (CNC), which since the time of Cárdenas has been the agrarian sector's predominant organization.

The labor sector exhibits less homogeneity than its agrarian counterpart. The Mexican Workers Federation (CTM) is the largest single labor organization, claiming over two million members. Its membership is probably far closer to one million. In an effort to retain its predominant position within Mexican organized labor and within the labor sector of the official party during the 1950s, the CTM joined with a number of other labor confederations and large industrial unions to form a front known as the Workers Unity Bloc (BUO). This development encouraged the more leftist rival confederations to unite in opposition, and in 1960 the latter group joined in the National Confederation of Mexican Workers (CNT). Despite several attempts

---

[17] *Latin American Digest* 3 (January 1969): 1.

[18] On these charges and others see Pablo Gonzáles Casanova, *La Democracia en México* (Mexico: Ediciones ERA, 1965), pp. 22ff.; and Brandenburg, *Making of Modern Mexico*, pp. 156ff.

since the 1920s to unite all of Mexican organized labor into a single powerful confederation, there is today neither a clearly predominant confederation nor an obvious trend toward further unification. The labor scene is one of fluidity, marked by coalitions and confederations of individual unions which are constantly open to realignment. While some labor unions support such opposition parties as the Popular Socialist Party, almost all are members of the official party's labor sector which numbers somewhere near two million.

The popular sector of the party is organized within the National Confederation of Popular Organizations, the CNOP. It also has a total membership of close to two million, and is often referred to as Mexico's "organized middle class." It is far more diverse than the other two sectors of the PRI, and includes among other groups Mexico's government bureaucrats, teachers, private farmers, small merchants and industrialists, and professionals. Of the sector's various organizations the most powerful would seem to be the 400,000 member Government Employees Union (FSTSE). Measured by salaries, fringe benefits and patronage positions held, this organization has had remarkable success. And what has been true for the FSTSE is generally true for the popular sector as a whole. To a great extent this can be attributed to the middle-class nature of its membership. The professionally trained persons within this sector exhibit a much higher propensity for political action than do the less well-educated members of the agrarian and labor sectors.

In theory the three sectors play an active role in the naming of the PRI's candidates for all public offices from the presidency of the republic to the most insignificant municipal councilman. At all levels of government the party-affiliated interest groups assume control of the party's three sectors. Again theoretically, the sectors decide among themselves which elective offices are to be assigned to each sector, each sector selects its own candidates for the offices designated to it, and the three together support all the nominations made by the PRI.[19] The sector organizations at the national level theoretically nominate the candidate for the presidency, state-level sectoral groups nominate governors and senators, and local party interest groups choose the nominees for municipal offices.

Perhaps because of the theoretical role of the three sectors in the nomination process, and certainly because of the various interest groups which those sector groupings co-opt into the official party, one of the most prominent analysts of Mexican politics, Robert Scott, has portrayed the PRI as a dominant nonauthoritarian political institution which functions as an aggregator and balancer of the various interests represented within the ruling party.[20]

[19] Brandenburg, *Making of Modern Mexico*, pp. 172ff.; L. Vincent Padgett, *The Mexican Political System* (Boston: Houghton Mifflin Co., 1966), pp. 50ff.

[20] Robert E. Scott, *Mexican Government in Transition*, rev. ed. (Urbana: University of Illinois Press, 1964), chap. 1 and *passim*. In his excellent essay "Mexico: The Estab-

For example, he states that "as long as the present official party continues to work out a formula for satisfying a majority of the strongest influence associations, dissatisfying as few as possible, not only the aggregating function but the decision-making process itself will reside in it and not in the formal government." Elsewhere he argues that "the party forces a certain amount of adjustment and balance among the demands of the interests represented by associations belonging to its sector organizations," and that "the multiplying interests which must be accommodated in the decision-making process can be both represented and controlled through the good offices of the revolutionary party." He also states that "equilibrium has been achieved among the strongest sectors of economic and political life through the activities of the revolutionary party" and that the "political process" is "centered in the machinery" of that party. His analysis leaves the impression that the sectoral system within the PRI has provided a mechanism not only for the aggregation of interests of various member groups, but also, and more importantly, for a balanced representation of those interests in terms of policy formulation and outcome.[21]

Strong objections have been raised against this analysis of the role of the PRI in Mexican politics. As one critic stated the issue, "the official party cannot 'continue' interest satisfaction since this role in the Mexican political system has always been performed elsewhere. . . . And as for 'the decision-making process,' if this had actually resided in the official party instead of the Revolutionary Family inner council and in the formal government, Mexico probably would have become a worker's state long ago."[22]

Those who reject the interpretation of the PRI as the center of the Mexican political process have generally tended to view the party as an instrument for consolidating political support for the revolutionary elite.[23] Brandenburg refers to that elite as the Revolutionary Family; Padgett calls it the Revolutionary Coalition. The "Revolutionary Family," says Brandenburg, "is composed of the men who have run Mexico for over half a century, who

---

lished Revolution," written at about the same time as the revised edition of his *Mexican Government in Transition*, Scott was more inclined to emphasize the authoritarian and elitist aspects of the Mexican political system. See Lucian W. Pye and Sidney Verba (eds.), *Political Culture and Political Development* (Princeton, N.J.: Princeton University Press, 1965), chap. 9.

[21] Scott, *Mexican Government in Transition*, pp. 29, 32, 108, 145–46. In the revised conclusion to his book, written in 1964, Scott emphasized the "nearly captive relationship" of some of the interest associations to the political elite, but did not otherwise alter his analysis of the operation of the PRI and its sectors. See *ibid.*, pp. 315–16.

[22] Brandenburg, *Making of Modern Mexico*, p. 144.

[23] This view is shared by Brandenburg, Padgett, and Patricia Richmond among others. Scott himself emphasizes the overwhelming importance of the presidency vis-à-vis the PRI and all other political institutions in "Mexico: The Established Revolution."

have laid the policy-lines of the Revolution, and who today hold effective decision-making power." He suggests that this elite operates at three different levels. An inner council including the Family head and about twenty favorite sons "keeps the Revolution intact and rolling forward by understanding the relative power of the major vested interests—the economic, political, social, governmental, religious, educational and military order of Mexico." At this highest level the final word belongs to the head of the Family who, since 1934, has also been the president of Mexico.

A second level is occupied by some two hundred spokesmen from finance, commerce, industry and agriculture; from government ministries, agencies and state-owned industries; from the armed forces and veterans groups; and from labor unions, agrarian leagues and other active political groupings. It is from this level, Brandenburg argues, that new leadership is co-opted into the Revolutionary Family, and not from the ranks of the PRI.

Only at the bottom level of the Family structure does the PRI appear. This level embraces the national bureaucracy, the armed forces, the PRI, "captive opposition parties" and state and local public administrations. "All these segments owe ultimate loyalty to the chief of state, and the orientation and timing of policies and programs under their charges depend upon instructions received from the President of Mexico. Failure to observe his dictates means an eclipse of prestige, discharge from position, or an even worse fate."[24]

Padgett's characterization of the Mexican political system stands somewhere between Brandenburg's elite description and Scott's "balanced interests" model, though it is much closer to the former. In his view Mexico is ruled by a Revolutionary Coalition which incorporates "that cluster of groups and leaders whose political prominence is directly or indirectly connected with the 'revolutionary' struggle and the victories that were won in that struggle. These are the men and groups who because of their connection with the Revolution have some influence, or at the very least, hope of gaining influence in decision-making within the Mexican political system."[25] Padgett conceives of the PRI more as a creature of the executive organizational network than as an independent and significant balancer of competing interests and demands. He also emphasizes several crucial functions which the official party does perform, among them the facilitating of political communication and the promotion of consensus within the elite and its various organizations. Even more important is the manner in which the PRI serves to legitimize the continuing control over Mexican politics by the Revolutionary Coalition. The

---

[24] Brandenburg, *Making of Modern Mexico*, pp. 3–6.
[25] Padgett, *Mexican Political System*, p. 34, n. 25.

mere existence of the party makes the selections of the nominees for president and lesser political offices seem less arbitrary, even though the party itself plays no significant role in these selections. And as an electoral instrument the party also provides a successful device for fulfilling the norm of electoral participation.[26]

From these major competing (and sometimes complementary) interpretations of the workings of the Mexican political system we can construct two simplified paradigms. One depicts the PRI as effectively representing its component sectoral groupings in the struggle over who gets what, when and how. While it stresses the power of the Mexican presidency, it also views the PRI and its interest groups as positioned at the center of the decision-making process, where party demands are reflected in government policies. The other paradigm portrays Mexico as governed by a small elite group emerging from the revolution and headed for three decades by the president of the republic, which in essence uses the PRI to facilitate its continued control over the destiny of Mexico. In this model the party is viewed as controlled by and responsive to the Revolutionary Coalition. The PRI's primary functions are to legitimize and implement the policies of the ruling political elite rather than to formulate its own. Which of the two models most closely approximates the reality of Mexican politics?

When we consider the years between 1940 and 1970, the burden of evidence clearly suggests that the PRI is better conceptualized as an apparatus through which the Revolutionary Coalition controls Mexican politics than as a mechanism for representing and implementing the demands of its component interest groups. In the first place, the economic analysis in the preceding two chapters underlines the implausibility of the first interpretation of Mexican politics. A government in which the demands of organized labor and Mexico's *campesinos* were effectively represented could neither have designed nor implemented the development strategy that has characterized Mexico's recent economic growth. In the long run that development strategy may well benefit all segments of Mexican society in an equitable manner, but in the long run, as Keynes said, we are all dead. And no segment of a society whose interests are effectively represented in its political system will voluntarily curtail its demands for over a generation while others reap the profits of its sacrifice. The Mexican government did distribute land, did devise and implement various welfare programs, and did support the organization of labor. But in measuring the size and effect of such efforts, we discover that they were modest indeed, and that by comparison most other Latin American countries have generally done more in all areas save the redistribution of land.

[26] *Ibid.*, pp. 61-62.

And even in that particular field of endeavor the results reveal at best an ambivalent commitment to the principles of agrarian reform as stated in the Mexican constitution.

In the second place, the first paradigm is weakened by the fact that most of the groups which have shared the fruits of Mexican growth are not represented in the official party. Two groups of particular importance are the Confederation of Chambers of Industry of Mexico (CONCAMIN) and the Confederation of National Chambers of Commerce (CONCANACO). These two organizations have both a semiofficial status and an extensive influence within the highest government circles.[27] According to law all but the smallest business firms must belong to one of the specialized chambers grouped within these two broad organizations. Scott himself has acknowledged that the role of CONCAMIN and CONCANACO in the political process can hardly be overstated, "for although business and commercial interests are not provided with access to governmental councils through the PRI's sectors they can and do make their voices heard through these organizations."[28] The government has found it very convenient to consult these national federations and their constituent chambers concerning administrative regulations and new legislation on matters affecting their interests. As a result, interaction between the various business chambers and the government is by now institutionalized and continuous. The chambers frequently phrase their demands in the form of proposed legislation; on other occasions they submit amendments to pending legislation at the invitation of the government. Their representatives now sit on numerous public-sector regulatory and advisory commissions and a host of other governmental bodies.

One of the chambers most effective in pressing its views upon the Mexican government through these channels has been the National Chamber of Manufacturing Industries (CNIT). This chamber has acted as the semiofficial spokesman for the new group of industrialists that appeared during the late 1930s and 1940s when the process of Mexican industrialization was rapidly accelerating.[29] By 1950 observers were already noting the effectiveness of this body in influencing government policies of protection and other incentives to new manufacturing enterprises. Its members were perhaps the first to advocate continuous and intimate contact and cooperation between the Mexican private sector and government in the process of industrialization. They,

---

[27] See Raymond Vernon, *The Dilemma of Mexico's Development: The Roles of the Private and Public Sectors* (Cambridge: Harvard University Press, 1963); Scott, *Mexican Government in Transition*, chap. 8; Padgett, *Mexican Political System*, chap. 5; and Sanford A. Mosk, *Industrial Revolution in Mexico* (Berkeley and Los Angeles: University of California Press, 1954).

[28] Scott, *Mexican Government in Transition*, p. 285.

[29] For a discussion of this "New Group" see Mosk, *Industrial Revolution in Mexico*, pp. 21ff.

more than the older established firms, needed tariff protection, tax incentives and government-financed assistance. In return for such support they endorsed government policies of land reform and social welfare, and the unionization of Mexican labor.

By the mid-1960s the enthusiasm of the CNIT for close and cordial relations with the government was increasingly being shared by the older, more established elements in the Mexican business community represented in CONCANACO and CONCAMIN. This seems a natural evolution of a trend begun during the years of Calles' ascendancy, interrupted by the Cárdenas presidency, and renewed again when Alemán became president in 1946. Alemán's inner circle was filled with what has been called the "Revolutionary Right," wealthy and influential businessmen whose affluence generally dates from the 1920-40 period. Intimates of Alemán were such successful businessmen as Luis Aguilár, Carlos Trouyet, Bruno Pagliai and Eloy Vallina. Since the 1940s elite members of the business community have increasingly accepted public posts at the behest of the government. By 1964 the relationship between Mexico's political and business elites had warmed to the point where most of the country's leading businessmen publicly supported the candidate of the PRI for the presidency, Gustavo Díaz Ordaz, despite the fact that the more conservative opposition party, the PAN, fielded its own candidate.

In light of the evidence revealed in both the structure and the welfare effects of Mexico's development strategy, as well as in the relationship between Mexico's political and economic elites, it is difficult to think of the official party as an institution which effectively represents and balances the interests of its three sectors in the Mexican political process. The evidence clearly calls into serious question the autonomy of the party's labor and peasant sectors, which represent the overwhelming majority of PRI membership yet receive so little in return for adherence to the institution.

Scott himself has recognized the difficulty in reconciling this kind of evidence with his general interpretation of Mexican politics, and in at least two instances has raised issues which, when closely examined, provide an entirely different view of the orientation and operation of the Mexican political system. At one point he observes that the PRI machinery "has managed to continue providing a workable system for satisfying (*or at least controlling*) the demands of the interest associations participating in Mexican politics." At another point he states that "*whether it is because their leaders have failed to represent them properly* or because their own social limitations have hindered the members of the lower class from supporting their leaders effectively the great mass of Mexico's population has not won nearly the share of the advantages of industrialization that its numbers warrant."[30]

[30] Scott, *Mexican Government in Transition*, pp. 172, 91. Emphasis added.

There is a great deal of evidence to suggest that the PRI's function as a control mechanism, parenthetical in Scott's view, is primary in the eyes of the Revolutionary Coalition. Furthermore, much of the behavior of the majority of the labor and agrarian sector leaders is highly inconsistent with the interests of those segments of the official party which they supposedly represent. Some light is shed on both the control and the leadership behavior aspects of the PRI by analyzing the party's methods of choosing new leadership.

*The Nominating Process*

The official party's candidate for the presidency always has, and most probably will for some time in the future, become the president of Mexico.[31] No other party, in the past or present, has been or is powerful enough to challenge the PRI in the presidential election. Perhaps the most serious opposition was mounted in 1940 by General Almazán; some observers feel that he actually received a majority of the votes in that election. "Officially," however, he received only 6 percent, while the PRI's candidate, Ávila Camacho, was given 94 percent.

The choice of the party's candidate every six years is made by the outgoing president after consultation with the inner circle of the Revolutionary Coalition. Since no one within this circle has ever publicly discussed the selection process, little of a specific nature is known about it. For example, it is not clear how many persons or groups outside the coalition are consulted during the search for a successor. Most observers limit these "outsiders" to a few vested interests not grouped within the structure of the PRI, and "sometimes" the sector leaders of the party.

Moreover, it is not clear what constraints, if any, operate upon the president as he chooses a successor. Some have argued that the two "wings" of the party, represented on the left by ex-President Cárdenas and his supporters and on the right by Miguel Alemán and his followers possess something like a veto power in the process. The choices since Alemán (1946–52), they suggest, have been candidates whose presumed policies would be acceptable, if not congenial, to each group.[32] While others deny that anything like a veto power exists and emphasize the complete freedom of the president to name a successor, the evidence does indicate that the three presidents since Alemán

[31] This analysis of the Mexican nominating process is based on interviews undertaken during two visits to Mexico since 1966 and the accounts in Brandenburg, *Making of Modern Mexico*; Scott, *Mexican Government in Transition*; González Casanova, *La Democracía*; Patricia McIntire Richmond, *Mexico: A Case Study of One-Party Politics* (Ph.D. dissertation, University of California, 1965); and González Navarro, "La Ideología de la revolución mexicana," "Social Aspects of the Mexican Revolution," and "Le Developpement economique."

[32] See for example Scott, *Mexican Government in Transition*, chap. 7.

have steered a political course somewhere between the generally socialist tendencies of the Cárdenas period and the business-oriented policies of the Alemán presidency.

The Mexican president is chosen by a very few men, and ultimately by the outgoing president. Since 1934 each new president has served in the cabinet of the outgoing chief of state. Not a single president has ever headed a labor union or *ejido* confederation. There is, however, evidence that organizations within the PRI try to influence the selection of the new president. Political activity of labor unions increases, new labor blocs are formed, and new worker demands are voiced with increasing frequency as the year of succession approaches. Other forms of conflict develop which cross sectoral lines. A perfect example emerged in 1969 when the CTM suddenly opened a campaign to organize agricultural workers and aroused the wrath of the CNC, which considered such activity as trespassing upon its political domain.[33] This clash developed approximately six months before the heir-apparent, Luis Echeverría Alvarez, was designated by outgoing President Díaz Ordaz, and can best be interpreted as an attempt by forces within the PRI to influence that selection.

If little else can be said with much certainty about the presidential selection process, there is more evidence available with regard to the designation of the rest of the PRI's candidates. The nominations for state governors are controlled by the president of the republic, and here as elsewhere the theory of party nominations decided upon by the three sectors in convention is at odds with the facts. A former governor of Baja California has given the following account of his own selection, and of the general process of leadership designation within the PRI:

> I was selected and previously designated by the President of the Republic, at that time my distinguished friend, Don Adolfo Ruiz Cortines, and *all the functionaries, large or small, in our country have been designated in the same way from 1928 to the present.* This is an axiomatic truth. . . . The chief executive can select good or bad functionaries and it is the public which receives the benefits or the evils that emanate from the behavior of the designated functionary. [After an aspirant is chosen by the President] the battle is won, the victory has been obtained in the waiting rooms of the government. Now the labor unions, the organized peasants, the popular sector, the party declare him the Official Candidate, and thus it is that the candidate is converted into the man of the day, a person with talent, honored in all respects and deemed a person with great revolutionary merits.[34]

[33] Daily accounts of the conflict appear in *Excelsior*, starting in May 1969.

[34] Braulio Maldonado, quoted in Richmond, *Mexico: A Case Study*, pp. 390-91. Emphasis added.

The selection of governors has been somewhat different in the home states of former presidents Cárdenas (Michoacán), Ávila Camacho (Puebla), and Ruiz Cortines (Veracruz). In these states the president of the republic has in most instances allowed the regional strongmen to choose new governors and control the "election" to most other public offices.[35]

In some cases when selecting gubernatorial candidates the president consults with his inner circle and state representatives of the PRI's sectors. In recent years the party has sent delegates to each state prior to nominations for all state offices and municipal posts, and these delegates consult with the sector leaders at that stage of the nominating process. However, their primary function is to guarantee the acceptance of the choices made in Mexico City by the president and those with whom he has consulted.[36] Indeed, some presidents both minimize the consultation process and name gubernatorial candidates over the strenuous objections of PRI sectoral groups within various states. Alemán's indifference to the wishes of labor groups was notorious. He chose Sanchez Colín to be the governor of the state of México although all the CTM leadership was opposed to the nomination. He also aroused great indignation by naming a nonresident, Ignacio Morones Prieto, as governor of Nuevo León.

As for the other PRI candidates for elected offices in Mexico, there is little doubt that they too are selected by the political elite rather than through a sectoral bargaining process at the PRI's nominating conventions. The federal legislature (sixty senators and now over two hundred deputies) is the province of the president, although he appears to allow certain groups within the PRI and other parties to participate in the selection process.[37]

The choices of the PRI for state legislatures and municipal governments are made either in Mexico City or the state capitals, depending upon the relationship between the president and the various state governors. The former PRI governor of Baja California has written that the established and regularly followed custom "is for municipal representatives to be selected directly from the federal capital with or without the intervention of the governor of the states."[38]

[35] González Casanova, *La Democracía*, pp. 38ff.; Brandenburg, *Making of Modern Mexico*, pp. 150ff. During the 1960s some PRI candidates in Michoacán were apparently chosen against the wishes of Cárdenas.

[36] See, for example, the evidence presented in Richmond, *Mexico: A Case Study*, pp. 368–69.

[37] According to Brandenburg the president typically chooses about one-third of the senators himself, and allows the party's sector leaders to name the rest. Brandenburg also estimates that since 1940 the president has personally picked about 20 percent of all federal deputies, while governors and regional strongmen have named another 15 percent and the opposition parties have been given 5 percent. The remaining 60 percent have emerged from the party's official sectors. Brandenburg, *Making of Modern Mexico*, p. 155.

[38] Quoted in Richmond, *Mexico: A Case Study*, p. 402.

At each level of government, then, PRI candidates are designated by the president in consultation with his closest political associates, state governors, and regional *caciques*. After these choices are made, the sectors of the party then "nominate" them at their conventions as instructed by the central executive committee of the party. Thus the seal of democratic "legitimacy" is awarded to the PRI's candidates, all but a fraction of whom are then elected to their various posts throughout the republic. Even many of those members of opposition parties who are given elected seats are chosen by the Revolutionary Coalition, presumably in return for their behavior as members of a "loyal opposition."[39]

In summary, the president stands at the apex of Mexico's political pyramid. He designates some elected officials who in turn designate literally all the rest. Office holders owe their selection not to interest groups which support them with their votes, but to those few within the political elite who have co-opted them into the political hierarchy. The municipal councilman owes allegiance to the regional *cacique* who chose him for the position. The *cacique* in turn, unless he is one of the very few regional strongmen still operating in Mexico, must count upon the good will of the governor in order to continue his dominance of local politics. And given the federal government's constitutional and fiscal dominance over Mexico's state governments, the governor cannot successfully retain either his position or his influence unless he has the approval of Mexico's president.

The singular lack of anything resembling legislative branch independence vis-à-vis the executive reflects the nature of the Mexican power hierarchy. At both the state and national level the will of the governors and the president prevails in all but the most bizarre circumstances.[40] At the national level anywhere from 60 percent to 95 percent of all legislation submitted by the president is adopted unanimously. And when opposing votes are cast, they almost never exceed 5 percent of the total vote.[41]

## The Labor Sector

Looking beneath the PRI's methods of selecting its official candidates for public office to the working of the party's labor and agrarian sectors themselves, we note a similar pattern of co-opted or imposed leadership and the consequent upward-flowing obligations and loyalties. With a few exceptions

[39] See Karl Schmitt, "Congressional Campaigning in Mexico: a View from the Provinces," *Journal of Inter-American Studies* 11 (January 1969): 93–110, for confirmation of this point in the 1967 congressional election in Mérida.

[40] Occasionally monumental corruption or misgovernment on the part of a state governor will lead to legislative revolt.

[41] González Casanova, *La Democracia*, pp. 26ff.

strong and independent labor unions do not exist in Mexico.[42] One reason for this pattern is the fact that ever since the revolution the Mexican government has been active in the affairs of organized labor; so too have labor leaders been widely engaged in Mexican politics. In the unstable years between 1910 and 1930 labor bosses were often able to mobilize support for various revolutionary political factions; in return political leaders who controlled the government were in a position to sponsor and support the organizational activities of favored labor groups. The search for mutually advantageous alliances continued throughout the years of the revolution and the chaotic decade of the 1920s that followed.

During most of these years "clubs were trumps," and Mexico's political generals held most of the clubs. Favored unions prospered; the rest perished. Thus, by the time the official party was formed, the pattern of union boss cooperation with political leadership was already institutionalized. In the Cárdenas years government sponsorship of organized labor, particularly those groups in conflict with foreign firms, increased the dependence of the labor movement upon the government at the same time that it swelled the numbers of organized workers.

Since 1940 two patterns can be observed in the relationship between union leaders and the government. One is the co-optive pattern, in which labor officials collaborate closely with the government. One commentator wrote of this group several years ago, "For two decades, the union boss has kept the rank and file in line, loyal to the Revolutionary regimes. His reward, besides the permanence of his tenure, sometimes comes in the form of a legislative office."[43] For thirty years the leaders of the biggest labor confederation, the CTM, have regularly been given seats in the federal legislature by the Mexican president. Since consecutive terms in either the Chamber of Deputies or the Senate are prohibited in Mexico, this CTM clique has rotated offices but never relinquished them. While retaining his place in the national legislature, Fidel Velázquez has also held the secretary generalship of the CTM since 1949.

The second pattern of union-government relations might best be called repressive, and was most clearly evidenced during the years of Alemán's presi-

---

[42] For descriptions of unionism and labor-government relations in Mexico see Vicente Fuentes Díaz, "Desarrollo y evolución del movimiento obrero a partir de 1929," *Ciencias políticas y sociales* 5 (July–September 1959); Richmond, *Mexico: A Case Study*, chap. 3 and *passim*; Padgett, *Mexican Political System,* chaps. 3 and 7; Scott, *Mexican Government in Transition,* chaps. 6–8; González Casanova *La Democracia*; Brandenburg, *Making of Modern Mexico,* chaps. 6 and 9; Alfonso López Aparacio, *El Movimiento obrero en México* (Mexico: Editorial Jus, 1958); and Robert Paul Millon, *Mexican Marxist: Vicente Lombardo Toledano* (Chapel Hill: University of North Carolina Press, 1966).

[43] Brandenburg, *Making of Modern Mexico*, p. 154.

dency. Perhaps the best description of the period would be one of total intervention by the government in union affairs. The government held wage increases in check while prices were rising at more than 10 percent a year, and labor opposition to Alemán's policies simply was not tolerated. The army was used to crush strikes, and government recognition of certain leftist unions was withdrawn. Many labor leaders openly critical of the regime were jailed, and others were forced to resign their offices. Then the government imposed its own union "leadership," a practice that Mexicans labeled "Charrismo Sindical" to emphasize the fact that the new officials represented the interests not of the union membership but of those who had chosen and imposed them.[44]

Throughout these years of repression and imposed leadership the co-opted union bosses of the CTM, led by Fidel Velázquez and the others in the group that Mexicans refer to as "the five little wolves," held the line for Alemán's policies and, not incidentally, their own sinecures. As a result the number of strikes declined, and the unity of the labor movement achieved under Cárdenas was fractured. By 1956 there were eight major labor federations and several independent industrial unions, all but one or two completely dominated by the government.

Since the mid-1950s a third pattern in union-government relations has emerged. There are some unions, like the electrical workers union, which have refused to join the government-oriented Workers' Unity Bloc, yet manage to be among the highest paid union workers in Mexico. In contrast, the members of many unions whose leaders belong to the Bloc and always support the government receive wages which barely match the legal minimums. It has been  argued that some of the privileged unions whose leaders retain some independence from the government have achieved their status through a complex set of relationships including presidential favor, dynamic union leadership, and the strategic nature of the industrial activity involved.[45] Like most other attempts to fathom the workings of the Mexican political system, this observation cannot be clearly substantiated; nevertheless it seems to offer the best explanation we have at present.

What is clear is that the Mexican government will still not tolerate much union opposition. Since the late 1950s the army has been utilized to suppress strikes; union leaders have been and continue to be imprisoned, and new leaders are imposed when dissidents are removed. The range of tolerated opposition is perhaps growing, but the seeming inconsistency in government policy has led one Mexican scholar to argue that independent leaders are now never sure whether their labor demands will be met by government support or repression.[46]

[44] Fuentes Díaz, "Desarrollo y evolución," pp. 337ff.

[45] Brandenburg, *Making of Modern Mexico*, p. 245.

[46] Fuentes Díaz, "Desarrollo y evolución," pp. 347ff.

What is also clear is the fact that the labor sector of the PRI cannot reasonably be characterized as an autonomous interest group (or set of interest groups) within the party. Like almost all Mexico's elected officials, the leaders of the sector are chosen by the president and his closest confidants. The majority of Mexico's labor leaders have been co-opted into the PRI structure by the Revolutionary Coalition in exchange for the support which their union membership can deliver. And the very fact that some unions which have remained outside the inner circle have made the most concrete gains in terms of salary and fringe benefits obviously suggests that the labor sector of the party is today better conceptualized as a mechanism for elite control of the labor movement than as an effective representative of labor interests.

### The Agrarian Sector

An examination of leadership designation within the agrarian sector of the PRI reveals much the same picture; in fact, the imposition of leaders from above is reported even more frequently than is the case for labor unions.[47] As with the labor sector, the interaction between organized peasant groups and Mexico's political elite began during the revolution and intensified during the 1920s. Again the political generals—perhaps better, the military politicians—used this organized source of support in their continuing struggle to control the Mexican presidency, and the very usefulness of such groups to the generals encouraged further agrarian organization.

With the appearance of the official party the peasant leagues became the nucleus of the agrarian sector. Their numbers grew with the spread of agrarian reform, and so did the practice of "*desde arribismo*," leadership "from above." At the lowest level of the agrarian sector oganization each *ejido* elects its own president and *ejidal* commission. Here the charges of imposition of leadership have been widespread and continuous for forty years. Eyler Simpson, examining the *ejidos* in the mid-1930s, noted the constant interference from municipal authorities, *caciques*, governors and federal deputies in *ejidal* elections.[48] These same charges still appear weekly throughout Mexico, and the claim is often made that the interference in elections is undertaken at the behest of local *hacendados*.[49] In addition to electoral frauds, imprisonment

---

[47] The reading of any Mexico City daily newspaper will confirm this observation over any given period.

[48] Eyler N. Simpson, *The Ejido: Mexico's Way Out* (Chapel Hill: University of North Carolina Press, 1937), pp. 335–440. For evidence of interference and imposition from above in the 1950s see Carlos Manuel Castillo, "La Economía agrícola en la región de el Bajío," *Problemas agrícolas e industriales de México* 8 (July–December 1956), chap. 10.

[49] One of the best sources of information on *ejidal* problems is the Mexico City newspaper, *El Día*.

and assassination not infrequently cut short the political careers of articulate and genuine *campesino* spokesmen.[50]

At the municipal and state levels, the selection of the PRI's agrarian sector leadership appears to be made in accordance with the wishes of state governors. In the various state conventions only a single slate of candidates is presented, and as one observer described the process, "the apathetic and sparse number of delegates accept their new officers by acclamation."[51] At the national level CNC leaders are of course designated by the president.

Corroborating evidence for this characterization of the politics of rural Mexico is supplied in countless glimpses of the PRI's activities provided by community studies and other forms of research undertaken in Mexico since 1929. Glen Fisher's study, one of the most enlightening treatments of the subject, focused on *ejidal* life in the state of Nayarit. Several of Fisher's observations help to penetrate the reality of agrarian politics in Mexico.

First, the small clique which ran the state branch of the PRI was in tight control of all political activity in Nayarit, and "constitutional processes seem to operate at their pleasure."[52] Second, the authority of this group extended down to the *municipio* level through its influence over the selection of local *presidentes municipales*. "This is easy since usually only the candidate of the 'official' party runs for office. Competition for the office must be carried out within the confines of the party." Third, through the *presidente municipal* the state PRI leadership then named the presidents of the local *ejidos*. In many instances *ejidal* elections were simply omitted and appointments made "*desde arribo*."

Finally, the system was cemented by a loyalty to the shared spoils of office. "In return for loyal support of the party for carrying out in the *ejido* the wishes of state politicians and the *presidente municipal*, the local village político can pursue the advantages of his position."[53] It bears repeating that Fisher's description of the imposition of *ejido* leadership for the covert purposes of those totally outside the agrarian sector of the party conforms to a pattern observed by investigators ever since the *ejidos* came into being over four decades ago.

---

[50] Such charges are made in *El Día* weekly, and the assassinations of the *ejidatario* spokesman Jaramillo Morelos and his entire family in 1962 was not an isolated occurrence. For further evidence of official and unofficial repression in rural Mexico see Bo Anderson and James D. Cockcroft, "Control and Cooptation in Mexican Politics," *International Journal of Comparative Sociology* 7 (March 1966): 21.

[51] Richmond, *Mexico: A Case Study*, pp. 228–29. For several examples of such procedures see *ibid.*, chap. 3.

[52] Glen Fisher, "Directed Culture Change in Nayarit, Mexico," in *Synoptic Studies of Mexican Culture*, edited by Robert Wauchope (New Orleans: Tulane University, Middle American Research Institute, 1957), p. 95.

[53] *Ibid.*

The members of the PRI's agrarian sector are the passive victims not only of state and local officials, but also of several major organs of the federal government. Both the Ejidal Bank and the Department of Agrarian Affairs are deeply involved in the administration of Mexico's *ejidos*. The former is the major—sometimes the only—source of credit for Mexico's two and a half million *ejidatario* families. The agrarian department is even more prominent in *ejidal* affairs, since it is charged with supervising elections for *ejido* presidents and commissioners, those officers charged with running *ejido* affairs for three-year periods. The department is also the federal agency which investigates the evasion of the laws regarding land tenure; its findings can open millions of hectares to Mexico's landless *campesinos*.

The records of both organizations cast considerable doubt on their commitment to serving the interests of the agrarian sector of the PRI. The Ejidal Bank has from its inception attempted to organize *ejidos* in accordance with its own interests, and always to the detriment of any aggressive and independent peasant leadership. As Clarence Senior noted in his study of the development of *ejidos* in the fertile Laguna region several decades ago, bank officials have often combined forces with state politicians to smother the emergence of indigenous *ejidal* spokesmen. In one instance the lengths to which the bank went to subvert independent leadership included the removal of an *ejidal* official who was exposing an organization that nightly stole thousands of pounds of cotton grown by Laguna *ejidatorios*. Such observations on the bank's activities are echoed in daily protests from individual *ejidatarios* throughout Mexico and occasionally from state and national CNC leadership itself.[54]

In addition to these activities, employees of the Ejidal Bank are more often accused of fraud and corruption than those of any other Mexican governmental agency. And in Mexico, being number one in corruption is a very high fence to ride at. Seldom does a year go by without the uncovering of a major scandal in the bank; charges of fraud at the local level are a weekly occurrence.[55]

There are two kinds of evidence that the Department of Agrarian Affairs does not effectively represent the interests of Mexico's *ejidatarios*. The first

[54] Clarence Senior, *Land Reform and Democracy* (Gainesville: University of Florida Press, 1958), p. 188. Similar activities are discussed in various works by prominent Mexican authors. See, for example, Jesús Silva Herzog, *El Agrarismo mexicano y la reforma agraria* (Mexico: Fondo de Cultura Económica, 1959); Lucio Mendieta y Núñez, *El Problema agrario de México* (Mexico: Editorial Porrua, 1964); and Moisés González Navarro, *La Confederación nacional campesina* (Mexico: B. Costa-Amic, 1968).

[55] The evidence for these observations can be found in any good Mexico City newspaper. The major scandal for 1969 involved the pilfering of $8 million by seven branch and agency managers, all employees of the bank. See the accounts of the charges beginning June 1, 1969 in *Excelsior*.

comes in the form of the department's interference in *ejidal* elections. It has the statutory duty to supervise such elections, and thus becomes the instrument by which those interests outside the *ejidos* control them for their own political and economic advantage. In a detailed study of the Bajio region made over a decade ago, Carlos Castillo documented the modus operandi of the department. He cited one instance in which an *ejidal* president imposed from outside the community was in danger of his very life due to the resentment of the imposition, and commented that in many *ejidos* where the department interfered in elections "conflict is the norm" for daily life.[56] The same resentment led to the killing of an *ejidal* president in the region of Nayarit while Glen Fisher, quoted above, was doing research for his study.

The second kind of evidence is found in the continued existence of vast private agricultural holdings in Mexico. The department does little about them for the obvious reason that it is far more influenced by pressures from without the agrarian sector of the PRI than from those within it. Most of Mexico's illegal landholdings are found in the north, and according to press reports and other scraps of information, many of them are in the possession of prominent revolutionary families.[57] In the Yaqui valley, for example, members of the Obregón, Tapia, and Calles families all own large contiguous holdings.[58] When informed of the land tenure situation in that region by *campesino* leaders during his presidential campaign in 1964, PRI presidential candidate Gustavo Díaz Ordaz is reported to have termed the situation "scandalous."[59] No more so, however, than other situations revealed by stories which appear each year denouncing the illegal landholdings of members, relatives and friends of the revolutionary elite. One such scandal erupted in 1962 when the names of many prominent politicians were identified as owners of huge holdings in Baja California.[60] One Mexico City newspaper pointed out at the time that while some of those accused denied the reports, their names had been linked with violations of the agrarian laws for twenty years.[61]

When land is held illegally by members and friends of the Revolutionary Coalition, both the state governors and the agrarian department are in a position to prevent any action to remedy the situation. The governors can simply reject or bury petitions for land presented by *campesinos*, and the department can take years to complete the legal details involved in making

[56] Castillo, "La Economía agrícola," p. 159.

[57] See Richmond, *Mexico: A Case Study*, pp. 119ff.

[58] Anderson and Cockcroft, "Control and Cooptation," p. 23.

[59] *Ibid.*, p. 24.

[60] See newspaper accounts in November 1962.

[61] *El Día*, November 14, 1962.

land transfers. Department officials, often in collusion with the owner of expropriated land, "prevent the completion of land grants, deprive *ejidatarios* of land which they have already received, and see to it that *campesino* leaders are arrested on false charges."[62] A classic example of *tortuguismo* ("a turtle's pace") appeared in June 1969 when, after twenty years of denials, the agrarian department admitted that there were fifty-three illegal haciendas in the state of Puebla and indicated that it was prepared to take action against them in the near future.[63]

Officials of the agrarian department usually benefit directly from their failure to represent the interests of Mexico's *ejidatarios* and landless peasants. They are often among those named as owners of illegal holdings, as was the case in the 1962 Baja California scandal. In the following year a chief of the department, Roberto Barrios, was charged with the illegal selling of *ejidal* lands within the Federal District. Implicated with him were the press secretary of the National Campesino Confederation itself (who also held a sinecure in the federal Chamber of Deputies) and the chief of the Bureau of Complaints in the Office of the Presidency.[64] More often, however, the department fails to respond to the interests of the agrarian sector of the party simply because that sector is not and never has been an autonomous and effective interest group in Mexican politics. Even more than the labor sector it is controlled from above, a captive of Mexico's revolutionary political elite.

## MEXICAN POLITICS: THE MANIFEST AND THE LATENT

The discrepancies which exist among the leading interpretations of the PRI and Mexican politics are of considerable magnitude. At one extreme are those interpretations which view Mexican politics as evolving steadily toward a democratic system of government and a fulfillment of the social goals of the revolution. They generally view the PRI as an institution which is actively involved in the process of "nation-building." Within this range of interpretation one scholar states that ever since 1910 Mexico "has organized to benefit the masses, either directly as in social revolution, or indirectly, as in political and economic revolution."[65] Another writes that "the attitude of the govern-

---

[62] Richmond, *Mexico: A Case Study*, pp. 122-23.

[63] *Excelsior*, June 13, 1969. A week later the department was asked by the CNC to examine a holding of 100,000 hectares in the state of Chihuahua. Such requests are made weekly in various states, usually with no concrete results. See *Excelsior*, June 19, 1969.

[64] Gonzáles Navarro, *La Confederación Nacional Campesina*, pp. 256-57.

[65] James W. Wilkie, *The Mexican Revolution: Federal Expenditure and Social Change Since 1910* (Berkeley and Los Angeles: University of California Press, 1968), p. 263.

ment toward the *ejidos* is constantly solicitous and paternalistic. . . ."[66] And we read that "the country's most important labor leaders are in a very real sense members of the small group which in part governs Mexico. They help to choose . . . the candidate for president every six years; they have marked influence on administration policy on a wide range of issues."[67]

Others holding to the same general view write that elections in Mexico "are a part of the educational process in the long and arduous task of . . . turning illiterate campesinos, Indians, and an uneducated and culturally backward people into Mexican citizens."[68] And scholars of this persuasion generally conclude that under the leadership of the Revolutionary Coalition "the Mexican Revolution has become synonymous with Mexican nationalism, no longer the exclusive property of one faction or approach, but a common enterprise of the overwhelming majority of modern Mexicans."[69]

It is clear from their writings that these observers have generally focused their attention upon the manifest goals of the revolution and the manifest functions of the PRI and of the Mexican government. For the most part they view the labor and agrarian sectors of the party as effective representatives of their interest groups, accepting at face value the government's "commitment" to Mexico's *ejidatarios* and contending that Mexico's unions "have for more than a generation been one of the principal power centers of Mexican society."[70] The existence of opposition parties and elections are most often interpreted by them at the manifest level, and suggest the emergence of a competitive democratic system of politics.

In marked contrast with this general interpretation of the PRI and the political system is that which emphasizes the nondemocratic, nonegalitarian and repressive aspects of Mexican politics. This latter view has been developed in most detail by Pablo González Casanova. In his opinion, somewhere between 50 and 70 percent of today's Mexicans are effectively barred from making any type of demand upon the political system. They are not allowed to organize politically, and any form of public protest on their part is quickly suffocated. "Supplication and silence win them little, but protest and organization are the traditional road to jail, exile and even death."[71] Among the organized minority, the labor and the agrarian sectors of the PRI are captives

[66] Vernon, *Dilemma*, p. 16.

[67] Robert J. Alexander, *Organized Labor in Latin America* (New York: Free Press, 1965), p. 197.

[68] Schmitt, "Congressional Campaigning," p. 97.

[69] Howard F. Cline, "Mexico: A Matured Latin-American Revolution, 1910–1960," *Annals of the American Academy of Political and Social Sciences* 334 (March 1961): 94.

[70] Vernon, *Dilemma*, p. 16; Alexander, *Organized Labor in Latin America*, p. 199.

[71] González Casanova, *La Democracia*, p. 123.

of the political elite, their leaders bribed and bought by the Revolutionary Coalition. Opposition parties are merely bourgeois interest groups organized to extract favors from the coalition. The Mexican governing elite is inclined neither to democratize its political institutions nor to devote increased resources to raising the standard of living of "marginal" Mexico.[72]

The González Casanova analysis appears to have captured more of the reality of Mexican politics than have those which emphasize the manifest functions of the official party, its sectors, the opposition parties, and the electoral process. The latent functions which these institutions perform, in particular the function of control of Mexican politics, have clearly predominated during the years since 1940.

The official party is used by the Revolutionary Coalition to control Mexican politics at two distinct levels. At the first level the PRI is used as a mechanism to attain majorities in municipal, state, and national elections. At the second it is used to control the various sectors of the party itself; the PRI structure provides access to large organized groups which can furnish the party with electoral majorities without granting those groups anything that could be reasonably labeled "effective representation."

One reason that the control aspect of the PRI has been neglected by many foreign observers is that the political elite does allow a substantial amount of pluralism in Mexican politics. Other parties are tolerated, indeed encouraged in some instances. An excellent example of the willingness to allow some opposition to develop is afforded by the recent electoral reforms which provided for some proportional representation in the federal Chamber of Deputies.

While a degree of political pluralism is not anathema to the Revolutionary Coalition, there is a great deal of evidence to suggest that effective competition will still not be tolerated. The most recent evidence involved the elections for municipal offices in Tijuana and Mexicali in 1968, and for the governorship of Yucatán in 1969. The two cities bordering the United States have a substantial degree of political and economic importance both in the state of Baja California and nationally. In each city the only opposition party in Mexico with any organized strength, the PAN, reportedly won the races for municipal president and obtained majorities in the city councils.[73] Shortly thereafter the state legislature, firmly controlled (as all of them are) by the PRI, annulled the election results.

The PRI loss of the municipal presidency of Mérida, the state capital of Yucatán, evoked a different response. In the 1967 municipal election in Mérida the PAN won political control and the PRI leaders allowed the results

[72] *Ibid.*, pp. 115ff.
[73] *Visión*, March 14, 1969.

to be validated. Since that time, however, the state government has constantly harassed the elected officials of Mérida, and in June of 1969 the state assumed control of the city's police force over the vociferous but ineffective opposition of Mérida's PAN officials.[74] When the Partido de Acción Nacional challenged the PRI in the gubernatorial contest later that fall, Yucatán witnessed one of the most violence-ridden campaigns in recent decades. The degree of skepticism which greeted the announcement of a PRI victory at the polls was high even in the Mexican setting.[75]

Throughout the past ten years the PAN, once very conservative and church-oriented but now competing with the PRI in the content of its socioeconomic pronouncements, has broadened its electoral support. The PRI's tolerance of competition, once risk-free, is just beginning to be tested. Given the rather contradictory evidence provided in Yucatán and Baja California, it is not at all clear whether the Revolutionary Coalition will respond to an effective challenge from the PAN at the polls with toleration or repression. It is manifest, however, that certain political challenges from the left will not be allowed. During the last presidential election, for example, the leftist *Frente Electoral del Pueblo* (FEP) was not allowed to register as a legal political party, and most of its leaders were jailed early in 1965.

At the second level of control, that is, at the level of the interest associations within the PRI itself, the willingness of the Revolutionary Coalition to expand the margins of genuine competition is yet to be documented. In fact the one major attempt during the 1960s to "democratize" procedures within the PRI was a total failure. Carlos Madrazo was named head of the party by President Díaz Ordaz in 1964, and during his brief term of office Madrazo attempted to introduce several reforms in party practices. In general he tried to strengthen the participation of party membership by reducing the number of decisions made behind closed doors by the party leadership. The method he chose was the party primary election at the municipal level; with it he hoped to replace the old nominating conventions which heretofore had listlessly approved the official slate of candidates presented to them. In 1965 such primaries were actually held in the states of Chihuahua and Baja California.

That a man convinced that the PRI had to democratize its methods of operation could be named head of the party would seem to indicate that some elements within the Revolutionary Coalition are willing to broaden the margins for competition. That Madrazo was removed from his post in less

---

[74] Daily reports of the conflict appear in leading Mexico City newspapers. See, for example, *Excelsior*, starting June 13, 1969.

[75] See accounts of the violence marking the campaign and election beginning October 2, 1969 in *Excelsior*.

than one year, and that all of his reforms went with him, suggests that the "reformers" are still in a decided minority.[76] In the five years since Madrazo's abrupt dismissal the PRI has continued to operate in its traditional manner. The disillusionment caused by the failure of the party to increase local-level participation and by the renewed imposition of nominees from above evidently led many former PRI adherents to support the victorious PAN candidates in Mérida and Hermosillo, the state capital of Sonora, in the 1967 elections.[77]

After his removal from the party's presidency Madrazo spoke often and openly about the "undemocratic and unresponsive" nature of the PRI. He condemned the entire system of choosing party leadership and warned of an increasing alienation from the PRI, especially among the young in Mexico.[78] In these public criticisms he was joined by another prominent former PRI leader and presidential aspirant, Manuel Moreno Sánchez. In a series of articles written for the Mexico City daily, *Excelsior*, in 1968 the latter castigated Mexico's political elite for rigging elections, choosing and imposing "obscure" and "ill-qualified" persons as PRI candidates for public office, and barring the emergence of any independent public opinion in Mexico. The result of such control, he argued, has been widespread corruption "which is never discussed much because each regime is indebted to its predecessor for being in power."[79]

### La Cosa Nuestra

The link observed by Moreno Sánchez between the PRI's control of Mexico and the problem of corruption, noted so often by those in a position to know, suggests a major reason why Mexico's Revolutionary Coalition as well as many of those co-opted into the PRI's hierarchy are unwilling to relinquish their dominant position in Mexican politics. Perhaps the most sweeping condemnation of the system established through the official party structure has been made by a one-time high government official and noted economist, Jesús Silva Herzog:

Politics degrades and corrupts everything. With painful frequency everything is subordinated to politics: government action, economic conve-

---

[76] Some of the opposition to Madrazo may well have been directed at his own political ambitions which, it was widely rumored, included the Mexican presidency. See, for example, the *New York Times*, December 29, 1967.

[77] *Latin American Digest* 3 (November 1968): 1.

[78] A summary of many of his views appeared in the *New York Times*, December 29, 1967.

[79] *Excelsior*, August 19, 1968. See also his articles in the issues of August 5, 12, and 26.

nience with regard to production, credit and technical expertise, etc.
There are big, medium and small politicians, giants and dwarfs, and one
finds them everywhere: in the offices and ante-rooms of public officials,
in schools, in labor unions, in cooperative societies and in the ejidos. The
politician is seldom considerate and honest, he is interested solely in
personal gain, he is the profiteer of the Revolution; on the ejido he
exploits the ejidatario, in the labor union he exploits the workers and
other employees, and in the schools he exploits his companions. *Politics is
the easiest and most profitable profession in Mexico.*

Immorality is the most alarming in the Federal Public Administration,
in the States and in the municipalities; the gangrene has spread, whether
from top to bottom or bottom to top we do not know. Many are the
public officials who have made fortunes in a few months without loss of
respectability. And this is the greatest of the evils. . . .[80]

The corruption and immorality of which Silva Herzog complained takes
many forms, some of which we have noted in reviewing the operation of the
political system. At the top of the political hierarchy, within the Revolutionary Coalition itself, major forms of personal gain have included both
illegal landholdings and unethical manipulation of public sector enterprises. A
former president of Mexico, Emilio Portes Gil, has publicly admitted the
accuracy of such charges, which have been well documented over the course
of the past three decades.[81] In doing so he also commented that "we must
recognize that administrative corruption has at times produced a climate of
virtual asphyxiation."[82]

Most often, of course, the personal gains derived from politics at the top
of the political system have not been obtained illegally. For example, the
nationalization of the oil industry in Mexico has proved highly profitable to
many leading politicians. First of all, the products from the state-owned
Pemex Company are generally transported by private trucking concerns,
usually the property of politicians. Second, when Pemex decided that filling
stations should remain in private hands the best locations were acquired by a
few revolutionary politicians, and an absence of competition converted a
filling station into an absolute monopoly. Finally, in the case of the few
petrochemical plants left to the private sector, politicians are conspicuous as
owners.

What happened as a result of the oil nationalization was not atypical. As
noted in chapter 2, the new group of industrialists which developed during
the late 1930s and 1940s often had very close personal connections with the

---

[80] Jesús Silva Herzog, "La Revolución mexicana en crisis," *Cuadernos americanos*
(1944): 33–34. Emphasis added.

[81] Silva Herzog, *El Agrarismo mexicano*, pp. 542ff.

[82] *Ibid.*, pp. 543–44.

revolutionary elite, and many of them got their start with public works contracts. In still other cases politicians in government positions have formed private enterprises to which they have then granted public contracts for government projects under their official control. Another variation on the same theme has been noted by a former minister of the treasury, Ramon Beteta. "Let us say that a public official knows that a highway is to be constructed and that he knows the person in charge of building or directing the work. He can buy, directly or indirectly, the land that will be affected by such a highway and thus obtain an advantageous position. This is not ethically right, but legally it is not a crime. And this kind of thing is quite common, much more so than people think."[83]

Whether through the direct sacking of the public coffers or through the use of the government apparatus in what Beteta calls the "less vulgar ways, unethical but legal," the co-opters and the co-opted who reach the top of the Mexican political ladder generally reap financial rewards that cushion their later years. "The top" includes cabinet members, managers of all the major state industries, directors of the large semiautonomous government agencies, commissions, banks and boards as well as the president of Mexico and his inner circle. During the six-year presidential term "the precise amount a cabinet minister or state-industry manager finally accumulates . . . largely depends on himself, although when grafting becomes excessive and injurious to his rule, the President of Mexico may step in and close some sources of a subordinate's income. The average minister or director finishes his term with two or three houses, a good library, two or three automobiles, a ranch, and $100,000 cash; about 25 directors and ministers hold posts from which they can leave office with fifty times that amount in cash."[84]

At the state level the stakes are lower, but the rules of the game are no different.[85] As one experienced observer commented, "our greatest problem in this state is that every four years we find ourselves obliged to turn out a rich governor. In the process of becoming rich, he bestows costly favors on relatives and friends, and he must also allow his subordinates to take at least enough to keep them quiet. . . . Would to God that a rich man would run for office!"[86] In another state which had just "elected" a former president of Mexico as its new governor the following comment was a commonplace: "We are glad that ex-President Abelardo Rodríguez is going to be our next gov-

---

[83] Quoted in Wilkie, *Mexican Revolution*, p. 8.

[84] Brandenburg, *Making of Modern Mexico*, p. 162.

[85] Here, as elsewhere in this chapter, the analysis is focused upon prevailing tendencies. Mexico, like any other country, has some scrupulously honest politicians and public servants.

[86] Quoted in Nathan L. Whetten, *Rural Mexico* (Chicago: University of Chicago Press, 1948), p. 549.

ernor because he is already a rich man and therefore won't need to accept so much graft as our previous governors. Perhaps he will be able to do something for the state of Sonora."[87]

At both the national and the state levels the chief executives, together with their inner circle of advisers and appointees to top administrative posts, retire at the end of their elective terms.[88] In doing so they do not lose their personal stake in seeing to it that the government of Mexico remains in the hands of persons favorably disposed toward their interests. Some departing officials are deeply involved in business enterprises that are dependent on governmental favor for credit and contracts.[89] Others hold large haciendas that can be broken up and distributed to the landless by any administration that should march to the beat of a different drummer. Indeed, with the passing of each administration the number of vested interests increases.

There is little reason, then, to wonder at the opposition which was raised to Madrazo's attempt to introduce free primary elections and other forms of direct participation in the official party's operations at the municipal level. Next in line would be primaries at the state level. And in the process the agrarian and labor sectors of the party might find their own spokesmen, ridding themselves of those so often imposed upon them at present. Such an evolution could only injure the special interests which the past thirty years of PRI politics have created. One small and insignificant yet highly revealing clash between such vested interests and the manifest goals of the revolution which the PRI publicly supports was observed and recorded in Nayarit over a decade ago. It is worth recounting because it captures in miniature all the ingredients of post-1930 Mexican politics, and because it demonstrates the general tendency of the latent or control aspects of Mexico's official party system to predominate over the manifest goals of the revolution to which that party pays homage.

Since the 1920s various Mexican governments have attempted to bring basic education to previously isolated rural areas. Thanks to the revolution and its aims, Mexico's work in rural education was undertaken long before comparable efforts were mounted in the rest of Latin America. In the late 1940s the government's Department of Education, in cooperation with UNESCO, engaged in what was called a Pilot Project in Basic Education in the state of Nayarit.[90] The program, in addition to incorporating basic education,

---

[87] *Ibid.*

[88] Some cabinet members occasionally retain their positions. For example, Antonio Ortíz Mena has now served for close to twelve consecutive years as secretary of the treasury.

[89] All businesses in Mexico are vulnerable to a host of governmental policies. See Vernon, *Dilemma*, chap. 1.

[90] The following account is drawn from Fisher, "Directed Culture Change."

was designed to "effect a more complete realization of cultural potentialities, democratic participation in community development, economic well-being and social justice."

The agricultural area in Nayarit chosen for the experiment consisted of *ejidal* lands. When the cultural mission from the Department of Education got to the valley, it discovered that the lands had been distributed in an illegal fashion. Some *ejidatarios* had as much as forty hectares of land; others had little or none. As Fisher commented, "*ejido* officials themselves are in the best position of all. It is said that in one *ejido* of 700 population, the president controls 100 hectares. . . . The president of another is building a nice house of his own in Santiago [a nearby town]." The mission leaders decided that the ideals of the pilot project could not be attained so long as the whole economic base rested on illegal procedures. They therefore turned to the agrarian department of the Mexican government to have the lands redistributed in accordance with Mexico's agrarian code.

Engineers from the agrarian department were sent to the valley, but the problem at issue was not resolved. "Far from adopting the methods of the Pilot Project, these engineers . . . according to rumors (heard many times, but not verified by this reporter) were open to bribes and worked in closer cooperation with the state political machine than with the Pilot Project. Land parcels were being reorganized, but with results no better than the previous situation." With the failure of the agrarian department to enforce the agrarian code, the Department of Education concluded that its program for integrated change of "culture" of the valley could not be carried out.

Why did the state *politicos* in Nayarit undermine the efforts of the Department of Education to have the *ejidal* lands redistributed according to law? Because, as Fisher points out, "the *ejido* system was an aid in reaching their goals of enjoying the benefits of political position. . . . Permitting certain members of the *ejido* communities to enjoy special privileges ensured their strong support for the political machine. As long as local *presidentes* of the *comisariados ejidales* received a personal gain from the unequal land distribution, they supported the higher authorities who allowed the system to continue."[91] An equitable redistribution of the land in question would have threatened the entire structure of political control; therefore it was not allowed to take place.

What happened in the little drama in Nayarit was that an attempt on the part of the Department of Education to implement the social goals of the Mexican revolution was effectively undermined by the latent operation of the revolution's own institutions. First, land distribution in the Nayarit *ejidos* was contrary to the revolution's goals of equal opportunity and in violation

[91] *Ibid.*, p. 153.

of agrarian statutes. Second, the *ejidal* presidents and commissions were not elected as prescribed, and therefore were not responsive to the desires and needs of *ejidal* members. Third, the agrarian sector of the PRI failed to act as a spokesman for the interests of its members and therefore offered no recourse for the victims of the illegalities. Fourth, the agrarian department did not implement the Mexican agrarian code, but instead worked in tandem with those state *políticos* who controlled the party's agrarian sector from without. The conflict which took place in Nayarit is repeated daily throughout Mexico, most often with the same result.

As Mexico enters the 1970s, political power within the country remains highly concentrated in the hands of the Revolutionary Family or Coalition, whose origins are found in the struggles of 1910-20 and whose political supremacy in Mexico was institutionalized with the founding of the official party in 1929. The coalition has exhibited enough coherence, self-consciousness, and will to common action in the years since 1930 to be accurately characterized as Mexico's political elite or, in S. F. Nadel's terminology, its "governing elite."[92] Top leaders retire every six years, but they choose their own successors. Admission to the elite circles is now controlled by revolutionary lineage and co-optation from above, not by demands or support from below. This leadership continues to decide who gets what, when and how.

The presence of a governing elite within a political system does not necessarily foreclose the possibility of "representative" government. Indeed, the view that a multiplicity of elites or leadership groups is compatible with democratic government has been expressed with increasing frequency by political scientists over the past two decades. An elite theory of democracy has emerged which bears very little resemblance to the classical democratic concepts found in the writings of such nineteenth-century interpreters as Jean-Jacques Rousseau and John Stuart Mill. Theorists of elitist democracy

---

[92] As Geraint Parry has noted, almost all definitions of the term "political elite" include the qualities of coherence, self-consciousness and unity vis-à-vis the rest of society. See Geraint Parry, *Political Elites* (New York: Frederick A. Praeger, 1969), pp. 31-32. Nadel distinguishes three types of elites: "social," "specialized" and "governing." The first two he conceives of as status groups. A social elite has no coercive power or monopoly over decision making, and exerts its influence indirectly. "Specialized" elites, the leaders of interest groups, are more directly involved in the political arena. They bargain with the political authorities on issues affecting their spheres of interest. Some of these specialized elites—for example, military officer groups and leading businessmen-bankers in less developed countries—may exercise a substantial degree of direct political influence. Nadel uses the phrase "governing elite" to refer to a country's political rulers, and argues that this group has "decisive pre-eminence" over both specialized and social elites, a pre-eminence deriving from its control over legislative and coercive authority. See S. F. Nadel, "The Concept of Social Elites," *International Social Science Bulletin* 8 (1956): 413-24. Nadel's distinctions offer an insightful characterization of elite relationships in the Mexican case.

argue that those outside a society's authority structure can and do gain access to political power and political influence through the competitive struggle among political elite groups for generalized as well as specific forms of support. As Talcott Parsons notes, the "key term in this approach is *access*. Those who have access to the political elite in the sense that sections of the latter, party leaders, office holders, officials of mass organizations, must consider how they will react to a given policy, have a share in the effective power, even if their participation is limited to voting every four years or less."[93]

The evidence introduced in chapters 3 through 5 suggests that in Mexico, however, access to the political elite by groups within two major sectors of the PRI and by the Mexican population in general is extremely limited. This lack of meaningful access is perhaps most fundamentally a result of the very carefully controlled nature of competition within the political elite, and thus the very limited bidding on the part of its members for support from labor and *campesino* organizations.[94] Therefore the characterization of the Mexican political system as one dominated by a governing elite goes beyond the assertion of a truism—that in every society political influence is distributed unevenly—to suggest that meaningful access to Mexico's authority structure is very limited, and that among those organizations often excluded from such access and influence are two of the three mainstays of the PRI itself, the labor and *campesino* sector organizations.

It follows that the economic development strategy which has emerged in Mexico over the past four decades is best understood as a reflection neither of official party interests nor of the sectoral demands within the PRI, but rather in terms of the interests and value-orientations of the country's self-renewing political elite. This conclusion raises two further sets of questions about the course of economic development in Mexico.

First, how can the interests and values of that governing group have encompassed both the programs to implement the social goals of the revolution which characterized the 1930s and the development strategy as it was constructed after 1940? Why has government policy favored Mexico's industrial-agricultural elite for the past thirty years when support from such groups was, at least during the early years, incidental to the Revolutionary Coalition's continued political hegemony? If not necessity, what factors have

---

[93] Quoted in Seymour Martin Lipset, *Revolution and Counterrevolution: Change and Persistence in Social Structures* (New York: Basic Books, 1968), pp. 430-31. See also Talcott Parsons, "Voting and the Equilibrium of the American Political System" in *American Voting Behavior*, edited by E. Burdick and A. Brodbeck (Glencoe, Ill.: Free Press, 1959), pp. 80-120. For an interesting summary discussion of the concepts of political elite groups and elitist democracy see Parry, *Political Elites.*

[94] See chapter 7 below.

accounted for this felicitous and fruitful cohabitation which Mexico's political leaders have taken the lead in developing? In sum, what motivations led Mexico's political leadership to choose the path to industrialization and economic development implicit in its economic and social policies? The following chapter will examine these questions.

Second, development strategy having been chosen, what political and social factors account for its successful implementation? Any government can adopt a set of internally consistent policies to promote economic growth; the evidence in the world around us is that few governments can implement such policies long enough to achieve the self-sustaining momentum which for several decades has characterized the Mexican economy. How has the Mexican political system contained the political and social stresses of the past thirty years within limits consistent with Mexico's development strategy? How has a system which has enriched its political and agricultural-industrial elites immeasurably while minimizing the welfare gains of the large majority of Mexico's population retained enough support to achieve political stability with a minimum of outright repression and a continuing claim to "legitimacy" apparently valid in the eyes of a remarkably high percentage of the Mexican people?[95] These questions are examined in chapter 7.

[95] See Gabriel A. Almond and Sidney Verba, *The Civic Culture* (Boston: Little, Brown & Co., 1963); and Scott, "Mexico, The Established Revolution" for evidence and interpretations of the high positive system affect noted in Mexico.

*Chapter 6*

# THE ROOTS OF MEXICAN POLITICS: THE SETTING, THE SEEKERS, AND THE SYSTEM

The origins of the present-day Mexican political system, its leaders and their values are deeply embedded in Mexico's nineteenth-century history. Indeed, their emergence begins one hundred years prior to the revolution of 1910. The political unity of the former Spanish colony was shattered by the very success of the war for independence, and Mexico soon displayed a socio-cultural fragmentation which for decades was to defy all efforts to reconstruct effective central government. Instead, government remained local, personal, and direct. Hidden behind imposing geographical barriers, many regions of Mexico obeyed only their local chieftains and recognized no other sources of authority. Military and political dispersion "was further increased by each hacienda that became, during this time, a political, military, and economic unit within its own borders."[1] During these decades of political chaos, however, one stratum of Mexican society slowly developed the capacity to master the centrifugal forces inherent in the Mexican mosaic. The goals of Mexico's nineteenth-century power seekers were for the most part very personal and parochial, but the effect of their efforts at mastery of Mexican politics was the creation of a nation where previously none had existed.

The political system which contributed immeasurably to the emergence of both political stability and economic development was first constructed during the rule of Porfirio Díaz (1876-1911). During these years, as noted earlier, Mexico experienced its first decades of modern economic growth. But the inherent inadequacies of the political system as it operated under the Porfirian dictatorship led almost inevitably to the Mexican revolution. And only after two further decades of political turmoil and resultant economic

[1]Frank Tannenbaum, *Peace by Revolution: Mexico After 1910*, 2nd ed. (New York: Columbia University Press, 1966), p. 90.

stagnation did the power seekers construct the much improved version of the Porfirian political system which for the past forty years has promoted and sustained economic development in Mexico.

## THE SETTING

The two major themes of interest in this chapter are (1) the origins and value orientations of Mexico's political elite, and (2) the political system which its members have developed and refined since the 1870s. By way of background, however, some attention must be given to the postindependence social and political setting from which that elite group emerged. In Mexico, as in most of Hispanic America, independence was accompanied by a collapse of political authority at the national level. The ensuing political instability in Mexico produced fifty-six different governments during the forty years between 1821 and 1861. No Mexican president completed an elective term after 1828.

The sudden collapse of authority in Mexico and elsewhere in Latin America after independence is generally attributable to the fact that a patrimonial state had lost its vital center.[2] In theory, colonial organization was shaped in a pyramid of power, with the king at the apex. Reality was quite different. As one scholar recently noted, "the organization of political power in the Indies . . . could be better compared to a circle whose radii come all from the crown."[3] According to another, "The king ruled and legislated; the king named the authorities and in his behalf justice was administered; settlers and Indians were vassals of the monarch; the king was owner of lands and water which he granted as rewards. . . . During the three centuries of Spanish colonialism, the king was everything."[4]

The crown, then, was the one and only source of true authority in the colonies. And with the disappearance of this single legitimizing political institution in 1821 there was none other to bind Mexican society together. "Decapitated, the government could not function, for the patrimonial regime had developed neither (1) the underpinning of contractual vassalic relationships that capacitate the component parts of a *feudal* regime for autonomous life;

[2] For an extended discussion, see Richard M. Morse, "The Heritage of Latin America," in *The Founding of New Societies*, edited by Louis Hartz (New York: Harcourt, Brace and World, 1964).

[3] Ricardo Zorraquín Becú, *La Organización política argentina en el periodo hispánico*, 2nd ed. (Buenos Aires: Editorial Perrot, 1962), quoted in Frank Jay Moreno, "The Spanish Colonial System: A Functional Approach," *Western Political Quarterly* 20 (June 1967): 316.

[4] Jesús de Galíndez, *Iberoamérica: su evolución política socio-económica, cultural e internacional* (New York: Las Americas Publishing Co., 1954), quoted in Moreno, "The Spanish Colonial System," p. 316.

nor (2) a nationalized legal order not dependent for its operation and claims to assent upon personalistic intervention by the highest authority."[5] With the collapse of regal authority the absence of anything resembling social cohesion in Mexico became immediately apparent. As one student of the period has put it, "There were indians, castes, nobles, soldiers, priests, merchants and lawyers but there were no citizens."[6] A similar conclusion was reached by a contemporary observer in 1847: "In Mexico that which is called national spirit cannot nor has been able to exist, for there is no nation."[7]

At the bottom of the social scale in this fragmented society were the Indians, who numbered some 55 percent of Mexico's six million inhabitants in 1821. The indigenous population had been placed in a class legally and socially apart from the rest of Mexican society by the Spanish conquerors. Indians were considered wards of the state and were subject to their own laws, a situation which entailed both advantages and disadvantages. On the one hand, the Indians were excused from some forms of taxation, and seldom subjected to fine or imprisonment. On the other hand they were denied citizenship, were forced to pay a tribute to the crown, were isolated into ghettos in urban areas, and in many other ways were legally prevented from rising above their subject status.[8]

About three-quarters of the Indian population continued to live in isolated rural communities which had been instituted and protected by crown policy ever since the sixteenth century. Subject to royal supervision, these communities had managed their internal affairs through their own elected officials. Each community was granted a legal charter and communal lands, and was equipped with a communal treasury. Although this local social unit constructed by crown officials did not envisage a return to the pre-Hispanic Indian community, "so well did it meet the needs of the Indian peasant that he could take it up and make it his own."[9] Developed almost four centuries ago, its features are still visible in Mexico's predominantly Indian communities today, and were of course even more prominent when Mexico achieved independence a century and a half ago.

[5] Morse, "Heritage of Latin America," p. 161. Morse applies this description to all of Hispanic America.

[6] L. N. McAlister, "Social Structure and Social Change in New Spain," *Hispanic American Historical Review* 43 (August 1963): 349-70.

[7] Quoted in Charles A. Hale, *Mexican Liberalism in the Age of Mora, 1821-1853* (New Haven: Yale University Press, 1968), p. 14.

[8] Many managed to evade the laws, however. See, for example, Eric Wolf's discussion of Indians in the Bajío region in his essay, "The Mexican Bajío in the Eighteenth Century," in *Synoptic Studies of Mexican Culture*, edited by Robert Wauchope (New Orleans: Tulane University, Middle American Research Institute, 1957), pp. 177-99.

[9] Eric R. Wolf, *Sons of the Shaking Earth* (Chicago: University of Chicago Press, Phoenix Books, 1959), p. 214.

For our purposes the most significant fact about these communities in 1821 was their contribution to the fragmentation of Mexican society. The isolated, autonomous, and self-sufficient nature of these corporate institutions reinforced the separateness which had characterized pre-Hispanic Indian life in Mexico. To the original legion of Indian tribes and languages were now added these geographical divisions of Indian society. This new localism so effectively prevented a consolidation of Indian interests and loyalties that throughout the centuries which followed their organization no two towns ever united in defense of common interests against the encroachment of the haciendas and other creole and mestizo forms of economic organization which gradually usurped Indian lands, waters and pastures.[10]

The depth to which this pattern of fragmentation was embedded in rural Mexico is evidenced in the fact that even after the 1910 revolution localism and particularism continued to overwhelm the forces for unity and homogeneity set in motion by the decade of upheaval. The following passage from a study undertaken during the 1920s of the Indian population adjacent to Mexico City offers vivid testimony to this observation:

> The native is incapable of comprehending the idea of the country. . . . He does not know that Mexico is a Republic nor do his rights and obligations as a citizen interest him. . . .
>
> The only manifestation of solidarity and love of country among the natives is the absolute and almost irrational affection that they feel for their village.
>
> Although it is impossible for them to understand not only the existence of the larger political entity of which they form a part, but also of the state or municipal government to which they belong, on the other hand they deeply love their village, and this affection is sometimes manifested in violent forms.
>
> The deepest hatred exists between the inhabitants of neighboring villages; old quarrels have divided them from time immemorial, and like nations that fight to the death for their autonomy the villages have their rural struggles. . . . It seems that time has not passed and that the organization of the villages is the same as in the ages of the [Spanish] viceroy. The hatreds and the sympathies have the same force and the same origins as they did three hundred years ago.
>
> The villages of San Francisco Mazapán and San Martín de las Pirámides are an eloquent testimony to this fact. They are divided by a street in such a fashion that to the outsider they form a single community. The inhabitants continuously go from one village to the other, and they have the same customs. Nevertheless, a deep and inextinguishable

[10] Charles Gibson, *The Aztecs under Spanish Rule* (Stanford, Cal.: Stanford University Press, 1964), p. 405.

hatred has divided them from time immemorial . . . without anyone today knowing the cause of this antipathy.[11]

Directly above the Indians on the social scale as it was inherited from colonial Mexico were the *castas*, the offspring of racially mixed liaisons. The predominant caste group was the mestizo, the product of Spanish-Indian unions. By 1821 the *castas* represented somewhere between one-third and one-half of the population of Mexico, and by the end of the century they were to predominate both numerically and politically.

On the eve of independence, however, their situation was quite different. The mestizos were generally rejected by both parental ethnic groups. Like the Indian, the mestizo faced innumerable legal barriers to his economic and social mobility. He could hold no political post, nor could he practice most of the professions. Certain residential areas were also forbidden to him. Some mestizos were able to move up from the caste into the *criollo* segment of Mexico's social structure as their economic circumstances improved, for the social lines in the country were always determined more by wealth and its accoutrements than by racial origins. But the lack of sizeable or growing commercial and manufacturing sectors in the Mexican economy severely limited the opportunities for economic and social mobility. In rural Mexico the spread of the hacienda system also constricted the development of a rural middle class through which the mestizo might have risen above his psychologically and economically frustrating caste status.[12]

So limited were the general economic opportunities and so oppressive were the social and cultural barriers to the integration of the *castas* into creole society that the mestizos eventually posed a serious problem for the colonial elite groups. The caste population in urban slums, often referred to as *léperos*, survived by begging, robbing and looting; on several occasions in the colonial years they were the center of riots that verged on full rebellion. Nor were such mestizo activities restricted to urban areas. "Banditry between Veracruz and Mexico City was endemic, and foolhardy indeed was the man who journeyed from any city to another without an escort. . . . The European interpreted these unwholesome activities as manifestations of a blood taint,

[11] Carlos Noriega Hope, "Apuntes etnográficos," in *La Población del valle de Teotihuacán*, edited by Manuel Gamio (Mexico: Dirección de Talleres Gráficos, 1922), Vol. 2, 263–64.

[12] In some regions of Mexico, particularly in the Bajío, industrial-commercial complexes did develop which provided opportunities for socio-economic advancement for both the Indian and caste populations. See, for example, Eric Wolf's excellent account in "The Mexican Bajío." But the Bajío region was an exception to the general pattern. See Hugh M. Hamill, Jr., *The Hidalgo Revolt* (Gainesville: University of Florida Press, 1966), pp. 48–52.

about which he could do little, instead of the harvest of a degrading system, about which he could have done much."[13]

At the apex of Mexico's society on the eve of independence was the "white" or European segment.[14] The fragmentation which characterized it was not cultural and geographical, as in the case of the Indian population, but rather a matter of class and status. With some obvious simplifications for the purposes of analysis we can speak of three divisions within this European segment. At the top, and therefore at the apex of the entire colonial social structure, were the *peninsulares*, the numerically inferior but politically and socially superior group whose members had been born in Spain. Below them were the *criollos*, those of Spanish descent born in Mexico. This creole group itself is best analyzed in two distinct segments, the European and the American creoles.[15]

The frictions and deep-seated hostilities which separated the *peninsulares* from the creoles resulted from the privileged position accorded to the former group in colonial Mexico. Outnumbered by at least twenty to one within a total "white" population slightly in excess of one million by 1821, the *peninsulares* controlled literally all of the top administrative positions within the colony as well as a large portion of Mexico's total wealth. With a few exceptions, high colonial offices in both church and state were bestowed upon them, and these crown officials in turn favored their European-born compatriots with lower echelon appointments and privileges.

Among the special concessions granted to the European-born were the generally very profitable private trading monopolies which enriched the *peninsulares* while tending to obstruct the spread of colonial manufacturing enterprises. In addition, they controlled the administration of government monopolies such as tobacco processing, which remained in the hands of Spanish-born officials throughout the colonial period. During the course of three centuries a small group of Spanish merchants controlled all legal import trade, and they limited the volume of European goods and charged exorbitant prices. Through a "tortured" interpretation of the original charters, these merchants were able to retain the commercial privilege for *peninsulares* alone, severely hampering creole trading activity. "The entire mercantile system,

[13] Charles C. Cumberland, *Mexico: The Struggle for Modernity* (London: Oxford University Press, 1968), pp. 57–58.

[14] It should be emphasized again that social distinctions were more economically and culturally than racially determined. Both Indian and mestizo could rise to the elite circles, though circumstances rarely permitted them to do so. For an excellent discussion of the problem applicable to all Latin America see Charles Wagley, "On the Concept of Social Race in the Americas," in *Contemporary Cultures and Societies of Latin America*, edited by Richard N. Adams and Dwight B. Heath (New York: Random House, 1965), pp. 531–45.

[15] This distinction is made by Hugh Hamill in *Hidalgo Revolt*, pp. 33ff.

with its emphasis on the economic advantages accruing to the [*peninsulares*] almost to the exclusion of the *criollo*, probably did more to push the creole toward independence than did any other single royal policy."[16] In addition to the wealth which the *peninsulares* were able to command as a result of their near monopoly on high church and state offices, their ownership of haciendas and mines in the colony further cemented their economic predominance within the white segment of Mexican society.

The creole population in Mexico bitterly resented its exclusion from the higher and more lucrative posts in colonial government. The depth of its resentment was partially due to the fact that creole exclusion from high administrative office in church and state severely limited their opportunities for upward economic and social mobility. Some *criollos* were able to live on the income they derived from entailed estates (*mayorazgos*), but the majority had to earn their living occupying minor administrative posts or practicing in the overcrowded and highly competitive professions, chiefly in law.[17] The lack of business opportunities and secular posts forced many young *criollos* to rely upon lower echelon church positions for sustenance—"far too many . . . for the seven bishoprics to absorb," wrote one eighteenth-century complainant. "Between the desire for a personal livelihood and the necessity of supporting an impoverished family, men were taking orders who were more inclined to empty people's pockets than to fill their souls."[18]

Not all creoles were frustrated by the lack of financial opportunity in the essentially static colonial Mexican economy.[19] A marked difference in economic well-being necessitates a distinction between what have been called the European and the American creole. The former maintained closer ties to Spain, perhaps because he was the son of a *peninsular* or because he had been educated in Europe. Often he retained business connections with Spain, or lived off the proceeds of a large hacienda. The fact that he was generally rich and propertied minimized the European creole's discontent with his secondary social status and led him to support the royalist cause in the abortive Hidalgo revolt against Spanish rule in 1810.

The American creole was generally neither rich nor a member of the colonial aristocracy. A significant portion of this group consisted of what have been called "*criollos de la plebe*," petty municipal officials, artisans, night watchmen and "unemployed riffraff."[20] The more industrious and ag-

---

[16] Cumberland, *Struggle for Modernity*, p. 106.

[17] Hamill, *Hidalgo Revolt*, chapter 1.

[18] *Ibid.*, p. 29.

[19] Again the dynamism of the Bajío economy, where mining, commercial agriculture and the beginnings of a manufacturing sector came together by the late eighteenth century, offers a sharp contrast to this generalization.

[20] Hamill, *Hidalgo Revolt*, p. 35.

gressive American creoles found employment as small ranchers, storekeepers, and members of the professions. Toward the end of the eighteenth century the growth of the colonial militia and professional army provided a new avenue of social and economic mobility. Indeed, the new army had as an explicitly stated aim the provision of status-conferring careers for creoles in the officer crops and the *castas* in the ranks.[21]

The fragmented nature of Mexican society and the absence of social cohesion inherent in the Mexican system of social stratification were vividly demonstrated during the decade between 1810 and 1820. The first attempt to achieve independence was instigated by some prominent members of the American creole group whose dissatisfaction with their place in society finally led them to seek an end to Spanish rule. But the Hidalgo revolt of 1810 immediately kindled the fierce resentments of Mexico's mestizos and some of the country's Indians, and their bloody uprising soon cooled the ardor of the creole class for independence. Concerned only with their own socio-economic standing, most creoles, American and European, rallied to the royalist cause in defense of their own class interests. The caste uprising was quickly crushed, but not before mestizo and Indian hatreds, concealed for centuries behind the masks of docility and submissiveness, had been revealed. In 1821 independence was won not for these elements of Mexican society, but for the creole class in general and in particular for the wealthier and more conservative elements within it that were repelled by the liberal tendencies of the new constitutionalist government in Spain. The successful revolt therefore involved little more than a minor shifting at the apex of Mexican society, where the conservative creole replaced the conservative *peninsular*. Beyond this the new rulers sought to retain the old patterns of stratification. Whether landowners, merchants, church officials or members of the army's officer class, the new ruling creoles shared the same narrow sense of class privilege of those *peninsulares* whom they replaced.

They opposed further change but, in the long run, did so unsuccessfully, for they had severed Mexico from the one institution whose legitimacy had been effective in restraining the centrifugal tendencies inherent in Mexican society for several hundred years—the Spanish crown. And when legitimacy failed, force inevitably prevailed. So began the open and often violent struggle for power in independent Mexico and the rise of Mexico's power seekers who rule the country today.

## THE SEEKERS

Because men cannot live together without entering into relationships of influence, all societies develop political systems which mirror those relation-

---

[21] McAlister, "Social Structure and Social Change," p. 369.

ships. And every society produces its power seekers, those who strive to increase their own influence by gaining control of the state. It is quite natural that the state should be at the center of struggles over power since it generally disposes of a significant portion of a society's resources and has an exclusive claim to the legitimate use of coercion in defense of a society's interests. The power gained through control of the state can be and has been used to seek a wide spectrum of goals, including among other things fame, security, respect, affection and wealth. "In its instrumental character, power is like money. Some men invest more effort in gaining money than others do; they do not necessarily do so because they value money, as such, more highly than others but because they see money as an instrument to other goals."[22] To comprehend the nature of twentieth-century Mexican development we must understand the goals sought by Mexico's power seekers and the motive forces which propelled them to their present predominant position in Mexican politics.

During the first years of independence, politics was still the province of the creole class in Mexico. But divisive tendencies within this elite proved its undoing, and within a half century political control had passed into the hands of Mexico's mestizo population.[23] The mestizo threw himself into the struggle for power that was precipitated by Mexican independence because he had so little to lose and so much to gain. As Eric Wolf has noted, his rise to power resembles the experience of the European middle class only superficially. In contrast to that segment of the European social spectrum which had both a place and a stake in constituted society, the mestizos shared

> not a common stake in society but a lack of such a stake; they shared *a common condition of social alienation*. . . . In their common estrangement from society, the petty official, the political fixer, the hard-pressed rancher, the hungry priest, found a common denominator with the Indian bereft of the protection of his community . . . the petty trader or cattle-rustler, the half employed pauper of the streets, the ragamuffin of the Thieves Market. Such men constituted neither a middle class nor a proletariat; they belonged to a social shadow-world.[24]

The mestizo was disinherited by both Mexican societies, Indian and creole. Without a place in the social order, he had lived for generations by his wits, his dissimulation. These qualities, cultivated for survival prior to independence, were of equal value after 1821. The adaptive nature of the

[22] Robert A. Dahl, *Modern Political Analysis* (Englewood Cliffs, N.J.: Prentice-Hall, 1965), p. 68.

[23] As Andrés Molina Enríquez noted, however, creole social and economic influence effectively blunted the forces of change which metizo political leadership might have entailed until after the revolution of 1910. See *Los Grandes problemas nacionales* (Mexico: Imprenta de A. Carranza e Hijos, 1909), chap. 5.

[24] Wolf, *Sons of the Shaking Earth*, p. 242. Emphasis added.

mestizo's personality allowed him to take full advantage of the opportunities for his own upward mobility presented by the social and economic instability which accompanied the ensuing period of political chaos.[25]

A further product of the mestizo's social marginality which proved invaluable in his rapid rise to political prominence in the nineteenth century was his attitude toward power and its uses. The mestizo valued power above all other personal attributes, for power was the one instrument "that would make people listen where society granted him no voice and obey where the law yielded him no authority. Where the Indian saw power as an attribute of office and redistributed it with care lest it attach itself to persons, the mestizo would value power as an attribute of the self, as *personal energy that could subjugate and subject people.*"[26]

The mestizo's pathological fascination with and craving for power was eventually to have serious adverse consequences for all attempts to introduce democratic forms of government in Mexico. The mestizo viewed power as an attribute of the self, not of the group; consequently the group was used by him to attain personal, not collective, goals. This conception also led him to view life as a constant combat. One wins or loses; there is no middle ground. To the present day this characteristic of mestizo psychology pervades Mexican public life. Almost a century after the mestizo's rise to power Octavio Paz was to write that the "conception of social life as combat fatally divides [Mexican] society into the strong and the weak. The strong—the hard, unscrupulous *chingones*—surround themselves with eager followers. This servility toward the strong, especially among the *politicos*, is one of the more deplorable consequences of the situation. Another, no less degrading, is the devotion to personalities rather than to principles. . . . The only thing of value is manliness, personal strength, a capacity for imposing oneself on others."[27]

The "Ishmaels" of Mexican society embraced the struggle for power in the decades following independence not only because they had so little to lose, but also because political and military power offered them the surest and best-recognized road to economic and social advancement. Spanish mercantilist policies and general economic conditions had limited the scope of colonial industrialization and left the commercial sector for the most part in the hands of the *peninsulares* and the creole elite. Rural Mexico was dominated by large haciendas and Indian pueblos. Finally, the Catholic Church, the country's largest landlord, may have held close to half of Mexico's total

[25] *Ibid.*, chap. 11; and Octavio Paz, *The Labyrinth of Solitude: Life and Thought in Mexico* (New York: Grove Press, 1961), chap. 2.

[26] Wolf, *Sons of the Shaking Earth*, p. 239. Emphasis added.

[27] Paz, *Labyrinth*, pp. 78-79. Paradoxically, this mestizo attitude toward power and personal relations, while wholly incompatible with democratic forms of government, has undoubtedly served to support political stability under Mexico's present regime. This point will be developed in the following chapter.

liquid wealth. This economic setting offered little room for mestizos on the make. The wars for independence plunged Mexico into a prolonged period of economic stagnation, further limiting the mobility opportunities available through economic enterprise. Furthermore, manual labor was held degrading in the creole value system, discouraging those mestizos influenced by *criollo* standards from undertaking many forms of economic activity. As before independence, therefore, public employment with its perquisites was universally desired and avidly sought.

The use of public office for personal enrichment in Mexico had for so long been a norm of elite behavior that a guide book for political aspirants, written in 1777, detailed the proceeds which colonial offices were thought to be worth.[28] Offices were purchased and sold, and some bright entrepreneurs "bought positions merely on speculation, tendering other offices in payment."[29] Under Spanish rule the crown was defrauded from the highest office to the lowest, and the forms which corruption took defy enumeration. With independence this pattern continued; only the beneficiaries changed.

The period between 1820 and 1850 has been aptly characterized as one of "ephemeral alignments for a massed assault on the treasury." Loyalties were reduced to the most personal kinds, "to the man who at the moment appeared most likely to promote one's own fortunes."[30] During these years of political and social disarray government service, particularly the military profession, offered the only dependable means of livelihood. Even the chaotic conditions did not prevent the collection of public revenues, whether by force, fraud, promises, or threats. As might be expected, the army was the chief beneficiary, and the military career the most profitable of the professions. The army "collected what money it could from the budget through rebellion, forced loans, pillage and theft," lending its support first to one presidential aspirant then another regardless of the candidate's political leanings.[31] Each overthrow offered significant opportunities for mobility. The lieutenant who participated in several successful uprisings was soon a general, and a Mexican general in those days was a very rich man. Thus the military element in Mexico destroyed at least a dozen federal governments between independence and the victory of Benito Juárez in the reform era, often aided by a civilian bureaucracy whose appetite for the spoils of office was as consuming as its own.

During this period, and under rules of the game which rewarded deceit and personalism rather than dedication and loyalty to institutions and ideas, the mestizo was baptized into Mexican politics. The opportunity was pre-

[28] Gibson, *The Aztecs*, p. 96.

[29] Ernest Henry Gruening, *Mexico and Its Heritage* (New York: Century Co., 1928), p. 20.

[30] *Ibid.*, p. 51.

[31] Tannenbaum, *Peace by Revolution*, p. 80.

sented because of a growing split in the ruling creole class. One segment, the conservatives, strove to minimize change in postindependence Mexican society and politics. They defended the corporate privileges of the church and the army, some from conviction and others from a belief that undermining either institution would inevitably call into question further privileges—specifically, their own. The church and the army, recognizing the mutual benefits to be derived from such solidarity, soon began to support each other's legal status and social position; together they successfully advocated high property and income qualifications for political office to ensure continued conservative rule.

The other segment of the creole class, generally referred to as the moderates, sought to break the corporate privilege that had elevated both church and army to a position of states within a state. Strongly influenced by the continental liberalism of Benjamin Constant and the attempts at Spanish reform under the Bourbons in the late eighteenth century, the moderates aimed at creating a juridically uniform and fiscally strong secular state.[32] In time the *moderados* came to view the church as particularly intolerable. Not only was it a separate juridical entity; it also absorbed a large percentage of the country's liquid capital which, its opponents felt, should be put to work creating Mexican industries and commercial agriculture. Furthermore, as the country's major property-holding institution it blocked another goal of the moderates—the development of a rural sector comprising family farms. Finally, the church was accused of financing the conservatives' hold over the government and the army, and of withholding support from moderate President Gomez Farías when he tried to repel the U.S. invasion of Mexico in 1847. Thus the church became the focus of the reform movement, and was at the vortex of the War of the Reform (1857-60). The conservative forces, defeated by a coalition of creole moderates and mestizo liberals, turned to the French for assistance. Napoleon III generously supplied them with an army and Archduke Maximilian, whose death in 1867 at the hands of the once-again victorious liberals finally dissolved the political power of Mexico's conservative creole aristocracy.

The mestizos emerged from the reform period with the political destiny of Mexico in their hands. Serving their apprenticeship in the army and the bureaucracy during the 1820s and 1830s, they maximized the advantages inherent in the creole split. At the national level a group of intellectual leaders appeared, consisting mostly of lawyers and bureaucrats, which pressed for the abolition of corporate privileges, the destruction of caste distinctions, and above all the confiscation of church property. Only by breaking the

[32] See Hale, *Mexican Liberalism*, especially chaps. 1 and 9 for an admirable exposition of the contending ideas in Mexican politics during this period.

power of the "haves" could the mestizos facilitate their own socio-economic mobility, and these so-called *puros* supplied much of the ideological support for the programs implemented by the liberals in the reform period.[33]

It was at the local and regional level, however, that the foundations of enduring mestizo political strength were developing. The collapse of centralized authority in independent Mexico gradually led to the appearance of those mestizo *caciques* who were to dominate their regions so forcefully and to oppose central government so successfully that it was said of one of them "not a leaf could stir in the entire territory without his consent."[34] These provincial *caciques*, particularly predominant in northern Mexico where mestizo *rancheros*, laborers and peasants outnumbered Indians, and where church activities were less pronounced, became the backbone of the liberal military forces which finally defeated both the conservative and the imperial armies.

So successful were these regional mestizo chieftains in concentrating power in their own hands, and so psychologically incapable were they of relinquishing their newly gained power to the civilian leaders of the liberal party, that civil strife and rebellion constantly punctuated the decade between the victory of the liberals in 1867 and the power grab of Porfirio Díaz in 1876. So long as its revered leader, Benito Juárez, lived, the civilian element in the liberal party withstood the challenge of the military *caciques*. The latter group was informally led by Díaz, who had emerged from the wars of the reform period as Mexico's leading military figure. Following the death of President Juárez the civilian element fell prey to internal dissension and external pressures, and in 1876 Díaz, supported by most of Mexico's new regional strongmen, finally succeeded in overthrowing the civilian regime.[35] Ishmaels no longer, the power seekers were home—at the apex of Mexican politics.

*THE SYSTEM*

Since its independence Mexico has experienced only two extended periods of political stability. The first covered the years between 1876 and 1911; Porfirio Díaz served as president for all but four of these years (1880–84). The second has covered the four decades since 1930. The problems faced by Díaz and the political system which he constructed to manage

[33] On the rise of the *puros* see Molina Enríquez, *Los Grandes problemas*, part 1, chap. 3; and François Chevalier, "Conservateurs et liberaux au Mexique," *Cahiers d'histoire mondiale* 8 (1964).

[34] Henry Bamford Parkes, *A History of Mexico* (Boston: Houghton Mifflin Co., 1950), p. 180.

[35] On the conflicts within the liberal party and the rise of the regional *caciques* see Vicente Fuentes Díaz, *Los Partidos políticos en México*, vol. 1, pp. 50ff.

them reveal so many startling similarities to the challenges which confronted the Revolutionary Coalition in the 1920s and the system which it developed in response to them that a few generalizations about Mexican politics, elite values and economic development can be set forth with some degree of assurance. Likewise, an understanding of the reasons for the ultimate failure of the Díaz system and of the improvements on that system developed by the Revolutionary Coalition provide some basis for interpreting the fundamental sources of stability in present-day Mexican politics.

## The Peace of Porfirio

Porfirio Díaz ruled Mexico for thirty-one years, twenty-seven of them consecutively. This political calm followed a period of fifty years during which governments fell on the average of more than once a year. An era of widespread violence, civil wars and rebellion gave way to one of relative tranquility, in which sporadic outbreaks of warfare were eliminated with singular dispatch. This relative political calm laid the foundations for several decades of modest but steady economic growth. So startling is the contrast between these trends in the Díaz period and the political turmoil and economic stagnation which preceded it that the rule of Porfirio Díaz was indeed "the political and economic miracle of nineteenth century Mexico."[36] What were the foundations of the political "miracle?"[37]

Francisco Madero, the man who led the overthrow of Díaz in 1911, contended that the dictator had but one fixed idea—to achieve power and hold it indefinitely.[38] Both the record of the Díaz years and the general mestizo conception of power and its personal attributes support Madero's contention. The passion to hold on to power was both a strength and a weakness in Díaz's system. In the short run it gave him a tremendous advantage over such predecessors as Benito Juárez, who had been concerned with

[36] Stanley R. Ross, *Francisco I. Madero: Apostle of Mexican Democracy* (New York: Columbia University Press, 1955), p. 20.

[37] The following analysis of politics under Díaz is based upon these works: Carleton Beals, *Porfirio Diaz: Dictator of Mexico* (Philadelphia: J. B. Lippincott, 1932); Francisco Bulnes, *El Verdadero Díaz y la revolución* (Mexico: Editoria Nacional, 1952); Francisco Bulnes, *The Whole Truth about Mexico* (New York: M. Bulnes Book Co., 1916); Daniel Cosío Villegas, *Historia moderna de México*, vol. 2, *La República restaurada*, and vol. 7, *El Porfiriato* (Mexico: Editorial Hermes, 1965); Charles C. Cumberland, *Mexican Revolution: Genesis under Madero* (Austin: University of Texas Press, 1952); Fuentes Díaz, *Los Partidos políticos*; Gruening, *Mexico and Its Heritage*; Francisco I. Madero, *La Sucesión presidencial en 1910* (San Pedro, Coahuila: n. p., 1908); Molina Enríquez, *Los Grandes problemas*; Moisés González Navarro, *Historia moderna de México*, vol. 4, *La Vida social* (Mexico: Editorial Hermes, 1957); Parkes, *History of Mexico*; Ross, *Madero*; and José C. Valadés, *El Porfirismo*, vol. 1 (Mexico: Antigua Librera Robredo, de José Porrua e Hijos, 1941), and Vol. 2 (Mexico: Editorial Patria, 1948).

[38] Madero, *La Sucesión presidencial*, pp. 118-19.

politics for *what* as well as for *whom.* Concerned only with retaining power, Díaz could follow two relatively simple precepts: (1) ignore those individuals and groups that lack the capacity for effective political action; and (2) buy off all those politically active groups and individuals that can be bought, and liquidate those that cannot.

Following the first precept, Díaz totally ignored the welfare of 35 percent of Mexico's population, the Indian segment.[39] The continued lack of social cohesion among Indian groups and the passivity which they assumed in relationships with mestizos and creoles made them the natural victims of the Díaz system of government. As related in chapter 2, it was often the remaining Indian farmlands, pastures and water rights that were used to pacify the more articulate groups in Mexico's political spectrum. By 1910 about 90 percent of Mexico's rural families owned no land, and approximately 85 percent of the country's Indian communities had lost all their holdings. The remaining 15 percent eked out a living on fractions of their former lands. In addition, some of Porfirio's closest friends became millionaires by selling Yaqui Indians into slavery. In the long run, of course, the policies dictated by this precept proved disastrous for the Díaz political system. They led directly to what has aptly been called the "last great Indian uprising," one of the two major strands of the Mexican Revolution of 1910.[40]

The Díaz policies toward the Indians were not very different from those of the dictator's creole and *peninsular* predecessors. It was with regard to the other elements in Mexican society, to which his second precept was applied, that the Díaz system revealed both its novelty and its striking resemblance to the present system of Mexican politics. In a country still fragmented geographically and culturally and lacking in social cohesion and legitimate institutions of authority, the most essential rule in the politics of stability was to buy off all possible individuals and groups capable of armed opposition. Therefore, rather than oppose those mestizo *caciques* who had risen to power in various regions of Mexico and in the federal army, as Juárez had done, Díaz made their strength his own. He did so by granting to those who cooperated rewards too great to be risked in revolt. The military barons among the *caciques* and army generals were granted state governorships (twenty-seven), *jefaturas políticas* (district political offices of which there were three hundred), and military commands which provided ample opportunity for

---

[39] Again it should be remembered that those Indians who left their pueblos and adopted mestizo mores were accepted as mestizos. The Indians who were ignored were those who continued to live as Indians, forming what Charles Wagley calls a "social race" as opposed to a biological race.

[40] The phrase belongs to M. L. Chávez Orozco. See François Chevalier, "Un Facteur décisif de la revolution agraire en Mexique: le soulevement de Zapata, 1911–1919," *Annales economies sociétés civilisations* 16 (January–February 1961).

personal enrichment. Monopolies on gambling establishments, houses of prostitution, and the supply of food and clothing for the army were the most common sources of revenue for such appointees, though the record is replete with more exotic approaches to social and economic mobility at this level of Mexican society under Díaz.[41]

While buying off the *cacique* generals, Díaz simultaneously weakened their capacity for revolt. He made some of them governors, then proceeded to shift their personal troops to far parts of Mexico where they were either placed under someone else's command or slowly disbanded. Some of these military governors held their offices for life; those whom Díaz retired, like Generals Treviño and Francisco Cantón, were given railway and other concessions which netted them millions of pesos. In other instances Díaz would balance the mestizo strongmen against each other to weaken their capacity for disturbing the Porfirian peace. A favorite practice was to place generals with large personal followings in states ruled by strong governors where each would checkmate the ambitions of the other. In the northeast, for example, where the mestizo generals Treviño and Maranja became governors, the leading military figure, Bernardo Reyes, was made chief of operations of the army. Years later, when Reyes himself, as governor of Nuevo León, was developing a large popular following, Díaz rebuilt the strength of General Treviño to retain a balance of ambitions which would leave Porfirio the ultimate arbiter of events, not only in the northeast but throughout Mexico.

Below the state level other *caciques* with strong regional bases of power were made *jefes políticos,* district political chiefs. At this level, as at the

---

[41] See for example Bulnes, *El Verdadero Díaz,* and *The Whole Truth.* Gruening captured the essence of the opportunities which cooperation with Díaz offered the *caciques,* as well as the nature of their own value-orientations, in the following passage: "General Bernardo Reyes became the great cacique of the [northern] frontier. *Jefe de Operaciones* over the vast states of Tamaulipas, Nuevo León, Coahuila, and Durango, he was also civil governor of Nuevo León, and drew both salaries. In addition, he received a 'gratification' of two thousand pesos monthly out of the extraordinary expenses of the war department, and had the disposal, without accounting, of eighty thousand pesos annually for a corps known as the Rurales of Tamaulipas, and of more than a hundred thousand for a similar armed force in Nuevo León. So much the national treasury records show officially. These sums represented but a fraction of his income.

"In Nuevo León, under his civil governorship, civil and criminal justice passed through the hands of his son-in-law, whom one retained if one wanted to win.

"In Puebla, General Mucio Martínez, governor for eighteen years, owned a dozen gambling-houses—prohibited by law. He likewise monopolized the state pulque supply. His gubernatorial office was worth 4,000,000 pesos to him.

"General Luis Torres of Sonora, who speculated in Yaquis, selling them arms at high prices through intermediaries, cleaning up on the campaign expenses in the war upon them, and netting so much per head for each of them sold into slavery in Yucatán, likewise emerged four times a peso millionaire.

"Generals Carlos Pacheco, Carlos Díaz Gutiérrez, Rafael Cravioto, Manuel Mondragón, Francisco Cantón and Jerónimo Treviño, starting with nothing, emerged as multimillionaires" (Gruening, *Mexico and Its Heritage,* p. 59).

higher levels, the Díaz precept was meticulously followed: buy off the strong by appealing to their desires for social and economic mobility, whatever the cost. Thus Díaz succeeded in pacifying the emergent mestizo regional and national military elite "by converting local tyranny into a general dictatorship, by converting the cacique into a policeman, a representative of the national government."[42] In a country so lacking in social cohesion, where loyalties never rose from the personal to the institutional level and where the very concept of political legitimacy was alien, the only way to tie the local political-military power elite to the central government was to satisfy its demands for economic and status advancement. This was the precept that pacified Mexico, clearly suggested in the Díaz slogan *pan o palo*, bread or stick. "If they will cooperate, feed them from the public treasury; if not, exterminate them."[43]

Those who were co-opted governed their various principalities ruthlessly, since any form of opposition was, per se, opposition to their own interests. All forms of resistance and criticism were crushed by the use of the army or the *rurales*, bandits turned policemen. Nonconformers were shot "while trying to flee," about 10,000 of them during the Porfiriato. Thousands of others were impressed into the army, impelled to migrate, or arrested and sent to forced labor camps in Yucatán and the Valle Nacional. So much for political opposition.

The structure of the political system as it emerged under Díaz bears a striking resemblance to that in Mexico today. First of all, once Díaz had pacified the new mestizo power elite through a judicious spread of governorships, military commands, contracts, concessions, and monopolies he was able to concentrate all effective political power in the federal government—more specifically, in the presidency. While the constitution of 1857 was never revoked, the federated republic, the division of powers and the democratic procedures set down in that document remained as fictitious as they are today. Díaz controlled, directly or indirectly, every government activity. "He made all appointments to Congress, to important jobs, cabinet posts, governorships."[44] By 1892 Díaz was naming all members of the federal chamber and senate. "First came the relatives of the President. . . . Next old comrades-in-arms or their sons. . . . Then relatives of generals, cabinet ministers and governors."[45] At the lower levels the district political chiefs were chosen directly by the president or in consultation with the various state governors, much as such second-level choices have been made in Mexico since the Peace

[42] Tannenbaum, *Peace by Revolution*, p. 145.

[43] Quoted in *ibid.*, p. 98.

[44] Beals, *Porfirio Díaz*, p. 287. All scholars of the Díaz period agree on this assessment.

[45] *Ibid.*, pp. 289–90.

of the PRI commenced in the 1930s. And, as today, all of the "official" candidates won their election contests.

Andrés Molina Enríquez, analyzing the Díaz system in 1908, summed it up in one phrase—*amistad personal.* In this *amigo* system governors were linked to the president, *jefes políticos* were linked to the governors, and the *presidentes municipales* were linked to the *jefes políticos.*[46] From bottom to top, each group within the political elite was indebted to the group above for the opportunities for mobility provided by their official positions. The salaries which came with the offices, and more importantly the opportunities for graft, illegal seizures of property, monopolies, concessions and all the other forms of personal enrichment, were dependent upon co-optation into the system. Therefore political loyalties, such as they were, all flowed upward as in Mexico today. And, as today, the "entire machinery of local, provincial, and national government became dependent upon the will of one man."[47]

That Díaz realized the necessity of meeting the demands of the mestizo power seekers is clearly revealed in the nature of his appointments. Over the first two decades of his rule almost all those chosen by him to serve as governors, generals, *jefes políticos,* ministers and in various other official capacities were mestizos.[48] Thus there slowly developed in Mexico a new mestizo elite which took its place beside the old creole aristocracy. Because of the social, psychological and economic configuration of Mexico during the nineteenth century, political—not economic—enterprise provided the maximum mobility opportunities; nothing reflected this fact better than the make-up of the Díaz political hierarchy prior to the late 1890s.

But Díaz did not pacify Mexico by responding to the demands of one group alone. In addition to his embrace of the leading mestizo power seekers, he devised a series of policies which placated all the other articulate but less potentially dangerous groups in Mexican society. First, to the old creole conservatives he offered a peace and a stability that left their economic interests intact. Their haciendas were untouched; indeed they thrived and expanded as the Díaz land policies further undermined the Indian pueblos. Since all judges were also Díaz appointees, Indian attempts to halt the land grab through the courts fell on deaf ears. Second, Díaz made peace with the church. The anticlerical legislation of the reform period was not enforced, and the church gradually reemerged as one of the most powerful social institutions in Mexico. This church policy pleased the old conservatives who, although kept out of political positions during the Díaz period, regained a social prominence and thereby lost all interest in opposing the dictator.

---

[46] Molina Enríquez, *Los Grandes problemas,* chap. 5.

[47] Ross, *Madero,* p. 23.

[48] See Molina Enríquez, *Los Grandes problemas,* chap. 5.

The former creole moderates and the newer European immigrants might have objected strenuously to the limited role allowed them in politics before the 1890s; again, however, Díaz's economic policies were so beneficial to their interests that opposition was never seriously considered. They formed the group from which Mexico's emerging entrepreneurs were drawn, and which was showered with state subsidies, tax exemptions, monopolies and various other incentives to promote the emergence of an industrial sector in Mexico. Other members of this new creole class found extremely profitable employment representing various foreign interests in Mexico, most often as lawyers for foreign corporations.

Finally, and definitely not forgotten, were the interests of a growing mestizo "middle class"—Mendieta y Núñez called them a white collar proletariat—which demanded employment consistent with its status orientations. In essence the demand was for white collar jobs, enough to employ the 10 to 15 percent of Mexico's population which was literate—at least semi-educated—by the end of the Díaz years. As many observers of the Mexican scene during the second half of the nineteenth century noted, all those mestizos with any education demanded "as an indisputable right" employment in the government bureaucracy.[49] Inheriting both the earlier Hispanic desire for public office and a distaste for physical forms of labor, the educated mestizos pressed their demands with increasing virulence after the War of the Reform broke the creole monopoly of political power.

Díaz recognized the potential for political instability inherent in a status-conscious and dissatisfied "educated unemployed" group, small as it was at the time. The problem that the group faced in Porfirian Mexico was the same as always: in an unindustrialized country with a rural sector dominated by haciendas, there were very few employment opportunities for a "middle class," especially one which wanted to work in offices. The economic growth during the Díaz years did increase the demand for white collar workers, but not at a pace fast enough to absorb the growing number of literate mestizos.[50] The Díaz response to the problem was to increase vastly the size of the Mexican bureaucracy. Between 1876 and 1910 the government payroll grew by 900 percent. Bulnes estimated that in 1876 16 percent of Mexico's literate population worked for the government at the national, state and municipal levels; by 1910 over 70 percent were employed in the bureaucracy.[51] Thus Porfirio's policy with regard to the growing educated mestizo class matched the motto he adopted toward the bureaucracy: "Feed the brute."[52] For a long time the policy worked. Díaz seemed the savior of the

[49] *Ibid.* See also Bulnes, *El Verdadero Díaz* and *The Whole Truth.*
[50] See Bulnes, *El Verdadero Díaz*, pp. 42, 261–65.
[51] *Ibid.*, p. 42.
[52] Quoted in Beals, *Porfirio Díaz*, p. 230.

middle class, "ever buffeted by previous governments, lost in armed turmoil, sunk in the wide gulf between Indian helots and feudal overlords."[53] As with his policy toward the Indian population, however, short-term success bore the seeds of long-term disaster.

Revolutions can perhaps best be analyzed in terms of both precipitating events, often superficial in themselves, and preconditions, the more fundamental causes. The precipitants of the Mexican revolution are of no concern to us here, but an understanding of the underlying causes is essential to our analysis. It reveals not only the fatal flaws in the Díaz system, but also the problems which the postrevolutionary Mexican political system would have to resolve in order to restore and maintain political stability.

The social upheaval that wracked Mexico between 1910 and 1920 was really two revolutions, not one. Both were in conflict with the Díaz regime, and they were also often at war with each other.

The first was the revolt of Indian Mexico. It was centered in Morelos and the adjoining states of Puebla, Guerrero, México and Hidalgo, heavy in indigenous population. It was a classic example of the peasant jacquerie, a spontaneous uprising on the part of a rural population which, in the face of new production methods and deteriorating standards of living, attempted to return to a "golden age" in its past.

During the Díaz years the attack on the remaining communal lands had been accelerated. Both the mestizo elite and the old and new creole aristocrats took full advantage of their predominant position in Mexican society to despoil the Indian pueblos of their land and livelihood. The spread and the intensity of the encroachment, the futility of legal recourse, the growing system of debt peonage and the trend toward near-famine conditions in rural Mexico provided the fundamental conditions for the Indian revolt. Like all jacqueries, it looked backward, not forward. It sought to restore ancient rights and privileges, most particularly the communal lands.[54] Led by Emiliano Zapata in the state of Morelos, the Indians fought one last battle against the encroachment of the sugar plantations and haciendas on their village lands. Both Zapata and his followers remained traditional in orientation, suspicious of non-Indian "outsiders," and unable or unwilling to cooperate for any length of time with the other major element in the revolution, the northern-led mestizo movement. Regardless of their parochialism, the tenacity with which those involved in the Indian uprising fought for the reestablishment of communal lands so dramatized the problem of the inequitable structure of land tenure in Mexico that the cry for *Tierra y Libertad* was

---

[53] *Ibid.*, p. 231.

[54] The classic analysis of the revolt in Morelos is Chevalier, "Un Facteur décisif." All Mexican scholars are now also indebted to John Womack, Jr. for his authoritative and engaging treatment of the revolt and its leader in *Zapata and the Mexican Revolution* (New York: Alfred A. Knopf, 1969).

soon enunciated by all the revolutionary elements in Mexican society. Land reform of some sort had clearly become a prerequisite to political stability.

Most of the participants in the second revolution—the mestizo revolution—looked not backward but, as usual, upward. What they saw was a closed door. The door had opened with the triumph of Díaz, and through it had passed the mestizo *caciques* whom the dictator embraced in his *amigo* system. They had become cabinet members, governors and generals. Rising with them had been the lesser power seekers who ruled at the district level, the *jefes políticos* and the *rurales* who served them. Indeed, the 1870s were the high tide of mestizo mobility. But then the door had swung shut, once again in Mexican history sharply limiting the opportunities for social and economic advancement. At the national, state, and even the local level, access to elite circles, political, economic or social, gradually contracted. Perhaps this process was most dramatically evidenced in the realm of politics.

By 1910 Díaz was eighty years old. Two of his cabinet members were older than he, and the youngest was fifty-five. Two of Mexico's twenty-seven governors were over eighty, six of them past seventy, and seventeen were sixty. The senate was described by a contemporary as an asylum for gouty decrepits, and the chamber as composed of a host of veterans relieved by a group of patriarchs. "Such an administration could not be called progressive, not even conservative; it was a home for the aged, with a standing account at the druggists."[55] The young mestizos who had come to power with Díaz grew old, but they still held the reins of power. And when they passed them on, it was generally to another member of the family. In Chihuahua the Terrazas clan had ruled for over fifty years. By 1910 the family held seven million acres of land, a million and half head of cattle, and was worth at least twenty-five million dollars. In the state of Sonora Ramón Corral and Luis Torres had ruled for over three decades. "The clan netted so much per head on each Yaqui sold into Yucatán slavery, stole Yaqui lands, trafficked in government military supplies, and cleaned up on campaign expenses." Owning a significant portion of the Cananea Copper Company, they "supplied the mines with workers, and kept them in stern order under frightful exploitation."[56] In Querétaro General Francisco González Cosío, sixty-eight years old in 1910, had been governor for twenty-six years and was a millionaire many times over. Tlaxcala, Aguascalientes, Tabasco, Veracruz and Guanajuato had each been governed for at least nineteen years by a single chief executive, and in almost all these cases the governors were millionaires.[57] At all levels of government the Díaz system suffered from a hardening of the political

[55] Bulnes, *The Whole Truth*, p. 117.

[56] *Ibid.*, pp. 373–74.

[57] These included Dehesa in Veracruz, General Mucio Martínez in Puebla, and General Fernando González in México, in addition to those already mentioned above. See Bulnes, *El Verdadero Díaz*, pp. 360–65.

arteries. The co-opted grew richer and older; the outsiders grew older and increasingly resentful.

The problem of access to social and economic mobility would have been relieved had the Mexican economic system provided alternate routes of advancement in significant proportions, but this was not yet the case. As noted in chapter 2, growth rates of employment in the industrial and service sectors of the economy were very low. Between 1895 and 1910 the growth of the work force in both sectors was perhaps less than 1 percent a year, so slow that the agricultural sector had to absorb an increasing percentage of the labor supply each year after 1900 (table 2-4). Thus the economic arteries of the Díaz system were themselves too constricted to mediate the rising discontent on the part of the literate and semiliterate mestizo group, a group which was growing as some limited educational reforms increased the numbers of schools and students.[58]

A further factor which aggravated mestizo discontent was the fast-growing gap between its own relative poverty and the riches of the new political and economic elites created during the Díaz years. In addition to the nouveau riche mestizo politicians and generals there appeared a new creole group, the ill-reputed *científicos*. Starting their careers as young and generally talented lawyers, economists and academicians of European or creole parentage, the *científicos* surrounded Díaz by the 1890s and strongly influenced the shaping of the dictator's economic policies. Initially dedicated to honesty in government, and to a program of economic and social development for Mexico that reflected their reading of Comte and Spencer, many of them succumbed to the opportunities for personal enrichment which their positions in the Díaz administration presented. As heads of the various federal departments they controlled not only the federal budget but also the machinery used to apportion concessions to foreign and domestic investors. "Into their hands fell the contracts for paving, lighting, local railways, roads. Mostly lawyers, they were also the legal representatives of the powerful foreign companies; they arranged banking and industrial concessions, secured special favors, expedited legal procedure, and milked all the teats of the cow."[59]

By the 1900s their idealism was gone. Now extremely wealthy industrialists, lawyers and bankers, the *científicos* aspired to total economic and political control of Mexico. By 1910 their influence with Díaz had grown to the point where they held three cabinet positions, eight subsecretariats, twelve governorships, twenty-five senatorial seats and half the seats in the Chamber of Deputies. Their rise to predominance stirred increasing resentment within

[58] Bulnes argues that this was the root cause of the revolution. See *ibid.*, pp. 261–65.
[59] Beals, *Porfirio Díaz*, p. 330.

both the mestizo masses and the new mestizo elite which had hoped to inherit the Díaz dictatorship. A behind-the-scenes struggle for power began as early as the 1890s, and during the final decade of the Porfiriato the ruling elite decisively split into the creole *científico* group led by Minister of the Treasury Limantour and the mestizo *cacique* group that looked toward General Bernardo Reyes for leadership.

By 1910 these fundamental problems had set the stage for the revolution that swept Mexico for a decade. At the apex of Mexican society a relatively new and extremely narrow elite, in conjunction with those foreign interests to which it was often closely attached, controlled literally all the wealth, political power and social position in the country. The new creole segment of the elite was hated by mestizo Mexico for its rapid rise, its close links with foreign interests, and its view that only "whites" were capable of ruling Mexico. Even the mestizo members of the elite, aging and dictatorial, were disliked for governing their districts and states as if they were personal property.

Beneath the elite group of the population was the bulk of the mestizo segment, gradually exposed to education and increasingly alienated from an economic and political system which provided it with little or no opportunity for mobility. Even those mestizos who found white collar employment were incensed by the gap which separated them from the elite circles. As Bulnes noted: "the hatred of the lower bureaucracies for the higher had assumed unheard-of proportions. The lower bureaucracy was not socialistic, but it wanted a new order of things through the intervention of any national liberator, it mattered not who, so long as the lower bureaucracy was actually relieved of the host of decrepits that weighed it down."[60]

If those members of the mestizo middle group with jobs sought a new order, even more so did the "outs" of the regime, "the professionals without clients, and the aspirants for public sinecures."[61] In rural Mexico this mestizo group was to furnish a great part of the revolution's military leadership: the *ranchero* who fought to retain his few acres of land and maintain a subsistence standard of living; the muleteer turned bandit under the pressure of the Porfirian dictatorship; the school teacher resentful of the social and economic limitations he faced. These were the "outs" who awaited only the right leader and the right moment for their revolution of access, of mobility.

Below the mestizos, as noted earlier, the Indian segment of Mexican society was also being driven toward revolt. It too needed only the right

---

[60] Bulnes, *The Whole Truth*, p. 142.

[61] Moisés González Navarro, *La Confederación Nacional Campesina* (Mexico: B. Costa-Amic, 1968), p. 45. See also the description of mestizo frustrations in Lucio Mendieta y Núñez, "Un Balance objetivo de la revolución mexicana," in *Revista mexicana de sociología* 23 (May–August, 1960): 529–42.

moment, a moment which came when the mestizo revolution in the north challenged the aging dictatorship in 1910.

The events which finally precipitated the revolution need not concern us here. Suffice it to say that the worsening of economic trends after 1905 aggravated all these problems, and in addition alienated a great number of elite circle families whose economic interests were endangered. When the revolt erupted, even the plutocracy gave Díaz little support.

## The Praetorian Interlude

The revolution, led initially by a political moderate and member of one of Mexico's great landholding families, forced Díaz into exile in less than one year. As he embarked for France, the dictator reputedly said, "Madero has unleashed a tiger; let us see if he can control him." He couldn't, and like most moderates who lead revolutions he was devoured by his own creation. But he was merely the first of many revolutionary leaders to pay the ultimate price before the tiger was finally leashed through the formation of the PRI twenty years later.

Madero was removed from the presidency and then murdered by former Díaz associates who attempted to regain control of Mexican politics. But the forces of reaction were soon crushed by the mestizo armies which were generally composed of and led by men from the north who would, from 1915 on, determine the destiny of Mexico. A very few, like Venustiano Carranza, were large landowners. Many more, like Alvaro Obregón, were *rancheros*. Others, like Saturnino Cedillo, began life as *campesinos*; still others, like Francisco Villa, were outlaws. But perhaps the majority of the leadership of the northerners had been employed as school teachers (Antonio Villareal, Plutarco Calles), muleteers and storekeepers (Pascual Orozco), bank tellers (Adolfo de la Huerta) and factory workers (Pablo González). Thus many of the emerging leaders were "middle class" in the Mexican setting. "They were 'self-made' men, brought up in poverty though not in dire want, and had always been sufficiently close to the toilers in the field, factory, and mine to understand how incurably the discrimination of the old Mexican social system weighed on the masses."[62]

Yet there was an ambivalence about these new leaders which has characterized the Revolutionary Coalition ever since its inception. They were the men who eventually wrote the constitution of 1917 and engineered a revolutionary transformation of Mexican society. At the same time, however, "though the revolutionary professions of love for the peon and the worker became current among the constitutionalist generals, the constitutionalist

---

[62] Gruening, *Mexico and Its Heritage*, p. 310.

movement had more of self-seeking than of idealism. It was not only a crusade, it was also a struggle for power."[63]

The northerners were natives of a desolate frontier region that had produced a hard and acquisitive mestizo breed; over the course of three centuries northern Mexico had been the scene of savage conflicts between Indian and Spaniard, Mexican and Anglo-Saxon. The armies of Obregón and "Pancho" Villa were raised from the mining camps and cattle ranches of the region, and the red-light towns on the U.S. border. Their slogans were land, liberty, and democracy, "but for most of them, as they rode southwards on troop trains . . . the Revolution meant power and plunder."[64]

From its very inception, then, the mestizo revolution and its accomplishments have represented an interplay of altruism and egoism, of a commitment to liberal reform and a desire for wealth and power in the nineteenth-century tradition of Mexican politics. The altruistic face of the revolution was most eloquently displayed at the Querétaro constitutional convention of 1916-17. The reform elements at the convention, supported by General Obregón and led by General Mújica, overrode the conservative tendencies of acting President Carranza and wrote what was then the world's most liberal constitution. The articles dealing with land reform, the rights of labor, and the commitment to democracy defined as "a way of life founded in the steady economic, social, and cultural improvement of the people" were unparalleled in 1917. Once again, during the Cárdenas presidency (1934-1940), the face of reform emerged with a force that profoundly altered the structure of rural Mexico. Close to one-half of the nation's arable land was taken from the remaining *hacendado* aristocrats and foreign owners and given to Mexico's Indian and mestizo *campesinos*. The organizational efforts of labor were supported and the state became labor's advocate in its conflicts with ownership, both native and foreign.

For the most part, however, it is not the reform strand of the revolution which has predominated in postrevolutionary Mexican leadership. From the very beginning the drive for social and economic mobility and political power on the part of the revolutionary leaders made a mockery of the revolution's own slogans, and turned institutions for reform into engines for personal advancement. With the collapse of the Díaz system the power and wealth which the state represented were once again up for grabs, and the praetorian struggle for mobility via political office was resumed.

The revolutionary army that destroyed the Díaz regime became the most important political force in Mexico, and remained so for close to thirty years. The reason for military predominance was the same as it had been throughout

[63] Parkes, *History of Mexico*, pp. 338-39.

[64] *Ibid.*, p. 339.

the nineteenth century: Mexico still lacked political institutions with any strength or widely recognized claim to legitimacy. The Díaz system had remained a personal system, without institutions and without any means of handling the problem of succession. With the dictator's departure, the search for political stability had to start, as in 1821, from the beginning.

Clubs were once again trumps, but even the clubs were fragmented. The new mestizo generals had created their own armies, and the loyalties of these soldiers never went beyond their own *jefes*. The generals became regional *caudillos* whose local power could not be shaken by the first postrevolutionary presidents. Thus the condition of the states changed from prerevolutionary "satrapies held in bondage to the central government by an officer loyal to the dictator into autonomous fiefs ruled by the local military commanders. The battalions and regiments of the various states were loyal only to the military governors or, if the governor was a civilian, to a [chief of military operations]."[65]

In the early postrevolutionary years the generals themselves were often state governors. Just prior to 1920 eighteen out of thirty governorships were held by generals and colonels, half of whom had totally ignored the electoral process and "simply shot their way into office."[66] Where the military *caciques* did not control the governorships directly, their interests were well protected through bargains, explicit and implicit, with the civilian authorities.[67]

Whether in or out of office, the military *caciques* played their trumps for their own social and economic advancement. Examples are legion, and none is better than that of Plutarco Calles, the poor school teacher who became a revolutionary general, cabinet officer under President Obregón (1920-24), president of Mexico (1924-28), and founder of the PRI. His personal fortune was estimated at "no less than twenty million pesos."[68] He acquired enough real estate to put his heirs into the "political *hacendado*" class, that revolutionary group which in many instances appropriated for itself estates of the former creole and mestizo aristocracy. By the early 1930s Calles, the president who first gave real impetus to land reform and who supported organized labor during the 1920s, "settled at Cuernavaca, where he lived surrounded by wealthy revolutionaries, on what was popularly known as the Street of the

[65] Edwin Lieuwen, *Mexican Militarism: The Political Rise and Fall of the Revolutionary Army 1910-1940* (Albuquerque: University of New Mexico Press, 1968), p. 36.

[66] *Ibid.*, p. 36.

[67] "The [civilian] governor must come to an understanding or carry out one previously made with the *jefe de operaciones*. Sometimes state executive and federal commander work jointly; sometimes they agree on 'spheres of influence,' distinct and exclusive purviews for each. The military generally have the gambling houses." Gruening, *Mexico and Its Heritage*, p. 486.

[68] Lieuwen, *Mexican Militarism*, p. 90.

Forty Thieves. . . ."[69] He was the center of a group of revolutionary millionaires that included Abelardo Rodríguez, Aarón Saenz, Alberto Pani, Luis
León and Puig Casauranc among others.

General Abelardo Rodríguez accumulated one of Mexico's largest revolutionary fortunes. A former baseball player, he served Calles as governor of
Baja California, minister of war, and for a year as president. "In the border
towns of Tijuana, Ensenada and Mexicali, Governor Rodríguez was the principal entrepreneur in the horseracing, casino, and brothel business. Subsequently, he invested in real estate, food processing, stocks, and banking.
When he became President in 1932 his fortune was over 100 million pesos."[70]
General Aarón Saenz used his military rank and personal friendship with the
two strongmen of the 1920s, Obregón and Calles, to make a fortune. He
became one of the wealthiest contractors in Mexico, starting as did a host of
other military businessmen with government contracts. Another conspicuous
general-contractor was Juan Almazán. He made millions from construction
projects and real estate during the 1920s while he was serving as minister of
public works and communications. By the late 1930s another military-
political figure, General Amaro, owned the finest string of polo ponies in
Mexico, several rural estates and more than one magnificent home in Mexico
City. Other leading military figures who emerged from the revolution and the
1920s as millionaires were Roberto Cruz, Antonio Guerrero, Eulogio Ortíz,
Rodrigo Quevado Moreno, and Miguel Acosta.

Military fortunes were accumulated by those generals and colonels who
remained loyal to the two men who controlled the Mexican presidency
between 1920 and 1934, Generals Obregón and Calles. As in the Díaz system,
loyalty was rewarded with lucre, and the sources of wealth were very similar
to those of the earlier period. The traditional pattern reemerged at the state
level as well. Governorships were used as they had been under Díaz to build
personal fortunes, and the local and district office holders were given carte
blanche to steal, embezzle and murder so long as they could deliver the
needed support to keep the governor and his coterie in power. One revolutionary commented in 1923 that Mexico had two honest governors out of
twenty-eight, and reasoned that "the best that can be hoped for, generally
speaking, is not a governor who will not enrich himself through his office, for
nearly all do, but one who while stealing will do *something* for his state. The
majority take all they can and leave nothing."[71]

The governors' machines were cemented by spoils. Offices, commissions,
concessions, "and often connivance at illegal despoilments for which any

[69] Parkes, *History of Mexico*, p. 393.
[70] Lieuwen, *Mexican Militarism*, pp. 91–92.
[71] Quoted in Gruening, *Mexico and Its Heritage*, p. 485.

unusual situation or social dislocation, such as agrarian reform or rebellion, real or alleged" provided the means for enriching those followers of the chief executive.[72] State regimes also solidified their power in several other ways. Sometimes they murdered leaders of opposition movements; at other times they simply drove them from the state or kept them in jail indefinitely. Often they installed their own supporters as officers of recently organized labor unions; the more ambitious organized state-wide labor organizations. And always they fought to control the *ejidos* within the state by imposing their own choices as *ejidal* commissioners. Almost all of the *ejidos* were soon controlled by politicians who used them as salable commodities on the political market. *Ejidos* became the civilian politician's equivalent of a general's troops. The politician or militia chief who could deliver the votes of an *ejido* for a governor was assured of a prominent spot in the state political machinery and of all the emoluments which the post entailed; a *cacique* who strung together several *ejidos* into a state agrarian league had a good shot at the governorship itself.[73] By the early 1930s all of Mexico's states had developed peasants' confederations. Sometimes founded by men who were committed to the reform strand of the revolution, most of these leagues soon became instruments of personal advancement. As one Mexican commentator wrote in 1934, "The history of peasant political organizations, however optimistic we may wish to be, has been a history of failure.... [It] reveals the same grave defects as that of the labor organizations: personalism and politicians and bosses with unlimited ambitions who have used the organizations for their own gains."[74]

The praetorian period of Mexican politics thus witnessed the reemergence of the mestizo military politician, the caudillo whose regional military strength gained him a governorship or the presidency. Some of them were committed to the revolution's reform program, as the land reform measures undertaken by both Obregón and Calles suggest. In fact some of those revolutionaries most bent on personal economic and social advancement were also the most reform-minded where their personal interests were not at stake. Guadalupe Zuno became a millionaire many times over while governor of Jalisco, but at the same time introduced more roads, schools and other public improvements during his term than all other governors save Carrillo Puerto in Yucatán.[75]

Nevertheless, the politics of egoism predominated throughout the period. The mestizo *caciques* exhibited the same personal value-orientations as those of their Díaz period predecessors. Without a recognized *jefe maximo*, how-

---

[72] *Ibid.*, p. 486.

[73] See Eyler N. Simpson, *The Ejido: Mexico's Way Out* (Chapel Hill: University of North Carolina Press, 1937), especially chaps. 19 and 23.

[74] Quoted in *ibid.*, p. 350.

[75] Quoted in Gruening, *Mexico and Its Heritage*, p. 443.

ever, the period was marked by recurrent civil strife. In 1920, 1923, 1927, and 1929 the nation was wracked by rebellion as disappointed military aspirants for the presidency contested the issue with arms. They chose a military rather than a political campaign because, then as now, the "official" candidate—the one supported by the outgoing president—was always assured of winning. The government tallied the votes, and at both the state and national levels the practice of *imposición* was the norm. At stake nationally was control of the federal government and all the opportunities for personal gain that went with it, and that prize tempted a major segment of the revolutionary army to join a leading *caudillo* in revolt each time a presidential "election" approached.

The rebellion of 1929 was to be the last serious challenge to the federal government in Mexico. In that year the Revolutionary Coalition, led by Calles, put together the "official" party. Through it the coalition has ruled Mexico for forty years; since 1940 it has done so without serious threat of overthrow by bullets or ballots. Several factors help to account for the initial success of the official party in pacifying Mexico. In the first place, Calles was able to capitalize upon a crucial event, the assassination of President-elect Obregón. He convinced the rest of the regional caudillos that a civilian must be given the presidency, warning that to name a military man would result in another serious rebellion by other dissatisfied generals. After the military leaders agreed upon an interim choice, Calles further persuaded them that only the organization of a political party—within which their interests would be represented and their conflicts mediated—could prevent further rebellions and solidify their joint political predominance in Mexico.

The regional strongmen were in a mood to listen. Many of the leading military figures had been killed in the rebellions of 1920, 1923, and 1927, and many more were removed in the revolt of 1929. Thus the most ambitious aspirants for the presidency were dead; many others had been removed from the army in the purges that followed each revolt. Furthermore, the remainder were slowly being subjected to two kinds of pressures which increased their willingness to enter the official party. The first entailed a series of reforms within the army which aimed at professionalizing the military and reducing the elements of personalism which had previously bound the troops to individual officers. The second involved the changing personal fortunes of the remaining generals. As noted above, many were becoming extremely wealthy as a result of their loyalty to Calles. The richer they got, the more they had to lose in an unsuccessful revolt. Of the five *divisionarios*, the leading generals of Mexico between 1929 and 1935, four were millionaires: Calles, Minister of War Amaro, Governor Cedillo of San Luis Potosí, and Minister of Communications and Public Works Juan Almazán. Other generals continued to hold over half of the governorships and the major cabinet posts well into the 1930s.

In these circumstances the official party was formed, at that time "an amalgam of local political machines," generally dominated by military figures.[76] Within a decade, however, the power of the political generals had been undermined and the political system that governs Mexico today had emerged. The first step in this direction was taken by Calles. From behind the scenes he dominated party matters until 1935, gradually strengthening the party bureaucracy and weakening the provincial bases of personal power accommodated in the original party organization. The second step was taken by Cárdenas who, as noted in chapter 4, brought organized labor and the *ejidal* leagues into the party on a sectoral basis to counteract the power of Calles and the old political generals allied with him.

In bringing these two huge interest groupings into the revolutionary party where they could easily be dominated by national-level sector organizations, Cárdenas not only strengthened his position vis-à-vis Calles and the other conservative generals and businessmen in his circle, but also took a major step toward centralizing all political control in Mexico City. Whatever Cárdenas' intentions, the realities of Mexican politics dictated that the labor and *campesino* sectors would be run by leaders co-opted into the political hierarchy from below or imposed by the hierarchy from above.

The Cárdenas years also witnessed the emergence of the Mexican presidency as the vital center of the Mexican political system. Of the five leading military figures in the 1930s, Cárdenas broke the power of four: Calles, Amaro, Cedillo and Almazán. The fifth, Cárdenas himself, aided the cause of presidential primacy immensely by retiring from the office at the end of his legal term and not attempting to run the country from behind the scenes as Calles had done from 1929 to 1935. In addition, Cárdenas popularized the presidency to a degree unknown in Mexican history. He set the campaign style to which all future PRI candidates have adhered by traveling throughout the nation by airplane, train and automobile, meeting and talking with the humble as well as the exalted. He continued to travel across Mexico during his six-year term, and this personal contact and exposure together with his policies for land reform and labor organization gradually elevated not only Cárdenas but also the office of the president of the republic to the point where a political institution in Mexico acquired a degree of legitimacy unparalleled since the ties with the Spanish crown were sundered in 1821.

When Cárdenas retired from the presidency in 1940 he passed on to his hand-picked successor, General Avila Camacho, a political party which had vastly broadened its membership and increased its capacity to incorporate new groups into Mexican political life. Thus far that incorporation has not generally redounded to the benefit of either the labor or the *campesino* sectors of the PRI. In terms of political stability, however, it is clear that the

[76] Scott, *Mexican Government in Transition*, p. 122.

control of these groups by the leadership of the official party has had two significant effects. First, it has minimized the divisiveness and conflict which have so often accompanied the initial appearance of lower social strata in political life. Through the mechanism of the PRI the Mexican *campesino* and laborer have been granted a limited form of political citizenship, an opportunity for some participation—if wholly ceremonial—in the choice of political leadership. At the same time the coalition has used the PRI to control carefully the demands of these new groups in accord with its own interests. Second, the PRI has provided the means by which the coalition can continue to hold power in Mexico while observing enough of our present-day democratic norms to minimize both the appearance and, to a great extent, the reality of dictatorial government. The broadening of the official party has allowed the coalition to legitimize its continued control through the electoral process. Even in disputed elections, such as the presidential contest in 1940, the PRI's claim to victory inherits an almost a priori validity which flows directly from the size and diversity of the interest groups "represented" in the party.

Since 1940 no presidential election has been closely contested. In that year, and again in 1946 and 1952, disappointed military aspirants for the presidency deserted the PRI; some formed their own parties and campaigned for the office. The dismal failure of these attempts strengthened the PRI and reinforced the willingness of the bypassed aspirants within it to accept the choice of the outgoing president and remain in the party.

The end of the praetorian period of Mexican politics was further marked by the emergence of a series of civilian presidents. Miguel Alemán, who served from 1946 to 1952, was "a lawyer by training and a politician by dedication."[77] He was the first of a succession of presidents whose entire adult lives have been spent working within the machinery of Mexican politics. He served as the campaign manager for Avila Camacho, the man who preceded him in the presidency and who chose Alemán as his successor. He also held the post of minister of interior (*Gobernación*) in the cabinet of his predecessor, a pattern followed by Presidents Ruiz Cortines (1952-58), Díaz Ordaz (1964-70), and Echeverría Alvarez (1970-    ). All presidents since Alemán have previously served as heads of a major ministry and—with the exception of Echeverría Alvarez—as either senators or governors.

## THE REVOLUTIONARY COALITION AND MEXICO'S DEVELOPMENT STRATEGY

At the end of chapter 5 two questions were posed. The first was: why did Mexico's Revolutionary Coalition pursue the development strategy analyzed

---

[77] Ramón Eduardo Ruíz, *Mexico: The Challenge of Poverty and Illiteracy* (San Marino, Cal.: Huntington Library, 1963), p. 70.

in chapters 3 and 4? What interests and value-orientations led this self-renewing political elite to adopt an approach built upon high profits, low wages, forced savings through inflation, regressive taxation and low tax rates, minimum expenditures on social programs and a maximum concentration of public sector expenditures on projects directly related to increased economic output? The second question was: how did the coalition get away with it? Stated more analytically, how has a political system which has greatly enriched its political and agricultural-industrial elites while generally minimizing welfare gains for the great majority of Mexico's population maintained that degree of political stability vital for continued economic development? An understanding of Mexico's power seekers and their rise to prominence provides a crucial perspective from which to answer the first question; for the second an understanding of the socio-cultural setting of Mexican politics and of the system developed by the power seekers is equally imperative.

The policies and programs shaped by the Mexican government to promote economic development over the past thirty years are an accurate reflection of the interests and value-orientations of the political elite that controls Mexico today. Perhaps the point can best be illustrated by recalling Samuel Huntington's discussion of the characteristics of praetorian society. We have already noted that praetorianism, defined as active intervention of the military in government, had ended in Mexico by 1940. Considered somewhat more broadly, however, there is an element of praetorianism in Mexican politics which is traceable from the very beginnings of independence politics to the present day. That element involves both the norms of political behavior in Mexican society and the values held by the politician himself.

It will be remembered that Huntington contrasts sharply the political behavior in an institutionalized society from that of a praetorian society. He argues that in institutionalized political systems "politicians expand their loyalties from social group to political institution and political community as they mount the ladder of authority."[78] Contrasted with this behavior is that common in praetorian societies, societies which lack agreement as to the legitimate and authoritative methods for resolving conflicts and in which social forces confront each other "nakedly." In such societies, Huntington argues, "the successful politician simply transfers his identity and loyalty from one social group to another. . . . The individuals who mount the ladder to wealth and power simply transfer their allegiance from the masses to the oligarchy. They are absorbed or captured by a social force with narrower interests than that to which they previously owed allegience."[79]

Huntington has characterized the Mexican political system before the development of the PRI as praetorian, and nobody would disagree with him.

[78] Huntington, *Political Order*, p. 197.
[79] *Ibid.*, p. 197.

But he views the post-1940 Mexican political system as institutionalized, and here there is a crucial sense in which his argument is unconvincing. It is true that Mexico has developed a political institution through which conflict is refined, moderated, and mediated. It is also the case that the institution—the official party—has ended the fragmentation of power in Mexico and covered itself with enough legitimacy to develop authoritative methods of conflict resolution generally accepted by all major segments of Mexican society. In these important structural and functional aspects of political life, Mexico is an "institutionalized polity."

But what about political behavior? What about the questions of allegiances, loyalties and identities? Do members of the Revolutionary Coalition and those co-opted by them expand their loyalties as they rise in the Mexican political hierarchy, or do they narrow them? Do their allegiances move toward a broadened political community, or do they instead tend to be captured by "narrower interests," by the "oligarchy"?

The evidence suggests that in Mexico, both yesterday and today, any broadening of allegiances on the part of Mexico's mestizo politicians has been and continues to be severely limited by their own personal concerns for power and socio-economic mobility. Throughout the nineteenth century politics served as the premier path to wealth and power. All other avenues of mobility were sharply constricted by the structure of the Mexican economy and the pattern of ownership of productive resources. There were no industrial or commercial sectors to speak of, and within what did exist literally all upper echelon positions were held by either foreigners or members of the creole aristocracy. Likewise, landholding was perhaps as concentrated as it has ever been in any country at any time in history. Thus politics attracted the strong and ambitious elements of the *desheredados*, the disinherited and socially alienated mestizos who had nothing to lose and everything to gain.

The mestizo *caciques* who fought their way to the top of the Mexican political structure, as noted earlier, valued personal power as much as wealth. To them social life was combat, and power was that "personal energy that would subjugate and subject people."[80] Driven by desire for wealth, power and status, Mexico's mestizo *caciques* moved from a position of social marginality to one of political preponderance between 1820 and 1870.

The political and socio-economic consequences of mestizo politics emerged for the first time during the Díaz dictatorship. Then, as now, we see personalism prevail in the political realm, and from the lowest to the highest levels of the political structure loyalties flow upward from the appointee to the appointer, from the co-optee to the co-opter, from the follower to his *patrón.* Constitutions and other less fundamental laws are most often honored in the breach, especially in the case of elections. Those in power count

[80] Wolf, *Sons of the Shaking Earth*, p. 239.

the ballots, and they win all elections save those they decide to lose. Dissent, when allowed, is carefully controlled. Finally, opposition on the part of the lowest stratum of society, the Indian stratum, is simply not tolerated; statutes protecting its interests are not enforced.

The socio-economic consequences of the Mexican mestizo system of politics are also clearly delineated in the Díaz period. Political posts are used to accumulate personal wealth. The more important the post, the larger the fortune. Local politicians do well when judged by local standards, but the big money goes to the governors, generals, and cabinet members. Their official positions, as in the old Hispanic-American tradition, are considered as ownership of a source of income, to be exploited for all the personal gain the holder is capable of grasping. The uneducated often amass their fortunes crudely, using such methods as confiscation, fraud and extortion. The better-educated prefer somewhat more delicate means such as the use of official information, influence over the awarding of public contracts, and the "adjusting" of all those bureaucratic regulations which govern private economic initiative in Mexico. The end result of such political entrepreneurship in the Díaz period was the birth of a new monied elite, a new mestizo economic aristocracy which took its place beside the creole elite. At that point the mobility which first accompanied the mestizo seizure of political control froze.

This pattern occurred in the Díaz system because the mestizo politicians neither broadened loyalties nor identified with a larger political community. Their personal desires for wealth and power drove them to demand access to elite circles, but never destruction of the existing aristocracy. They were climbers, not levelers; and once they reached the top they joined elite society and shut the door on all but their personal followers. True, they were increasingly in conflict with the *científicos* toward the latter half of the Díaz dictatorship, but that conflict resulted from the apparently growing influence of the latter group. Members of the new mestizo elite fought the creole aristocracy when they felt their own social and economic position to be challenged by it; otherwise they were content to share the spoils with it.

The pattern of politics which emerged after the revolution bears a striking resemblance to that of the Díaz period, and clearly suggests a consistency in mestizo political behavior that still shapes Mexican political life. Again in the political realm a system emerges which is characterized by personalism and upward-flowing loyalties that severely limit the ability and/or commitment on the part of Mexican politicians to represent the interests of their presumed constituencies, whether the latter be geographical or sectoral in nature. Within the PRI selections are made from above for almost all elective and nonelective posts; within the party's sectors the Revolutionary Coalition also chooses those labor and *campesino* leaders who are to be elevated through party ranks. The co-opted take their orders from above, since their opportunities for advancement depend more upon choices from above than support from below. Constitutions and elections were as meaningless in the 1920s and early 1930s as they were in the Díaz period. Again the candidate whose supporters controlled the counting of the ballots won the elections, and the practice of imposing favored cohorts upon the electorate was the order of the day. In the years since 1940 this practice has changed only slightly. The willingness of the Revolutionary Coalition to conduct free elections constituted no threat to its control of Mexico until quite recently, and events of the past decade suggest that a serious electoral challenge to the PRI may simply not be allowed for some decades to come.

The socio-economic consequences of the postrevolutionary mestizo system are close to a carbon copy of those experienced during the Díaz period, with one highly significant exception to be considered in the following chapter. Again politics has been and continues to be used as an avenue to personal fortune and social mobility. So common is this trait that even those *políticos* who have showed some interest in and commitment to social reform have used political office in the best mestizo tradition. The classic case is Calles, the reformer of the 1910s and 1920s, who by the 1930s was one of Mexico's large landholders, a millionaire surrounded by other revolutionary millionaires. He ended by opposing both land redistribution and the organization of labor. Like all the other revolutionaries, he was publicly committed to the "no reelection" dictate of the Mexican constitution; yet he personally ruled Mexico for close to six years after he retired from the presidency. He espoused the revolutionary cry for "effective suffrage"; yet he imposed his son Rodolfo as governor of Sonora, his son Plutarco as governor of Nuevo León, and tried to bequeath Tamaulipas to his son Alfredo.

But Calles only followed a life style led by most of the other *caciques* from the north who eventually constituted the Revolutionary Coalition. Saturnino Cedillo, an agrarian radical, died one of the largest landholders in all Mexico. Miguel Alemán, son of a liberal revolutionary general, allowed graft and corruption to reach new heights during his presidency and retired to join former Calles intimates Aarón Saenz and ex-President Abelardo Rodríguez as one of the wealthiest members of the coalition. Beneath the upper echelons, as noted in the previous chapter, the fortunes have been smaller but the behavior the same.

That behavior and the value-orientations which produce it suggest why the members of the mestizo elite that emerged in firm control of Mexican politics by the 1940s have favored and promoted the present pattern of economic development in Mexico. Regardless of the depth of their commitment to the reform strand of the revolution, their use of political power to enhance their own social and economic mobility transformed them from a "white collar proletariat" into wealthy members of a new mestizo aristocracy. Again, as in the reform period, theirs was above all a revolution of access, not a leveling movement which sought to eradicate distinctions. The very force of the revolution did in fact remove much of the Díaz elite circle from the Mexican scene, but this aristocracy was as much a victim of the ravages of war as of any conscious social policy on the part of the northern revolutionaries.

Once these men became wealthy, any commitment which they might have had to the reform strand of the revolution ebbed. They now owned land, which set them against agrarian reform; they owned construction firms and small manufacturing concerns, which set them against further support for organized labor. They were opposed to the reform programs of President Cárdenas, and this opposition was one of the considerations which led Cárdenas to choose as his successor a general whose views were more compatible with the emerging conservative consensus within the revolutionary elite.

Thus, when World War II provided Mexico with the opportunity and incentive to undertake a program of rapid industrialization, the country was in the hands of a political elite which was on at least four major counts prepared to adopt the kind of economic development strategy that surfaced in post-1940 Mexico. In the first place, a significant portion of the coalition's charter members were now in a position to profit greatly from the emerging approach to growth. They owned much of the arable land which benefited from Alemán's huge irrigation projects, and many revolutionary politicians and generals soon appeared as part of Mexico's new agricultural elite. Others thrived on government contract work, and made fortunes in the construction field and in industrial projects undertaken by the public sector since 1940.[81] Still others, investing in small manufacturing concerns, were in a position to benefit from the high profit/low tax drive toward industrialization.

In the second place, the same values which had motivated earlier mestizo power seekers affected the *políticos* who have presided over Mexico since 1940. They too have viewed politics as a means of personal mobility, and strive not to level the postrevolutionary economic and social elites in Mexico but to join them. They are not simply open to bribes that the economic elite can easily afford and often provide; they are also attracted to the status which that elite has in its power to convey.

In the third place, by the 1940s the official party had grown in such a way that the development strategy chosen was as politically feasible as it was personally profitable. After Cárdenas brought the *campesino* and labor sectors into the party, the ambitions of the sectoral leaders combined with the authoritarian characteristics of the Revolutionary Coalition to capture those groups for the coalition's own purposes. It should be remembered that only

[81] See chap. 5 above.

eight years after Cárdenas left the presidency Alemán had suffocated what was left of independent leadership of the labor movement and had imposed his own choices upon it. Thereafter the coalition held laborer and peasant under tight and effective control, and could implement a development strategy that often overlooked the interests of these groups even though they formed the mass base of the official party.

In contrast, the coalition could not so easily control the activities of Mexico's growing industrial and commercial elites. Had the Mexican development strategy included such measures as high rates of taxation, increased wages, and continued efforts to restructure land tenure, this group might simply have deposited its savings abroad and choked off a major source of investment capital. This option has always been open to Mexico's entrepreneurial group, and has been a constant source of concern to the Mexican government. Nor is the concern unwarranted. When President López Mateos spoke of governing "on the extreme left within the Constitution" shortly after his term began in December 1958, approximately $250 million from the Mexican private sector fled the country in a matter of days; this was one of the major factors that led the president to soften both his words and actions very soon afterward. Thus a felicitous conjunction of personal goals and practical politics helped to shape Mexico's development strategy for the 1940s and 1950s.

Many Mexican scholars would want to broaden the analysis of the political feasibility of the strategy adopted to include an examination of the influence of the United States on its formulation. They would argue that particularly during the 1920s U.S. diplomatic pressure over petroleum and other matters influenced the shaping of Mexican development policies, as did the U.S.-Mexican tensions which followed the oil expropriations of 1938. There can be little doubt that Mexico's governing elite had to give serious consideration to the foreign repercussions of its domestic policies, particularly with reference to the United States. First, there was a general concern that United States and other foreign business interests in Mexico were ready and willing to finance Mexican opposition to the PRI leadership when foreign interests were jeopardized during the years of reform following the revolution. And second, there was a constant recognition of the degree to which the health of the Mexican economy depended upon access to U.S. markets and—at times—U.S. capital. At no time since 1940 has the United States consumed much less than 65 percent of Mexico's annual exports. Under these circumstances the chosen strategy of development passed the test of international as well as domestic feasibility; it is clear that most, although by no means all, of Mexico's post-1940 development policies have met with the approval of both the United States government and U.S. business interests in Mexico.

Nevertheless, the argument must not be carried to the point where U.S. pressures are portrayed as decisive in the shaping of Mexico's strategy. The history of United States–Mexican diplomacy since the revolution is at the very least somewhat ambiguous on this point. On many occasions Mexico has acted abrasively, if not belligerently, in its relations with the United States and the U.S. foreign investor and suffered no ill consequences, political or economic. Many incidents between 1915 and 1920 testify to this fact, as do other events during the Cárdenas years, including the expropriation of U.S. oil properties. The record suggests that Mexican tenacity often combined with U.S. domestic factors to limit the ability and/or willingness of the United States to intervene in Mexican affairs; this pattern seems to have become more pronounced with the passage of the years since 1920. Furthermore, the U.S. business community in Mexico has never exhibited a united front for any length of time. To cite but one instance, when the expropriated oil companies demanded sanctions against Mexico, other major U.S. enterprises still in the Mexican market strongly opposed any measures which might have imperiled their own interests.

Only a careful study of the diplomatic record would reveal the true degree to which a fear of United States responses to more radical approaches to Mexican development conditioned the emergence of the development strategy discussed above. But a cursory reading suggests that Mexico's rulers were possessed with more flexibility than they chose to exercise. And certainly there was no pressing need for Mexico's social and economic policies to exhibit the "plus royaliste que le roi" quality which rapidly emerged. Stated all too briefly, this study suggests that the entente cordiale best expressed in the relationship between President Calles and U.S. Ambassador Dwight Morrow was dictated as much by a consensus of values on major social and economic issues as by considerations of realpolitik.

In the fourth place, as Manuel Moreno Sánchez noted, "each regime is indebted to its predecessor for being in power." In the process of Mexican politics each administration builds a set of vested interests which its grateful successor is naturally loath to disturb. A particularly corrupt regime, like that of Alemán, may produce some adverse reaction on the part of the following administration, but this is the exception rather than the rule. With the passing of each six-year administration, the top positions in the Mexican political and bureaucratic hierarchy are vacated. Some of the retiring *políticos* turn their wealth and talent toward private-sector economic enterprise; others retain their close contacts within the Revolutionary Coalition and continue to thrive on profits derived from public-sector expenditures. In either case they are likely to support government policies which distribute welfare gains from economic growth in Mexico in about the same way that they have over the past three decades. They now find themselves in those upper-income deciles which have reaped the rewards of growth, and they have no commitment to reforms which might alter the present distribution of gains to their detriment.

The second mestizo system, run through the PRI, is highly institutionalized in comparison with its Díaz-period predecessor. This accounts in great part for its continuing success. But the behavior of its power seekers is perhaps as praetorian as it was in the Díaz system. It would be difficult indeed to argue that their loyalties or identities broaden as they rise through the machinery of Mexican politics. Far more frequent, as we have noted so often, are examples of an initial commitment to the reform strand of the revolution being diluted as elevation affords greater opportunity for personal mobility. The number of Mexican politicians who succumb to the attractions of social and economic elite status appears far larger than those who retain allegiance to the labor, *campesino*, and even middle class segments of the population that constitute the PRI. Calles, not Cárdenas, most closely approximates the modal behavior of the mestizo revolutionary and his heirs.

This same kind of behavior froze social and economic mobility in the Díaz years, and eventually destroyed the Peace of Porfirio. Yet the Peace of the PRI, already forty years old, still appears viable. How has the second mestizo political system improved upon the original, and what aspects of the present-day Mexican economy and society explain its continued success, a success of fundamental importance in the process of Mexico's economic development?

*Chapter 7*

# THE PEACE OF THE PRI

The political system developed by Mexico's Revolutionary Coalition is now entering its fifth decade of operation. For forty years it has provided political stability, an accomplishment both superior to that of the first mestizo system developed under Díaz and unprecedented in the history of independent Mexico. What are the factors which account for its effectiveness?

One way to identify some of them is to examine the manner in which the present system has resolved the two fundamental problems that eventually destroyed the Peace of Porfirio: how has it eased or contained the pressures which drove Indian Mexico to revolt in 1911? and how has it managed the problem created by demands for social and economic advancement on the part of Mexico's educated mestizo population? In addition to these two salient historical problems of Mexican politics, however, the past three decades of rapid economic growth and social change may well be expected to have introduced further challenges to stable government in Mexico. A broader perspective is needed if we are to examine those newer challenges and to identify all the major factors which have contributed to the longevity and effectiveness of Mexico's present political system.

One of the most thoughtful and productive approaches to the study of political systems and their capacity to persist has been developed by David Easton. In his view, the major function of a political system is "the authoritative allocation of values," most easily understood as the formulation of those government decisions which are binding on society.[1] If a political system is to persist it must be able to make policy decisions and take the action necessary for their implementation; to do so successfully it must manage to induce most members of society to accept these decisions as binding.[2] In exploring

[1] David Easton, *A Systems Analysis of Political Life* (New York: John Wiley and Sons, Inc., 1965), chap. 2 and *passim*.

[2] *Ibid.*, pp. 23-24.

the capacity of a political system to persist, Easton focuses upon two broad categories of factors which are worth considering in some detail with regard to Mexico. The first entails the *demands* made upon a political system by the society in which it functions, and the second encompasses the *supports* generated for the system. Demands may threaten the life of a political system when they begin to exceed the capacity of the system to respond with relevant and authoritative policies, or what Easton calls system outputs. A successful political system must develop either an output capability to match increased demands, or the means by which to control and limit their number.

The quantity and variety of demands made upon governments have grown dramatically in the twentieth century. The development of industrial societies has increased the proportion of the total population that is aware of government activity and which makes demands upon public authorities, and has also broadened the nature and scope of those demands. The phrases mercantilism, laissez faire, welfare state, and socialism not only highlight the differing emphases which have marked governmental outputs over the past several centuries, but also implicitly reveal the changing nature and growing number of demands upon political systems in western societies today.

For over a decade the ubiquitous discussion of "the revolution of rising expectations" in the less-developed countries of the world has led people to believe that the pattern of increasing demands upon political systems experienced in the industrialized societies of the West has been rapidly emerging in Asia, Africa and Latin America as well. If the Mexican political system has been faced with such a revolution, how has it managed to respond successfully to new demands? If, on the other hand, "rising expectations" have not challenged the Mexican government, what are the factors which have held Mexican demands in check?

Viewed from the other side of Easton's equation, how has the Mexican system developed sources of support within Mexican society? Supports are best conceptualized in two general categories: diffuse and specific. The latter types are developed through concrete government policies; for example, support is gained from interests within the oil industry by instituting a system of depletion allowances. In contrast, diffuse support "is independent of the effects of daily [governmental] outputs. It consists of a reserve of support that enables a system to weather the many storms when outputs cannot be balanced off against inputs of demands."[3] Diffuse support, reflected in such feelings as patriotism, loyalty and good will, may be directed toward the nation, the regime, or the particular authorities in power. Regardless of the sentiment involved or the particular object toward which it is directed, the major characteristic of diffuse support is that it constitutes a reserve of politi-

[3]*Ibid.*, p. 273.

cal good will. An attachment to a political object for its own sake, "it taps deep political sentiments and is not easily depleted through disappointment with outputs."[4] How has the Mexican political system generated these supports for the political community, for the regime constituted by the Revolutionary Coalition and the PRI, and for the authorities who govern Mexico from one administration to the next?

The record of stability in Mexico since 1929 indicates that the present political system has succeeded in one or more of the following ways: (1) limiting the number of demands upon it; (2) increasing its capacity to meet growing demands; (3) stimulating diffuse support for the political system; and (4) retaining the specific support of the politically relevant members of Mexican society, that is, those members who control enough of the society's total resources to threaten the system's stability if they choose to do so. The only other factor which could account for stability—and that only in the short run—would be an increased application of coercion by governmental authorities. There is no clear evidence, however, that the use of coercion as an instrument of political control is on the rise in Mexico. In fact, despite its continued use—especially in rural Mexico—the incidence of coercive methods in Mexican political life has probably declined considerably during the course of the past four decades.[5] Mexico's present stability, therefore, would seem to be rooted in a mixture of the four possible trends in demands and supports outlined above. We will consider each of them more closely after examining the means by which the Revolutionary Coalition has dealt with the two salient challenges to stability inherited from the Díaz period.

## LAND AND MOBILITY

The problem posed for political stability by the agrarian revolt of 1911 was intrinsically much easier to resolve than that which was reflected in the mestizo revolution of mobility. All that was necessary to silence the demands of the landless *campesino* was to alter the structure of land tenure, to break up the great haciendas which dominated rural Mexico and redistribute the land to a new group of smallholders. All elements of the revolutionary leadership eventually pledged themselves to some mode of agrarian reform, and the process of official redistribution began as early as 1915. (The rate and structure of the process are illustrated in tables 7 and 8 of chapter 2.) Between

[4] *Ibid.*, p. 274.

[5] Unfortunately this estimate is only impressionistic, based upon secondary sources for the earlier years and a reading of Mexican newspapers during the 1960s. The latter source does suggest a rise in the use of coercion in the second half of the 1960s, as do several highly publicized events in Mexico City since the summer of 1968. But the apparent rise may simply reflect an expanding press coverage.

1915 and 1940 over one and a half million Mexican families received land under the redistribution program, and since that time another one million have been granted *ejidal* parcels. By 1940 close to 42 percent of those Mexicans employed in agriculture worked their own land, *ejidal* or private. While that figure has dropped in the following three decades due to the rapid rate of population growth, approximately one-third of Mexico's agricultural workers now possess at least some land of their own.

In a political sense the agrarian reform program in Mexico has had some profoundly stabilizing consequences.[6] First, those peasants who received plots of land were transformed from political dissidents into supporters of any regime that allowed them to retain those holdings, small as they might be. Second, the redistribution program gave hope to all those who had yet to benefit directly from it. Even today, a half century later, that hope has not been entirely eradicated since each new political administration publicly commits itself to agrarian reform and redistributes land throughout its term of office. Third, after the breakup of the old haciendas in the central and southern plateau regions of Mexico many of the poorest *campesinos* were no longer exposed directly to the rural rich. Most of the large privately owned commercial farms which have appeared since the 1930s are located in the north and northwest, far from the concentrated Indian population of central Mexico. Thus an age-old source of friction in rural Mexico has been greatly diminished. Fourth, the breakup of the hacienda system and the redistribution programs that followed created major social and economic mobility opportunities for the most highly motivated members of those pueblos and hacienda communities touched by reform. As Oscar Lewis has illustrated in his study of Tepoztlán, the revolution and the creation of the *ejidos* shattered many of the barriers to social and economic mobility which had previously restrained the more individualistic and commercialistic members of the community.[7] The more these ambitious individuals gained from the fruits of reform, the greater was their commitment to the new political regime that emerged during the 1920s and 1930s.

A noted student of rural Mexico recently related the revolution's agrarian reform program to the success of Mexico's present political system as follows:

> Is it not true that ejidal policies, social peace, and political stability go hand in hand? Are (or were) they not—to a very great extent—all facets of a single historical phenomenon? . . . It is very probable that the political

---

[6] See the references cited in chapter 3, and Rodolfo Stavenhagen, "Aspectos sociales de la estructura agraria en México," in *Neolatifundismo y explotación* (Mexico: Editorial Nuestro Tiempo, 1968), pp. 11–55.

[7] See Oscar Lewis, *Life in a Mexican Village: Tepoztlán Restudied* (Urbana: University of Illinois Press, 1963), chap. 21 and *passim*.

stability is linked with the absence of serious social tensions, and even with some possibilities of expression being available for the majority of the population, *which is concerned above all with preserving results already achieved, even if these have now become more or less illusory from the economic point of view.*[8]

If land reform responded directly to the demands inherent in the Indian revolt of 1911 it also indirectly assisted in relieving those pressures which had led to the mestizo revolt of 1910. The overall effect of the revolution and the consequent program of land redistribution benefited many of those northerners who were driven to revolt by the lack of opportunities for social and economic advancement during the later decades of the Díaz dictatorship. Leading *caciques* in the northern movement of the 1910s often became the large landowners of the 1920s and 1930s. Hundreds of less renowned *jefes*, on their own initiative or as officers of the revolutionary army, turned the establishment of *ejidos* to their own advantage. Sometimes they held most of the *ejidal* lands for themselves and their followers; on other occasions they simply raked off the profits from the sale of *ejidal* produce.

The problem posed for political stability by the mestizo drive for mobility was inherently much more difficult to resolve than that of land hunger on the part of Mexico's predominantly Indian *campesinos*. The latter problem could be eased for decades by a program of land reform. But how could the Revolutionary Coalition avoid a gradual freezing of the postrevolutionary elite and the consequent constriction of mobility of the type that had dragged the Díaz system to destruction? As noted in the preceding chapter, the personal value-orientations and the resulting behavior of the coalition's members were very similar to those of their predecessors in the Díaz regime. Indeed, during the years that Calles ruled the country through his chosen presidents it seemed quite probable that another elite circle might emerge around him as it had around Díaz; that wealth, social status and political power would concentrate in fewer and fewer hands; and that the delicate fabric of Mexican society might be shredded again a decade or so hence by frustrated aspirants for political place, economic gain, and social position. How were the Revolutionary Coalition and its political system eventually protected against the potentially destructive consequences of their own deeply entrenched pattern of praetorian behavior?

One way to protect the system and those whom it benefited was to ensure the continuous circulation of office holders within the political structure. As long as politics remained a major avenue of social and economic

---

[8] François Chevalier, "The Ejido and Political Stability in Mexico," in *The Politics of Conformity in Latin America*, edited by Claudio Veliz (London: Oxford University Press, 1967), p. 190. Emphasis added.

advancement in Mexico it was essential to avoid the sclerosis that had gripped and killed the Díaz political system. A second way to guard against freezing the Mexican elite was to develop greater opportunities for mestizo mobility outside of the political system itself. Throughout Mexican history politics had to a great extent attracted the ambitious because other careers were generally foreclosed. When economic development in the years after 1940 finally began to provide employment opportunities for an educated white collar group, the present Mexican political system was gradually relieved of a burden which it and its predecessors had borne for more than a century.

## Mobility via Politics

The arteries of mobility in Mexico's present political system have not hardened as they did in the Díaz period. The Mexican Senate and Chamber of Deputies are filled with men in their forties and fifties; some are in their thirties. Governors are not eighty, nor are presidents. Ever since Cárdenas broke the grip of Calles over the PRI and the political system, periodic access to all political positions in Mexico has characterized the operation of Mexican politics. In almost no cases are offices filled for more than one term by the same man. Presidents serve for six years and then retire; most senior officials in their administrations retire with them. The same pattern prevails at the state level, where governors serve for six years and then relinquish office to their successors. Even at the municipal level the practice of "no re-election" is the norm. In the second mestizo system a successful politician climbs to the top of the political pyramid and then retires, making room for the next in line.

Circulation takes place within the upper levels of the bureaucracy as well as in elective offices. On occasion the changes involve little more than switching jobs among a certain group of individuals; bureau chiefs change ministries, and state enterprise managers exchange seats. Nevertheless the principle of circulation is upheld, and new groups of advisors are brought into the system.

It has been estimated that every six-year change in presidential administrations witnesses a turnover of 18,000 elective offices and more than 25,000 appointive posts. Of those positions about half provide good to excellent incomes, licit and otherwise.[9] The better-educated members of the Mexican middle class who choose to follow government careers have increasingly entered the political system through the civil service, while their less-educated counterparts often enter via lower-echelon elective offices under PRI sponsorship. Through whatever route—career civil service, PRI politics, the military,

[9] Brandenburg, *Making of Modern Mexico*, pp. 157–58.

or state-owned enterprise—the "ambitious Mexican who rises to the top of the politico-bureaucratic heap . . . rarely needs more than six years to accumulate sufficient capital to retire for life."[10]

While the behavior of many members of the PRI's political hierarchy closely resembles that of their Díaz period predecessors, the effects on the present political system are quite different. Because politics still offers excellent opportunities for personal gain, those co-opted by the Revolutionary Coalition supply the system with the same loyalty and strength that their predecessors gave to the Díaz machine. However, since the established norms of the present regime dictate a continuous turnover of offices, such behavior no longer leads to a constriction of mobility via politics nor to a group of aging authorities who lose touch with their environment and its demands on political leadership. The norm of no reelection guarantees that the Revolutionary Coalition will give very serious thought every six years to the choice of new leadership, a practice which forces those who control the Mexican political system to give at least indirect consideration to the changing environmental parameters of Mexican politics.

In addition to the constant turnover in political and bureaucratic posts, there is another way in which present political elite behavior may be contrasted with that of the Díaz period. In the present system co-optation is not limited to relatives and followers of the coalition's members alone. With each election and each new administration the PRI has elevated an increasing number of persons who are neither relatives, allies, nor *campadres* of the ex-presidents or regional strongmen.[11] The ability and willingness of the political elite to co-opt talented and ambitious young men without previous political connections assures the political system of a broadening base of support, drains opposition parties and movements of potential sources of leadership, and contributes directly to a meaningful circulation within the political hierarchy.

## Mobility via Economic Development

It was noted in the previous chapter that the pattern of economic development in the Díaz years was not buoyant enough to ease the stress imposed upon the political system by mestizo mobility demands. There was some growth, but it was not of the magnitude needed to provide the middle class, white collar positions which educated mestizos sought. Since 1940 the relative contributions of the political and economic systems in managing the problem of mobility have been quite different. If the Peace of the PRI has

[10] *Ibid.*, pp. 161–62.

[11] Pablo González Casanova, *La Democracia en México* (Mexico: Ediciones ERA, 1965), pp. 39–40.

sustained Mexico's present rate of economic growth, Mexican economic development has in turn significantly eased the resolution of the perennial problem of Mexican politics and thus contributed directly to political stability.

Upper and middle class Mexicans constituted less than 17 percent of the total Mexican population in 1940. By 1963 that figure had approximately doubled. More than 30 percent of Mexico's families in 1963 were earning over $1,200 per year, and the rate and structure of economic growth since then suggest that the proportion of the total population which we can designate as middle class or above by income has continued to increase fairly rapidly.[12]

TABLE 7-1.  CLASS AND OCCUPATIONAL STRUCTURE, 1940-1960

| Class | 1940 | 1950 | 1960 |
|---|---|---|---|
| Upper Class[a] | 2.9 | 2.0 | 6.5 |
| Middle Class[b] | 12.6 | 25.0 | 33.5 |
| Transitional[c] | 6.5 | 20.0 | 20.0 |
| Popular[d] | 78.0 | 53.0 | 40.0 |
| Total | 100.0 | 100.0 | 100.0 |

Source: Howard F. Cline, *Mexico: Revolution to Evolution, 1940-1960* (London: Oxford University Press, 1962), chap. 11.  Since Cline's measurements include both income and occupation some occupational categories are found in both the transitional and the middle class sectors.

[a]Managerial and professional.
[b]Professional, technical, office workers, small tradesmen, artisans.
[c]Small tradesmen, semiskilled artisans, miners, petroleum labor, service employees.
[d]Service employees, manual and day laborers, agriculturists, others.

Viewed from the perspective of occupational structure, Mexico's pattern of economic growth has considerably expanded the employment opportunities for the white collar worker. It has been estimated that by 1960 approximately 40 percent of the Mexican work force were employed in upper or middle class occupations as professionals, managers, technicians, office workers, small tradesmen and artisans.[13] The comparable figure for such forms of employment in 1940 was 15.5 percent. These estimates suggest an increase in these occupations of over 150 percent during the two decades following 1940. Other statistical attempts to isolate the size of upper and middle class Mexico at the end of the 1950s—measured in terms of income, occupation, or some combination of the two—arrive at figures closer to 30

[12] See table 4-2.

[13] Howard F. Cline, *Mexico: Revolution to Evolution, 1940-1960* (London: Oxford University Press, 1962), chap. 11.

percent.[14] Even if we accept the lower estimates as a closer approximation to the reality of the Mexican social structure at the beginning of the 1960s, it is clear that the past three decades of industrialization have witnessed a degree of social and economic mobility unsurpassed during any other period of Mexican history.[15]

As the present political system has avoided a growing concentration of political power in the hands of a few unchanging individuals, so too has recent economic development in Mexico avoided a repetition of the pattern established in the Díaz period. There has been a distinct lessening of the concentration of income within the top 5 percent of Mexican families in recent years. The proportion of total Mexican income going to the top 2.5 percent fell from about 32 percent in 1950 to 16 percent in 1963; and that going to the top 5 percent has dropped from approximately 40 percent to 26 percent over the same years. Those who have gained relatively are those located in the seventh, eighth and ninth deciles; their proportion of total income has risen from 26 percent to 37 percent.

The point of these statistics on income distribution, as of those on the circulation of posts in the political system, is not that economic and political power in Mexico is fairly evenly distributed; we have already documented the great degree of concentration of both political and economic resources. What the statistics do illustrate is the circulating nature of the elite within the political system and a trend toward less income concentration within the uppermost income groups. Both of these factors have considerably broadened the range of opportunities for social and economic mobility in post-1940 Mexico, and in doing so have contributed immeasurably to the Peace of the PRI.

## MEXICAN STABILITY: THE BROADER PERSPECTIVE

Land redistribution, political elite circulation and rapid economic growth have all helped to mediate the two challenges to political stability in Mexico that were the most prominent at least as late as the 1920s and 1930s. But other ingredients contributing to stability since those years can only be iden-

[14] See Arturo González Cosío, "Clases y estratos sociales," *México: cincuenta años de revolución* (Mexico: Fondo de Cultura Económica, 1961) 2: 54 and *passim*; and Ifigenia de Navarette, *La Distribución del ingreso y el desarrollo económico de México* (Mexico, D.F.: Instituto de Investigaciones Económicas, Escuela Nacional de Economía, 1960).

[15] All attempts to measure the size of the Mexican middle and upper classes suffer from both statistical and analytical difficulties. Data on income levels and occupational structure are incomplete. Furthermore, how can agreement be reached on what income level or occupation qualifies as "middle class"? What is important for political stability is that upward-aspiring individuals *feel* that they are entering the "middle class." Their view, and not the statisticians', is the relevant variable.

tified if we broaden our frame of reference in an attempt to encompass all the significant variables. For this purpose we can apply the systematic framework for political analysis described in the introduction to this chapter. What is the nature of the demands which various segments of Mexican society have made upon their political system? Have these demands reached the point at which it makes sense to speak of a revolution of rising expectations which strains the PRI system in Mexico? How has the political system responded to new demands? How has it stimulated specific and diffuse support? How has it limited the number of demands upon the system, and/or increased its capacity to respond to them with governmental outputs? And more specifically, how has it retained the support of those members of Mexican society whose control over resources enables them to threaten political stability if their interests are jeopardized? In short, how has the mix of demands, supports and governmental policy outputs in Mexico produced forty years of political stability and helped to sustain more than three decades of rapid economic growth?

## Limited Demands and Liberal Support

One of the surprising aspects of political life in Mexico over the past four decades has been the limited nature of the demands made upon Mexico's political system. They have been limited in two senses: first, in terms of the proportion of the total population involved in the creation of demands; and second, in terms of the resources required by the government to satisfy them. Equally interesting is the extensive nature of what we have called diffuse support for the Mexican political system, that support which is given to the present regime and its authorities without a quid pro quo. It is found at practically all levels of Mexican society, and clearly binds to the political system major segments which might otherwise seek a radical restructuring of Mexican politics. In the following discussion both the demand and support variables in the present system will be considered.

The welfare effects of economic development in Mexico over the past three decades indicate that at least the bottom half of Mexican society (in income terms) either makes very few demands upon the political system or finds its demands generally unfulfilled. Chapter 4 suggested that the bottom 20-30 percent of Mexico's families may in fact have suffered from absolute declines in their standards of living, and that the bottom five deciles have clearly suffered a relative decline in income during a period of rapid economic growth and emerging affluence at the upper levels of Mexican society. Most of the families in the bottom half of the income scale are located in rural Mexico, and they are the victims of the government's dual agricultural policy. The government has consistently allocated a major portion of its expenditures for the construction of an infrastructure to support large private commercial farms, has preached agrarian reform while redistributing arable land at a slowing pace between 1940 and 1958, has often ignored obvious violations of agrarian statutes, and has in other ways contributed to the emergence of Mexico's new agricultural dualism.

Despite their disadvantaged position in the Mexican social spectrum and the continued lack of governmental response to their social and economic needs, the members of this segment of Mexican society have raised few political demands to challenge the capabilities of the present political system. Three major factors appear to be responsible for the limited nature of their demands. The first encompasses what might best be called the political culture of this group, that is, its "attitudes toward the political system and its various parts, and attitude toward the role of the self in the system."[16] The second involves the capacity of the Mexican economy to satisfy mestizo mobility aspirations. The third includes the structure and functioning of the official party, particularly its capacity to limit effective competition among elite groups. If such competition had not been carefully controlled, different factions would undoubtedly have attempted to mobilize support among the disadvantaged half of Mexican society; and if they had succeeded the nature of Mexican politics would be radically different from what it is today.

How can we characterize the political culture of the "have-nots" of Mexican society? How does this predominantly rural group relate to the political system? Recent discussions of political culture have distinguished three modal types: parochial, subject, and participant.[17] For our purposes the most significant feature of the parochial individual is that he expects nothing of the political system. In some cases this results from his lack of knowledge about the government and its operations; in other cases suspicion and mistrust dictate a dissociation between the parochial and his government. Unlike the parochials, those sharing subject and participant orientations do relate themselves directly to the national political process, though in quite different ways. The subject is both aware of the government and affectively oriented to it. But his relationship with it is "toward the system on the general level, and toward the output, administrative, or 'downward flow' side of the political system; it is essentially a passive relationship."[18] The participant, in contrast, is one who identifies with political system inputs as well as outputs. He is a member of interest groups and associations that attempt to influence policy

[16] Gabriel A. Almond and Sidney Verba, The Civic Culture: Political Attitudes and Democracy in Five Nations (Princeton, N.J.: Princeton University Press, 1963), p. 13.

[17] Ibid., chap. 1; Lucian W. Pye and Sidney Verba, eds., Political Culture and Political Development (Princeton, N.J.: Princeton University Press, 1965), passim, and especially chap. 9, "Mexico: The Established Revolution," by Robert E. Scott.

[18] Almond and Verba, Civic Culture, p. 19. Emphasis added.

formulation; he is the political party member, the voter, the political "activist" even if only in election years.

## The Parochial Culture

Parochials will rarely make demands upon the political system. They are village-oriented traditionalists, generally contented with their isolated and passive life. Robert Scott has estimated that 90 percent of the Mexican population was parochial in its political orientation at the time of the revolution, and that 25 percent remain so today.[19] In 1910 this segment endangered political stability not because it was making increasing demands upon the Díaz system, but rather because its traditional institutions and sources of livelihood were being destroyed by the enclosure movement of the late 1800s. Under the regime of the PRI this quarter of the Mexican population, thanks to the revolution and land reform, has thus far not been a source of stress on the political system. Possessing tiny plots of land, certificates promising land, or the vague hopes of ownership sometime in the future, Mexico's parochials, half of them still Indian in orientation, generally ask for no more. Their interests can most often be ignored, preserving the political system's resources for allocation in response to the demands coming from the more articulate and powerful segments of Mexican society.

The cultural and psychological characteristics of the parochial segment of the Mexican population that serve to limit its involvement in politics have been noted by historians and anthropologists for decades. If one were to compile a list of the characteristic traits of this stratum of Mexican society, as noted by such distinguished scholars as Samuel Ramos, Octavio Paz, Manuel Gamio, Eric Wolf, Oscar Lewis, Frank Tannenbaum and Sol Tax, the most repeated words would be apathy, passivity, fatalism, resignation, stoicism, distrust, and feelings of inferiority.[20] The psychological impact of the conquest, the accompanying destruction of Indian society, and the child-parent relationship which developed between Indian and Spaniard in the centuries

[19] Scott, "Mexico: The Established Revolution," pp. 335-45.

[20] Consult the following works: Manuel Gamio, ed., *La Población del valle de Teotihuacán* (Mexico: Dirección de Talleres Gráficos, 1922); Oscar Lewis, *The Children of Sanchez* (New York: Random House, Vintage Books, 1967); Oscar Lewis, *Pedro Martinez* (New York: Random House, Vintage Books, 1967); Oscar Lewis, *Five Families: Mexican Case Studies in the Culture of Poverty* (New York: Science Edition, 1962); Oscar Lewis, *Life in a Mexican Village: Tepoztlán Restudied* (Urbana: University of Illinois Press, 1963); Octavio Paz, *The Labyrinth of Solitude: Life and Thought in Mexico* (New York: Grove Press, 1961); Samuel Ramos, *Profile of Man and Culture in Mexico*, translated by Peter G. Earle (Austin: University of Texas Press, 1962); Frank Tannenbaum, *Peace by Revolution: Mexico After 1910*, 2nd ed. (New York: Columbia University Press, 1966); and Sol Tax, ed., *Heritage of Conquest* (Glencoe, Ill.: Free Press, 1952).

following the conquest all contributed to the Indian's passive acceptance of his subordinate position in Mexican society. Nor is this pattern of interethnic relations unique to Mexico; it is generally evidenced in all those Latin American countries in which large Indian populations survived the conquest.[21]

The way in which such personality types develop and perpetuate themselves over generations has been analyzed most cogently by Everett Hagen, who has noted how parental behavior patterns instill the same personal attributes of passivity, ineffectiveness and apathy in children.[22] In the Mexican case patterns of behavior derived from childhood experiences and cultural norms were reinforced by the results of the Indians' daily contact with Spaniards and mestizos. As Tannenbaum noted years ago, Mexican history has been one of constant conflict between white and Indian.

> No general statements . . . concerning the racial distribution of Mexico, the cultural divergence between the races, or the strife between the whites, the *mestizos*, and the Indians, give an idea of the persistent conflict that has shaped the relationships between these groups. It is only upon examination of details, the little things, in attitudes, and the physical bearing, that the depth of the separation can be sensed. The white has exploited; the *mestizo* has played a double game when he could, having been now the partner of the white man, and now of the Indian. The Indian has retired into the mountains when he could, otherwise into himself. He has refused to learn the Spanish language; refused to take over the conquerers' customs; refused to share in the white man's interests; refused to be a part of the game as it was being played. In part, he could not participate because he was not allowed to.[23]

Over four hundred years of racial oppression have left a mark upon the Indian which the revolution failed to eradicate. The predominance of the white man, his social prestige, his economic prerogatives, his capacity to use political institutions and military power to maintain his position reinforced the psycho-cultural processes analyzed by Hagen to instill in the Mexican Indian not only distrust and hatred, but also docility, apathy and submissiveness. He expects nothing from government but to be cheated by it. As Lewis noted of the Indians in Tepoztlán, the motives of everyone are suspected

---

[21] For its development in Mexico see especially Eric R. Wolf, *Sons of the Shaking Earth* (Chicago: University of Chicago Press, Phoenix Books, 1959), chap. 10; Charles Gibson, *The Aztecs Under Spanish Rule* (Stanford, Cal.: Stanford University Press, 1964); and the literature reviewed in Gordon Hewes, "Mexicans in Search of the Mexican: Notes on Mexican National Character Studies," *American Journal of Economics and Sociology* 13 (January 1954): 209–23; and John Leddy Phelan, "México y lo Mexicano," *Hispanic American Historical Review* 36 (August 1956): 309–18.

[22] Everett Hagen, *On the Theory of Social Change* (Homewood, Ill.: Dorsey Press, 1962).

[23] Tannenbaum, *Peace by Revolution*, p. 27.

from the nation's highest officials to the local priest and even one's relatives. It is generally assumed that all people in positions of power will use it to their own advantage at the expense of others. "Honest government or leadership is considered an impossibility; altruism is not understood."[24]

Thus as much as 25 percent of today's Mexican population is either so isolated and ill-informed as to be incapable of comprehending the workings of the Mexican political system, or is so distrustful of "white" authorities as to avoid contact with the national political system whenever possible. The behavior of this group is often marked by anomic violence, the reports of which fill Mexican newspapers weekly. Village fights village, and local political figures and *campesino* leaders are assassinated. However, this behavior is a far cry from "the calculated, organized and purposive political violence that is a common feature of Latin American politics."[25] Because it has no broader purposes, such behavior over the past forty years has neither threatened the political system directly, in the form of a military challenge, nor indirectly, in the form of disturbances requiring a significant allocation of governmental resources to be controlled.

## The Subject Culture

A much larger and more important group than the parochials in terms of Mexican political stability is that which, broadly speaking, shares the political orientations characteristic of a subject political culture. Scott has estimated that close to two-thirds of the Mexican people presently relate to the political system as subjects; they are aware of government and its activities, approve or disapprove of its various aspects and programs, but remain essentially passive in relation to it rather than participating in civic and interest group activities. It is within this segment—we will call it the subject segment—that we find what one author has labeled "the ambivalent Mexican." He is the man who, on the one hand, supports the revolution and the political institutions that have emerged since the 1930s and, on the other hand, is quite cynical about Mexican politics and political leaders.[26] His cynicism and distrust with regard to the operations of the present system generally lead him to avoid political activity and to expect little or nothing for himself from the government.

[24] Lewis, *Life in a Mexican Village*, p. 292. Lewis adds that "The frank, direct person, if he exists anywhere in Tepoztlán, is considered naive or the greatest rogue of all, so powerful or shameless as to have no need to conceal his deeds or thoughts."

[25] Martin Needler, *Political Development in Latin America: Instability, Violence, and Evolutionary Change* (New York: Random House, 1968), p. 106. This book is one of the most insightful, well-organized and cogently written studies of the problems of political development in Latin America to appear during the 1960s.

[26] Joseph A. Kahl, *The Measurement of Modernism* (Austin: University of Texas Press, 1968), p. 114; and Almond and Verba, *Civic Culture*, chaps. 1, 2.

The ambivalent Mexican is revealed in two recent survey studies which concentrated wholly or in part upon Mexicans' feelings about their political history and present government.[27] The samples in the first survey, presented in a study entitled *The Civic Culture*, were taken from cities with a population of 10,000 and above; we can therefore be reasonably sure that the views of the Indian and otherwise rural-oriented Mexican parochials are not represented.[28] Within the urban environment, however, an attempt was made to obtain a representative cross section of the Mexican population. For our purposes the most salient finding of the survey was that a great number of Mexicans bear a strong reserve of good will for their political system and its institutions. They do so despite the fact that they are often alienated from its day-to-day operations and from the officials who work within it, and they expect little from it in the sense of specific governmental policy outputs. In the terminology we have been using in this chapter, their demands upon the political system remain low because they view actual governmental operations and political-bureaucratic behavior with a great deal of cynicism; at the same time they remain a strong source of diffuse support for the system through their attachment to its revolutionary symbolism and manifest goals.

Responses to several questions in the *Civic Culture* survey illustrate both the general alienation which characterizes Mexicans' attitudes toward their government and their lack of expectations with regard to government outputs. When asked to estimate the degree of impact which activity on the part of the national government had on their lives, 66 percent of the Mexican respondents answered "no effect," 23 percent "some effect" and 7 percent "great effect." As indicated in table 7-2, these responses contrast sharply with those gathered in the other four countries sampled in the same survey.

A follow-up question was worded thus: "On the whole, do the activities of the national government tend to improve conditions in this country, or would we be better off without them?"[29] The responses, shown in table 7-3, again illustrate the relatively low opinion which many Mexicans have about the operations of their national government. One-fifth of those questioned felt that government activity was detrimental to national life, and only 58 percent viewed government operations as beneficial. Combining the results of the two questions the authors of the survey note that "only a minority of the

[27] The results of the two surveys are reported in Almond and Verba, *Civic Culture*; and Kahl, *Measurement of Modernism*.

[28] See Almond and Verba, *Civic Culture*, p. 46. Over one-third of those surveyed were migrants from rural areas, and some of the newest arrivals undoubtedly retained a partially parochial orientation. For an interesting analysis of the migrant group within the survey which documents this assertion see Wayne A. Cornelius, Jr., "Urbanization as an Agent in Latin American Political Instability: The Case of Mexico," *American Political Science Review* 62 (September 1969): 823-57.

[29] Almond and Verba, *Civic Culture*, p. 81.

TABLE 7-2. ESTIMATED DEGREE OF IMPACT OF NATIONAL GOVERNMENT
ON DAILY LIFE

| Percentage of Respondents Who Say National Government Has | Mexico | Italy | Germany | U.K. | U.S. |
|---|---|---|---|---|---|
| Great effect | 7 | 23 | 38 | 33 | 41 |
| Some effect | 23 | 31 | 32 | 40 | 44 |
| No effect | 66 | 19 | 17 | 23 | 11 |
| Other | – | 3 | – | – | – |
| Don't know | 3 | 24 | 12 | 4 | 4 |

Source: Gabriel A. Almond and Sidney Verba, *The Civic Culture: Political Attitudes and Democracy in Five Nations* (Princeton, N.J.: Princeton University Press, 1963), p. 80.

TABLE 7-3. CHARACTER OF IMPACT OF NATIONAL GOVERNMENT

| Percentage Who Say | Mexico | Italy | Germany | U.K. | U.S. |
|---|---|---|---|---|---|
| National government improves conditions | 58 | 66 | 61 | 77 | 76 |
| Sometimes improves conditions, sometimes does not | 18 | 20 | 30 | 15 | 19 |
| Better off without national government | 19 | 5 | 3 | 3 | 3 |
| Other | 5 | 8 | 5 | 4 | 2 |

Source: Almond and Verba, *Civic Culture*, p. 82.

Mexicans (less than one-third) attributes significance to the government, and even among this third a substantial proportion either takes a skeptical position on the benefits of government or rejects it as largely harmful in its effects."[30]

Mexican feelings of alienation and distrust with regard to their government were also revealed in another set of responses. Those surveyed in each of the five countries investigated were asked in several ways what kind of treatment they would expect to receive from government officials and the police. The responses are shown in table 7-4. Again it is the Mexican who is the most alienated, in this instance considerably more so than even his Italian counterpart. And it is worth noting once more that the Mexican survey sampled only urban Mexicans, and not those rural residents who might be expected to have shown more suspicion of government authorities. If over half of those questioned from this urban sample did not expect equal treatment, a representative sampling of Mexican society would surely have revealed that at least 80 percent of the population shared these feelings.

[30] *Ibid.*, p. 82.

TABLE 7-4. EXPECTATION OF TREATMENT BY GOVERNMENTAL BUREAUCRACY AND POLICE*

| Percentage Who Say | Mexico | | Italy | | Germany | | U.K. | | U.S. | |
|---|---|---|---|---|---|---|---|---|---|---|
| | Bur. | Pol. | Bur. | Pol. | Bur. | Pol. | Bur. | Pol. | Bur. | Pol. |
| They expect equal treatment | 42 | 32 | 53 | 56 | 65 | 72 | 83 | 89 | 83 | 85 |
| They don't expect equal treatment | 50 | 57 | 13 | 10 | 9 | 5 | 7 | 6 | 9 | 8 |
| Depends | 5 | 5 | 17 | 15 | 19 | 15 | 6 | 4 | 4 | 5 |
| Other | – | – | 6 | 6 | – | – | – | – | – | – |
| Don't know | 3 | 5 | 11 | 13 | 7 | 8 | 2 | – | 4 | 2 |

Source: Almond and Verba, *Civic Culture*, p. 108.

*Actual texts of the questions: "Suppose there were some question that you had to take to a government office—for example, a tax question or housing regulation. Do you think you would be given equal treatment—I mean, would you be treated as well as anyone else?" "If you had some trouble with the police—a traffic violation maybe, or were accused of a minor offense—do you think you would be given equal treatment? That is, would you be treated as well as anyone else?"

Two further findings from the survey are of interest to us. One was that the Mexicans were the most poorly informed of the five groups investigated. "Approximately half the Mexican respondents—including many who say they follow politics—could not name correctly any political leader or any government department."[31] The second finding was that, measured in terms of voluntary association membership and more direct forms of political activity, the Mexicans exhibited lower frequencies of political performance than any of the other four national groups surveyed.

A recent investigation of Mexican factory workers adds corroborating evidence to this profile of the subject culture in Mexico. Joseph Kahl's findings reveal the same high degree of cynicism and alienation toward their government and political system on the part of Mexicans well above the lowest income levels. He notes that 59 percent of his urban sample believed that labor officials, generally a part of the PRI hierarchy, had no interest in the welfare of members of their unions. He quotes from a typical response to questions about the operation of politics in Mexico given by an "articulate and ambitious" foreman in a small-town textile mill with four years of primary education:

> For me the national elections are a myth. . . . Everything spent on campaigns and tours should be spent to help the people with hospitals, places to find work, instead of spending millions and millions of pesos uselessly. If the government is going to pick the man who will be President, why not just say so openly?
> Besides, I'm not a follower of any party, nor do I think any of them are legal or any good. They're not serious. Just take a look at Señor _____, director of the PRI; he has his bunch of friends, and from them, chooses So-and-So to be mayor, and so on. Unfortunately, in small towns the behaviour of those fellows is notorious. They don't help the progress of the towns at all.
> I left politics because it is a dirty business.[32]

If the frustrations with the operations of the PRI and the Revolutionary Coalition led such men to voice increasing demands or to oppose the government outright, this alienation and latent hostility would rapidly become a source of severe stress upon Mexico's present political system. Yet, for over forty years, this subject segment of Mexican society—encompassing over half of the total population—has neither increased notably its demands nor even lost its belief that the political system is somehow moving in the right direction.[33]

[31] *Ibid.*, p. 96.

[32] Kahl, *Measurement of Modernism*, pp. 114–15.

[33] For example, the same shop foreman quoted above also says of his country that "the future of Mexico is very good in general, because Mexico in every respect is a

The *Civic Culture* survey discussed previously adduced some interesting evidence on this point. One of the questions asked was, "Speaking generally, what are the things about this country that you are most proud of?" The results are presented in table 7–5. Thirty percent of the Mexican respondents expressed pride in their political system despite the fact that they mistrust it,

TABLE 7–5. ASPECTS OF NATION IN WHICH RESPONDENTS REPORT PRIDE

| Percentage Who Say They Are Proud of | Mexico | Italy | Germany | U.K. | U.S. |
|---|---|---|---|---|---|
| Governmental, political institutions | 30 | 3 | 7 | 46 | 85 |
| Social legislation | 2 | 1 | 6 | 18 | 13 |
| Position in international affairs | 3 | 2 | 5 | 11 | 5 |
| Economic system | 24 | 3 | 33 | 10 | 23 |
| Characteristics of people | 15 | 11 | 36 | 18 | 7 |
| Spiritual virtues and religion | 8 | 6 | 3 | 1 | 3 |
| Contributions to the arts | 9 | 16 | 11 | 6 | 1 |
| Contributions to science | 1 | 3 | 12 | 7 | 3 |
| Physical attributes of country | 22 | 25 | 17 | 10 | 5 |
| Nothing or don't know | 16 | 27 | 15 | 10 | 4 |
| Other | 14 | 21 | 3 | 11 | 9 |
| Total % of responses* | 144 | 118 | 148 | 148 | 158 |

Source: Almond and Verba, *Civic Culture*, p. 102.
*Percentages exceed one hundred because of multiple responses.

expect little personally from it, and generally view the politicians and bureaucrats within the system as corrupt men bent solely upon personal advancement. Where the Italian is both alienated from the day-to-day operation of politics and has no pride in his political institutions, the ambivalent Mexican manages to meld alienation and pride, a remarkably fruitful conjunction of attitudes for the Mexican strategy of economic development. Much of this diffuse support results from the revolution and the manifest goals that emerged from it. Two-thirds of Mexico's respondents indicated that they could name some of the goals of the revolution, and they listed, among others, democracy, political liberty and equality, economic welfare, agrarian reform, social equality and national freedom.[34] These same respondents were then asked if the goals they listed had been realized, or if people were still working to achieve them. "Of the respondents . . . 25% thought the goals had

---

forward-looking country and is ahead of all the others in Latin America. It is, taking into account all the countries of the world, for its doctrine, for its *politics*, for its mission in favor of peace and neutrality and respect for the rights of others. . . ." *Ibid.*, p. 115. Emphasis added.

[34] Almond and Verba, *Civic Culture*, p. 104.

been realized, 61% thought that people were still working to attain them, and 14% thought they had been forgotten."[35]

The findings from Kahl's survey of Mexican workers are quite similar. He notes that 78 percent of his respondents felt that Mexico was "better off" as a result of the revolution. "They say that things are slowly improving, for they see 'progress' around them in the form of new schools, hospitals, roads, and industries."[36] In the words of our shop foreman, personally disgusted with Mexican politics, "the future of Mexico, as everybody knows, is developing rapidly."[37]

The inculcation of a sense of legitimacy is probably the single most effective device for raising and sustaining the level of diffuse support for a political system. When citizens sense a conformity between their own feelings of what is right and the goals of their political regime, their inclination to accept political decisions as binding is greatly enhanced. As Easton has noted, "On a day-to-day basis, if there is a strong inner conviction of the moral validity of the authorities or regime, support may persist even in the face of repeated deprivations attributed to the outputs of the authorities or their failure to àct."[38] The evidence drawn from the two surveys cited above, both undertaken within the past ten years, indicates that while the great majority of Mexicans hold a very low opinion of Mexican authorities, a large percentage of them continue to associate the present regime with the manifest goals of the revolution. In doing so they imbue the regime with a sense of legitimacy which considerably lessens the sources of stress that might otherwise endanger Mexico's present political stability.

Regardless of the policies which it has adopted in the years since 1929, the regime of the Revolutionary Coalition has never ceased to preach its commitment to those goals. They have linked the PRI and the Mexican presidency to land reform, social justice, the rights of labor, and democracy— by word far more often than by deed—and in so doing, they have legitimized these two political structures to a degree hitherto unknown in postcolonial Mexico. The survey data indicate that many Mexicans still believe that the regime is implementing the manifest goals of the revolution, and their recognition of both the latent goals and the resulting praetorian behavior of the system's politicians and bureaucrats has not dissolved their pride in Mexico's political institutions.

The legitimating ideology with which the regime has managed to surround itself is only one of four major factors that help to account for the political quiescence of the subject segment of Mexican society. The second we have

---

[35] *Ibid.*, p. 104.

[36] Kahl, *Measurement of Modernism*, p. 114.

[37] *Ibid.*, p. 115.

[38] Easton, *Systems Analysis*, p. 278.

already noted in discussing the growing opportunities for social and economic mobility in Mexico during the Peace of the PRI. We have been examining here the political attitudes of the urban lower and middle classes, those persons who have experienced upward mobility themselves or have witnessed advancement among their families and friends. It is interesting to note in table 7-5, for example, that 24 percent of all the Mexican respondents to the question "what are the things about this country that you are most proud of?" named the Mexican economic system as a major source of pride. Only in Germany was the economic system mentioned more frequently, and the corresponding figure for the United States was only 23 percent. While other factors—such as native pride in the nationalized oil industry and the constant governmental propaganda about economic development—help to account for the high level of approval of the Mexican economy, it is also quite probable that the obvious opportunities which the economy has presented for advancement have conditioned this favorable response. The shop foreman quoted above had risen to his position with only four years of primary education; it is understandable that he viewed the future of Mexico as bright.

The crucial point is not that mobility in Mexico is higher than in many other Latin American countries. Kahl's comparative study of Brazil and Mexico, for example, suggests that the rates of upward movement in the two countries are quite similar; and another recent work suggests that mobility opportunities for the lower classes in the urban Colombian setting are at least as great as those in Mexico.[39] The point is rather that the Mexican economy has provided excellent opportunities for the really ambitious mestizo. As Whiteford's comparative study of the Mexican city of Querétaro and the Colombian city of Popayán demonstrates, a new group—what he calls the lower upper class—has appeared in Mexico since 1940, comprising "energetic men of the Lower Middle Class who acquired the franchises for the new goods and services coming into the region and built productive businesses out of nothing."[40] Members of this new group are now "at the top of the social scale" in both their own minds and the minds of most other Querétaños.[41] Their rise has been witnessed by all and grudgingly admired by most. Thus the rapidity of Mexican economic development has contributed to political stability not only by providing ample advancement opportunities for the most ambitious members of the Mexican lower and middle classes, but also by demonstrating to those who have not yet reaped the benefits of growth that such opportunities exist.

[39] Kahl, *Measurement of Modernism*, appendix B; and Andrew Hunter Whiteford, *Two Cities of Latin America* (Garden City, N.Y.: Doubleday & Co., Anchor Books, 1964), p. 135.

[40] Whiteford, *Two Cities*, p. 220.

[41] *Ibid.*, p. 224.

The third factor which helps to account for the political quiescence of this large middle group in Mexico is the specific nature of its political culture. Certain psycho-cultural attributes of this broad mestizo group, while quite different from those which limit the rural and Indian-oriented Mexican's participation in politics, are just as effective in controlling its demands. The attributes are those which, as Octavio Paz has noted, fatally divide Mexican mestizo society into the strong and the weak, and turn social life into continuous combat. The best-known and still most persuasive analysis of the problem is found in Samuel Ramos's *Profile of Man and Culture in Mexico.* What Ramos attempted was a psychoanalysis of the Mexican mestizo, and what he uncovered was a deep feeling of inferiority that has pervaded Mexican society for generations. He traces the origins of these feelings to the conquest and to the gradual emergence of that mestizo segment of Mexican society scorned by Indian and Spaniard alike. Lacking values of his own, the mestizo has desperately copied those of others—the Spanish, the French, and even the North Americans—but has failed to rid himself of a fundamental sense of personal worthlessness. These feelings of inferiority have led to both a profound sense of self-distrust and "an unjustified distrust of others, in addition to a hypersensitivity in his contact with other men."[42] The mestizo's life is devoted to an affirmation of his own individuality at the cost of others. The following excerpt from Ramos's study summarizes those portions of his analysis which are most relevant for our purposes:

> Self-obsession and constant attention to one's ego imply, naturally enough, a corresponding lack of interest in others, an incomprehension of the lives of one's fellow men. In brief, one's reactions to the sentiment of inferiority lead to militant individualism, which damages in varying degree one's feeling toward the community. Undeniably, the will to cooperative action and to collective discipline is weak in Mexico. In general, our life tends to dispersion and anarchy, to the obvious detriment of social solidarity.[43]

Exceptions have been taken to Ramos's methodology, particularly to his reliance on Adler's theory of resentment. Nevertheless, most Mexican scholars feel that his observations are still valid. As Octavio Paz notes, "Ramos has given us an extremely penetrating description of the attitudes that make each one of us a closed, inaccessible being."[44]

The two surveys cited earlier add some quantitative evidence on the degree of distrust and interpersonal hostility that exist in Mexico. Already noted is the fact that fewer Mexicans are members of clubs, organizations or

[42] Ramos, *Profile*, p. 62.

[43] *Ibid.*, p. 128.

[44] Paz, *Labyrinth of Solitude*, p. 160.

active political groups than their counterparts in the United States, Great Britain, Germany, or Italy. And in Kahl's study of urban workers in Brazil and Mexico one survey item dramatically demonstrates the pervasive sense of mistrust in the latter country. The item reads, "People help persons who have helped them not so much because it is right but because it is good business." The responses were as follows:[45]

|                    | Brazil | Mexico |
|--------------------|--------|--------|
| Agree very much    | 13     | 41     |
| Agree a little     | 8      | 41     |
| Disagree a little  | 11     | 11     |
| Disagree very much | 68     | 7      |
| Total              | 100    | 100    |

In emphasizing the distrust which pervades interpersonal relationships in Mexico and sets sharp limits on personal contacts and social cohesion outside the family setting, Kahl quotes one interviewee as saying "the best friend is the one who will be the traitor."[46]

Citizens who view their fellow men in this manner do not overload a political system with organized demands. They may rely on extended family structures for support, or perhaps develop some limited sense of community within their own barrio.[47] But their deep sense of distrust and wholly justified cynicism about politics prevents them from entering into broader associations to voice political demands and to influence governmental policy decisions. In factories they look no further than the boss or the labor leader, the patrón upon whom they continue to depend while not really trusting him either. And whenever these forms of personalism and paternalism characterize a potentially political relationship, the development of political organizations based upon a clear recognition of common interest is once again prevented. The psychological and cultural barriers to a rapid growth in political activity on the part of the 50 to 60 percent of Mexican society examined here, like the barriers restraining the parochial stratum discussed above, suggest that the very social and cultural environment within which the Mexican political system operates has served admirably to limit a potential source of stress on the present regime.

The enduring nature of these barriers is further illustrated when we consider the political behavior of this subject group from a slightly different

[45] Kahl, Measurement of Modernism, p. 82.
[46] Ibid., p. 82.
[47] See Lewis, Five Families, pp. 62ff.

frame of reference. It was from this vast mestizo segment of Mexican society that those individuals appeared who led the struggles to organize labor unions and agrarian leagues during the 1910s and 1920s. Viewed in historical perspective, this new leadership, itself rooted in the subject political culture, had an opportunity to begin the process of breaking the barriers to political participation in Mexico. However, these leaders proved incapable of doing so because they, too, were the willing or unwilling victims of Mexico's political heritage.

What happened was that most of the leaders of the labor and *campesino* movements behaved much like their military counterparts: regardless of initial intentions, they eventually used their organizations for their own socioeconomic mobility. In doing so they undercut not only the manifest goals of the revolution but also the opportunity to broaden the bases of social solidarity and the capacity for cooperative action. Within the labor movement unions were "continuously the instruments, and almost as often the victims, of political intrigue and personal ambition."[48] The fault was not solely that of the labor leaders; they, like their unions, were often the pawns of the period's military politicians. Presidential support or opposition could make or break national labor confederations, as could the inclinations of the powerful caudillos at the regional level. But the union leadership contributed greatly to the process by joining the game for personal advantage and forsaking the development of anything resembling labor movement solidarity.

Nowhere was this praetorian behavior better exemplified than within the largest and by far the most favored confederation of the 1920s, the Confederación Regional de Obreros Mexicanos.[49] How did the leaders of the confederation use their power? First, to crush as many competing confederations and independent labor unions as possible. As a result "rival unions soon learned to hate each other far more bitterly than any of them hated the capitalists."[50] Second, to amass personal fortunes. An "immense majority" of the CROM leaders literally bathed in affluence by the end of the 1920s.[51]

> They built themselves a magnificent country estate, with swimming pools, and a steel-girded *fronton* court ... became the owners of hotels and even, through intermediaries, of factories. Morones [the chief of the CROM who served several years as minister of industry] himself acquired

[48] Marjorie Ruth Clark, *Organized Labor in Mexico* (Chapel Hill: University of North Carolina Press, 1934), p. 70.

[49] See Alfonso López Aparicio, *El Movimiento obrero en México* (Mexico: Editorial Jus, 1958), pp. 187ff.

[50] Henry Bamford Parkes, *A History of Mexico* (Boston: Houghton Mifflin Co., 1950), p. 376.

[51] Vicente Fuentes Díaz, "Desarrollo y evolución del movimiento obrero a partir de 1929," *Ciencias políticas y sociales* 5 (July–September 1959): 326.

the habit of wearing expensive diamond rings which, he explained to critics, he was keeping as a reserve fund which the working class could use in time of need.[52]

As Gruening noted, life for Morones and his CROM associates was lifted "to a plane of luxury unequalled except by millionaires' country clubs in the United States."[53]

Third, labor officials used their power to improve working conditions somewhat. Wages were increased for many CROM members during the 1920s, and systematic indemnities for industrial accidents and dismissals were gradually introduced. Also introduced, however, was the practice of blackmailing management for the strict benefit of union leadership. Industrialists who contributed to the financing of the CROM leaders' new life style were guaranteed immunity from labor disputes.[54]

Like Calles and the military-business circle which formed around him, the CROM leaders softened their commitment to the manifest goals of the revolution as they climbed the socio-economic ladder. By the late 1920s they too were calling for an end to "radical" reforms and for collaboration with the business community in building a new Mexico. Their prescription for Mexican development may well have been correct, but their private behavior mocked their public statesmanship, shattered the beginnings of labor solidarity and laid the groundwork for the captive labor movement that emerged within the official party in the following decades. Indeed, the "five little wolves" of the Mexican labor movement, led by the CTM chief Fidel Velázquez, were all CROM officials during the 1920s. As one historian of these early years concluded, most union officials "failed to remember that they were labor leaders except in a very limited sense, and even then they apparently forgot all too often."[55]

The same behavioral pattern characterized the majority of the power seekers who organized the peasant leagues. Once again the initial commitments to social reform—where they did exist—were most often diluted as the mobilization of political strength put the new leaders in a position to reap the personal rewards which the political system had to offer. As noted in the previous chapter, throughout Mexico ejidos and peasant leagues quickly became the captives of ambitious mestizo politicians. All that need be added here is that, as in the case of the labor unions, social solidarity that might

[52] Parkes, History of Mexico, p. 383.

[53] Ernest Henry Gruening, Mexico and Its Heritage (New York: Century Co., 1928), p. 390.

[54] Parkes, History of Mexico, p. 383; Robert Paul Millon, Mexican Marxist: Vicente Lombardo Toledano (Chapel Hill: University of North Carolina Press, 1966), p. 15.

[55] Clark, Organized Labor, p. 121.

have eventuated in a broad political movement was undermined from within as well as without. Within each *ejido* and each league there were those who fought for reform only to betray it when they themselves reached positions of leadership. Most of the new *ejidal* officials behaved in the same way that the rural *caciques* before them had behaved, and proceeded to commit the same kinds of abuses that all the power holders before them had committed.[56] Time and again the poorer *campesinos* in a village—the *agraristas*—would win the battle for land reform only to produce a leader from within their own group who would tyrannize them once again. Eyler Simpson details countless cases like that in the village of Tapilula where a poor leader of the *agrarista* element, upon winning control of the *ejido*, transformed it "into a feudal estate of which he was the absolute master."[57] Or that which took place in Remedios, where the once landless *agrarista* chief Pablo Martínez used his leadership position in the local *ejido* to build a modest fortune which included ownership of a hotel, a motion picture theater, a cock fighting ring and a reputed net worth of 100,000 pesos.[58]

The behavior of the power seekers who used both rural and urban institutions of reform to advance their own fortunes—ultimately to the detriment of whatever group they presumably represented—accurately reflects the patterns which Ramos sketched and attempted to explain in his *Profile of Man and Culture in Mexico*. Distrusting themselves, and therefore everyone else, these emergent leaders were generally no more willing or able than their predecessors to sacrifice opportunities for personal ego satisfaction to the development of broader social and political solidarities. The men leading the labor movement and the peasant leagues treated power as a personal possession. Like their mestizo forebears of the nineteenth century, they strove for primacy "in a world in which everything is seen as superior or inferior."[59] And their antisocial behavior simply reinforced that distrust of politicians and apathy toward political participation which has continued to characterize the vast majority of the Mexican population to the present day.

The fourth and final significant factor accounting for the limited nature of the demands made upon the present political system by the subject segment of Mexican society is attributable not to the socio-cultural environment but to the structure and functioning of the present system itself. The most important aspect of that system in terms of limiting demands and enhancing political stability has been its growing capacity to control—if not entirely prevent—elite competition for political power. A lesser, but still important,

---

[56] See the reports of Mexican government officials on this type of behavior cited in Eyler N. Simpson, *The Ejido: Mexico's Way Out* (Chapel Hill: University of North Carolina Press, 1937), chap. 19.

[57] *Ibid.*, p. 370.

[58] *Ibid.*, p. 434.

[59] Ramos, *Profile*, p. 128.

aspect has been a general ability of the system to detect discontent and deal with it speedily enough to avoid potential threats to stability. Both aspects are worth some detailed consideration.

If the regime constructed by Calles and the rest of the Revolutionary Coalition had not developed the capacity to limit elite competition for control of the political system and its spoils, some of the cultural and psychological barriers to greater participation in political life might well have been considerably weakened as ambitious individuals sought continuously to construct new sources of political strength. Such an outcome would have been in character both with a general pattern of Latin American politics and with the Mexican system as it developed during the two decades between 1910 and 1930. As has been noted with regard to Latin America in general, the lack of political institutions recognized as legitimate by most citizens has created a pattern of politics in which various contenders for political power—those who seek to control the allocation of the resources and other values at the disposal of the state—mobilize and apply a broad range of power capabilities.[60] These capabilities encompass all those properties which enable an individual or group to be politically influential, and include among others the capacity to influence military forces, to create civic disruption, and to develop electoral support. Money, votes, clubs, all are "legitimate" political tender in Latin America because no one of them is any more legitimate than the rest. In the struggle for control of the state in the Latin American legitimacy vacuum the power seekers use whatever resources and talents they have at their control. The number of military coups d'état in Latin America over the past several years demonstrates once again that the capacity to win elections is but one of several forms of political capabilities in the nations of the region, and, at least during some short- and medium-term periods, not a very influential one at that.

Mexican politics between 1910 and 1930 conformed closely to the Latin American pattern. Military caudillos mobilized their private armies; lesser *caciques* and politicians constructed political machines out of *ejidos* and peasant leagues; other enterprising mestizos applied their organizational talents to the mobilizing of political capabilities through the creation of labor unions. As Easton has noted about the political process in countries where the hold of a single elite group has recently been broken, "The rise in the degree of political involvement . . . is often refracted through competing leaderships. . . . Members may seek out leaders to express their wants; or *leaders may locate followers necessary to the fulfillment of their own ambitions.*"[61] In Mexico during this period it was the power seekers who took the lead in

---

[60] See Charles W. Anderson, *Politics and Economic Change in Latin America* (Princeton: D. van Nostrand Co., 1967), chap. 4 for an excellent discussion of the points noted summarily here.

[61] Easton, *Systems Analysis*, p. 111. Emphasis added.

mobilizing new groups into the political process to achieve their personal goals. In the contest which developed peasant leagues and labor unions served as sources of both military and electoral strength. Armed units supplied by labor leaders helped Carranza and Obregón to crush Villa; other labor divisions later supported Obregón in his successful revolt against Carranza. *Ejidal* peasants were used in military conflicts during the 1920s, and later formed a major source of support for Cárdenas in his political struggles with Calles and other military elements during the 1930s.

Had the conflict among the power seekers continued uncontrolled, it is quite probable that both organized labor and the *campesino* leagues would eventually have become far more politicized than they are today. Indeed, it is one of the many paradoxes of modern Mexico that such a vast percentage of the Mexican population remains nonpolitical despite its revolutionary heritage. All analysts of the process of politicization—the movement from a lack of perception of the role of government in one's life toward a recognition of its relevance and into active involvement in politics—have emphasized the prominent place of revolution in activating this process and drawing the bulk of society into political life.[62] Thus both the revolution and the entry of organized labor and the *campesino* leagues into the praetorian politics of the 1910s and 1920s might have been expected to overcome the cultural and psychological restraints, the alienation and apathy that characterized attitudes toward politics of perhaps 90 percent of Mexico's total population at the end of the Díaz era. So, too, might the impact of the Cárdenas years have been expected to give the process of politicization a momentum which could not be easily checked.

The restraints persisted, however, because aggressive competition for political power was brought to a close by 1940. From that date to the present the political regime as run by the Revolutionary Coalition through the institutions of the presidency and the official party has faced no serious challenge to its near total control of Mexican political life. And once the regime's primacy was established the power seekers altered their patterns of political behavior. Military opposition was futile; so, too, was a challenge at the polls. The regime controlled the counting of the ballots at all levels of government, and probably also the affections of a majority of those who voted. In either case the regime's hold over the country was secured. Thus began that process noted in the previous chapter whereby every six years fewer and fewer disappointed aspirants for power broke away from the PRI. They, like the *campesinos*, adopted a policy of waiting and hoping. The next sexennial

[62] See, for example, Daniel Goldrich, "Comparative Study of Politicization" in *Contemporary Cultures and Societies of Latin America*, edited by Dwight B. Heath and Richard N. Adams. (New York: Random House, 1965), pp. 361–78.

shuffle of political leadership might brighten their prospects, while opposition would be fruitless.

Undoubtedly, active competition for political office occurs within the official party. Reports of the maneuverings which precede the PRI's choice of candidates every six years can be found in all the standard accounts of Mexican politics, and no attempt is being made here to deny the existence of power struggles within the confines of the Revolutionary Coalition and its PRI structure. The crucial point, however, is that the competition today is so hidden from the Mexican public that it smothers rather than invites the mobilization of Mexicans into the political process except in the most ceremonial ways. The political selection process is almost totally veiled from the public, and even from the party's sector organizations themselves. The Mexican president consults with the members of his inner circle in choosing his successor, a circle which may not even include representatives of the party's major sectors. Governors are chosen in almost the same manner, and so on down the line.

One of the clearly established norms of behavior now attached to this process is that there shall be no public campaigning on the part of leading aspirants for the PRI nomination. The system of selection dictates that all contenders maintain a scrupulous public silence, and any open discussion by party members of the probable choice is denounced as "futurism." The power moves take place behind the scenes, although almost no one who is in a position to know just how the moves are made has ever written or spoken publicly about them. Braulio Maldonado is an exception, and his description of the selection process at the gubernatorial level was discussed in chapter 5. In fact, so little is actually known about the process that "Mexicologists" seldom agree on their interpretation of the occult events. The student demonstrations in Mexico City in the summer and fall of 1968, for example, were thought by some to be the work of left-wing elements in the PRI who were trying to embarrass the presidential candidacies of a few PRI "hard liners." Other commentators attributed the same demonstrations to right-wing elements in the party that were presumably trying to embarrass some of the PRI "soft liners." Still others, unsatisfied by such pedestrian hypotheses, sought to implicate the C.I.A.[63]

It is not necessary to follow all the court intrigue, however, to recognize how the evolution of the PRI and the Mexican presidency has smothered the public aspects of elite competition for political power and place, and in doing so has braked the process of political mobilization that accompanied the fight for office as late as the 1930s. A labor leader or CNC official may indeed

[63] For the various interpretations see the Mexico City press, September through December 1968.

derive some leverage from the fact that he somehow "represents" a major interest group in the party; but if that group is not privy to the process, it is neither encouraged to become politically active in his support, nor aroused to see that he bargains in its own best interests. Thus all but a few individuals are left without any active role whatsoever in the selection process for all major government offices. They are brought into the political picture only when it is time for the shouting, and they shout for a slate of candidates they have had little or no voice in choosing. As long as the Revolutionary Coalition controls the only party which can win elections, it can control and limit the competition for political power. If the Partido de Acción Nacional is ever allowed to evolve to the point where it represents a significant threat to PRI predominance, open competition among elites may once again appear in Mexico.

In addition to limiting elite competition to the confines of the party's inner sanctum, the structure of the PRI has provided the present political system with a growing communications network that gives the regime the capacity to detect and deal with political stress before minor irritants become major crises. Despite the fact that the party is used less as an aggregator of interests than as a mechanism of control, officials in the lower echelons of the labor and *campesino* sectors keep the PRI and the present regime in touch with local and regional moods. Whether the regime responds to dissension with coercion or conciliation, it is at least aware of discontent as it arises. And although the official party does not provide its major sectors with effective representation, it does provide to individuals and groups within them various channels of access to party and governmental officials through which grievances are sometimes redressed.

An interesting case study in the operation of these channels to resolve conflict in *ejidal* communities is given by Vincent Padgett. He demonstrates how a group of *ejidatarios* was able to rid its *ejido* of dishonest government by using the several forms of recourse open to it. The group petitioned the federal delegate from the national agrarian office, the state agrarian league, and the state governor. As Padgett notes, an eventual alignment of the latter two authority structures produced "a just arrangement according to the relevant provisions of Mexican law found in the Agrarian Code." His familiarity with the Mexican political system, however, led Padgett to conclude that "although the *ejidatarios* of Ignacio Romero Vargas succeeded in deposing their delinquent officials, this should not be interpreted to mean that like situations can always be resolved according to the rule of law and the wishes of the majority."[64] Indeed, the example he cites may well be more the

---

[64] L. Vincent Padgett, *The Mexican Political System* (Boston: Houghton Mifflin Co., 1966), pp. 119–20.

exception than the rule. As noted in chapter 5, the response of the political system to gross violations of the agrarian laws in Nayarit was to do nothing. In terms of political stability, however, the important point is that the regime is kept in touch with that large majority of the Mexican population which is for the most part politically apathetic, thus reserving for the political system the option to respond to local pressures before major problems arise.

Thus far the regime has responded to Mexico's cycles of discontent with piecemeal measures designed to ease mounting pressures without significantly altering existing government policies. It temporarily increases the rate of land redistribution, the size of the increments in legal minimum wages, and the pace of public housing construction. At the local and regional level the regime sometimes conciliates opposition groups which form within the peasant and labor sectors, and at other times co-opts the leaders of dissident factions—a technique frequently employed by the PRI at all levels of government. Such methods of conciliation minimize the necessity for coercive action, add to the government's aura of legitimacy, and undermine the development of an aggressively led opposition.

The fact that the communications network exists does not guarantee that it will always operate successfully. The 1968 student demonstrations in Mexico City undoubtedly caught the Revolutionary Coalition off guard. Only when about 200 persons were shot and killed on the night of October 2 by the police and army in the "Battle of Tlatelolco" was Mexico's political tranquility reestablished.[65] However, on the very same evening in late August of that year that several hundred thousand Mexican students were marching in protest toward the presidential palace in Mexico City, Chicago was being wracked by the turmoil accompanying the opening of the Democratic convention. If the Mexican president and his party were out of touch with some emerging political problems in 1968, so was the American president and most of his party. Events of that year throughout the world suggest that all political systems, from the most repressive to the most representative, are prone to occasional communications failures. Thus far there is very little evidence that the Mexican system suffers from a serious structural weakness in this regard.

At the beginning of the discussion of political demands and supports in the Mexican setting it was asserted that the demands on Mexico's political system over the past four decades had been quite limited in two senses: first, in terms of the proportion of the total population involved in the creation of demands; and second, in terms of the resources required by the government to satisfy them. Having examined the parochial and subject political cultures in Mexico, we are in a position to verify that assertion. As noted, the two

[65] Estimates of the number of fatalities vary between 50 and 300. The *New York Times* settled on 200. See the *New York Times*, October 6, 1969.

cultures together probably encompass close to 90 percent of the entire Mexican population.[66] Our examination has revealed how the cognitive, affective, and evaluative attitudes of these two broad segments of Mexican society toward their political system sharply limit the number and nature of their demands. They know little about government, expect little from it, and in many instances desire only to be left alone by it. Their primary socialization experiences in the family and at school most often breed in them patterns of distrust and hostility which obstruct the formation of loyalties stretching much beyond the nuclear or extended family structure. As political followers, they fear that their allegiances will be betrayed; as political leaders, they perpetuate the pattern of betrayal. The attitudes affecting political participation formed in the early years are reinforced by actual experiences in adult life, and the mold continues with as yet insignificant change from one generation to the next.

The parochial and the subject Mexicans have generally expected so little from government that they appear to have been satisfied with what are, for the most part, symbolic governmental outputs that continue to link the present regime to the manifest goals of the revolution. Thus the government has been able to operate with a minimal claim on Mexico's resources; as noted in chapter 3, it was not until the mid-1960s that total public sector revenues rose above 13 percent of gross national product, or that total government taxes rose above 10 percent. Furthermore, 40 percent of the aggregate resources captured by the political system were channeled directly into economic development projects, and not into social expenditures on schools, housing, public health, and rural development.

## Mexico's Participants: Demands and Support at the Top

The remaining 10 percent of Mexican society, sharing a participant political culture, does articulate political demands and in other ways participates actively in political life. In this stratum are found the upper-middle income groups that comprise the government bureaucracy and the upper-income segments of Mexican society prominent in the economy's private sector. Within the PRI structure itself the popular sector officials serve as articulate spokesmen for the state bureaucrats organized in the Government Employees Union. The growing salaries and fringe benefits won by this group, as well as the rising number of political posts allocated to it every six years, testify to the nature of its demands and the degree of its political effectiveness in influencing the shape of government policy.

[66] This is Scott's estimate. Corroborating evidence can be found in González Casanova, *La Democracia.* See especially chap. 5, "La Sociedad plural."

Outside of the official party, yet deeply involved in the articulation of demands and the shaping of policy outcomes, is Mexico's organized private sector. Two of the most powerful business organizations, the National Confederation of Chambers of Industry and the National Confederation of Chambers of Commerce, play a major role in the formulation of those government policies which affect their immediate business interests. They are consulted directly and continuously through a host of intergovernmental and decentralized agencies and commissions, and in many instances they themselves draft the legislation which is eventually approved by the government. Their influence is reflected in the content of all those special policies adopted to promote economic growth in Mexico: high tariffs, import licensing, tax rebates, special forms of government financial assistance, and so forth. Even more noticeable is their influence in shaping the overall impact of government policies on Mexican society. As noted, those policies have not challenged the interests of the highest income groups in Mexico. The total tax burden, for example, remains among the lowest in Latin America, and the overall tax system is still regressive in its impact after four decades of PRI politics. Commenting on the inequities of Mexican taxation, Nicholas Kaldor noted that the system was "unjust because it favors income from capital over income from labor, owing to a vast multitude of omissions and exemptions *that have no parallel in other countries sharing Mexico's economic and social objectives.*"[67] Needless to say, the economic and social objectives of Mexico's top 10 percent—the participant group being examined here—are very well served by Mexican tax policies, as they are by most of the other authoritative allocations of resources made by the present political system.

The continued support which this segment of Mexican society gives to the present regime is, then, what we have called specific support. It is support which is contingent upon the favorable nature of the system's outputs, and thus far the outputs have met with the approval of Mexico's post-1940 economic elite groups. Having noted the growing community of interest between the country's economic and political elites since 1940, this finding comes as no surprise. Nor is it surprising that by the time of the 1964 presidential election the relationship between the political regime and the industrial community had become so mellow that most of Mexico's business leaders publicly and effusively endorsed the candidacy of Gustavo Díaz Ordaz, the standard-bearer of the Party of Revolutionary Institutions. What other regime could better organize the "left" (or masses) to support the policies of the "right" (or elites)?

[67] This quote from Kaldor's highly critical study of the Mexican tax system—a study which the government sponsored but then refused to make public—is found in González Casanova, *La Democracía*, p. 131. Emphasis added.

The support of the politically relevant members of Mexican society—individuals and groups whose financial, military or organizational-political resources give them a major political power capability—has been solidified by a very broad range of government policy outputs which cater to their interests. In rural Mexico the regime has allowed the old *caciques* to retain much of their influence. While the PRI and its leaders claim to have diluted the power and position of these local power figures, much of the evidence points to a continuing pattern of accommodation between local *jefes* and national political leadership.[68] In urban Mexico the examples of accommodation, as suggested by the growing ties between the national political and economic elites and the parameters of Mexican fiscal, monetary and other economic development policies, require no further elaboration.[69]

It is interesting to note that even at the participant level of Mexican society, where demands are made on the Mexican government, the resources required by the political system to meet those demands are minimal. In effect, the demands are met by transferring their resource cost to the rest of Mexican society in a somewhat hidden manner. High tariffs and import quotas are policies which win the support of the politically relevant groups in Mexico; the cost of such policies is paid by the Mexican consumer. Forced savings through inflation during the 1940s and 1950s achieved the same effect. It was costless to the political system in terms of the economic resources the government itself had to raise, yet the policy won the support of the economic elite groups at the ultimate expense of most segments of the Mexican labor force. Eventually inflation began to cost the political system in terms of labor unrest, however, and the forced savings route to rapid growth was abandoned by the late 1950s. As the capacity of so many income groups in other Latin American countries—particularly in Chile—to protect themselves against the redistributive effects of inflation indicates, some "costless" policies favoring elite groups can operate for only limited durations. Over much of the period we are considering the Mexican political

---

[68] For some interesting evidence see Philip B. Taylor, Jr., "The Mexican Elections of 1958: Affirmation of Authoritarianism," *Western Political Quarterly* 13 (September 1960): 722–44; Richmond, *Mexico: A Case Study*, pp. 175ff and pp. 460ff; and chap. 5 above.

[69] David Apter has noted how the clash between what he labels traditional, modernizing, and accommodative elites can produce intense conflict in modernizing societies. The capacity of the Mexican political elite of the present regime to accommodate the demands of both the rural *caciques*—the traditional rural elite figures—and the new industrial and commercial groups—the modernizing elites—cements what might otherwise prove to be conflicting elite groups. The *caciques*, of course, are not "traditional" in the sense that the *hacendados* were, though each group has opposed "modernization" when the process threatened its own spheres of influence. See David E. Apter, *The Politics of Modernization* (Chicago: University of Chicago Press, 1965), especially chap. 4.

system was blessed with a flexibility that is narrowing as the level of economic sophistication in middle and lower class Mexico rises.

In historical perspective it is clear that the easing of the two sources of stress which eventually destroyed the Peace of Porfirio contributed significantly to the political stability which has characterized Mexico since the 1930s. Land reform reduced the resentments of rural Mexico and returned it to its traditional state of political apathy; accelerated rates of economic development and emerging patterns of circulation within the political elite expanded the arteries of middle class mestizo mobility. These changes help to account for the initial success of the present political system in achieving that degree of political stability necessary for sustained economic development. However, the Peace of the PRI is now entering its fifth decade, and rapid economic growth its fourth. How has the regime of the Revolutionary Coalition "gotten away with it" for so long a period? What other factors have contributed to its successful implementation of a development strategy whose welfare consequences might have seemed destined to create growing political instability and consequent economic stagnation?

The answers have been seen to lie in the psychological and cultural parameters of the Mexican development process, and in the modus operandi of the PRI regime. The psychological and cultural barriers to political participation have proved so enduring that close to 90 percent of Mexican society has absorbed the welfare effects of Mexican economic growth without putting undue stress upon the Mexican political system. The elements of distrust, hostility and consequent political apathy have proved so pervasive that the Mexican political system has seldom been required to respond to demands upon it by broad segments of society.[70] To put the matter in an only slightly overstated way, below the elite levels the present political regime has only needed to gain the support of ambitious individuals in order to persist. It has often responded to labor "demands" by providing a few labor leaders with lucrative sinecures; it has eased rural pressures by elevating individual peasant

---

[70] One psychological root of political nonparticipation has perhaps not been given the attention it deserves in the earlier discussion. It has to do with the persistence of a conflicted and often violent involvement at the local level in Mexican life. The fact that Mexico has one of the world's highest homicide rates merely confirms the observations of all commentators familiar with Mexican society with regard to the high level of passions and violence which pervade daily life. Eric Wolf has argued convincingly that the very intensity of personal dyadic conflicts constrains attempts at political participation. Surely this aspect of the Mexican psychological makeup helps to explain the absence of cohesion within Mexican political and social groups and the repeated failures to develop interest groups with broadened loyalties during the 1920s and 1930s.

leaders into the ranks of the PRI's *campesino* sector. In the Mexican setting stress on the political system is generally relieved not by accommodating mass group demands, but rather by co-opting the potential spokesmen for such demands.

Political systems which must deal with more cohesive social groups do not have the Mexican option. In the case of Argentina, for example, the Argentine political system must partially meet the demands of major segments of organized labor or suffer from stress on the system which has on several occasions in recent history led directly to economic stagnation. Yet, when the system has satisfied labor demands, it has inevitably lost the support of major social, economic and military elite groups. That loss of support also endangers political stability and compounds the difficulties of sustaining the process of economic development.

How long the psychological, cultural and political factors noted in the Mexican case can check the formation of more cohesive social units, a broader participation in Mexican politics, and the growing demands which will inevitably accompany such participation, is impossible to predict. All that can be said with certainty is that these factors have proved remarkably resilient in cushioning the welfare impact of Mexico's economic "miracle" and in constraining any "revolution of rising expectations" for the past three decades, and show few signs of disintegration on the eve of the fourth.[71]

---

[71] See Wayne Cornelius, "Urbanization as an Agent in Latin American Instability" and Barry Ames, "Bases of Support for Mexico's Dominant Party," *American Political Science Review* 63 (March, 1970): 153–67 for some well documented evidence supporting this general conclusion.

*Chapter 8*

# THE DYNAMICS OF
# MEXICAN DEVELOPMENT

Mexico, like almost all other Latin American countries *en vias de desarrollo*, enters the decade of the 1970s with justified concern about its prospects for continued rapid economic development. Some of the problems facing the Mexican economy are indeed profound, and past success is no guarantee of effective future performance. What are the present challenges to the Mexican economy? And what does Mexico's political heritage suggest about the capacity of the present political system and its leadership to meet those challenges?

## *OBSTACLES TO RAPID GROWTH*

The major Mexican economic problem for the 1970s and beyond is posed by the country's present demographic trends. The overall rate of population growth in Mexico is now 3.5 percent a year. The trends which have pushed this figure steadily upward over the past four decades are a rising birth rate (46.0 per thousand in 1960), a falling death rate (11.5 per thousand in 1960) and a life expectancy that is presently estimated at 62 years. Somewhere between 45 and 50 percent of the present Mexican population is under fifteen years of age. This distribution places a tremendous burden upon the Mexican educational system and severely limits the savings capacity of the great majority of Mexican families. In addition, rural-urban migration patterns have caused Mexico's urban population to grow at an annual rate of 5 percent ever since 1940, eventually necessitating the rapid expansion of urban social and economic infrastructure expenditures.[1]

Mexico enters the 1970s with a population of approximately 51 million. Current calculations (which may prove to be on the low side) project a demographic growth rate of 3.5 percent for the next ten years; by 1980 the

[1] Statistics derived from Raúl Benítez Zenteno and Gustavo Cabrera Acevedo, *Proyecciones de la población de México* (Banco de México, 1966).

Mexican population will have reached 72 million.[2] By the latter date the proportion of the population under fifteen years of age will still be close to 50 percent. While the rapid trend toward urbanization will continue, rural population is expected to grow at 1.5 percent a year throughout the 1970s.

In the face of these demographic trends the Mexican economy must continue to expand at a fast pace if per capita income is to rise significantly over the next ten years. Yet these same trends pose serious difficulties for rapid growth. As noted, they tend to decrease the aggregate Mexican propensity to save, and they require increasing expenditures on education and other forms of "social investment" which generally have a lesser impact on short-term growth rates than other forms of investment. Furthermore, they will aggravate the problem of creating employment opportunities for a rapidly expanding work force. During the 1960s over three million landless farm laborers in rural Mexico experienced increasing difficulties in finding work. Their per capita rate of employment fell from 194 days per year in 1950 to 100 days in 1960; over the same ten-year period their real income dropped by 18 percent. All indications are that the 1970 census will reveal a continued deterioration in their rate of employment and their standard of living. Although the degree to which "disguised unemployment" actually exists in Latin America and other regions of the world has become a hotly debated issue within the economic development community, there is little doubt that such unemployment constitutes a problem of considerable and growing dimensions in today's Mexico.

Part of the difficulty in the present Mexican employment picture is attributable to the educational profile of the Mexican work force. While the educational system continues to expand yearly, the dropout rate remains very high. For every one hundred students entering primary school only nine enroll in secondary school; of those nine only two enter college. And only 12 percent of those entering college are graduated.[3]

In 1965, only two-thirds of Mexico's population in the 6–14 year age group was enrolled in primary education. In rural Mexico most primary schools offered no education beyond the fourth grade. At the secondary level, 28 percent of the 14–18 year age group was enrolled; in higher education (the 19–24 age group) the ratio fell to 3 percent. As this educational picture suggests, unskilled school drop-outs are pressing into the labor force

---

[2] The projections assume a 10 percent decline in fertility over the decade, although there are reasons to believe that such a decline may not take place. See Victor L. Urquidi, "An Overview of Mexican Economic Development," *Weltwirtschaftliches Archiv* 101 (1968): 13–14.

[3] *Ibid.*, p. 14. See also Victor L. Urquidi and A. Lajous Vargas, *Educacíon superior, ciencia y tecnología en el desarrollo económico de México* (Mexico, D.F.: El Colegio de México, 1967).

from an early age, earning minimum wages or less, and finding only partial or sporadic employment.[4]

According to the 1960 census figures, 65 percent of the Mexican population above the age of fifteen was literate, a proportion slightly above that in Brazil (61 percent), Peru (61 percent) and Venezuela (63 percent), and well below the corresponding figures for Argentina (91 percent), Chile (84 percent) and Colombia (73 percent). While the literacy rate continues to increase in Mexico, it is worrisome to note that it is rising more slowly than in most other Latin American countries.[5] This is due both to the rapid increase in Mexico's population and to the government's limited expenditures on education. Mexico has traditionally channeled fewer funds (measured as a percentage of GNP) into education than almost any other major Latin American nation. In 1965, for example, public expenditure on education in Mexico represented 2.1 percent of GNP. Corresponding figures for other Latin American countries during the early 1960s were as follows: Argentina, 3.3 percent; Bolivia, 4.3 percent; Brazil, 3.0 percent; Chile, 3.6 percent; Colombia, 3.1 percent; and Peru, 4.9 percent. During the past decade Mexican expenditures on education increased rapidly, but by 1968 still represented less than 3 percent of Mexico's national product.[6]

The changing structure of public-sector investment in Mexico during the past decade reveals the inevitable response to the growing need for expanded programs in health, education and welfare. The figures in table 8-1 indicate that throughout the 1960s approximately 23 percent of all public-sector investment was being allocated to the various social welfare fields; the 1935-60 average was 15 percent, and even for the 1950s the ratio had not reached 16 percent (table 3-5).

If the Mexican government were capable of meeting the increasing demands for educational and other social expenditures without cutting back on its other investment programs, concern with the present demographic trends would be somewhat eased. For the past thirty years the public sector has accounted for some 30 percent of the country's aggregate investment, most of it in the form of highly productive industrial and agricultural projects. While the figures available for the 1960s reveal no decline in that ratio, they do indicate that the Mexican government has had to rely increasingly on public borrowing in order to finance that investment. Over the five-year period from 1964 through 1968 public-sector savings covered only 64 percent of its investment, a proportion substantially lower than that of previous years

---

[4] Urquidi, "An Overview of Mexican Economic Development," p. 14.

[5] See *América en cifras, 1967: situación cultural: educación y otros aspectos culturales* (Washington, D.C.: Panamerican Union, 1969), p. 6.

[6] Urquidi, "An Overview of Mexican Economic Development," p. 9; United Nations, *Statistical Yearbook, 1967* (New York: United Nations, 1968).

TABLE 8-1. DISTRIBUTION OF GROSS PUBLIC CAPITAL FORMATION, 1960–1968 (percent)

| Years | Total | Agriculture | Industry | Transport and Communication | Social Welfare | Administration and Defense | Unspecified |
|---|---|---|---|---|---|---|---|
| | (1) | (2) | (3) | (4) | (5) | (6) | (7) |
| 1960 | 100 | 6.9 | 31.2 | 36.0 | 22.5 | 2.3 | 1.1 |
| 1961 | 100 | 9.2 | 44.4 | 27.0 | 16.9 | 2.5 | — |
| 1962 | 100 | 7.6 | 38.8 | 28.8 | 21.0 | 3.5 | 0.4 |
| 1963 | 100 | 10.2 | 33.1 | 24.6 | 28.8 | 3.2 | — |
| 1964 | 100 | 13.6 | 30.5 | 21.0 | 31.8 | 3.0 | — |
| 1965 | 100 | 9.4 | 44.5 | 26.5 | 16.9 | 2.7 | — |
| 1966 | 100 | 9.1 | 42.5 | 24.8 | 21.9 | 1.7 | — |
| 1967 | 100 | 10.6 | 39.5 | 24.7 | 23.5 | 1.6 | — |
| 1968 | 100 | 13.1 | 39.4 | 23.0 | 22.7 | 1.9 | — |
| 1960–68 | 100 | 10.4 | 38.9 | 25.3 | 23.2 | 2.4 | — |

Source: Calculated from data supplied by the Dirección de Inversiones, Secretaría de la Presidencia.

(table 3-7). The second major challenge to economic development during the  1970s is thus the necessity for the Mexican government to augment its revenues.

There is some evidence that the challenge may be met with success. In 1960, total public sector income—government tax revenues plus net earnings from public enterprises and other state agencies—accounted for 12.4 percent of Mexico's gross national product. By 1964 that figure had risen to 14.8 percent. A series of minor tax reforms since that time has considerably increased revenues derived from direct taxation on corporate and individual incomes. By the end of the 1960s, income taxes were providing approximately one-half of the federal government's revenues. Furthermore, the income elasticity of income tax proceeds appeared to be considerably above unity (the growth in these revenues, after adjustments for tax reforms, exceeded the aggregate growth rate of the Mexican economy). With its increased reliance on such direct forms of taxation, the Mexican government may well be able to augment public sector revenues as a percentage of national product during the course of the 1970s.

The capacity of the government to expand its revenues is intimately linked to a third challenge to continued economic development in Mexico, that of sustaining and possibly increasing Mexico's present rate of savings. Domestic saving in Mexico as a percentage of national product rose from 8 percent in 1940 to 17 percent by 1967. While this growth in the capacity to generate domestic sources of investment represents a marked achievement, Mexico's burgeoning population necessitates an even greater allocation of GNP for investment purposes if economic growth is to continue to raise per capita income at a rapid rate. Over the past decade Mexico has been investing at an annual rate of 20 percent of GNP, and foreign investment has filled the gap between Mexico's domestic savings and total Mexican investment. Direct private foreign investment has contributed approximately one-third of these foreign resources in recent years, or about 6 percent of Mexico's annual fixed capital investment.[7] Public-sector borrowing has accounted for the rest.

The growing reliance upon foreign borrowing to finance Mexico's public sector investment programs, reflected in tables 8-2 and 8-3, has reached a point where amortization and interest payments on foreign loans to the Mexican government and its agencies measure close to 30 percent of Mexico's annual export earnings. The confidence of both public and private investors abroad in the economic future of Mexico and the capacity of the public sector to meet its financial commitments has permitted Mexico to borrow heavily throughout the 1960s. It may well be, however, that the present level

[7]Carlos Quintana, "Resultado de una encuesta sobre inversión extranjera en México," *Comercio exterior* 19 (August 1969): 590.

TABLE 8-2. MEXICO'S BALANCE OF PAYMENTS, 1955-1968: LONG-TERM CAPITAL ACCOUNT ITEMS (in millions of U.S. dollars)

| Year | Private Foreign Direct Investment | Foreign Loans to Public Sector | | |
|---|---|---|---|---|
| | | Received | Repaid | Net |
| 1955 | 105.4 | 102.7 | 64.5 | 38.2 |
| 1956 | 126.4 | 114.7 | 79.3 | 35.4 |
| 1957 | 131.6 | 158.2 | 82.3 | 75.9 |
| 1958 | 100.3 | 238.9 | 137.9 | 101.0 |
| 1959 | 81.1 | 221.0 | 158.4 | 62.2 |
| 1960 | -38.1[a] | 332.8 | 167.3 | 165.5[a] |
| 1961 | 119.3 | 357.3 | 183.7 | 173.6 |
| 1962 | 126.5 | 400.9 | 267.9 | 133.0 |
| 1963 | 117.5 | 385.6 | 195.3 | 190.3 |
| 1964 | 161.9 | 695.3 | 334.9 | 360.4 |
| 1965 | 213.9 | 344.2 | 343.4 | 0.8 |
| 1966 | 109.1[b] | 540.9 | 444.3 | 96.6 |
| 1967 | -24.2[a,b] | 701.0 | 446.4 | 254.6 |
| 1968[c] | 115.0[b] | 698.0 | 550.1 | 147.8 |

Source: Derived from Banco de México, *Informe anual*, various issues.
[a]Reflects disinvestment by foreign companies.
[b]Excludes reinvested earnings.
[c]Preliminary.

TABLE 8-3. AMORTIZATION AND INTEREST PAYMENTS ON MEDIUM- AND LONG-TERM EXTERNAL PUBLIC DEBT (as a percentage of total receipts from Mexico's current international transactions)

| | |
|---|---|
| 1960 | 12 |
| 1961 | 14 |
| 1962 | 20 |
| 1963 | 16 |
| 1964 | 21 |
| 1965 | 21 |
| 1966 | 24 |
| 1967 | 26 |
| 1968 | 28 |

Source: Derived from Banco de México, *Informe anual*, various issues.

and structure of foreign debt will not allow as extensive a use of foreign savings for Mexico's public sector investment programs in the coming decade. If Mexico is to avoid further international indebtedness and at the same time to sustain the level of per capita income advances experienced over the past thirty years, it must increase still further domestic rates of savings and investment.

In addition to these three major problems, one can list at least two others only slightly less salient. First, can Mexico meet the challenge presented by rural poverty and unrest during the 1970s?[8] Will government programs be reoriented toward assisting the *minifundista* and the landless *campesino*? Will agricultural extension services be expanded to bring to subsistence agriculture the fruits of agricultural research? Will opportunities for employment be developed for the growing numbers of landless peasants, either through further land redistribution or through programs for regional industrialization? The problem of marshaling the public and private resources required to improve conditions in rural Mexico reflects all the major challenges to continued development noted earlier.

And, to take the final problem, can Mexico expand its capacity to export rapidly enough to avoid a serious foreign exchange bottleneck?[9] During the 1960s Mexico's imports have grown at a rate of 12 percent a year while its exports of goods and services have increased at an average yearly rate of approximately 7 percent. Close to 85 percent of Mexico's merchandise imports consist of industrial materials and capital goods; restrictions on such imports would tend to check the pace of Mexican industrialization. If international demand for its traditional agricultural commodities continues to be weak, can Mexico diversify its industrial exports rapidly enough to avoid debilitating import restrictions? There is some encouragement in the fact that 1968 and 1969 witnessed considerable improvement in the foreign sales of Mexican manufactured goods. Automobile engines, spare auto and truck parts, electrical machinery, iron and steel sheeting and piping, and many other industrial products contributed to a notable recovery in export earnings in 1968. In addition, preliminary figures for 1969 revealed a further increase of 16.9 percent in export earnings on manufactured goods.[10]

## THE DILEMMA OF MEXICO'S DEVELOPMENT: A REPRISE

For any developing nation, the listing of major obstacles to continued economic growth is a relatively easy task. All such countries confront serious problems, and Mexico is certainly no exception. Indeed, just ten years ago such a listing was undertaken for Mexico, accompanied by a pessimistic prediction with regard to the prospects for continued rapid growth. Nevertheless, the difficulties which Mexico faced at the beginning of the 1960s failed to slow its growth rate perceptibly. It is worth recalling that for the past ten years the factors responsible for sustained economic development in Mexico

[8] Reports of rural discontent seem to be on the rise. See, for example, Eduardo L. Venezian and William K. Gamble, *The Agricultural Development of Mexico: Its Structure and Growth Since 1950* (New York: Frederick A. Praeger, 1969), pp. 192ff. However, this may reflect broader press coverage rather than an increased incidence of violence. No good quantitative study exists on the subject.

[9] See appendix, tables 1–5.

[10] *Comercio exterior* 19 (August 1969): 570–71; 20 (March 1970): 189–91.

have revealed far more resilience than had been predicted. Boom conditions for traditional Mexican exports did come to an end by the close of the 1950s, but the aggregate growth rate since then has averaged 6.4 percent. Where did the predictions of a slackening in the growth process err?

In the first place the increasing diversity of its major exports has enabled Mexico to avoid stagnation in aggregate foreign sales. In many developing countries the leading export product may constitute anywhere from one-third to one-half of total export earnings. In the Mexican case the major export commodity, cotton, constitutes slightly less than one-fifth of merchandise export receipts. Coffee, livestock, tomatoes, sugar and fish each represent another 5 to 7 percent, and processed foods and a growing list of manufactured products constitute the rest. This gradual diversification of Mexico's exports is slowly but steadily decreasing the extent of its vulnerability to changing demand conditions in the international market. In addition, the rapid rise in earnings from tourism and border trade has eased the difficulties caused by the relative decline in traditional export sales during the 1960s.

In the second place, Mexico's private businessmen apparently failed to share some economists' concern with regard to the limited size of the Mexican domestic market. The best available estimates reveal that private sector investment averaged 15.2 percent of Mexican gross national product between 1954 and 1960, fell to 12.6 percent for the following two years, and then recovered to an average of 14.5 percent a year during the period from 1963 through 1967.[11] These figures suggest that the decline in private investment during the 1959–62 period reflected private-sector anxieties concerning the domestic impact of the Cuban revolution and the policies to be followed by the new administration of President Adolfo López Mateos. When it became clear that the regime of the PRI was not to be shaken by events in Cuba and that López Mateos had no intention of radically restructuring either the pattern of Mexican income distribution or the prevailing economic policies that had so greatly benefited Mexico's leading business groups, private investment returned to what seems to have become a normal level of close to 15 percent of Mexican national product.

The recovery of private investment during the 1960s suggests that the limitations to continued economic development constituted by the size of the Mexican domestic market may have been exaggerated, and illustrates the need for careful empirical analysis of this question both in Mexico and elsewhere.[12] Early in the 1960s it was estimated that between two-thirds and

[11] See table 3–4.

[12] One interesting study during the past decade reached the conclusion that the Mexican market would be large enough by 1970 to make feasible the domestic production of such items as machine tools, steam engines and turbines, transformers,

three-quarters of the Mexican population was outside the market for many modern-day products. Nevertheless, throughout the 1960s existing industries have expanded and new manufacturing enterprises have been constructed; output from the manufacturing sector since 1965 has increased at an annual rate of close to 10 percent. These trends have developed without the major alterations in income distribution which some commentators have felt were necessary to induce continued private-sector investment and industrial expansion.

The studies of Mexican income distribution examined in chapter 3 and the general trends in the economy since those studies were made suggest that by 1970 approximately 30 percent of the Mexican population, or about 15 million persons, had family incomes ranging from $1,400 to $8,000 per year. Perhaps the size of the Mexican market for modern manufactured products implied by these rough calculations is large enough to support continued industrial expansion in Mexico. Only the passage of time or detailed empirical study will resolve the issue. In the interim, many economists will continue to emphasize market size both in Mexico and in other developing countries as an impediment to rapid growth; others will cite with approval the opposite conclusion reached by Simon Kuznets. He argues, on the basis of his own exhaustive studies on the process of economic growth, that the patterns of income distribution characterizing underdeveloped countries today are not too different from those observed in the presently developed countries in the 1920s and 1930s, and he sees little reason to believe that they constitute a major impediment to rapid industrialization in countries of Mexico's population size.[13]

One significant economic trend during the 1960s suggests that the size of the domestic market for consumer manufactures is now growing more rapidly than at any other period in recent Mexican history. Throughout the past decade the wages paid to much of Mexico's industrial labor force have been increasing at rates well in advance of the Mexican cost of living index. While real wages may not have kept pace with the increases in productivity, they have clearly expanded the real purchasing power of workers in the industrial sector by perhaps 2 to 3 percent a year. It appears that the passage of a new labor law at the end of 1969 will continue this trend. If all of the provisions of the new labor code are implemented they will contribute to an elevated

pumps and compressors, and locomotives. See Alan S. Manne, "Key Sectors of the Mexican Economy, 1960 -1970," in *Studies in Process Analysis*, edited by Alan S. Manne and Harry M. Markowitz, pp. 381 –400 (New York: John Wiley and Sons, 1963).

[13] Simon Kuznets, "Quantitative Aspects of the Economic Growth of Nations, VIII. Distribution of Income by Size," in *Economic Development and Cultural Change* 11 (January 1963): 68–69.

standard of living for the laborers who are covered in terms of both increased salaries and broader fringe benefits.[14]

Another potential bottleneck to Mexican economic development in the 1960s failed to materialize when the government demonstrated a capacity to expand its revenues more rapidly than had been predicted. As we noted, during the 1960s total revenues rose from 12.4 percent of Mexican GNP to a figure estimated somewhat above 15 percent.[15] Changes in Mexican tax laws have been marginal, and no attempt has been made to implement Nicholas Kaldor's proposals for tax reform submitted in 1960. The government, after inviting Kaldor to study Mexico's tax structure, refused even to make public his suggestions. Nevertheless, the minor changes introduced throughout the decade have probably reshaped the Mexican tax system enough to provide the government with revenues that will grow faster than aggregate national product during the 1970s. In the tax field as elsewhere, changes in governmental policy which adversely affect the interests of Mexico's political "participants" come very slowly. But slow change should not be confused with no change. Mexico's incrementalist approach to policy formulation for sustained economic growth may eventually prove unequal to the tasks implied by present Mexican demographic trends; as yet, however, a pessimistic prognostication appears premature.

The view that pessimism is still unwarranted is rooted in the interpretation of Mexican politics developed in the last three chapters. What emerges is the portrait of a political system in many ways ideally suited to promote and sustain the process of economic development. Perhaps this point can best be made by comparing the interpretation developed in this study with that offered several years ago in a major work on Mexico's political economy. Its prognosis for further rapid growth was decidedly pessimistic, reflecting a strong doubt that the Mexican political system possessed the capacity to sustain the development process at rates comparable with those of the 1940s and early 1950s. How did *The Dilemma of Mexico's Development* arrive at a conclusion which contrasts sharply with that presented in this study?

In the view of its author, Raymond Vernon, the Mexican government was reduced to virtual immobility by a broad range of demands upon it ranging from the far left to the far right. The aggregate effect of the demands and the government's inability—or unwillingness—to reject any of them was to interdict any consistent course of action to promote continued economic develop-

[14] For a discussion of the new law and its possible impact, see *Visión* 38 (January 30, 1970): 40ff.

[15] The 15 percent plus estimate is based on the growth in revenues by 1964 recorded in table 3-8 (14.8 percent), the growing importance of income taxes in the revenue structure since that year, and the increasing profits of several major public-sector enterprises.

ment. Pressures from the left prevented the government from reducing the prominence of the public sector and thereby encouraging expanded investment on the part of Mexico's private business groups; they also prohibited an expanded reliance on foreign private investors. Pressures from the right blocked effective redistribution of income through higher tax rates and transfer payments; they also checked further measures for land redistribution and the allocation of proportionally greater resources to an attack on Mexico's rural problems.

Vernon argued that the growing immobility was traceable to two fundamental threats to political stability. The first came from the "dangerous pressures" within the official party. He wrote that "one can look in vain for a tight ideological bond cementing its many splinters," and that "all of these splinters must have some measure of access *and some significant degree of persuasion* upon the policies of the presidency if the pitch of dissension inside the PRI is to be held within tolerable limits." The second challenge came from other "threatening forces" in Mexican society, constituted essentially by powerful commercial and industrial groups "whose economic power and potential political strength have won them a special right to the ear of key ministers or the president himself."[16] Paralyzed by these competing pressures, the Mexican government was pictured as wandering aimlessly between left and right, squandering its resources and incapable of acting decisively to sustain the growth process.

Our examination of the Mexican development strategy, its welfare consequences, the operation of the present political regime and the origins and development of Mexican mestizo politics all support quite a different interpretation of the Mexican political system. In the first place, there is very little evidence that the "splinters" within the party have a significant degree of persuasion upon the policies of the presidency, and a great deal of evidence to the contrary. Indeed, two of the three major sectors of the PRI seem better characterized as captives of the Revolutionary Coalition and the presidency than as groups with access to and significant influence upon Mexican policy formulation. The dualism in Mexican agricultural development since the 1930s, the minimal nature of public-sector resources channeled to the *ejidos*, the constant abuse of the rights of *ejidatarios* by government agencies, and the degree of evasion of agrarian statutes by members of the Revolutionary Coalition itself, all mock the public homage which every PRI politician pays to Mexico's novel agrarian experiment and to the *campesino* sector of the party.

[16] Raymond Vernon, *The Dilemma of Mexico's Development: The Roles of the Private and Public Sectors* (Cambridge: Harvard University Press, 1963), pp. 14–15. Emphasis added.

The labor sector has fared better within the PRI; wage trends for some industrial groups during the 1960s and the passage of the new labor law reveal that its adherence to the Revolutionary Coalition has not gone altogether unrewarded. Nevertheless, when looked at over the period of the past three decades, it is difficult not to think of the labor sector as another captive of the present political regime. Both the praetorian behavior of its (often imposed) leadership and the aggregate welfare impact of economic growth since 1940 support this contention, as does the fact that some of the unions whose members have benefited the most from economic development over the past three decades are precisely those unions not closely tied to the official party and its aging labor-sector leaders.

Because Vernon found no "tight ideological bond" cementing the various groups within the PRI, he assumed that only policies which pleased every faction could contain and control dangerous dissension within the party. But ideological bonds always have been, and will continue to be, of minimal relevance to the politics of mestizo Mexico. In both the first and second mestizo systems political loyalties, to the extent that they existed, were personal. Whether under Díaz or under the regime of the PRI, loyalties have been given to individuals, not ideas; and they have been given on the clear understanding that the reward for loyalty is personal advancement. What actually holds the present regime together is not a set of uncoordinated policies that pleases all sectors and paralyzes the government, but rather a system of mobility that attracts the personal allegiance of spokesmen for all the PRI sectors from the bottom to the top of the party hierarchy. And the strength which that structure of personal loyalties has given the Revolutionary Coalition has allowed it—Vernon's statement to the contrary notwithstanding—to suppress discontent and opposition in some instances and disregard them in others. Suppression was used during the 1940s and late 1950s to manage labor unrest; it has been and continues to be used much more frequently, if less visibly, in rural Mexico. And the killing of perhaps 200 persons and the wounding of hundreds of others by units of the Mexican army and police in an effort to terminate the student demonstrations in Mexico City in October of 1968 indicate that suppression will continue to be used whenever the present regime is convinced of the necessity for such action.

Vernon's analysis of interest groups outside the structure of the PRI and the demands which they make upon the political system was much more accurate than his interpretation of the political forces within the official party. The business community in general, and specifically those groups with economic power and potential political strength, (e.g., the national chambers of commerce and industry and major banking complexes) are in a position to threaten the stability of the present political regime if their interests are not adequately represented in the policy-making process. However, as all the evidence presented in this study indicates, these are the very groups whose demands have been met, and whose interests have not only been protected but expanded over the past thirty years. Given the value-orientations of Mexico's mestizo politicians and the norms of Mexican political behavior, it seems almost inevitable that the mutually profitable modus vivendi between Mexico's new economic and political elites should have developed as it has since 1940.

## THE DYNAMICS OF MEXICO'S DEVELOPMENT

For over thirty years the present political regime has retained the capacity to govern Mexico in a manner consonant with rapid economic development. Its major contributions to economic growth have been two. First, it has provided more than three decades of political stability, a setting that has encouraged the emergence of a dynamic private-sector response to the entrepreneurial opportunities in the Mexican market. It has made that market even more attractive through the legislation of a comprehensive set of governmental policies designed specifically to raise the rates of domestic saving and investment. One dramatic result has been the rise in Mexican private-sector investment from less than 5 percent of national product in the 1940–46 period to an average of more than 14 percent ever since the mid-1950s.

Second, the present regime has developed the capacity to concentrate public sector resources on the promotion of rapid economic growth. During the 1940s and 1950s close to 40 percent of all public-sector revenues were channeled into investment projects. Furthermore, as noted in chapter 3, most of those investments were of a type that added substantially to the immediate productivity of all other Mexican investment. The bottleneck-breaking nature of many public-sector projects has made a major contribution to the fluid and flexible nature of the Mexican economy over the past three decades. The Mexican government has been able to concentrate public-sector revenues in crucial infrastructure and industrial investment programs *precisely because it has not had to respond to the demands of all the groups within the PRI.* By making only insignificant expenditures on programs of agricultural extension, *ejidal* credit, rural and urban education, housing, and other welfare programs, the government has been able to channel a larger proportion of its limited resources into major development projects than all other industrializing nations of Latin America. Likewise, most of the government policies designed to encourage the expansion of private investment have sacrificed the short-term interests of the Mexican laborer and *campesino*, and have concentrated the fruits of growth in the hands of a new industrial-agricultural elite.

Four major factors account for much of the PRI regime's success. First, the program of agrarian reform eventually produced a state of political quiescence in rural Mexico. Second, the increasing opportunities for socio-economic mobility offered by the turnover of political offices within the PRI and by the rapid pace of industrialization eased the traditional Mexican political problem of managing discontent among the educated mestizo segment of society. Third, the development within the official party of the capacity to smother elite competition for political office perceptibly slowed the mobilization of large segments of Mexican society into active participation in political life. And fourth, the traditional cultural and psychological barriers to political participation continued to limit both the extent and the nature of political demands coming from Mexico's parochial and subject groups, which together comprise close to 90 percent of Mexico's total population.

It has been argued by almost all observers of the process of modern economic development that the socio-economic changes introduced by economic growth greatly increase the likelihood of expanded political participation and broadened political demands from members of society. In the Mexican case, however, the value-orientations and behavioral norms of mestizo political leadership, the structure and functioning of the official party, and the psychological and cultural heritage of the Mexican people have all conspired to slow the growth of the Mexican polity, stabilize the process of change in Mexican society, and accelerate the growth of the Mexican economy.

The contribution of the Revolutionary Coalition and the PRI regime to economic development does not appear to have resulted from an overriding commitment to Mexican industrialization. The major goals of its leadership have been—and continue to be—the retention of its own hegemony over Mexican politics and the enjoyment of the socio-economic advantages that accompany political position in Mexico. Mexican political and business elites have gradually been melding, and when the vested interests of the economic elite are involved in a political decision, the present governing group has been less development-oriented than would be suggested by its public pronouncements. This pattern of behavior on its part accounts for the continuous dilution of the social and political programs of the revolution since the 1930s. Perhaps the best example of the regime's sacrifice of sound measures that would accelerate growth is to be found in the area of tax reform. Advisers, foreign and domestic, have been urging reform for years with only marginal results.

But despite such lapses, the regime has nevertheless played a crucial role in the process of Mexican industrialization. While "traditional" in the mestizo political sense, Mexico's political leaders have easily accommodated themselves to the social and cultural changes accompanying economic development. They have filled government posts with well-trained economists and other "modernizers"; in some instances these government officials have been outspoken critics of the PRI and its policies. Jesús Silva Herzog, one of the present regime's most articulate enemies, was employed in the ministry of the treasury for many years. Victor Urquidi, a highly respected Mexican economist, spent many years officially advising the government at the same time that he exposed its inactions in his scholarly writings. And Ifigenia de Navarrete, author of a critical study of government policies during the 1950s, has served for several years as a special economic adviser to the president of Mexico.

If the present regime has created a place for Mexico's modernizers, it has also successfully accommodated Mexico's traditional powerholders, the rural *caciques*. While the power of these traditional figures has diminished over the past three decades, the ability of the Revolutionary Coalition during the early decades to incorporate them into a political regime that was moving ahead with industrialization was crucial to the success of Mexican development. Accommodating the traditional rural leadership provided the country with the stability upon which Mexico's development strategy depended; accommodating the modernizing urban elites gradually expanded Mexico's capacity for self-generating economic development. The fee which the coalition's leaders charged for performing as the brokers of Mexican development enriched almost all of them immeasurably; in the long run their political performance will probably enrich the entire nation. In the interim "realists" will praise their "constructive" achievements, while "idealists" will censure their "betrayal" of the manifest goals of the revolution; these emotionally irreconcilable points of view are equally valid. There is no question that the social and political goals of the Mexican revolution as enunciated ever since 1910 have been endlessly sacrificed on the altar of mestizo political ambitions. But neither is there clear evidence that economic development can be achieved in any society without sustained sacrifices on the part of lower income groups. In the Mexican case the rhetoric of the revolution raised hopes that another path to development might be found; it was not. Therein lies both the betrayal of the Mexican dream and the roots of the Mexican success.

## THE 1970s AND BEYOND

For the past three decades the operation of the Mexican political system has had a profound impact upon the course of economic development. It has kept the peace, it has marshaled close to 40 percent of the public sector's total revenues for economic investment purposes, and it has induced growing private-sector investment in Mexico's economic future. In the 1970s and beyond Mexico will face a continuing series of challenges to rapid economic growth. It faced them during the 1960s with a remarkable degree of success, and will most probably continue to do so as long as the Mexican political system can (1) stabilize the process of social change inherent in periods of rapid industrialization, (2) limit those political demands which would shrink the Mexican government's capacity to generate internal savings, and (3) induce continued private sector initiatives in the growth process. What are the probabilities that the present political system can provide these requisites for sustained economic development in Mexico?

There are two major reasons for believing that they will remain fairly high for some time to come. The first involves the nature of the restraints on active political participation in Mexico. It has been noted that the vast majority of the Mexican people make few, if any, demands upon their political system. The "parochials" know little about government and are alienated from it; the "subjects" are likewise alienated by the operation of Mexican politics at all levels of government, and they expect little from it. The point which needs emphasis in the present context is that such attitudes are likely to persist for many years, despite the pace of economic growth and the consequent changes in Mexican social structure.

Basic political attitudes and values, like the general attitude and value structure of any society, appear to be set quite firmly at an early age. They are formed in the family, at school, and in contact with one's peer group. Part of the socialization process through which basic attitudes affecting political behavior are developed results from explicit teaching, both in the home and in school. However, it is probable that the attitudes an individual develops toward the political process derive less from direct and explicit teaching than from indirect inferences drawn from experience not intended to have an effect on politics. Indeed, as Sidney Verba has argued, children learn basic lessons about the nature of authority and about the trustworthiness of others in early social situations which are devoid of explicit political content. Yet these are the primary experiences from which children generalize as they develop a set of attitudes toward politics.[17]

Attitudes regarding authority and interpersonal trust are among the most important in conditioning later political beliefs and perceptions. In the Mexican setting we have noted the unusually high degree of distrust which seems to pervade all segments of the population. It is a factor that has been affirmed by all analysts who have attempted character sketches of various segments of Mexican society, and it has been statistically measured by recent survey studies. As long as high levels of interpersonal distrust and alienation from political structures continue to permeate Mexican society, the demands upon the political system will tend to be limited. And since such basic attitudes, growing as they do out of childhood experiences, are subject only to slow and marginal change within each generation, a revolution of rising ex-

[17] Sidney Verba, "Comparative Political Culture," in *Political Culture and Political Development*, edited by Lucian W. Pye and Sidney Verba (Princeton, N.J.: Princeton University Press, 1965), p. 552.

pectations with regard to what government can and should do for the parochial and subject segments of Mexican society will not emerge rapidly. If this judgment is correct, it suggests that the incremental approach of the Mexican government to redressing the present welfare imbalance—an approach highlighted during the 1960s by marginal tax reforms, gradual changes in the allocation of public-sector funds in favor of welfare expenditures and subsistence farming, and increases of approximately 7 percent a year in legal minimum wages—may succeed both politically and economically in sustaining the process of economic development in Mexico.

The second major reason for believing that both the stability of the present political system and the PRI's capacity to cope successfully with the problems of growth will be sustained for some time to come involves the continuing ability of the present regime to smother open political competition. The major factor responsible for the mobilization of new strata of society into participatory politics in Mexico, as in most of Latin America, has been elite competition for control of the political process. That competition had been particularly strenuous in Mexico before the Peace of the PRI because few other avenues of socio-economic mobility existed. But the structuring of the official party and the gradual emergence of the Mexican presidency as the undisputed center of political power and authority finally brought an end to open contests for political control of the country. Whatever the nature of the hidden competition within the PRI hierarchy, open efforts of ambitious mestizo power seekers to increase their political power by mobilizing new groups of supporters into political life have greatly diminished over the past three decades. Some of the "have-nots" outside the party structure still develop support in their attempts to influence governmental policy; the appearance of new leaders and new groups in the political process was clearly illustrated during the 1960s when the Independent Peasant Confederation emerged to dramatize the problem of salinization of the soil in northwestern Mexico.[18] Nevertheless, the PRI and its governing hierarchy continue to demonstrate the capacity either to co-opt emerging local leaders into the party structure or to resolve the issues which give rise to independent leadership.

Judging by the smoothness with which Mexico's two most recent presidents have chosen their successors, the Mexican chief executive's command over the PRI, its sectors, and the Revolutionary Coalition appear to be strengthening with the passage of time. In 1958, maneuvering within and among the various party sectors in attempts to influence the choice of the party candidate led to open displays of dissension and conflict, especially

[18] See L. Vincent Padgett, *The Mexican Political System* (Boston: Houghton Mifflin Co., 1966), pp. 121ff.

within the labor sector. In 1963, however, when Gustavo Díaz Ordaz was named to succeed the late Adolfo López Mateos, little public controversy was noticeable. And in 1969, when Díaz Ordaz chose his minister of interior, Luis Echeverría Alvarez, to be the next president of Mexico, the transfer of power within the coalition was accompanied by less public evidence of disharmony than has ever attended the rite of PRI succession since the party's birth in 1929.[19] So long as the official party can successfully co-opt new sources of potential opposition leadership and mask from the public the sexennial bargaining process which takes place within the PRI, the mobilization of new groups into participatory politics will be limited and the psychological and cultural restraints on further political participation will be reinforced by the modus operandi of the regime of the Revolutionary Coalition.

Balanced against the two factors which prompt a prediction of continuity in both political stability and economic development in the 1970s are two possible sources of serious political stress. The first involves at least a localized tendency on the part of Mexico's urban voters to manifest their discontent with the present regime by supporting the only sizeable opposition party, the Party of National Action (PAN). The second political problem, more difficult to document, involves the possibility of increasing rural unrest in consequence of deteriorating rural standards of living.

[19] Those who believe that the massive student demonstrations of 1968 were directly attributable to the political machinations of various candidates for the presidency within the PRI will strongly disagree with the above assessment of the transfer of power from Díaz Ordaz to Luis Echeverría Alvarez. Some argue, for example, that the permit for the initial large demonstration on July 26, 1968, was granted by Minister of Interior Echeverría Alvarez in order to undermine support for a rival candidate, Alfonso Corona del Rosal, then mayor of Mexico City. Once the demonstrations got out of hand, right-wing elements within the party, led by the military, began to demand that force be used to end the student protest. On the night of October 2 thousands of soldiers and policemen, and scores of tanks, bazookas and machine guns were used to crush the demonstration at the Plaza of the Three Cultures. Another group has argued that the demonstrations were fomented by the liberal wing of the PRI in order to discredit the candidacies of both Corona del Rosal and Echeverría Alvarez.

There are two reasons why it is difficult to give credence to these interpretations. First, they are impossible to document. Those who might be in a position to evaluate them won't talk, as is evidenced by the widely differing interpretations of the events found in the Mexico City press reports at the time of the disturbances. Second, these interpretations imply that President Díaz Ordaz simply sat by mutely and paralyzed while members of his own cabinet and innermost circle turned Mexico City upside down on the very eve of the Olympic Games, whose success were of financial as well as symbolic importance to the Díaz Ordaz government. It is almost impossible to believe that the president fiddled while Mexico City burned, oblivious to the activities of his own confidants or powerless to control them.

Whatever the truth may be, it is worth emphasizing that social and political tranquility has prevailed in Mexico since October of 1968. Throughout 1969 the moves to influence the choice of a successor were made behind the scenes and almost without public incident.

With regard to the first problem a recent statistical study of Mexican voting patterns by José Luis Reyna has demonstrated that those Mexican states exhibiting the highest degree of economic development are also those with the lowest voter turnout in national elections. Furthermore, they are the states in which opposition parties receive the highest percentage of total votes cast.[20] Reyna's findings suggest that the Mexican middle class does not support the PRI to the same degree as laborers and *campesino* groups.

Several recent elections have illustrated the growing degree of middle class alienation from the PRI. In 1967 many former PRI supporters voted for the PAN candidates during municipal elections in the states of Sonora and Yucatán; as a result, PAN candidates won the mayoralties of both state capitals (Hermosillo and Mérida, respectively). During 1968 the PRI apparently suffered two further urban defeats, this time in the northwestern cities of Tijuana and Mexicali. Although the PRI-controlled state legislature of Baja California refused to confirm the election results, newspaper accounts reported that the PAN candidates won both the municipal presidencies and the control of the city councils.[21]

In each contest local and state issues undoubtedly influenced the election results. It would therefore be risky to interpret these few cases as convincing evidence of a strong middle class trend away from the PRI toward the increasingly centrist Partido de Acción Nacional. Nevertheless, coming as they did shortly after Carlos Madrazo's unsuccessful efforts to democratize the workings of the PRI at the local level, these election results did signify at least a temporary disgust among urban voters with both the quality of PRI candidates and with the refusal of the PRI leadership to open the party's nominating procedures to greater popular participation.[22]

The response of the official party's leadership to middle class dissent over the past several years suggests that the Revolutionary Coalition has little inten-

---

[20] José Luis Reyna, "Desarrollo económico: distribución del poder, y participación política: el caso mexicano," *Ciencias políticas y sociales* 50 (October-December 1965): 469-86. Barry Ames has also recently demonstrated that in Mexico (1) low levels of urbanization are associated with high PRI percentages of total votes cast, and (2) the presence of opposition parties is associated with a low voter turnout. However, his study suggests that voter turnout is relatively unaffected by level of economic development. See his observations and statistical analysis presented in "Bases of Support for Mexico's Dominant Party," *American Political Science Review* 64 (March 1970): 153-67.

[21] See chapter 5 above.

[22] See *Visión* (March 14, 1969), pp. 21-24. That such a trend did not exist during the 1950s and the first half of the 1960s is demonstrated by Barry Ames in his "Bases of Support for Mexico's Dominant Party." Wayne A. Cornelius, Jr. has noted the dangers of failing to examine the local circumstances surrounding some recent electoral setbacks for the PRI. See his comments on Baja California in "Urbanization as an Agent in Latin American Political Instability," *American Political Science Review* 63 (September 1969): 853-54.

tion of restructuring its method of internal operation or of allowing itself to be voted out of office. As yet it has resisted any democratization of the PRI's nominating processes. Furthermore, while permitting the adverse election results of 1967 in Mérida to stand, the PRI initiated some tactics of at best dubious legality to obstruct the PAN administration of that city ever since. And during the 1969 election campaign PRI supporters resorted increasingly to violence to disrupt major public appearances of Yucatán's PAN gubernatorial candidate, Manuel Correa Rachó.[23] By the time of the election the lives of both the PRI and the PAN candidates were endangered, and this uneasy situation was directly attributable to the violent tactics first introduced by PRI supporters. The PRI candidate was eventually declared the winner despite widespread charges of fraud which were given a great deal of credence in press reports of the election.

Another indication that the Revolutionary Coalition shows little inclination to "grease all the squeaky wheels" is reflected in the choice of Luis Echeverría Alvarez as Mexico's *jefe máximo* for the next six years (1970-76). Like all but one of Mexico's presidents since 1946, Echeverría Alvarez served as the minister of interior in the cabinet of his predecessor. As minister of *gobernación* in Mexico for the past six years, Echeverría Alvarez has been directly responsible for domestic political affairs and internal security. Like all but one of Mexico's recent presidents, he is a lawyer who has spent most of his adult life working within the inner sanctum of the PRI machinery. In the Mexican political context he has generally been considered a representative of the center-right elements within the PRI, a man from whom little in the way of major economic or political reform can be expected on the basis of his public record prior to 1970. In this respect his candidacy appeared to signify "more of the same" for the next six years in both economic policy and political operation.

His nomination was a disappointment to liberal circles. University groups in particular had held Echeverría Alvarez partially responsible for the conflict between the government and Mexico's university students, and have been sharply critical of the harshness with which student leaders have been treated since the 1968 student demonstrations; as late as the spring of 1970 more than 100 of them were still being held in jail without having been able to obtain either release on bail or firm trial dates. Moderates within PRI circles as well as liberals outside the party had urged that Díaz Ordaz name Dr. Emilio Martínez Manautou as his successor. Dr. Manatou, secretary of the presidency for the last several years of the 1960s, had spoken openly in favor

---

[23] See accounts of the campaign in *Excelsior*, October 4, October 6, and October 8, 1969, and especially the editorial on the campaign in *Excelsior*, October 6, 1969, p. 6-A.

of a series of reforms which would gradually have shifted the benefits of Mexican economic development toward lower income groups. Apparently, however, Mexico's present political leadership is as yet unprepared to change its incrementalist approach to the challenges of economic development, and undisturbed by the increasingly vocal criticism of PRI politics heard among middle class Mexicans both in and out of the universities.

Nor is it clear that this criticism and lack of strong middle class support at the polls should be a major source of concern to the PRI leadership. Barring unpredictable economic or political events, the PRI should be able to retain its political predominance throughout the 1970s without resorting to increased electoral fraud. Its organizational base and its association with the goals of the revolution in the minds of so many Mexican people suggest that any erosion of its capacity to win elections will occur only gradually. Indeed, between 1952 and 1967 the percentage of total votes going to the PRI rose in all but three of Mexico's thirty-two states; the average increase was 11 percent. Furthermore, over those same years there is no statistical evidence to suggest that rapidly urbanizing states "are becoming less strong for the PRI."[24] The extent to which fraud has affected these trends is impossible to determine, but press reports do not suggest any marked increase in electoral illegalities over the period as a whole. In view of these indicators there is no reason to believe that the loss of some municipal councils and even a few seats in state and national legislatures will endanger the PRI's control over the national political apparatus.

The events connected with the Battle of Tlatelolco in 1968 make it clear that the PRI leadership will not hesitate to incur the criticism of middle class Mexico in dealing with challenges to the present status quo. Rather than accede to some quite reasonable student demands in that year—most of them concerning police methods and political prisoners—the government ruthlessly crushed the massive demonstrations at a probable cost of over 200 lives.[25] Probably, as many critics of the present regime claimed in 1968, the government was caught off guard by the events which led to the demonstrations. However that may be, the indecisiveness which characterized the government's initial responses soon disappeared. Since this application of domestic overkill the government has been in firm control of events. On the first anniversary of the Battle of Tlatelolco hard-line tactics again prevailed, and they were succesful. As the *New York Times* noted, "An overwhelming display of armed policemen and army units around Tlatelolco and the periphery of university centers, as well as in high schools, reduced incidents by students who planned to commemorate the shooting to a few score arrests

[24] Barry Ames, "Bases of Support for Mexico's Dominant Party," p. 166.
[25] *New York Times*, October 6, 1969.

of young people wearing black armbands and scattering anti-government leaflets."[26]

Since 1968 Mexico has apparently returned to that state of stability which has characterized the Peace of the PRI for more than three decades, and if the government chooses to improve its relations with Mexico's student groups at some time in the future it will probably be bargaining from a position of strength, not weakness. The degree of repression which a government can employ without undermining its own strength varies from one country to the next, and is dependent upon the cultural and psychological parameters of its political system as well as upon the country's political history. In the Mexican setting it is not at all clear that the actions of the government in 1968 have seriously undermined former sources of support. One might even hazard the guess that the PRI leadership took the actions it did while calculating that the use of force would terminate the student disturbances without damaging the strength of the present regime over the long run. Less speculative is the conclusion that middle-class discontent does not yet appear to be a major source of concern to the Revolutionary Coalition. The present leadership enters the 1970s with an apparently undiminished capacity to accommodate or suppress urban dissent as it sees fit without risking any rapid erosion of its control over Mexican politics.

The other possible source of political stress involves the rapidly expanding landless *campesino* population. It is estimated that this segment of Mexico's rural labor force, over three million in number by 1960, will reach five million by 1980. The per capita hours of employment of these farms laborers are falling, as is their standard of living, already at the subsistence level. During the 1960s the sporadic outbreaks of rural violence, the invasions of privately held farmlands, and other forms of rural protest seemed to be increasing in comparison with the previous decade. Trends are difficult to measure because the reporting of such incidents is very incomplete. However, the picture of rural poverty that can be drawn from the 1960 census data and several recent investigations lends an aura of validity to reports of growing rural unrest. Peasants with land—however marginal—seldom revolt. Peasants without land, without job opportunities, and with falling standards of living do revolt, even if anomically and without clearly articulated purposes. Therefore, it is not beyond the realm of possibility that Mexico's political stability could be shaken during the 1970s by at least sporadic outbreaks of rural violence, especially if the land reform program is soon terminated. The likelihood of serious rural unrest will noticeably increase if middle class dissidents from urban Mexico attempt to capitalize upon *campesino* discontent in order to change the structure and policy orientations of the present regime.

[26] *Ibid.*

The fact that a new personality becomes the most powerful man in Mexican politics every six years entails one great advantage. The new president has an opportunity to assess the political picture and to initiate a series of adjustments in the policies of his predecessors in consequence of that assessment. Mexico's latest *jefe máximo*, Echeverría Alvarez, has indicated that he plans to make the socio-economic progress of the country's peasants the main concern of his administration.[27] Such pledges in Mexican politics have a long history of being honored in the breach, and there is not much in the new president's public background to suggest that his approach to the problems of rural Mexico will encompass more than continuing marginal adjustments in favor of the impoverished rural sector.

However, it would be a mistake to assume that Echeverría's presidential policies can be accurately predicted on the basis of his public record to date. Presidents dominate the Mexican political scene to such a degree that cabinet members do little more than implement presidential decisions. Indeed, wherever one is placed in the Mexican political hierarchy, his continued upward mobility is generally dependent upon the degree to which his behavior accords with the wishes of his immediate superiors. Only now that Echeverría is at the top of "the greasy pole" are his personal values and policy predelictions free to emerge.

Beyond the possibility that his own preferences might tend to alter present policies as they affect rural Mexico, there are two specific reasons for believing that Echeverría will make some adjustments in the allocation of government resources in favor of the rural poor. First, it is infinitely easier for the Mexican government to "move to the left" on rural questions than it is for most Latin American governments. The ideological underpinnings for almost every imaginable type of agrarian reform have been a vital part of the country's folklore for close to six decades. Furthermore, no traditional *hacendado* class remains to obstruct whatever measures might be taken to help Mexico's marginal farmers and landless *campesinos*. The major resistance forthcoming would be from those individuals and groups connected to the Revolutionary Family itself that have thus far evaded the intent if not always the letter of the agrarian reform statutes.

Second, Mexico's political elite is highly pragmatic. Indeed, it is probably the most pragmatic of all ruling groups in the developing world today. The commitment of Mexico's mestizo power seekers to their own social and economic mobility has left them generally uninterested in ideology and so eclectic in their approach to the problems of government that some commentators have emphasized their "lack of doctrine or direction."[28] Why

[27] *New York Times*, November 17, 1969, p. 11.
[28] Vernon, *Dilemma*, p. 131.

those same commentators interpret the lack of doctrine as a weakness is quite unclear. The very absence of commitment to any particular *weltanschauung* leaves Mexico's political leadership with a freedom of choice in many policy fields unequaled by that of most other governments. Its overriding concern is with what will work to resolve those problems which might threaten the predominance of the PRI structure. Therefore, if the new president is convinced that a change in priorities is needed to keep the peace in rural Mexico, the next six years will witness that change. If such changes have not occurred in the past, the reason is less that the government was paralyzed by *immobilisme* than that it did not view rural discontent with much alarm. Thus far, at any rate, its judgment that rural unrest has not constituted a major challenge to political stability has been accurate.

If, however, the government's response to the potential political stress represented by rural Mexico, like that of the Díaz regime, is for whatever reason too little and too late, the Peace of the PRI could become a relic of the past. As Samuel Huntington has recently noted, political stability in most modernizing countries is dependent to a considerable degree upon the capacity of the government to "build a bridge to the countryside."[29] It is in the urban setting that rapidly expanding groups of the populace are being mobilized for active participation in political life. The military, the intelligentsia, other organized middle-class groups and organized labor within the cities are relatively eager to contest for political power. Such a contest inevitably breeds instability where strong political organizations and broadly recognized legitimate political institutions and modes of political behavior are lacking. Mexico has thus far avoided the instability accompanying urban-dominated praetorian politics through the development of the official party and its capacity to retain rural support for the programs of the Revolutionary Coalition. If and when that rural support is undermined to the point where the predominance of the PRI can be effectively challenged by other political organizations, not only the pattern of Mexican politics but also the parameters of Mexican economic development will be significantly altered.

The probability of such change during the 1970s, however, seems fairly remote. The organizational strength of the PRI, the firmness of purpose—however praetorian—of its leadership, and the enduring impact of Mexico's psychological and cultural heritage all suggest that continuity rather than change will be the hallmark of Mexican politics as well as of Mexican economic development during the 1970s. If continuity does prevail, it will only serve to emphasize still further the remarkable resilience of the present political regime, a regime which is itself a fascinating mixture of continuity and

[29] Samuel P. Huntington, *Political Order in Changing Societies* (New Haven: Yale University Press, 1968), p. 209.

change in Mexico's political heritage. It has been said of the men who ruled Mexico a century ago that their "capacity for graft far outweighed their ability to govern."[30] Of the men who rule Mexico under the Peace of the PRI one can say without fear of serious contradiction that the scales are in far better balance.

[30] Charles C. Cumberland, *Mexico: The Struggle for Modernity* (London: Oxford University Press, 1968), p. 147.

*Appendix*

# BALANCE OF PAYMENTS DATA

(All data for tables 1-5 taken from Banco de México, *Informe anual*, various issues.)

TABLE 1. MERCHANDISE EXPORTS, INCLUDING GOLD AND SILVER

| Year | Total (million $) | Change from Previous Year (percent) |
|------|------|------|
| 1958 | 758.0 | |
| 1959 | 756.1 | -0.2 |
| 1960 | 786.4 | +4.0 |
| 1961 | 844.3 | +7.4 |
| 1962 | 944.0 | +11.8 |
| 1963 | 987.2 | +4.6 |
| 1964 | 1,068.6 | +8.2 |
| 1965 | 1,158.2 | +8.4 |
| 1966 | 1,207.4 | +4.2 |
| 1967 | 1,155.5 | -4.3 |
| 1968[a] | 1,252.6 | +8.4 |

[a]Preliminary data.

TABLE 2. RECEIPTS FROM TOURISM AND BORDER TRADE

| Year | Total (million $) | Change from Previous Year (percent) |
|------|------|------|
| 1958 | 450 | |
| 1959 | 496 | +10.2 |
| 1960 | 521 | +5.0 |
| 1961 | 557 | +6.9 |
| 1962 | 586 | +5.2 |
| 1963 | 657 | +12.1 |
| 1964 | 704 | +7.2 |
| 1965 | 774 | +9.9 |
| 1966 | 875 | +13.0 |
| 1967 | 958 | +9.5 |
| 1968[a] | 1,142 | +19.2 |

[a]Preliminary data.

TABLE 3.  MERCHANDISE IMPORTS

| Year | Total (million $) | Change from Previous Year (percent) |
|---|---|---|
| 1959 | 1,006.6 | |
| 1960 | 1,186.4 | +17.9 |
| 1961 | 1,138.6 | −4.0 |
| 1962 | 1,143.0 | +3.9 |
| 1963 | 1,239.7 | +8.5 |
| 1964 | 1,493.0 | +20.4 |
| 1965 | 1,559.6 | +4.5 |
| 1966 | 1,605.2 | +2.9 |
| 1967 | 1,748.3 | +8.9 |
| 1968[a] | 1,960.1 | +12.1 |

[a]Preliminary data.

TABLE 4.  EXPENDITURES ON TOURISM AND BORDER TRANSACTIONS

| Year | Total (million $) | Change from Previous Year (percent) |
|---|---|---|
| 1962 | 279.3 | |
| 1963 | 349.5 | +25.1 |
| 1964 | 376.8 | +7.8 |
| 1965 | 414.2 | +9.9 |
| 1966 | 478.8 | +15.6 |
| 1967 | 526.3 | +9.9 |
| 1968[a] | 643.8 | +22.3 |

[a]Preliminary data.

TABLE 5.  CURRENT ACCOUNT BALANCE (millions of dollars)

| Year | Amount |
|---|---|
| 1959 | −31.7 |
| 1960 | −174.0 |
| 1961 | −62.4 |
| 1962 | −93.7 |
| 1963 | −206.0 |
| 1964 | −406.5 |
| 1965 | −375.7 |
| 1966 | −296.1 |
| 1967 | −506.3 |
| 1968[a] | −622.5 |

[a]Preliminary data

TABLE 6.  INTERNATIONAL  RESERVES–GOLD,  FOREIGN  EXCHANGE,  AND
GOLD TRANCHE POSITION (millions of dollars)

| Year | Amount |
|------|--------|
| 1960 | 438 |
| 1961 | 411 |
| 1962 | 428 |
| 1963 | 548 |
| 1964 | 587 |
| 1965 | 537 |
| 1966 | 564 |
| 1967 | 586 |
| 1968 | 657 |

Source: International Monetary Fund, *Financial Statistics.*

# SELECTED BIBLIOGRAPHY

## BOOKS

Adams, Richard N., and Heath, Dwight B., eds. *Contemporary Culture and Societies of Latin America*. New York: Random House, 1965.

Alexander, Robert J. *Organized Labor in Latin America*. New York: Free Press, 1965.

Almond, Gabriel A., and Powell, G. Bingham, Jr. *Comparative Politics: A Developmental Approach*. Boston: Little, Brown & Co., 1966.

Almond, Gabriel A., and Verba, Sidney. *The Civic Culture: Political Attitudes and Democracy in Five Nations*. Princeton, N.J.: Princeton University Press, for the Center of International Studies, 1963.

*América en cifras, 1967: situación cultural: educación y otros aspectos culturales*. Washington, D.C.: Panamerican Union, 1969.

Anderson, Charles W. *Politics and Economic Change in Latin America*. Princeton: D. Van Nostrand Co., 1967.

Anderson, Charles W., and Glade, William P. Jr. *The Political Economy of Mexico: Two Studies*. Madison: University of Wisconsin Press, 1963.

Anguiano Equihua, Roberto. *Las Finanzas del sector público en México*. Mexico: Universidad Nacional Autónoma de México, Ciudad Universitaria, 1968.

Apter, David E. *The Politics of Modernization*. Chicago: University of Chicago Press, 1965.

Ashby, Joe C. *Organized Labor and the Mexican Revolution Under Lazaro Cárdenas*. Chapel Hill: University of North Carolina Press, 1963.

Baer, Werner. *Industrialization and Economic Development in Brazil*. Homewood, Ill.: Richard D. Irwin, 1965.

Baer, Werner, and Kerstenetzky, Isaac, eds. *Inflation and Growth in Latin America*. Homewood, Ill.: Richard D. Irwin, 1954.

Banco de México. *Encuesta sobre ingresos y gastos familiares en México, 1963*. Mexico: Banco de México, 1967.

Beals, Carleton. *Porfirio Díaz: Dictator of Mexico*. Philadelphia: J. B. Lippincott, 1932.

Benítez Zenteno, Raúl, and Cabrera Acevedo, Gustavo. *Proyecciones de la población de México*. Mexico: Banco de México, 1966.

Black, C. E. *The Dynamics of Modernization*. New York: Harper and Row, 1966.

Braibanti, Ralph, and Spengler, Joseph J., eds. *Tradition, Values, and Socio-Economic Development*. Durham, N.C.: Duke University Press, 1961.

Branch, H. N. *The Mexican Constitution of 1917 Compared with the Constitution of 1857*. Philadelphia: American Academy of Political and Social Science, 1917.

Brandenburg, Frank. *The Making of Modern Mexico*. Englewood Cliffs, N.J.: Prentice-Hall, 1964. '

Brothers, Dwight S., and Solís M., Leopoldo. *Mexican Financial Development*. Austin: University of Texas Press, 1966.

Bulnes, Francisco. *El Verdadero Díaz y la revolución*. Mexico: Editora Nacional, 1952.

Bulnes, Francisco. *The Whole Truth About Mexico*. New York: M. Bulnes Book Co., 1916.

Cabrera, Luis. *Obras políticas del lic. Blas Urrea*. Mexico: Imprenta Nacional, 1921.

Cabrera, Luis. *Veinte años despues*. Mexico: n.p., 1937.

Clark, Marjorie Ruth. *Organized Labor in Mexico*. Chapel Hill: University of North Carolina Press, 1934.

Cline, Howard F. *Mexico: Revolution to Evolution, 1940-1960*. London: Oxford University Press, 1962.

Cline, Howard F. *The United States and Mexico*. Rev. ed. New York: Atheneum, 1966.

Combined Mexican Working Party. *The Economic Development of Mexico*. Baltimore: Johns Hopkins Press, for the International Bank for Reconstruction and Development, 1953.

Cosío Villegas, Daniel. *American Extremes*. Austin: University of Texas Press, 1964.

Cosío Villegas, Daniel, ed. *Historia moderna de México*. Vol. 2, *La República restaurada—la vida económica*; vol. 7, *El Porfiriato—la vida económica*, books 1 and 2. Mexico: Editorial Hermes, 1965.

*IV censo agrícola ganadero y ejidal. 1960 resumen general*. Mexico, D.F.: Departamento General de Estadísticas, 1965.

Cumberland, Charles C. *Mexican Revolution: Genesis Under Madero*. Austin: University of Texas Press, 1952.

Cumberland, Charles C. *Mexico: The Struggle for Modernity*. London: Oxford University Press, 1968.

Davis, Tom, ed. *Mexico's Recent Economic Growth*. Austin: University of Texas Press for the Institute of Latin American Studies, 1967.

de la Peña, Moisés T. *El Pueblo y su tierra: mito y realidad de la reforma agraria en México*. Mexico, D.F.: Cuadernos Americanos, 1964.

de Vries, Egbert, and Medina Echevarría, José, eds. *Social Aspects of Economic Development in Latin America*. The Hague: Mouton & Co., UNESCO, 1963.

*Diario de los debates del congreso constituyente, 1916–1917*. Mexico, D.F.: Talleres Gráficos de la Nación, 1960.

Easton, David. *A Systems Analysis of Political Life*. New York: John Wiley and Sons, 1965.

Eckstein, Salomon. *El Marco macroeconómico del problema agrario Mexicano*. Photoduplicated. Mexico: Centro de Investigaciones Agrarias, 1968.

Editorial Nuestro Tiempo, eds. *Ensayos sobre las clases sociales en México*. Mexico, D.F.: Editorial Nuestro Tiempo, 1968.

Editorial Nuestro Tiempo, eds. *Neolatifundismo y explotación: de Emiliano Zapata a Anderson Clayton & Co*. Mexico, D.F.: Editorial Nuestro Tiempo, 1968.

Everett, Mike. *The Evolution of the Mexican Wage Structure, 1939–63*. Manuscript. Revised version. Mexico, D.F.: El Colegio de México, February 1968.

Fuentes Díaz, Vicente. *Los Partidos políticos en México*. Vols. 1, 2. Mexico: Edición del Autor, 1954–1956.

Gamio, Manuel, ed. *La Población del valle de Teotihuacán*. Vols. 1, 2. Mexico: Dirección de Talleres Graficos, 1922.

German Parra, Manuel. *La Industrialización de México*. Mexico: Imprenta Universitaria, 1954.

Germani, Gino. *Política y sociedad en una época de transición: de la sociedad tradicional a la sociedad de masas*. Buenos Aires: Editorial Paidos, 1962.

Gibson, Charles. *The Aztecs Under Spanish Rule*. Stanford, Cal.: Stanford University Press, 1964.

Goldsmith, Raymond W. *The Financial Development of Mexico*. Paris: Development Centre of the Organisation for Economic Co-operation and Development, 1966.

González Casanova, Pablo. *La Democracia en México*. Mexico: Ediciones ERA, 1965.

González Navarro, Moisés. *La Confederación nacional campesina*. Mexico: B. Costa-Amic, 1968.

Gruening, Ernest Henry. *Mexico and Its Heritage*. New York: Century Co., 1928.

Hagen, Everett. *On the Theory of Social Change*. Homewood, Ill.: Dorsey Press, 1962.

Hale, Charles A. *Mexican Liberalism in the Age of Mora, 1821–1853*. New Haven: Yale University Press, 1968.

Hamill, Hugh M., Jr. *The Hidalgo Revolt*. Gainesville: University of Florida Press, 1966.

Harbison, Frederick, and Myers, Charles N. *Education, Manpower and Economic Growth*. New York: McGraw-Hill Book Co., 1964.

Hertford, Reed. *Principal Historical and Economic Issues in Mexican Agricultural Development*. Mimeographed.

Hirschman, Albert O., ed. *Latin American Issues: Essays and Comments*. New York: Twentieth Century Fund, 1961.

Holt, Robert T., and Turner, John E. *The Political Basis of Economic Development: An Exploration in Comparative Political Analysis*. Princeton, N.J.: D. Van Nostrand Co., 1966.

Hoselitz, Bert F., and Moore, Wilbert E., eds. *Industrialization and Society*. UNESCO: Mouton & Co., 1963.

Huntington, Samuel P. *Political Order in Changing Societies*. New Haven: Yale University Press, 1968.

Iturriaga, José E. *La Estructura social y cultural de México*. Mexico: Fondo de Cultura Económica, 1951.

Johnson, John J., ed. *Continuity and Change in Latin America*. Stanford, Cal.: Stanford University Press, 1964.

Johnson, John J. *The Military and Society in Latin America*. Stanford, Cal.: Stanford University Press, 1964.

Johnson, John J. *Political Change in Latin America: The Emergence of the Middle Sectors*. Stanford, Cal.: Stanford University Press, 1958.

Johnson, William Weber. *Heroic Mexico*. Garden City, N.Y.: Doubleday & Co., 1968.

Kahl, Joseph A. *The Measurement of Modernism*. Austin: University of Texas Press, 1968.

Kuznets, Simon. *Postwar Economic Growth: Four Lectures*. Cambridge: Harvard University Press, Belknap Press, 1964.

LaPalombara, Joseph, and Weiner, Myron, eds. *Political Parties and Political Development*. Princeton, N.J.: Princeton University Press, 1966.

Lewis, Oscar. *The Children of Sanchez*. New York: Random House, Vintage Books, 1961.

Lewis, Oscar. *Five Families: Mexican Case Studies in the Culture of Poverty*. New York: Science Edition, 1962.

Lewis, Oscar. *Life in a Mexican Village: Tepoztlán Restudied*. Urbana: University of Illinois Press, 1963.

Lewis, Oscar. *Pedro Martinez*. New York: Random House, Vintage Books, 1967.

Lieuwen, Edwin. *Mexican Militarism: The Political Rise and Fall of the Revolutionary Army 1910-1940*. Albuquerque: University of New Mexico Press, 1968.

Lipset, Seymour Martin. *Political Man: The Social Bases of Politics*. Garden City, N.Y.: Doubleday and Co., 1960.

Lipset, Seymour Martin. *Revolution and Counterrevolution: Change and Persistence in Social Structures*. New York: Basic Books, 1968.

López Aparicio, Alfonso. *El Movimiento obrero en México*. Mexico: Editorial Jus, 1958.

Martz, John D., ed. *The Dynamics of Change in Latin American Politics*. Englewood Cliffs, N.J.: Prentice-Hall, 1965.

Medina Echevarría, José, and Higgins, Benjamin, eds. *Social Aspects of Economic Development in Latin America*. Vol. 2. The Hague: Mouton & Co., UNESCO, 1963.

Meisel, James H. *The Myth of the Ruling Class: Gaetano Mosca and the Elite*. Ann Arbor: University of Michigan Press, 1958.

Mendieta y Núñez, Lucio. *El Problema agrario de México*. Mexico: Editorial Porrua, 1964.

Meyer, Michael C. *Mexican Rebel: Pascual Orozco and the Mexican Revolution 1910-1915*. Lincoln: University of Nebraska Press, 1967.

Millon, Robert Paul. *Mexican Marxist: Vicente Lombardo Toledano*. Chapel Hill: University of North Carolina Press, 1966.

Molina Enríquez, Andrés. *Los Grandes problemas nacionales*. Mexico: Imprenta de A. Carranza e Hijos, 1909.

Moreno, Daniel. *Los Hombres de la revolución*. Mexico: Libro Mex, 1960.

Mosk, Sanford A. *Industrial Revolution in Mexico*. Berkeley and Los Angeles: University of California Press, 1954.

Myers, Charles N. *Education and National Development in Mexico*. Princeton, N.J.: Princeton University, Industrial Relations Section, 1965.

Nacional Financiera. *50 Años de revolución mexicana de cifras*. Mexico, 1963.

Nacional Financiera. *La Economía mexicana en cifras*. Various issues.

Navarrete, Ifigenia M. de. *La Distribución del ingreso y el desarrollo económico de México*. Mexico, D.F.: Instituto de Investigaciones Económicas, Escuela Nacional de Economía, 1960.

Needler, Martin. *Political Development in Latin America: Instability, Violence, and Evolutionary Change*. New York: Random House, 1968.

Ochoa Campos, Moisés. *La Revolución Mexicana*. Vols. 1, 2. Mexico, Biblioteca del Instituto Nacional de Estudios Históricos de la Revolución Mexicana, 1966.

Ortega y Gasset, José. *Invertebrate Spain*. Translated by Mildred Adams. New York: W. W. Norton and Company, 1937.

Padgett, L. Vincent. *The Mexican Political System*. Boston: Houghton Mifflin Co., 1966.

Paní, Alberto J. *Apuntes Autobiográficos*. Mexico: Manuel Porrua, 1950.

Parkes, Henry Bamford. *A History of Mexico*. Boston: Houghton Mifflin Co., 1950.

Parry, Geraint. *Political Elites*. New York: Frederick A. Praeger, 1969.

Paz, Octavio. *The Labyrinth of Solitude: Life and Thought in Mexico*. New York: Grove Press, 1961.

Portes Gil, Emilio. *Quince años de política mexicana*. Mexico: Ediciones Botas, 1941.

Pye, Lucian W., and Verba, Sidney, eds. *Political Culture and Political Development*. Princeton, N.J.: Princeton University Press, 1965.

Quirk, Robert E. *The Mexican Revolution: 1914-1915*. Bloomington, Ind.: Indiana University Press, 1960.

Ramos, Samuel. *Profile of Man and Culture in Mexico*. Translated by Peter G. Earle. Austin: University of Texas Press, 1962.

Redfield, Robert. *A Village that Chose Progress*. Chicago: University of Chicago Press, 1950.

Reynolds, Clark. *The Mexican Economy: Twentieth Century Structure and Growth*. New Haven: Yale University Press, forthcoming.

Richmond, Patricia McIntire. *Mexico: A Case Study of One-Party Politics*. Ph.D. dissertation, University of California, 1965. Microfilm, Library of Congress.

Ross, Stanley R. *Francisco I. Madero: Apostle of Mexican Democracy*. New York: Columbia University Press, 1955.

Ruíz, Ramón Eduardo. *Mexico: The Challenge of Poverty and Illiteracy*. San Marino, Cal.: Huntington Library, 1963.

Rustow, Dankwart A. *A World of Nations: Problems of Political Modernization*. Washington, D.C.: Brookings Institution, 1967.

Scott, Robert E. *Mexican Government in Transition*. Rev. ed. Urbana: University of Illinois Press, 1964.

Secretaría de la Presidencia, Dirección de Inversiones Públicas. *México, inversión pública federal 1925-1963*. Mexico, 1964.

Senior, Clarence. *Land Reform and Democracy*. Gainesville: University of Florida Press, 1958.

Siegel, Barry N. *Inflación y desarrollo: las experiencias de México*. Mexico, D.F.: Centro de Estudios Monetarios Latinoamericanos, 1960.

Sierra, Justus, ed. *Mexico: Its Social Evolution*. Mexico: J. Ballesca & Co., 1900.

Silva Herzog, Jesús. *El Agrarismo mexicano y la reforma agraria*. 2nd ed. Mexico: Fondo de Cultura Económica, 1964.

Silvert, Kalman H., ed. *Expectant Peoples*. New York: Random House, Vintage Books, 1967.

Simpson, Eyler N. *The Ejido: Mexico's Way Out*. Chapel Hill: University of North Carolina Press, 1937.

Tannenbaum, Frank. *Peace by Revolution: Mexico After 1910*. 2nd ed. New York: Columbia University Press, 1966.

Tax, Sol, ed. *Heritage of Conquest*. Glencoe Ill.: Free Press, 1952.

Tax, Sol. *Penny Capitalism: A Guatemalan Indian Economy*. Chicago: University of Chicago Press, 1953.

Turner, Frederick C. *The Dynamics of Mexican Nationalism*. Chapel Hill: University of North Carolina Press, 1968.

United Nations. Department of Economic Affairs. *National Income and its Distribution in Under-developed Countries*. New York: United Nations Statistical Office, 1951.

United States. Agency for International Development. *A Review of Alliance for Progress Goals*. Washington, D.C.: Government Printing Office, 1969.

United States. Department of Agriculture. *Changes in Agriculture in 26 Developing Nations: 1948 to 1963*. Washington, D.C.: Department of Agriculture, Economic Research Service, November 1965.

United States, Department of Commerce. *U.S. Business Investment in Foreign Countries.* Washington, D.C.: Government Printing Office, 1960.

Urquidi, Victor L., and Vargas, A. Lajous. *Educación superior, ciencia y tecnología en el desarrollo económico de México.* Mexico, D.F.: El Colegio de México, 1967.

Valadés, José C. *El Porfirismo.* Vol. 1. Mexico: Antigua Libería Robredo, de Jose Porrua e Hijos, 1941.

Valadés, José C. *El Porfirismo.* Vol. 2. Mexico: Editorial Patria, 1948.

Vasconcelos, José. *Aspects of Mexican Civilization.* Chicago: University of Chicago Press, 1926.

Veliz, Claudio, ed. *Obstacles to Change in Latin America.* London: Oxford University Press, 1967.

Venezian, Eduardo L., and Gamble, William K. *The Agricultural Development of Mexico: Its Structure and Growth Since 1950.* New York: Frederick A. Praeger, 1969.

Vernon, Raymond. *The Dilemma of Mexico's Development: The Roles of the Private and Public Sectors.* Cambridge: Harvard University Press, 1963.

Vernon, Raymond, ed. *Public Policy and Private Enterprise in Mexico.* Cambridge: Harvard University Press, 1964.

Wauchope, Robert, ed. *Synoptic Studies of Mexican Culture.* New Orleans: Tulane University, Middle American Research Institute, 1957.

Whetten, Nathan L. *Rural Mexico.* Chicago: University of Chicago Press, 1948.

Whiteford, Andrew Hunter. *Two Cities of Latin America.* Garden City, N.Y.: Doubleday & Co., Anchor Books, 1964.

Wilkie, James W. *The Mexican Revolution: Federal Expenditure and Social Change Since 1910.* Berkeley and Los Angeles: University of California Press, 1968.

Wolf, Eric R. *Peasant Wars of the Twentieth Century.* New York: Harper and Row, 1969.

Wolf, Eric. R. *Sons of the Shaking Earth.* Chicago: University of Chicago Press, Phoenix Books, 1959.

Womack, John, Jr. *Zapata and The Mexican Revolution.* New York: Alfred A. Knopf, 1969.

## ARTICLES

Ames, Barry. "Bases of Support for Mexico's Dominant Party." *American Political Science Review* 64 (March 1970): 153–67.

Anderson, Bo, and Cockcroft, James D. "Control and Cooptation in Mexican Politics." *International Journal of Comparative Sociology*, 7 (March 1966): 11–28.

Apter, David E. "A Comparative Method for the Study of Politics." *American Journal of Sociology* 64 (November 1958).

Bazant, Jan. "Tres revoluciones mexicanas." *Historia mexicana* 10 (October– December 1960): 220–42.

Blasier, Cole. "Studies of Social Revolution: Origins in Mexico, Bolivia, and Cuba." *Latin American Research Review* 2 (1967): 28-64.

Borah, Woodrow. "Colonial Institutions and Contemporary Latin America: Political and Economic Life." *Hispanic American Historical Review* 43 (August 1963): 371-79.

Brothers, Dwight S. Review of Raymond Vernon, *Dilemma of Mexico's Development: The Roles of the Private and Public Sectors. American Economic Review* 54 (March 1964): 155-57.

Brothers, Dwight, and Solís M., Leopoldo "Recent Financial Experience in Mexico." *Economía latinoamericana* 2 (July 1965): 77-98.

Castillo, Carlos Manuel. "La Economía agrícola en la región de el Bajío." *Problemas agrícolas e industriales de México* 8 (July-December 1956): 3-221.

Chevalier, François. "Un Facteur decisif de la revolution agraire au Mexique: le soulevement de Zapata, 1911-1919." *Annales economies sociétés civilisations* 16 (January-February 1961): 66-82.

Cline, Howard F. "Mexico: A Matured Latin American Revolution, 1910-1960." *Annals of the American Academy of Political and Social Sciences* 334 (March 1961): 84-94.

Cornelius, Wayne A., Jr. "Urbanization as an Agent in Latin American Political Instability," *American Political Science Review* 63 (September 1969): 833-57.

Davis, Tom. "Dualism, Stagnation and Inequality: The Impact of Pension Legislation in the Chilean Labor Market." *Industrial and Labor Relations Review* 17 (April 1964): 380-98.

Davis, Tom. "Eight Decades of Inflation in Chile, 1879-1959: A Political Interpretation." *Journal of Political Economy* 71 (August 1963): 389-97.

Deutsch, Karl W. "Social Mobilization and Political Development." *American Political Science Review* 55 (September 1961): 493-514.

Díaz-Alejandro, Carlos F. "An Interpretation of Argentine Economic Growth Since 1930." *Journal of Development Studies* 3 (October 1966, January 1967): 14-41, 155-77.

Dovring, Folke. "Land Reform and Productivity: The Mexican Case, Analysis of Census Data." Madison: University of Wisconsin, Land Tenure Center 63 (January 1969).

Fuentes Díaz, Vicente. "Desarrollo y evolución del movimiento obrero a partir de 1929." *Ciencias políticas y sociales* 5 (July-September 1959): 325-48.

Germani, Gino, and Silvert, Kalman. "Politics, Social Structure and Military Intervention in Latin America." *Archives européennes de sociologie* 2 (1961): 62-81.

Glade, William P., Jr. "The Enigma of Mexico's Dilemma." *Economic Development and Cultural Change* 13 (April 1965): 366-76.

Gonzáles Cosío, Arturo. "Clases y estratos sociales." In *México: cincuenta años de revolución*, Vol. 2. Mexico: Fondo de Cultura Económica, 1961.

Gonzáles Navarro, Moisés. "Le Developpement economique et social du Mexique." *Annales economies sociétés civilisations* 21 (July–August 1966): 842–58.

González Navarro, Moisés. "La Ideología de la revolución mexicana." *Historia mexicana* 10 (April–June 1961): 628–36.

Gonzáles Navarro, Moisés. "Social Aspects of the Mexican Revolution." *Cahiers d'histoire mondiale* 8 (1964): 281–89.

Hewes, Gordon. "Mexicans in Search of the Mexican: Notes on Mexican National Character Studies." *American Journal of Economics and Sociology* 13 (January 1954): 209–23.

Horton, D. E. "Land Reform and Economic Development in Latin America, the Mexican Case." *Illinois Agricultural Economics* 8 (January 1968): 9–20.

Hoselitz, Bert F. "Economic Growth in Latin America." *First International Conference of Economic History.* The Hague: Mouton & Co., 1960, pp. 87–102.

Iturribarría, Jorge Fernando. "Limantour y la caída de Porfirio Díaz." *Historia mexicana* 10 (October–December 1960): 243–81.

López Rosado, Diego, and Noyola Vázquez, Juan F. "Los Salarios reales en México, 1939–1950." *El Trimestre económico* 18 (April–June 1951): 201–9.

Maddox, James G. "Economic Growth and Revolution in Mexico." *Land Economics* 36 (August 1960): 266–78.

Manne, Alan S. "Key Sectors of the Mexican Economy, 1960–1970." In *Studies in Process Analysis,* edited by Alan S. Manne and Harry M. Markowitz, pp. 381–400. New York: John Wiley and Sons, 1963.

McAlister, L. N. "Social Structure and Social Change in New Spain." *Hispanic American Historical Review* 43 (August 1963): 349–70.

Mendieta y Núñez, Lucio. "Un Balance objetivo de la revolución mexicana." *Revista mexicana de sociología* 23 (May–August 1960): 529–42.

Moreno, Frank Jay. "The Spanish Colonial System: A Functional Approach." *Western Political Quarterly* 20 (June 1967): 308–20.

Morse, Richard M. "The Heritage of Latin America." In *The Founding of New Societies,* edited by Louis Hartz, pp. 123–77. New York: Harcourt, Brace and World, 1964.

Nadel, S. F. "The Concept of Social Elites." *International Social Science Bulletin* 8 (1956): 413–24.

Nash, Manning. "Economic Nationalism in Mexico." In *Economic Nationalism in Old and New States,* edited by Harry G. Johnson, pp. 71–84. Chicago: University of Chicago Press, 1967.

Olson, Mancur, Jr. "Rapid Economic Growth as a Destabilizing Force." *Journal of Economic History* 23 (December 1963): 529–52.

Phelan, John Leddy. "México y lo mexicano." *Hispanic American Historical Review* 36 (August 1956): 309–18.

Quintana, Carlos. "Resultado de una encuesta sobre inversión extranjera en México." *Comercio exterior* 19 (August 1969): 589–98.

Reyna, José Luis. "Desarrollo económico: distribución del poder, y participación política: el caso mexicano." *Ciencias políticas y sociales* 50 (October-December 1967): 469-86.

Rosenzweig, Fernando. "El Desarrollo económico de México de 1877 a 1911." *El Trimestre económico* 32 (July-September 1965): 405-54.

Schmitt, Karl. "Congressional Campaigning in Mexico: a View from the Provinces." *Journal of Inter-American Studies* 11 (January 1969): 93-110.

Scott, James C. "Corruption, Machine Politics, and Political Change." *American Political Science Review* 63 (December 1969): 1142-58.

Silva Herzog, Jesús. "La revolución mexicana en crisis." Reprinted from *Cuadernos americanos* (1944).

Simonsen, Mario Henrique. "Brazilian Inflation: Postwar Experience and Outcome of the 1964 Reforms." In *Economic Development Issues: Latin America*, pp. 261-340. New York: Committee for Economic Development, 1967.

Solís M., Leopoldo. "Hacia un análisis general a largo plazo del desarrollo económico de México." *Demografía y economía* 1 (1967): 40-91.

Stavenhagen, Rodolfo. "Aspectos sociales de la estructura agraria en México." In *Neolatifundismo y explotación*. Mexico: Editorial Nuestro Tiempo, 1968, pp. 11-55.

Stavenhagen, Rodolfo. "Social Aspects of Agrarian Structure in Mexico." *Social Research* 33 (Autumn 1966): 463-85.

Stone, Lawrence. "Theories of Revolution." *World Politics* 18 (January 1966): 159-76.

Sturmthal, Adolf. "Economic Development, Income Distribution and Capital Formation in Mexico." *Journal of Political Economy* 63 (June 1955): 183-201.

Taylor, Philip B., Jr. "The Mexican Elections of 1958: Affirmation of Authoritarianism." *Western Political Quarterly* 13 (September 1960): 722-44.

United Nations. Economic Commission for Latin America. "Income Distribution in Latin America." *Economic Bulletin for Latin America* 12 (October 1967): 38-60.

Wolf, Eric R. "The Mexican Bajío in the Eighteenth Century." In *Synoptic Studies of Mexican Culture*, edited by Robert Wauchope, pp. 177-99. New Orleans: Tulane University, Middle American Research Institute, 1957.

# INDEX

Access, political, 130, 219
Achievement motivation of Indiana, 37–38
Acosta, Miguel, 159
Agrarian leagues. *See Ejidal* leagues
Agrarian reform [land reform]: and business support, 109; of Calles, Plutarco Elías); of Cárdenas (*see* Cárdenas, Lázaro); code, constitution, laws, statutes, etc., 31, 60, 78, 89–90, 108, 157, 202; conservative effects of, 64 (n. 41); and demands of rural class, 64–65, 83, 107, 175–77, 183, 184, 207, 221; and economic growth rate, 30, 31–32, 36, 64–65; *hacendados'* power broken by, 36, 37, 39, 91, 157, 175; of Obregón (*see* Obregón, Alvaro); and political stability, 153, 176–77, 230–31; as redistribution of land, 31–32, 33, 34, 39, 65 (n. 43), 83, 91, 107–8, 128–29, 157, 175–76, 203; social overhead expenditures minimized by, 65 (n. 43); violations of laws, 118, 119–20, 125, 128–29, 183, 203, 219, 231
Agrarian revolt of 1911. *See* Indians, in Mexico, uprising of
Agrarian sector of PRI [*campesino* sector], 98, 100, 103, 110, 168–69; and communications network of PRI, 202; effectiveness as interest group, 120, 121, 129, 162, 219; selection of leaders, 116–22, 127, 166, 207–8. *See also Ejidal* leagues
*Agraristas*, and *ejidal* system, 32, 198
Agricultural Credit Bank, 36
Agricultural elite: government policy toward (since 1940), 101, 130, 131, 221; lack of political power after revolu-

tion, 97–98; origins of, 9; revolutionary politicians and generals as (after World War II), 168. *See also* Governing elite
Agricultural extension services, 86, 215, 221
Agricultural implements, purchase by rural poor, 59
Agricultural work force [rural labor]: under Díaz, 21, 154; under hacienda system, 24; income, 77–83; since *1935*, 59, 63 (n. 39), 64, 73 (n. 9), 81, 210, 215, 231; and presidential elections, 111
Agriculture: in Argentina, government investment in, 67; in Latin America, growth of production, 69; role in industrialization, 58
—in Mexico: during colonial period, 25, 139 (n. 19); government investment in, 44, 45; production in *1810–67*, 13; production in *1877–1911*, 13, 18, 27, 30, 32; production in *1940–70*, 7, 36, 38, 41, 42, 43, 45, 58–65, 69, 83. *See also* Agrarian reform
Aguascalientes (state), governor of, 153
Aguilár, Luis, 109
*Alcabala*, 13, 19
Alemán, Miguel: and Avila Camacho, 163; and business, 109, 111; as civilian president, 163; federal expenditures under, 66; and graft and corruption, 167, 170; and gubernatorial elections, 112; and industrialization, 48; investment in irrigation, 81, 168; and labor, 112, 114–15, 169; land distribution under, 33, 34; as representative of right "wing" of PRI, 110
Alexander, Robert J., on labor leaders in Mexico, 121

Payne: